THE BOOK OF THE
GOLDEN RETRIEVER

Title page: This handsome drawing of a Golden Retriever was done for this book by prominent artist John Weiss, of Sharon Center, Ohio. A very talented young man, Mr. Weiss is also a great dog lover and we appreciate so lovely a gift as this portrait to help enhance the beauty and interest of *The Book of the Golden Retriever.*

Front cover: Great winning bitch Am., Can. Ch. Russo's Pepperhill Poppy. Owned by Pepperhill Kennels, Barbara and Jeffrey Pepper.

Back cover: The magnificent late Am., Can. Ch. and O.T. Ch. Sunstreak of Culynwood, C.D., T.D., W.C.X., Can. C.D. Owned by Dave and Suzi Bluford, Dasu Goldens.

THE BOOK OF THE
GOLDEN RETRIEVER

by Anna Katherine Nicholas
*with special sections by Robert Stebbins, Mrs.
Ludell L. Beckwith, and Dr. Joseph P. Sayres*

0-87666-738-8

Distributed in the UNITED STATES by T.F.H. Publications, Inc., 211 West Sylvania Avenue, Neptune City, NJ 07753; in CANADA by H & L Pet Supplies Inc., 27 Kingston Crescent, Kitchener, Ontario N2B 2T6; Rolf C. Hagen Ltd., 3225 Sartelon Street, Montreal 382 Quebec; in ENGLAND by T.F.H. (Great Britain) Ltd., 11 Ormside Way, Holmethorpe Industrial Estate, Redhill, Surrey RH1 2PX; in AUSTRALIA AND THE SOUTH PACIFIC by T.F.H. (Australia) Pty. Ltd., Box 149, Brookvale 2100 N.S.W., Australia; in NEW ZEALAND by Ross Haines & Son, Ltd., 18 Monmouth Street, Grey Lynn, Auckland 2 New Zealand; in SINGAPORE AND MALAYSIA by MPH Distributors Pte., 71-77 Stamford Road, Singapore 0617; in the PHILIPPINES by Bio-Research, 5 Lippay Street, San Lorenzo Village, Makati, Rizal; in SOUTH AFRICA by Multipet Pty. Ltd., 30 Turners Avenue, Durban 4001. Published by T.F.H. Publications Inc., Ltd., the British Crown Colony of Hong Kong.

Contents

Nancy Sauer and her Golden, D.J.'s Stormy Thunderbolt, C.D.X., Can. C.D., winner of the *Dog World* Award, enjoy a walk together along the shores of Lake Michigan, May 1982. Nancy personally trained and handled "Thunder" to his titles.

In Appreciation

The Golden Retriever fancy has surely been most friendly, helpful, and cooperative to me in the preparation of this book, for which I am enormously grateful. The interest and support have been heartwarming and will never be forgotten.

Special appreciation goes to Mrs. Ludell L. Beckwith who has written a comprehensive and excellent chapter on judging the Golden Retriever. We present it with tremendous pride, as this is a lady who thoroughly knows and understands the breed and whose words we consider to be of tremendous value.

Having always been of the opinion that Bob Stebbins possesses very special talent when it comes to making a Golden arrive in the ring looking its best, we asked him if he could possibly find time to do a chapter on grooming and coat care for us. To our delight he was most willing, and we feel both proud and honored to present his chapter.

Our excellent veterinarian, Dr. Joseph P. Sayres, is an old and highly respected friend. His "Veterinarian's Corner" is a part of the book we consider to be of special merit, and we are fortunate to be able to provide it for our readers.

Barbara and Jeff Pepper loaned me reams of research material, contacted many people for photos and kennel information, and in general helped me tremendously both through their discussions with me about the fancy and by their tireless efforts to gather as much information as possible. The same is true of Linda and Bob Stebbins, who put me in touch with the owners of some of the earlier "greats" and made it possible for me to contact and include them. Roy and Doug Holloway went "all out" to contact former clients and friends and ask that they submit material. In fact, it was Doug who spent an evening visiting Mrs. Lloyd M. Case, telling her about this book and getting her to send me fabulous books and albums from her late husband's collection; these sources made it possible for me to bring you photos of the great Celloyd dogs and those dogs which Lloyd handled for other owners, as well as facts and information from the books written on Goldens many years ago. Bobby Barlow also assisted me greatly by providing me with current addresses of breeders for whom he had handled leading winners early in the fancy's history.

Here at home, Marcia Foy helped do research, did the copy-reading, contacted folks from whom we needed pictures, and made the work easier for me in a million ways.

All of the Golden Retriever fanciers who so enthusiastically supported and assisted me have made this book possible. Thank you, one and all!

Anna Katherine Nicholas

A lovely head-profile of Ch. Sir Richard of Fleetwood, C.D., owned by Pepperhill Farms, Barbara and Jeffrey Pepper, Putnam Valley, New York. Photo by Alton Anderson.

About the Author

Since early childhood, Anna Katherine Nicholas has been involved with dogs. Her first pets were a Boston Terrier, an Airedale, and a German Shepherd Dog. Then, in 1925, came the first Pekingese, a gift from a family friend who raised them. Now her home is shared with a Miniature Poodle and a dozen or so Beagles, including her noted Best in Show and National Specialty winner, Champion Rockaplenty's Wild Oats, an internationally famous Beagle sire, who as a show dog was top Beagle in the nation in 1973. She also owns Champion Foyscroft True Blue Lou and, in co-ownership with Marcia Foy who lives with her, Champion Foyscroft Triple Mitey Migit.

Miss Nicholas is best known in the Dog Fancy as a writer and as a judge. Her first magazine articles were about Pekingese, published in *Dog News* magazine about 1930. This was followed by a widely acclaimed breed column, "Peeking at the Pekingese," which appeared continuously for at least two decades, originally in *Dogdom* and, when that magazine ceased to exist, in *Popular Dogs*.

During the 1940s she was Boxer columnist for the American Kennel Club *Gazette* and a featured East Coast representative for *Boxer Briefs*. More recently, many of her articles of general interest to the dog fancy have appeared in *Popular Dogs, Pure-Bred Dogs, American Kennel Gazette*, and *Show Dogs*. She is presently a featured columnist for *Dog World, Canine Chronicle*, and *Kennel Review* in the United States and *Dog Fancier* in Canada. Her *Dog World* column, "Here, There and Everywhere," was the Dog Writers Association of America selection for Best Series in a dog magazine which was awarded her for 1979. And for 1981 her feature article, "Faster Is Not Better" published in the *Canine Chronicle* was one of four nominated for the Best Feature Article Award from the Dog Writers Association. She also has been a columnist for *World of the Working Dog*.

It was during the 1930s that Miss Nicholas' first book, *The Pekingese*, was published by the Judy Publishing Company. This book completely sold out two editions and is now an eagerly sought after collector's item, as is her *The Skye Terrier Book*, published through the Skye Terrier Club of America during the early 1960s.

Miss Nicholas won the Dog Writers Association of America award in 1970 for the Best Technical Book of the Year with her *Nicholas Guide to Dog Judging*. Then in 1979 the revision of this book again won the Dog Writers Association of America Best Technical Book Award, the first time ever that a revision has been so honored by this association.

In the early 1970s Miss Nicholas co-authored with Joan Brearley five breed books for T.F.H. Publications. These were *This is the Bichon Frise, The Wonderful World of Beagles and Beagling, The Book of the Pekingese, This is the Skye Terrier*, and *The Book of the Boxer. The Wonderful World of Beagles and Beagling* won a Dog Writers Association of America Honorable Mention Award the year that it was published.

All of Miss Nicholas' recent releases from T.F.H. have been received with enthusiasm and acclaim; these include *Successful Dog Show Exhibiting, The Book of the Rottweiler, The Book of the Poodle, The Book of the Labrador Retriever,* and *The Book of the English Springer Spaniel.*

In addition to her four Dog Writers Association of America awards, Miss Nicholas has received the Gaines "Fido" as Dog Writer of the Year and two "Winkies" from *Kennel Review* as Dog Journalist of the Year on separate occasions.

Ch. Alstone Sutter Creek Charade, U.D., completing title at Framingham in 1973. Undoubtedly one of Britain's finest exports, strongly influential in New England breeding programs. Owner-handler Susan Breakell, Sutter Creek Kennels, Norton, Massachusetts.

CHAPTER ONE

Origin and Development in Great Britain

Noranby Tweedledum, by Sandy of Wavertree ex Yellow Nell, exemplifies the beautiful head of the "old type" Golden. This dog, active during the early 1920s, had field trial Certificates of Merit to his credit.

Throughout my authorship of books on numerous breeds of dog, I have had occasion to do considerable research into breed histories. Many of these are very cut and dried, with little variation in what one reads. This, however, is not so with the Golden Retriever; this breed has two entirely different schools of thought concerning the breed's origin.

The Tale of the Circus Dogs

The story of the background of the Golden Retriever which follows was described in all of the Golden literature I have been able to find dated earlier than the mid-1950s. (This includes the summary description of the breed in *Hutchinson's Encyclopaedia*; the historical backgrounds outlined in *The Book of the Golden Retriever*, written by the famous Golden breeder Mrs. W.M. Charlesworth and published in England during the late 1930s; the 1950 *Yearbook of the Golden Retriever Club of America*; *The Golden Retriever* by H. Edwin Shaul, published in 1954; and *Retriever Gun Dogs*, published in 1945 and written by William D. Brown, who not only quotes the following story but also mentions the existence of a second version of the origin.)

A British sportsman named Sir Dudley Marjoribanks, who later became Lord Tweedmouth, was on a visit in 1860 to the seaside resort of Brighton where he saw a troupe of performing dogs (said to have been the first ever to appear in Great Britain). So fascinated did he become with the intelligence and skill of these dogs that Sir Dudley promptly decided he must have a pair to breed and train for field work at his estate in Scotland. The Russian trainer, however, refused to break up the troupe, saying that to do so would ruin his entire act. But Sir Dudley was not to be discouraged, and finally a solution agreeable to both parties was reached when he agreed to purchase the entire group of eight. Returning with them to Guisachan, as his estate was called, Sir Dudley was said to have embarked on a breeding program based entirely on his original purchase.

The Russian dogs came from a breed long known in their native country as Russian Retrievers, or Russian Trackers. They are described as having been especially hardy dogs of tremendous endurance. They were used principally as herders, and it was not unusual for the shepherds to provide them with a shelter and a cache of food, leave them on their own to tend the flocks over the winter months, and then return to find all in good order in the spring. Low-set in build, the Russian Retrievers, or Trackers, are described as having possessed especially beautiful heads, usually with dark eyes and dark pigmentation, although albinos occasionally did appear; heavy coats, usually wavy or curly, with dense, abundant undercoat; good round feet; excellent neck and shoulders; massive bone; and strong powerful hindquarters. They ranged in color from so pale as to appear almost white to cream or pale biscuit. Their tails were often curled over their backs, in keeping with the Arctic dogs, and always of good length. These early dogs frequently weighed up to one hundred pounds and stood about thirty inches at the withers. The dense coat which so well protected them from the rigorous winters in the Caucasus Mountains, where they were best known, served equally well as a shield against the attacks of wild animals.

From 1860 to 1870, Lord Tweedmouth (Sir Dudley) worked to establish his Guisachan Retrievers, breeding them without introduction of an outcross and using them for hunting deer. The dogs, as he is said to have noted when first seeing them, were, indeed, of superior intelligence; but at the same time the dogs were big and cumbersome, so many of Sir Dudley's fellow sportsmen were not impressed with them.

Thus it was, as the story goes, that in 1870, after due thought and consideration, Lord Tweedmouth decided to try a Bloodhound out-cross for the purpose of further developing the good tracking tendencies of his dogs. This version of the story specifically stated that this cross was a single event and that it was done only on this one occasion for the reason stated. The result was said to be a smaller dog, a more refined coat texture, and a slightly darker shade of coat, with general build and conformation similar to that of a Foxhound. It is further said that for at least several following generations the appearance of a wrinkled forehead, longer ears more typical of a Bloodhound, and a tendency to show "haw" in the eyes was not uncommon.

Lord Tweedmouth presented some of the offspring of the dogs he was breeding to friends who obviously believed them to be Russian Trackers, or Russian Retrievers. One friend, the Honorable W. le Poer Trench, retained them and bred them, keeping the blood pure by making no outcross. He had at one point tried unsuccessfully to find more of these dogs and purchase them from Russia, but when this proved impossible (we are not told whether this was due to unavailability or refusal to sell), he continued inbreeding those he had received from Lord Tweedmouth and their descendants. His favorite dog was St. Hubert's Peter, described as especially typical. This dog eventually was presented as a gift to King George V of England.

Dogs from Lord Tweedmouth's kennel, and their descendants, went also to Lord Harcourt, Lord Ilchester, Lord Portsmouth, and Lord Shrewsbury. There were definite differences of

This is St. Hubert's Peter, the Hon. W. le Poer Trench's most famous "Russian Retriever," said to have been a direct descendant of the Guisachan Retrievers owned by Lord Tweedmouth in the 1860s.

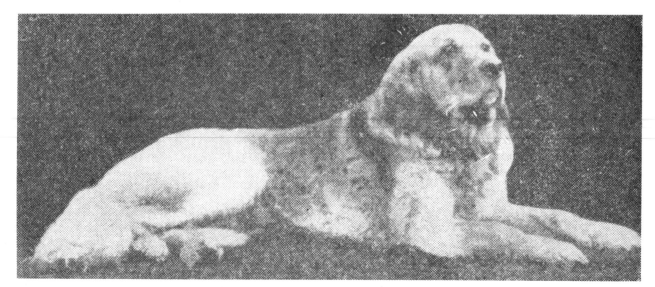

type among them, as we understand that some strongly resembled the supposedly original Russian dogs while others distinctly favored the Bloodhound. Was Lord Tweedmouth secretly chuckling as he fed his friends, and the public, what according to future revelations may have been pure fiction about the foundation dogs?

The Key to the Origin

The key dog in the heritage of the Golden Retriever seems without dispute to have been one named Nous. For decades Golden fanciers had had this dog described to them as "the best from the circus troupe," but in the face of later developments, doubt about this was created.

It would seem that there were skeptics in England who had never quite "bought" the story of the circus dogs. Among them, evidently, was the third Lord Tweedmouth who toward the close of the 1920s revealed the fact that he knew his grandfather had obtained a yellow retriever during a trip to Brighton at the time when the Russian Trackers were supposed to have accompanied his grandfather home and that this was the dog his grandfather had used in his breeding program. Whether he had also brought back a troupe of circus dogs at the same time is not revealed; but according to the kennel records of the first Lord Tweedmouth, verified to have been written by his own hand, Nous had been acquired in the early 1860s, of Lord Chichester's breeding. The story goes that Nous was from black Flat-coat parents and was the only yellow in an otherwise all-black litter. It is said that Lord Tweedmouth bought him from a cobbler at Brighton who had taken him in settlement of an unpaid debt.

Authority has it that although Lord Tweedmouth's handwritten kennel records were precisely kept, and date back to a considerably earlier time than the Brighton purchase or purchases, they make mention only of the yellow Retriever. Could it be that the circus dogs were purchased by Lord Tweedmouth but never actually used in his breeding program and therefore not recorded? Or had there ever been any such acquisition at all? It is interesting to speculate—but we shall never know for sure!

During 1952, a complete revelation of the discovery found in Lord Tweedmouth's handwritten records was told to the world through the pages of *Country Life* magazine, released at that time, it is said, by a grand-nephew, Lord Il-

This is Nous, the dog in the background of Golden history. He was owned by Lord Tweedmouth and is the dog around which a controversy in Golden history revolves.

chester. Since Lord Tweedmouth himself must have been responsible for the telling of the original version about the circus dogs (as how else could it have been known?), speculation must have been high regarding the entire matter. Why, if untrue, had the story been permitted to circulate in the first place? Why was the story never denied during Lord Tweedmouth's lifetime? Could it have been a complete hoax? Or a monstrous joke? Or just a plain misunderstanding?

We shall now set aside the romantic version of the origin of the Guisachan Retrievers and move on to the one now believed and generally accepted. Nous remains the cornerstone, but now he is believed to be an English-bred yellow Retriever.

According to the currently accepted history of the Golden Retriever, a liver-colored Tweed Water Spaniel named Belle, duly recorded in

This was Lord Harcourt's Culham Copper, one of the first Goldens ever exhibited in England in about 1908. Mrs. Charlesworth bred her original bitch, Noranby Beauty, to him in 1912 and puppies from the mating were among the foundation dogs in her Noranby strain.

Lord Tweedmouth's records, was bred to Nous and produced, in 1868, four yellow puppies eventually named Ada, Cowslip, Crocus, and Primrose. Tweed Water Spaniels, native to that area, were of a light liver shade and, to quote from an early description of these spaniels, had coats "so close in curl as to give the idea that they had originally been a cross from a smooth-haired dog, long in tail, ears heavy in flesh and hard like a hound's, only slightly feathered. Forelegs feathered behind, hind-legs smooth, head conical and lips slightly pendulous." These have elsewhere been described as reminiscent of small English Retrievers.

Lord Tweedmouth intensified the introduction of the Tweed Water Spaniel into his strain when he bred Cowslip to Tweed (the latter is the name Lord Tweedmouth used to indicate another Tweed Water Spaniel belonging to him); then one of these puppies, Topsy, was bred to Sambo, assumed to have been a black Retriever. From Topsy and Sambo, a bitch named Zoe was born. Zoe, in turn, was line-bred back to Crocus and produced three yellow puppies in 1881. Thus, a strain of Guisachans was officially established on the records. We understand that both Flat-coats and Labradors were used in the breeding programs toward the turn of the century, and I have seen an Irish Setter outcross as well as a Bloodhound outcross mentioned as having played a role in the earliest type-setting of the Golden.

Around 1870, Lord Tweedmouth presented some of his dogs to friends, as we have previously mentioned. These gentlemen, along with Lord Tweedmouth, became the earliest to establish Golden Retriever breeding programs in England, their dogs strongly resembling the modern Goldens of today.

Development in the 1900s

Playing an important role in the early development of Goldens, at the Earl of Ilchester's kennel, was Ada, from the original Nous–Belle litter, and Lord Harcourt's Culham Brass and Culham Copper. Lord Harcourt was the first to exhibit Goldens in an English dog show ring, and the best known of his Goldens were Brass and Copper plus a third one, Culham Tip. This was in 1908-1909, when Goldens had not yet been recognized as a separate breed but were lumped together with the others simply as "Retrievers."

Colonel le Poer Trench, who had so obviously believed in the Russian Trackers and tried unsuccessfully to obtain more of them in their homeland, was in competition with the descendants of Lord Tweedmouth's dogs until about 1914. Shortly after the turn of the century, Mrs. W.M. Charlesworth, a very dedicated lady who established Noranby Kennels (possibly the world's most famous for Goldens), started off when she bred her bitch, Noranby Beauty, to

Culham Brass; then, in 1912, she took this same bitch to Culham Copper. These two litters, along with Culham Tip, were of very special importance to the foundation of the breed as it is known today. Also very important was a bitch named Yellow Nell, owned by Mr. Hall and descended from Ingestre Scamp and Ingestre Tyne.

It was Mrs. Charlesworth who, about five years after establishing her kennel, was instrumental in the formation of the Golden Retriever Club of England, and shortly thereafter she helped obtain official recognition of Goldens as a separate breed to be registered as "Golden or Yellow Retrievers." At the great Crufts Dog Show in 1908, only eight Goldens appeared in competition. By 1934, the total ran well into three figures—an example of the steady and fast rise in the popularity of these dogs.

By 1911, Mrs. R.M. Grigg, Lady Harris, and Lord Shrewsbury had joined with Mrs. Charlesworth and Lord Harcourt in being consistent exhibitors, followed shortly thereafter by Captain H.F.H. Hardy, who was the first to win with the breed in open field trials, his Vixie running second in the Gamekeepers National Association in 1912. Mrs. Charlesworth took Certificates of Merit there with Tweedledum and with Noranby Sandy. All three of these Goldens were from the influential Yellow Nell line.

Noranby Sandy was sold by Mrs. Charlesworth to Colonel Hendley in 1913. During this time Captain St. John Loftus showed Braunston Gleam and Mr. F.W. Herbert showed Coquette. The following year the Honorable Mrs. Grigg entered competition with Noranby Dandelion, purchased from Mrs. Charlesworth, and bred some noted winners from her when mated to Noranby Campfire (the first Golden to achieve championship), litter-brother to Mr. Hordern's well-known Noranby Cadmium, another Golden that was winning well that year. Mrs. Grigg became a loyal and successful Golden fancier and owned the breed's third champion in England, Bess of Kentford, who finished in 1923. Other Golden fanciers active during this period were Mr. King, with some splendid examples of Culham breeding; Mr. Mills, with Astley Storm; and Mr. Everitt, with Fearless Don.

Ottershaw Kennels, which exported some dogs to America during the 1930s, was established in 1915 and was based on Noranby Balfour

(Culham Brass ex Noranby Beauty). W.S. Hunt was the owner.

Following World War I, activity in Goldens really started to surge. The first postwar champion to finish and the second for the breed in England was Mr. R. Herman's Balcombe Boy, who went on to become the first dual champion. Mrs. Grigg's Bess of Kentford, as mentioned, was the third champion for the breed; and Cornelius, owned by Mrs. K. Evers Swindell, and Flight of Kent, owned by His Highness Maharajah Dhiraj of Patalia, were close behind during that same year.

The Honorable Mrs. Carnegie appeared on the scene with Glory of Fyning, by Noranby Balfour, around this time and started an active and prominent kennel, where, with Glory as the foundation, quality and type excelled. Other breeders or exhibitors of the period included Mr. Braybrook, Mr. Matthews, and Mr. Meade,

Above: Noranby Sandy, born in 1910, was sold in 1913 by Mrs. Charlesworth to Col. Hendley. Sandy was a winner of a Certificate of Merit at the Gamekeepers National Association Trials in 1912. **Below:** Noranby Sandy displaying good form in the field at the beginning of this century.

all three of whom owned dual-purpose dogs. Also active, of course, was Mr. Herman and Dual Champion Balcombe Boy, to whom reference has already been made.

To Lord Brocket went the thrill of winning the first Golden Retriever Trials in 1921 with the nicely bred Ottershaw Brilliant, sired by Noranby Sandy.

1922 was the year when Mrs. Carnegie's Heydown Gunner, by her Glory of Fyning, gained Best Dog of the Year, this honor in bitches having previously gone to Mrs. Charlesworth's Noranby Daydream, who became a champion in 1924.

Champion Cornelius, a grandson of Noranby Campfire, who became a respected pillar of the breed, started out in 1923 for Mrs. Evers Swindell. Another important event that year was the debut of Champion John of Auchencheyne

Ch. Kelso of Aldgrove had been formerly known as Speedwell Kelso. A son of Ch. Michael of Moreton, this dog was bred by Mrs. K. Evers Swindell and owned by Miss E.L. Mottram. Mrs. Swindell owned a prominent pillar of the breed in her Cornelius, a grandson of Ch. Noranby Campfire, born in 1923 and still "going strong" in the early 1930s.

One of the greatest of all early Goldens, and the first of the breed to gain show championship, was the handsome dog Ch. Noranby Campfire, born July 1912, owned by Mrs. W.M. Charlesworth. Campfire gained his first Challenge Certificate in 1913, followed by two more that same year, giving him the title. Following World War I he obtained, in 1921, a Certificate of Merit in field trial competition.

An outstanding field trial winner, Ch. Noranby Jeptha is pictured winning the Ulster Gun Dog League Trials. During 1928 alone she gained honors at six trials, bettering her 1927 record by one, and still gaining recognition in 1931. She was born in 1925 and was bred by Mrs. Charlesworth.

One of England's important dual champions, Noranby Destiny, a representative of Mrs. Charlesworth's famed Noranby Kennel, so prominent from earliest recognition of the breed in England right through the first half-dozen decades of the 1900s.

in field trials, where he also did well for his owner, Captain Hardy.

No book on this breed could possibly be complete without a tribute to Mrs. W.W. Charlesworth for her dedication, loyalty, and devotion to Goldens from the early days to the 1950s. She and her dogs made history and contributed to breed progress both in England and, through their descendants, in North America. Mrs. Charlesworth was no fly-by-night fancier. She stuck with her breed, working long and hard to bring recognition to Goldens and to increase their popularity and appreciation. She was a very knowledgeable lady, a true student of her breed.

Among Mrs. Charlesworth's dogs were Champion Noranby Daydream, Champion Noranby Diana, Champion Noranby Jeptha, Champion Noranby Dutiful, Champion Noranby Deidre,

Three of Mrs. Charlesworth's Noranby dogs showing the type and quality Golden appearing in England during the 1920s and 1930s. Note the difference in depth of color of these Goldens.

More Noranby Goldens, typical of England's finest in the days of the breed's development.

and Champion Noranby Destiny. One of her first homebred dogs, Noranby Campfire, won his first Challenge Certificate in 1913 when he was one year old and during that same year he won two more certificates; thus he became the first Golden ever to attain championship, preceding Dual Champion Balcombe Boy, the first dual champion on record, by eight years. In 1921, following the close of World War I, Campfire returned to competition attaining a Certificate of Merit in Field Trials. The establishment of the Noranby type of Golden played a large part in the early history of the breed, and the kennel was truly a dominant force in the establishment and development of superior dogs.

Mrs. Grigg, of Kentford Goldens, was also a busy early exhibitor. Following World War I, her champions included Champion Bess of Kentford, Champion Rip of Kentford, and Champion Kib of Kentford. Champion Mischief of Kentford, although owned by Maharajah Dhiraj (his second champion), also carried her kennel name.

Mrs. Swindell, in addition to Cornelius, also had a champion in Speedwell Beryl, in 1929; and in 1933, she had Champion Speedwell Molly, followed, in 1934, by Champion Speedwell Brandy.

Mrs. J.D. Cottingham was busily making records through the mid-1920s and 1930s. Champion Cubbington Diver and Vic of Woolley gained titles for her in 1926, Champion Banner of Woolley and Champion Reine of Woolley in 1927, Champion Diver of Woolley in 1929, Champion Merry Rose of Woolley in 1930, Champion Mist of Woolley in 1936, and Champion Bachelor of Woolley in 1937. Plainly, the Woolley Kennel has been one with which to reckon, and we find the name often repeated in

Mrs. Cottingham in the garden with some of her Goldens from the 1920s and the 1930s. At the extreme left is the famed English Ch. Reine of Woolley. At the extreme right are Ch. Diver of Woolley, winner of highest show honors in England for Goldens in 1929, and Ch. Vic of Woolley. The dogs in the center include Rex, Vesta, and Champion Diver of Woolley, all of whom played their roles in British Golden History. Mrs. Cottingham was a very prominent and successful breeder-exhibitor.

pedigrees of dogs imported to the United States or bred from those coming from Great Britain.

J. Eccles, the owner of Champion Haulstone Dan, also had Champion Haulstone Sprig and Field Trial Champions Haulstone Brook and Haulstone Larry.

H. Wentworth-Smith finished Cubstone Bess in 1932, Champion Bingo of Yelme and Champion Gaiety Girl of Yelme in 1935, and Chief of Yelme in 1937.

Development After World War II

From 1939, when C. Walker's Champion Hazelgilt and Mrs. Wentworth-Smith's Champion Kandyd of Skroy completed their titles, until 1947, no Golden Retriever became a champion in Great Britain. These were the war years, when normal activities ground to a halt until peace had been won.

The first two postwar English champions were Mrs. Charlesworth's Noranby Destiny and Mrs. I.M. Parsons's Torrdale Happy Lad, both gaining their titles during 1947. Three followed in 1948: Alexander of Elsiville, owned by Mrs. E.L. Ford; Culzean Sulia, owned by Mrs. Porter; and Stubblesdown Golden Lass, owned by W.E. Hickmott.

The forties closed with five champions in 1949, representing some long-time breeders happy at again being in the ring with their dogs. They were Susan of Westley, belonging to Miss Joan Gill; Dorcas Gardenia, belonging to Mrs. H.T. Stonex; Golden Girl of Morinda, owned

by Mrs. E.A. Saunders; Dorcas Glorious of Slat, making it two that year for Mrs. Stonex; and Colin of Rosecott, owned by Mrs. R.G. Clark.

Joan Gill with her Westley dogs really started piling up the records in this postwar period, and by the latter part of the 1950s she had become the only British kennel to have produced six champions since the war's end, twice as many as any other kennel. (She also had a young dog with two Challenge Certificates to his credit at the time.) These winners included Champion William of Westley in 1950, Champion Sally of Westley and Champion Simon of Westley in 1955, and International Dual Champion (English and Irish) David of Westley. David, owned by Miss Ross, was the winner of four Challenge Certificates, seven Irish Green Stars, plus other show awards and twenty-four field trial awards including eight firsts. Champion Sally of Westley had a total of at least nine Challenge Certificates, and Champion Simon of Westley won the Gold Cup for the Best Golden Dog or Bitch at Crufts, having won at a field trial for the second successive year, this time with 283 Goldens entered.

One of the world's most famous kennels of Goldens is "of Yeo," owned by Mrs. Lucille Sawtell which exported dogs to many other countries, adding greatly to show competition and breeding programs all over the world. Champion Masterpiece of Yeo was going strong for the kennel in the late 1950s, as the sire of International Champion Masterstroke of Yeo, Field

Ch. Cubstone Bess, born July 1927, won Challenge Certificates and a qualifying certificate at the Golden Retriever Club's trials at Brocket Hall during 1932. Owned by Mr. Wentworth Smith and bred by Mr. L. Bryon.

Dr. T.R. Wilshaw was owner of this lovely daughter of Ch. Diver of Woolley, top winning show Golden of 1929. She was Ch. Goldgleam of Aldgrove, bred by H.L. Jenner, and she gained her first Challenge Certificate at the Scottish Kennel Club event in 1931.

Ch. Haulstone Marker, by Ch. Michael of Moreton, was born in 1928, bred by Mr. J. Eccles, and owned by H.L. Jenner.

Ch. Donkelve Jester, by Ch. Michael of Moreton, was born in 1929, bred by Lt. Com. A.M. Willoughby, shown at one period by Miss D.M. Turner, and later owned by Mrs. Vernon Wentworth.

Trial Champion Musicmaker of Yeo, and grand-sire of Champion Chip of Butlers and Field Champion Mazurka of Wynford. A son of Champion Anningsley Fox ex Princess of Slat, Masterpiece sired a number of successful show and working Goldens in Holland, Switzerland, Brazil, and the West Indies as well as in England and the United States.

English Champion Ringmaster of Yeo, a most impressive dog, has contributed much quality to the breed. His son, English Champion Figaro of Yeo, was imported in the early 1960s by Mrs. Charles Engelhard of New Jersey, to whose kennel he proved an invaluable addition. Another son of Ringmaster, Champion Toddytavern Kummel of Yeo, has also made his presence felt as a show dog and as a sire.

Mrs. Sawtell has written a very excellent book on Golden Retrievers which I have thoroughly enjoyed reading. She is a knowledgeable lady who has made a sizeable contribution to the quality and future of her breed.

We have heard many words of praise for the Camrose dogs, and we note their continuous presence in important pedigrees. Mrs. J. Tudor

is the owner, and some of her leading winners and producers have included Champion Camrose Fantango, Champion Camrose Tantara, Champion Camrose Lucius, Champion Camrose Loretta, Champion Camrose Jessica, Champion Camrose Talleyrand of Anbria, and Champion Camrose Tamarisk.

Mrs. Harrison's Boltby dogs are also familiar to fanciers in the United States. Champion Boltby Skylon achieved no small accomplishment by winning a total of at least twenty-three Challenge Certificates. Other Boltby dogs, all known for their outstanding quality have achieved success and fame, too.

Mrs. Wentworth-Smith has placed special emphasis on hard-working shooting dogs at her "of Yelme" Kennels. She was one of England's early breeders, and she was extremely successful. One of the most famous winners from here, Champion Dernar of Yelme, distinguished himself in both the field and show ring.

Thus we give you a background on some of England's winning Goldens, from the breed's early days through the 1960s. At least several of these kennels are still active and producing well.

Ch. Featherquest Jay's Blond Tom, November 1955 - February 1969, bred by Rachel Page Elliot and owned by Lyle R. Ring. He produced more than sixteen champions, one of them being the great Am., Can., Bda. Ch. Star Spray Maria's Rayo Del Sol.

CHAPTER TWO

Arrival and Development in the United States

Ch. Cragmount's Hi Lo, one of the important Goldens in breed history, winning the Sporting Group for Mrs. Charles W. Engelhard, at Valley Forge Kennel Club in 1966. H. Terry Correll handling.

It was in about 1918 that Freeman Lloyd, the eminent sportsman and *Field and Stream* editor, wrote an article stating his belief that North America's first Goldens had reached here from Siberia by way of Alaska, citing as his reason that he had in his possession photographs of Alaskan sled dogs whose appearance was strongly similar to this breed. Perhaps the sled dogs did resemble Goldens, and possibly they, or their ancestors, had accompanied Russian fishermen into Alaska. This theory, however, completely disregards the fact that it has been thoroughly well established that Golden Retrievers were originally created in Scotland by Lord Tweedmouth and his friends; the only question which remains in the minds of some people is whether they had used the Russian Trackers or the black-bred yellow retriever for their purpose.

It seems to me that the most logical manner for the breed to have arrived in North America is as described by the very knowledgeable and devoted early fancier Colonel S.S. Magoffin, a breeder and student of Goldens, who was the earliest important figure in their development and progress on this continent.

From friends in Canada who were staunch Golden fanciers, Colonel Magoffin learned that Goldens had arrived in Canada around the turn of the century from Great Britain, brought there by retired English army officers. This certainly fits in with what we have already discussed about the breed's early development in Scotland. We share Colonel Magoffin's acceptance of this as being the actual route by which Goldens arrived in the United States, as it does, indeed, make sense.

The 1930s and 1940s

Colonel Magoffin's contributions to the early establishment of Goldens in the United States in the 1930s is almost indescribable. He owned the first American Kennel Club champion of record of the breed, an imported English-bred dog who eventually became American and Canadian Champion Speedwell Pluto and was, additionally, the first of the breed to win a Best in Show in the United States, at the Puget Sound Kennel Club, December 2nd and 3rd 1933; Pluto was also the first to win a Sporting Group (at the 1932 Pacific International Kennel Club on October 21st through 23rd). We have read that

Pluto was a most perfect specimen of the breed, correct and beautiful in every way.

Soon after World War I, Colonel Magoffin had decided to breed Goldens, doing so purely as a hobby to produce good gun dogs to share with his friends. He and Mrs. Magoffin were originally from Minnesota and made frequent visits there for hunting, which almost certainly accounts for the fact that the original nucleus of Golden activity and interest in the United States was in that area. His Canadian friends encouraged his interest in establishing his own kennel, Rockhaven; and upon Mr. Armstrong's death the Colonel purchased the Gilnockie Goldens to interbreed with his own. People who enjoy tracing pedigrees back many generations will find the Rockhaven and Gilnockie kennel names behind many of our fine present-day strains.

For his foundation breeding stock, in addition to the aforementioned Pluto, Colonel Magoffin selected two bitches, Saffron Chipmunk and Saffron Penelope, both sired by English Champion Haulstone Dan. From these bitches, with Pluto as the sire, came the background for Rockhaven dogs.

In addition to the first American champion, Pluto, Colonel Magoffin had the second and third as well, the latter being also the first American-bred owner-bred Golden to gain the title. These two were Wilderness Tangerine, imported from England, and Rockhaven Harold, the homebred. Five other Goldens owned by other fanciers but bred by Colonel Magoffin also finished during the 1930s. American and Canadian Champion Speedwell Pluto became the first Golden Retriever Club of America Outstanding Sire on the strength of Canadian and American Champion Rockhaven Harold, Champion Rockhaven Rory, Champion Rockhaven Moonshine**, and Champion Rockhaven Danny.

Champion Rockhaven Rory, incidentally, became the second Outstanding Sire in the Golden Retriever Club of America Hall of Fame, Rockhaven Tuck the third Outstanding Sire, Rockhaven Ben Bolt the fourth, and Rockhaven Pluto Boy the fifth.

The official recognition of Goldens as a separate breed by the American Kennel Club took place in 1932. Among the earliest Golden champions finished during the 1930s were two belonging to Michael A. Clemans of New Jersey,

**For an explanation of "star champions," refer to the section entitled "Star Champions" in Chapter Nine.

A pair of famous Goldens: Ch. Tonkahof Bang (Ch. Goldwood Pluto ex Buff of Golden Valley) and Ch. Tonka Belle of Woodend (Rockhaven Tuck ex Rockhaven Judy), Tonkahof Kennels. These two were the sire and dam of Dual Ch. Tonkahof Esther Belle.

namely Alaisdair of Highstead, from England, and the Scottish import Lady Burns. Mr. Clemens also finished a homebred, Woodsman of Frantelle, in July 1941 and four others during 1947; they were Roger of Elsiville, imported, and the homebreds Frantelle's Fiddler, Frantelle's Diana, and Flare of Frantelle. These were soon joined by Champion Indian Field's Fairy Gold, also a homebred and sired by Fiddler.

Henry B. Christian, owner of Champion Rockhaven Rory, had a really super kennel during this period. Goldwood, which he and Mrs. Christian operated at Bear Lake, Minnesota, was established in 1933. Sprite of Aldgrove, an importation, was the second to finish from here. Then came Goldwood Sonia, bred by Ralph G. Boalt. There were also Champion Goldwood Pluto, Field Champion Goldwood Tuck, and three famous obedience dogs: Goldwood Toby, U.D.; Goldwood Michael, C.D.X.; and Goldwood Topshot, C.D.

Ottershaw Kennels finished the English import Ottershaw Collette in November 1936. Mrs. P. Moore did likewise with Veta of Wooley, also imported, the following month.

John K. Wallace, from St. Louis, Missouri, was an important figure in the breed. He finished two importations in 1937, Speedwell Tango and Bingo of Yelme; and in 1938 Rockhaven Whitebridge Nobby became a champion for this gentleman, who had then established his kennel name of Whitebridge.

Mrs. A.W. Smith, from Ipswich, Massachu-

Ch. Tonkahof Bang, born 1941, was bred by Henry Norton who co-owned him with J. MacGaheran. This Best in Show winner of the 1940s was by Ch. Goldwood Pluto.

Am., Can. Ch. Des Lac's Lassie, C.D., a grand-daughter of National Field Ch. King Midas of Woodend, was the fifth Golden to win Best in Show in the U.S., in 1950.

setts, finished two homebreds in 1938, Champion Frieda and Champion Alexander. The latter dog later belonged to Taramar Kennels owned by Mr. and Mrs. Theodore Rehm, who were very important in the breed in the eastern United States. Alexander became an Outstanding Sire in the Hall of Fame for Champion Mastland's Lucky Penny, Champion Alex of Taramar, and Champion Twin Hill Missy's Boy.

Ben L. Boalt of Gunnerman Kennels at Random Lake, Wisconsin, finished Champion Rockhaven Moonshine and Champion Rockhaven Glory, both bred by Colonel Magoffin; and F.R. Purvis put title on another bred by Colonel Magoffin, Rockhaven Danny. C.H. Clark finished Champion MacGregor of Three Acres, J.C. Thompson, Jr., finished Champion Toby of Willow Loch, and Mrs. F.C. Brown had the final champion of 1939 and the first of 1940 with Headisland Peter and Willowbank Gunner.

Two Goldens attained Best in Show honors during the 1930s: American and Canadian Champion Speedwell Pluto in 1933 and Champion Toby of Willow Loch at St. Paul Kennel Club in April 1938. The next Golden to win Best in Show in the United States was Champion Tonkahof Bang**, owned by J. MacGaheran and H. Norton, at St. Paul Kennel Club in April 1945. The latter dog was an Outstanding Sire with at least ten champions to his credit.

The big Group-winning Golden of the 1930s was Champion Rockhaven Rory; his three wins during the 1930s were followed by a fourth in 1941. Champion Rockhaven Danny also had a

Group One, at Puget Sound in 1937, as did Champion Beavertail Butch at St. Paul in September 1939.

The first multiple Best in Show winner for Golden Retrievers was Champion Czar of Wildwood, owned by Eric S. Johnson. This dog took six Best in Show awards, including Golden Gate and Beverly Riviera, between February 1946 and July 1950.

Champion Des Lac's Lassie, owned by Bart W. Foster, was Best in Show at Nebraska Kennel Club, March 1949. Champion Auric of Wildwood (a Canadian and American champion son of Czar) took the top award at Beverly Riviera for Frank L. Root in May 1949. Rockhaven Jack became Alaska's first Best in Show Golden in August 1949.

Ch. Auric of Wildwood, by Ch. Czar of Wildwood ex Winsome Winnie of Wildwood (granddaughter of Ch. Rockhaven Rory), was born in 1946 and was an early Best in Show dog in the U.S. Owned by Frank L. Root and bred by Eric S. Johnson.

Ch. Featherquest Blond Tom taking Best of Breed, Lloyd Case handling, and Ch. Golden Girl Enid taking Best of Opposite Sex, Lyle Ring handling, at the Golden Retriever Club Specialty at Willimantic, Connecticut, May 1960. Charles A. Schwartz is judging. Both of these splendid Goldens were owned by Lyle R. Ring and Pauline T. Ring, Westport Point, Massachusetts, leading fanciers of their day.

Dual Champion, Amateur Field Champion Squawkie Hill Dapper Dexter, born January 1948. Owned by Dr. Gerald W. Howe.

Bart Foster's Des Lac's Goldens were dominant producers along with being important winners. Canadian and American Champion Des Lac's Laddie of Rip's Pride was the sire of at least eight Goldens who have distinguished themselves in the show ring. This kennel was located at Winona, Minnesota.

Another early kennel which had particular impact on the breed was Featherquest, owned by Dr. and Mrs. Mark D. Elliott, where Goldens were bred for field, obedience, and show. Rachel Page Elliott is still an active and extremely knowledgeable lady in the dog fancy.

Golden Knoll has been a legendary kennel over the years. Mr. and Mrs. Russell S. Peterson owned many fantastic winners, and the dogs are to be found everywhere in present-day pedigrees.

Mr. and Mrs. Ben L. Boalt of Gunnerman Kennels and Ralph G. Boalt of Stilrovin were highly influential in the early development of Goldens in the United States. The Gunnerman Goldens were especially impressive in the field. Among the Stilrovin greats were Dual Champion Stilrovin Nitro Express, Champion Stilrovin Red Head Reliance, Dual Champion Stilrovin Rip's Pride, Field Champion Stilrovin Super Speed, Field Champion Stilrovin Katherine, Champion Stilrovin Shur Shot, Canadian Champion Stilrovin Victor, and Champion Krasnodar of Kingswere. Kingswere, another famous Golden kennel, was owned by Mariel King who became at one period Mrs. Ralph G. Boalt, so these two kennels evidently merged at least for awhile.

I recall with great admiration the Taramar Kennels owned by Mr. and Mrs. Theodore A. Rehm. Established in the 1940s, Taramar owned Mastlands Lucky Penny, a fine dog named Champion Alexander (by Donkelve Punch ex Ottershaw Norma), and many others including the noted Champion Noranby Baloo of Taramar, from Mrs. Charlesworth's kennel.

Baloo, a litter-sister to England's first postwar Golden champion, was Best of Breed at Morris and Essex in 1948 and won the Golden Retriever Club of America Specialty in 1946. Mr. and Mrs. Rehm were very dedicated fanciers and gave much time and energy on behalf of Goldens through their club activities.

Just as this book is nearing completion we have learned of the death of a most devoted Golden breeder, the well-known veterinarian Dr. Irene Kraft of White Plains, New York. She graduated from the Royal College of Veterinary Surgeons in London in 1939 and opened her practice on North Broadway in White Plains in 1941. Dr. Kraft, who numbered many well-known Goldens among her patients, practiced for more than forty years and had a most loyal following among dog and cat owners in her area. As a Golden breeder, she owned the Nerissida Kennels, and among her succesful winners were Champion Prince Oberon of Nerissida, Champion Stormy Weather of Nerissida, and Champion Nerissida's Finderne Folly. Dr. Kraft was active in club work in the eastern part of the country.

Golden Retriever winners at Morris and Essex in 1948. Best of Breed, Ch. Noranby Baloo of Taramar. Best of Opposite Sex, Ch. Duffy's Golden Desire. Handling were Bill Harvey, left, and Lloyd Case. Photo courtesy of Mrs. Lloyd M. Case.

Ch. Prince Alexander with Lloyd M. Case at the Windham County Kennel Club show.

The 1950s and Early 1960s

Elizabeth Tuttle's Champion Prince Alexander had two Bests in Show on his record for the beginning of the 1950s, at Tidewater and Longshore in April and June 1950, with a total of six Bests in Show during 1950 and 1951, along with numerous Groups to his credit.

Champion Golden Knoll's Shur Shot was the other early Best in Show Golden during the early 1950s, with no less than a dozen on the record during 1950 and 1951 alone. This dog was of tremendous importance to the breed as a sire, and the many champions to his credit include Canadian and American Champion Golden Knoll's King Alphonzo who took twenty Bests in Show between 1952 and 1955. Shur Shot was owned by Mrs. R.S. Peterson, and King Alphonzo was owned by Andre J. Penny, then later by N. Bruce Ashby. Both of these dogs added long lists of names to the roll of champions in America. Their contribution to the breed was inestimable! Shur Shot was by Champion Stilrovin Shur Shot ex Kingdale's Toast. He was born November 8th 1949.

Some of the other Goldens who gained the supreme award of Best in Show during the 1950s were Champion Cindy's Cheveleck, owned by Mrs. J.L. Powers, in 1951; Champion Joel of Claymr, owned by Mrs. Hertha Spooner-Franck, in 1951; Champion Copper's Czar Again, owned by Brackendale Kennels, at Providence and Danville in 1955; Champion Gilder of Elsiville, Des Lac's Kennels, in 1951; Champion Golden Knoll's Town Talk, owned by Major D.A. Smith, Jr., in June 1956; Dual Champion Lorelei's Golden Rockbottom in 1952 for R.M. Bischoff; Champion Prince Copper of Malibu in 1951 and 1952 for Dr. N.K. Forster; Champion Chee Chee of Sprucewood, once in 1951 and twice in 1953 for Mr. and Mrs. M.C. Zwang; Champion Sprucewood's Chocki, seven times in 1956 for Mrs. Zwang; and Champion Sprucewood's Chore Boy in 1955 for Mrs. H.D. Barbour.

Above: The great and magnificent Ch. Golden Knoll's King Alphonzo taking Best in Show at the Minneapolis Kennel Club on May 13th 1955. **Below:** The early Best in Show winner, Ch. Golden Knoll's Shur Shot, by Ch. Stilrovin Shur Shot ex Kingdale's Toast, owned by the Golden Knoll Kennels of Mrs. Russell S. Peterson at Waterloo, Iowa. Shur Shot took three Best in Show awards in 1950.

Two great friends of the Golden Retriever, who many times competed in the ring—both top handlers, both with splendid dogs. On the left is Harold Correll and on the right is Lloyd M. Case during a tight moment as the judge's examination of the dogs is underway.

A very famous and influential kennel in both Golden Retrievers and Dachshunds was Celloyd, owned by Mr. and Mrs. Lloyd Case at Torrington, Connecticut. The Cases bred both breeds and produced many outstanding dogs. Additionally, Lloyd was a highly successful handler and dogs belonging to his clients and shown by him piled up some very historic records during the mid-1900s. We are grateful to Mrs. Case for having shared her many photos of these dogs with us and are proud to have them included in our illustrations—these were top-flight show dogs who also were dominant producers.

Lloyd M. Case with one of the Goldens for which his Celloyd Kennels was noted.

The handsome Ch. Golden Pine's Brown Bear at Windham County Kennel Club 1959 adding still another Group first to his imposing record.

Above: This is Ch. Celloyd Country Squire, a noted winner of the 1950s, who gained his title between September 3rd and December 1st 1956 with four majors among his credits. Bred and owned by Celloyd Kennels, Mr. and Mrs. Lloyd M. Case, Torrington, Connecticut.

Left: Lloyd M. Case, owner, with a couple of Golden friends at his Celloyd Kennels.

Other famous, highly successful Golden breeders were Mr. and Mrs. Reinhard M. Bischoff at New Milford, Connecticut. Lorelei Hill was their kennel name, and it was synonymous with big winners of true quality. Champion Lorelei's Golden Rockbottom was one of their top dogs, born in 1948, by Champion Lorelei's Golden Rip ex Lorelei's Golden Tanya. Among this dog's victories were forty-five times Best Golden Retriever, including Westminster and Morris and Essex, plus twenty Group placements in the days when shows were not so plentiful nor dogs so widely campaigned as now.

Mrs. Patricia Corey was a leading Long Island Golden breeder, her Goldendoor Kennels managed by James A. Cowie. Here were to be found Champion Fancy of Goldendoor (Best of Breed at the Eastern Regional in 1955), Cham-

Four of Mrs. Patricia Corey's beautiful Golden door dogs, from the 1950s. Left to right: Ch. Fancy of Goldendoor, Ch. Candy of Goldendoor, Ch. Tabby of Goldendoor, and Ch. Lorelei's Sam.

The lovely Ch. Lorelei's Golden Rip in his last picture, taken in the 1940s and dedicated to his friends. Courtesy of Mrs. Lloyd M. Case, Celloyd Kennels, Torrington, Connecticut.

pion Candy of Goldendoor, English and American Champion Boltby Annabel, Champion Alreesford Nord Desprez, Champion Stubbings Golden Anubie, and Champion Lorelei's Sam, among others.

Another famous breeder on Long Island was Mrs. James M. Austin of Catawba Kennels. Mrs. Austin was active in numerous breeds of dogs, including several toy breeds and Labrador Retrievers, but the Goldens were among her special favorites. Champion Stormy Weather of Catawba was one of her big winners. Field Trial Champion Stilrovin Katherine and Stilrovin Victory, and the homebreds Copper Penny of Catawba and Copper Coin of Catawba, were others which she enjoyed. Mrs. Edmond Poor, better known for her Labradors, also had a Golden, Sun Glow of Catawba, bred by Mrs. Austin.

Mr. and Mrs. William A. Metz, who are associated with so many of the Sporting breeds, have also done well with Goldens. Theirs have included Champion Sir John of Sandywood, Champion Finderne Folly's Encore, and Champion Ironstreams Sir Launcelot.

Mrs. Charles W. Engelhard, Jr., in Far Hills, New Jersey owned one of the finest, most in-fluential Golden Kennels in the United States around the 1960s. Her dogs were of the highest quality, and their importance in breed development speaks for itself when one considers that these were the Cragmount Goldens.

At the 1960 Westminster, Mrs. Engelhard was showing Champion Finderne Gold Cloud of Kent and Champion Prince of Ranee. The two stunning homebreds, Champion Cragmount's Peter and Champion Cragmount's Hi-Lo, could have a whole chapter written on themselves alone. Peter was Top Golden in the United States in 1962, and at three years old he had chalked up three Bests in Show in keen Eastern competition, plus fifteen Sporting Group firsts. Hi-Lo, a highly consistent winner, was Golden of the Year for 1965 and 1966.

Mrs. Engelhard imported the superb English Champion Figaro of Yeo in about 1963. He came here fresh from three Bests in Show in England, and his last time in the ring there won the Northern Golden Retriever Association Specialty in 1962 over 142 dogs. Upon his arrival in the United States he won Best of Breed at the Golden Retriever Club of America National Specialty in 1963 and at the Eastern Regional in 1964, among his other successes.

Ch. Fancy of Goldendoor, left, and Ch. Czargold's Storm King at the Golden Retriever Club of America National Specialty, May 28th 1955.

Above: The great Ch. Cragmount's Hi Lo, by Ch. Golden Pine's Aces Hi ex Ch. Cragmount's Tiny Cloud, winning the Sporting Group at South Jersey Kennel Club, Vineland, New Jersey, October 22nd 1967. Judge, John W. Brady. H. Terry Correll handling for owner, Mrs. Charles W. Engelhard of Far Hills, New Jersey.

Right: Ch. Cragmount's Hi Lo winning the Group at Durham, North Carolina, March 25th 1966. Judge, Forest H. Hall. Handler, Terry Correll for Mrs. Charles W. Engelhard, Cragmount Goldens, Far Hills, New Jersey.

Above: Golden Retriever Club of America, June 20th 1954. Lloyd M. Case handling Ch. Czargold's Thor to a share of the honors.

Left: Ch. Star Spray's Rip of Glen de Fir at Concord Kennel Club, May 12th 1957. Lloyd M. Case, handling.

Right: Ch. Celloyd Golden Rogue at Great Barrington, August 25th 1957. Lloyd M. Case, handling.

Below: Ch. Celloyd's Storm King wins Best in Show at Providence County Kennel Club in 1955. Lloyd M. Case handling for owner H. Paul Warwick.

BEST DOG "IN" SHOW

Ch. Golden Pine's Brown Bear, owned by Mr. and Mrs. Josiah Semans of Rochester, New York, was handled exclusively to many fine wins around the 1950s by Lloyd M. Case.

Polly Chase of Glen Head, Long Island, was the owner of this outstanding Golden, Ch. Cherry Lane's Buff, handled here by the late Chuck Crane. Buff was a big winner in the 1950s.

Ch. Copper's Czar Again, whelped May 16th 1950, was bred by James Wellington. Czar Again was owned by H. Paul Warwick until 1953 when he was purchased by Celloyd Kennels, Mr. and Mrs. Lloyd M. Case of Torrington, Connecticut.

Lloyd M. Case winning Best in Show at Jacksonville, Florida, in 1952 with Ch. Copper's Czar Again. Photo courtesy of Mrs. Case.

Ch. Czargold's Storm King, owned by H. Paul Warwick, Brackendale Kennels, wins a Golden Retriever Specialty and first in the Sporting Group at Windham County Kennel Club, May 13th 1956. Handled exclusively by Lloyd M. Case.

The great Ch. Czargold's Storm King was by Ch. Prince Copper of Malibu ex Ch. Czar's Lassie. Highlights of this dog's career include Best in Show at Providence and Danville in 1955 with many Group firsts and placements.

Ch. Buckhead's Ricker finished title at Westbury Kennel Association during the 1950s. Handled by Lloyd M. Case.

Ch. Sprucewood's Chore Boy, by Am., Can. Ch. Golden Knoll's King Alphonzo ex Am., Can. Ch. Chee Chee of Sprucewood, was born March 16th 1954. He was from a litter of nine champions bred by Mr. and Mrs. Millard Zwang. Chore Boy was owned by Mrs. Henry Barbour of St. Paul, Minnesota.

Ch. Czarbella's Coppe Prince going Best of Breed at the Southern California Specialty at Kennel Club of Pasadena under Col. E.E. Ferguson, October 1957. Owners, Florence and Clancy Fox. Handler, George Sangster. Copper finished with four major show wins and Group placements at seventeen months of age and was Winners Dog at the Golden Retriever Club of America's Western Regional Area Specialty. Winner of many Groups and Bests in Show, Copper was California's top-winning Golden during the 1950s. Sired by Ch. Czarbella's Golden Boy ex Copper's Artistic Rhythm, he was bred by Gerald and Fleur Bergloff and was born January 6th 1956.

Ch. Yorkhill's Circus Clown, by Ch. Golden Knoll's Shur Shot, C.D., ex Goldpine Rigby, C.D.X., was born May 25th 1952, was bred by Mary Beth Gehan, and was owned by the Giralda Farms Kennels of Mrs. Geraldine R. Dodge.

Ch. Ruanme Blockbuster, by Ch. Ruanme Rory ex Ruanme Yankee Pride, was born on March 31st 1955, was bred by Barbara Miller, and was owned by Mrs. Geraldine R. Dodge, Giralda Farms, Madison, New Jersey.

Copper's Artistic Rhythm, handled by Evelyn Hale, winning the Brood Bitch Class at Pasadena's Specialty. She was owned by Gerald and Fleur Bergloff. Behind her is her son Ch. Czarbella's Copper Prince, top-winning California Golden of the 1950s, with George Sangster. Third in line is Copper's litter-brother, Ch. Maestro of Fleurcrest, C.D.X., owned and bred by the Bergloffs and handled by Jimmy Hale.

Left: Ch. Prince Royal of Los Altos, by Ch. Jason of Golden Anno Nueveo, U.D., ex Princess Pat of Los Altos, was born May 27th 1957, was bred by Mr. and Mrs. John Railton, and was owned by Mr. and Mrs. Oliver Wilhelm of Portolo Valley, California. He sired several champion get.

Below: Ch. Duke of Rochester, II, C.D., winning the Golden Retriever Club of America National Specialty, May 10th 1953. Chuck Crane handling for Mary Luise Semans, Golden Pine Kennels, Chesapeake, Virginia.

Above: Ch. Cragmount's Peter, by Ch. Finderne Gold Cloud of Kent ex Goldendoor Taffy, was the sire of Ch. Sunset's Happy Duke who in turn sired Am., Can., Bda. Ch. Cummings' Gold-Rush Charlie, Top Show Golden in the history of the breed, and Ch. Misty Morn's Sunset, C.D., T.D., W.C., Top Golden Sire in the history of the breed. Truly a dog whose contribution to the breed was inestimable! Owned by Mrs. Charles W. Engelhard, Cragmount Kennels, Far Hills, New Jersey, for whom he was an important winner and sire of the 1960s.

Right: Ch. Cheyenne Golden's King John, by Ch. Cheyenne Golden's King ex Cheyenne Golden's Sweet Sue, was born May 17th 1961. King John held the point record for Goldens in 1963 and 1964, and in both of those years he received from the Golden Retriever Club the Rockhaven Speedwell Pluto Trophy for the most show wins. He was bred and owned by Mr. and Mrs. William Herbert of Wichita, Kansas.

Ch. Golden Pine's Easy Ace winning under Miss Adele Colgate at Eastern Dog Club in 1960. Lloyd M. Case handling for Mary Luise Semans, Golden Pine Kennels, Chesapeake, Virginia.

Ch. Golden Pine's Easy Ace, W.C., Outstanding Sire, winning the Sporting Group, then on to Best American-bred in Show, at Amsterdam, New York, August 1960. Nancy Kelly Belsaas handling for owner Mary Luise Semans.

Am., Can., Bda. Ch. Star Spray Maria's Rayo Del Sol, a well-known winner of the late 1960s, was owned by Lyle and Pauline T. Ring, Westport, Massachusetts. Handled by Bill Trainor.

Am., Can., Bda. Ch. Star Spray Maria's Rayo Del Sol, known as "Jimmy," winning the Sporting Group at Ladies Dog Club, June 1st 1968, under Winifred Heckman. Handled by William Trainor for Mr. and Mrs. Lyle R. Ring.

Am., Can., Bda. Ch. Star Spray Maria's Rayo Del Sol winning the Garden State Golden Retriever Club Specialty in October 1972 from the Veterans Class. Nancy Ring Fenn handling for Pauline and Lyle Ring, Massachusetts. The Rings owned some of the greatest Goldens from the mid-1950s into the 70s and were noted for the quality of this dog and their other winners. At the Rings' small kennel the dogs received lots of personal attention, and all of the dogs were *real* retrievers as well as beautiful show winners.

Ch. Pathfinder of Lazy Pines, C.D.*, W.C., at Westminster in February 1967. Born March 25th 1965, Pathfinder was bred by Eugene R. Ferraro and was the foundation sire of Mrs. Janet L. Bunce's Wochica Kennels, Smithtown, New York. He was also Mrs. Bunce's personal pet.

The very famous Ch. Misty Morn's Sunset, C.D., at three years of age. Best of Breed 1968, 1969, and 1970 at the Garden State Golden Retriever Specialty and Best of Breed at the 1972 Eastern Regional of the Golden Retriever Club of America at Reston, Virginia, where he was also sire of the Winners Dog, Winners Bitch, and Best of Opposite Sex. A Golden Retriever Club of America Outstanding Sire, Sunset was by Ch. Sunset's Happy Duke (Ch. Cragmount's Peter ex Glen Willow's Happy Talk) from Amber Lady of Tercor Farm (Ch. Cragmount's Double Eagle ex Ch. Cragmount's Golden Wallis). Bred by the Rev. Edward French and owned by Peter and Rose Lewesky.

Cummings' Golden Doubloon taking Winners Dog at Westminster, February 10th 1970. By Bierly's Golden Sky ex Am., Can. Ch. Cummings' Golden Princess, Doubloon was born December 1966. Mrs. Mary W. Cummings, owner, Cummings' Goldens, Stillwater, New Jersey.

Above: Westminster Kennel Club, 1976. Owner Susan Taylor hugs Ch. Wochica's Okeechobee Jake following his third Best of Breed victory at this most prestigious of all dog shows in the United States. Jake is also noted for being the only Golden to have won the National three times, the third time at about nine years of age. **Below:** Ch. and O.T. Ch. Russo's Gold-Rush Sensation, U.D., the first dog of *any breed* to hold A.K.C. championship in both bench and obedience, and the first bench champion in A.K.C. history to be the Number One Obedience Dog (in 1977), all breeds. "Sadie" is owned by Edward L. Hamm (who handled her to her obedience victories) and L.C. Johnson.

Above: Am., Can. Ch. and O.T. Ch. Sunstreak of Culynwood, T.D., W.C.X., Can. C.D., the late and incomparable "Streaker," whose accomplishments in obedience and in the conformation ring combined to make him one of the all-time greats this breed has known. Dave and Suzi Bluford, owners, Dasu Goldens. **Below:** Am., Can. Ch. Ambertrail's Bargello Stitch, U.D.T., Can. U.D.T.X., W.C. Stitch, by Am., Can. Ch. High Farms Jantze of Curacao, T.D.X., W.C., Can. C.D., T.D.X., ex Can. Ch. Dolly, U.D., W.C. *** (qualified Open All Age), O.D., was bred by Michael Ducross and is owned by Barbara S. Tinker, Bargello Goldens. Stitch is the most titled Golden bitch in the United States, having seven American and seven Canadian titles. If she gets the last two titles (American T.C.X. and Canadian W.C.X.) during the fall of 1982, she will be the first Golden to do this. This would be a remarkable feat as she is only seven years old and has had five litters. She is an extraordinarily trainable truly tripurpose Golden.

This lovely English import is one owned by Nancy Garrison and is handled by William J. Trainor, to whom we owe thanks for use of the photo.

Facing page, top: Am., Can., Bda. Ch. Star Spray Maria's Rayo Del Sol, owned by Lyle and Pauline Ring, was handled by Bill Trainor to first in the Sporting Group at Ravenna in the late 1960s. **Facing page, bottom:** Ch. October's Foxy Lady, C.D., a multiple Group-winning and Group-placing bitch, has done some excellent winning under Linda and Bob Stebbins' handling. Owned by Katharine Gosling. **Right:** Ch. Briarmoor's Gold Drummer out in the snow. Owned by Briarmoor Goldens. **Below:** Bargello's Pomegranate, C.D., W.C., taking Best in Match at Southern Berkshire Golden Retriever Club Match Show. Barbara Tinker, owner.

Above: Am., Can. Ch. Bugaboo's Secret Treasure, a Best of Breed winner, by Ch. Sun Dance's Rarue ex Ch. Country Sun's Ms. Cricket. Owned by Bugaboo Kennels, John and Edie Shields.

Facing page: Bargello's Curry Cross Stitch is one of the fine Goldens at Bargello Kennels owned by Barbara Tinker.

Left: Ch. Kinni Kinnik's Tally of Gaylen, a multiple Group-winner, and a Best of Breed Specialty-winner, Fort Detroit Specialty 1977. Owned by Gayle L. Nash. **Below:** Ch. Camelot's Noble Fella, C.D.X., winning his eighth Best in Show, this one under Anne Rogers Clark, at Greater Miami Kennel Club in 1981. Handled by Bob Stebbins for owners, Kay Bickford and Margaret Zonghetti. **Facing page:** Ch. Beaumaris Aspen Hill Tessa, by Beaumaris Knightcap, C.D., ex Gold Coast's Golden Sandstorm, C.D., winning the Sporting Group from the classes in March 1981. Judge, Nelson Radcliffe. Owner, Anne Bissette.

Ch. Cloverdale's Golden Jake belongs to Vincent A. and Robert A. Indeglia, Narragansett, Rhode Island. Bred by Jane Zimmerman and Bob Stebbins and handled here by Linda Stebbins to win at Harrisburg in 1979.

Ch. Chebaco's Jacks Or Better taking Winners at Troy Kennel Club, 1980, handled by Bob Stebbins for Jeffrey and Judith Gowing.

Left: Ch. Gold-Rush Lightnin' owned by Gold-Rush Kennels.
Below: Apollo's Glance, a grandson of Ch. Eagle Ace of Tecor Farm, is the sire of the foundation bitch at Charms Kennels, Ginny Boyle, owner.

All of "Streaker's" intelligence and beauty are clearly apparent in this informal photograph of the magnificent late Am., Can. Ch. and O.T. Ch. Sunstreak of Culynwood, C.D., T.D., W.C.X., Can. C.D. Owned by Dave and Suzi Bluford, Dasu Goldens.

Left: Ch. Golden Glo's Margo, with Janet Sturz handling, winning second place in the highly competitive Westminster Junior Showmanship Class at Madison Square Garden in 1980. **Below:** Gosling's Precious Peronele, by Ch. Jolly October's Chevalier ex Ch. October's Foxy Lady, C.D., here is taking Best of Opposite Sex at West Volusia Kennel Club, December 1981. Owned by Kay Gosling. **Facing page:** Best in Show at Southern Colorado, Ch. Tempo's Frontier Bronco, who was bred by Peter and Sheila Huser, was purchased as a young puppy and shown to championship by the Arszmans of Frontier Kennels and is now co-owned by George and Vivian Wright, Gandalf Kennels. This dog, Number One Golden in 1981, is a son of the 1976 Number One Golden, Ch. Sun Dance's Rarue.

Above: Ch. Laurell's York, by Ch. Gold-Rush Lightnin' ex Ch. Laurell's Kilimanjaro, photographed with Bob Stebbins. Bred and owned by Thomas C. Kling and Laura Ellis Kling.

Facing page, top: This is Bierly's Golden Sky, first Golden owned by Mrs. Mary W. Cummings of the famous Cummings' Goldens. By Ruanme's Willard's Rex (grandson of Ch. Golden Knoll's Shur Shot, Ch. Des Lac's Goldie, C.D., and Ch. Lorelei's Marshgrass Rebel, C.D.) ex Gilda of Bryn Gweled (granddaughter of Ch. Ruanme Blockbuster and Ch. Ruanme Rory). Photographed at the Garden State Golden Retriever Specialty in October 1971. **Facing page, bottom:** Ch. Jolly Krishna Mr. Beau Jangles, C.D., by Ch. Sir Duncan of Woodbury ex Ch. Larkmill Genevieve, C.D., is owned by Sandra Haber, Schenectady, New York.

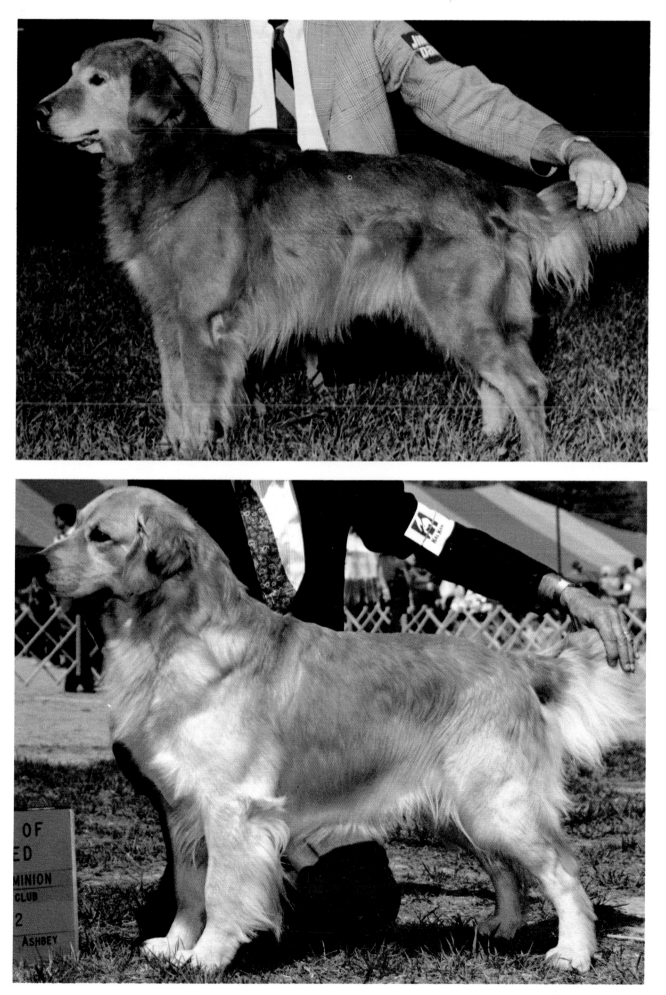

Am., Can. Ch. Duckdown's Unpredictable, C.D., W.C., owned by Laura Ellis Kling, is winning the Veterans Class at the Central Regional in 1978. Duckdown's Unpredictable was the sire of Amberac's Reeva Rustelle's first litter.

CHAPTER THREE

Kennels in the Continental United States

Ch. Amberac Sheza Q.T., by Ch. Amberac Ramala Ramblin' Rogue ex Ch. Amberac Yul B Ritzi, finished at sixteen months of age in seven shows. Shown taking Best of Winners for a five-point major at White River Golden Retriever Club Specialty, March 1982. Ellen Manke, owner, Amberac Goldens.

We are especially proud of our large, versatile, and interesting collection of kennel stories from breeders active in all facets of Golden Retriever endeavor. We think you will find them enlightening, and these will take up the discussion of United States breed history from the early 1960s until the present.

Amberac

Ellen Manke's well-known kennel, Amberac, has been in existence since about 1965, but its progress and true start in the breed were delayed because the first five bitches Ms. Manke owned turned out to be dysplastic. Thus she was very happy to locate and be able to own Amberac's Reeva Rustelle, "the bitch who started everything" for this kennel. Reeva, now ten years old and still going strong, is a Golden Retriever Club of America Outstanding Dam of five American champions with one finished in Canada, too.

In her very first litter, Reeva produced Champion Amberac's Mr. Beau Jangles, C.D., W.C., Champion Amberac's Joshua Jing, and Champion Amberac's Royal Rufus, C.D.X., W.C., all of them well known in Group competition. The

sire of this litter was the famous Champion Duckdown's Unpredictable, C.D., W.C., O.S.

Reeva's full sister, Amberac's Sungria De Ora, C.D., was the bitch who really kept the Amberac line going; she produced the bitch Amberac's Sunburst Sunbrave, W.C., O.D., co-owned by Judith Ciganek at the time of breeding. "Amber," bred to the Show Dog Hall of Fame member Champion Gold Coast Here Comes the Sun, C.D., produced Champion Amberac's Aristocrat, a Group winner, and Champion Amberac Sweet 'n' Sassy, who then produced Champion Amberac Ramala Ramblin Rogue, who just completed his title at two-and-a-half years of age and already has a champion daughter, Amberac Sheza Q.T. These dogs are mostly from litters which contained other champions as well; but in compiling this summary, Ms. Manke has stuck to those which have been key parts of her breeding program.

Q.T. finished in seven shows with the White River Specialty win of Winners Bitch and Best of Winners for a five-point major. She was reserve only twice, gaining five, five, four, and two points on the way to her title; and she was Best of Opposite Sex on most occasions.

Ch. Amberac Ramala Ramblin' Rogue, by Ch. Copper Lee Gold-Rush Apollo ex Ch. Amberac's Sweet 'n' Sassy, owned by Wesley and Janice Ravy, bred by Ellen Manke, Amberac Goldens. Pictured taking Best of Winners under judge Jane Forsyth.

Ch. Amberac Yul B Ritzi, bred and owned by Amberac Golden Kennels, Ellen Manke, Hartland, Wisconsin.

Another foundation bitch here is Champion Krishna's Klassic Fantasy, who has produced the gorgeous Champion Amberac's Yul B Ritzi, the dam of Q.T. and some other very promising littermates.

A famous winner not owned by Ms. Manke but bearing the Amberac kennel prefix is Champion Amberac's Asterling Aruba, a Group winner and the 1982 Westminster Best of Breed.

Amberac's Sunburst Sunbrave, W.C., O.D., produced the following: Champion Amberac's At A Girl Kindra, mother of a Leader Dog daughter and a U.D. son so far; Obedience Trial Champion Amberac's Sunrise Duke, owned by Mitch Schneider, the 1981 Gaines Regional Super Dog (Central) who placed third at the Gaines National in Texas; Champion Amberac's Aristocrat with Group placements; Champion Amberac's Sweet 'n' Sassy, with a champion son; and Canadian Champion Amberac Sweet Lady Autumnglo, with twelve points (including one major) in the United States.

Through research and study, Ms. Manke has come up with what she feels is a sound working line with the true Golden temperament. In selecting a sire to use on her bitches, she makes every effort to get as much information regarding littermates and parents as possible before making a final decision. Most of the breedings have turned out very well, but then some didn't. She usually gives a brood bitch two chances on two different sires; then if she does not produce the correct quality she is not used again. If considerable thought has gone into the selection of the parents, Ms. Manke then feels that the results should be the most favorable for the breeder and for those who eventually own the puppies.

O. T. Ch. Sunrise Duke, bred by Ellen Manke, Amberac Kennels. Owned by Mitch Schneider.

Ch. Amberac's 'At A Girl Kindra is one of the splendid Goldens owned and bred by Ellen Manke of Amberac Golden Retrievers, Hartland, Wisconsin.

Ashwel

Myra Moldawsky, of Tempe, Arizona, owns Ashwel Goldens, which despite being fairly young, is certainly off to an excellent start.

The very first champion here, Ashwel's Gold-Rush Logan, is a homebred out of Ashwel's very first litter. The second champion, Pepperhill's Peter Principal, was purchased from the Jeff Peppers of Pepperhill Farms. Both are producing well.

Peter Principal is by American and Canadian Champion Pepperhill's Basically Bear ex American and Canadian Champion Russo's Pepperhill Poppy. On the way to completing his title he gained his first two majors his first and second time out, Best of Breed over Best in Show

Ch. Ashwel's Gold-Rush Logan, by Am., Can., Bda. Ch. Cummings' Gold-Rush Charlie ex Wellesley's Lady Ashley, C.D., on the way to her title. Myra Moldawsky, owner, Tempe, Arizona.

Ch. Pepperhill's Peter Principle, by Am., Can. Ch. Pepperhill's Basically Bear ex Am., Can. Ch. Russo's Pepperhill Poppy. On the way to his title, Peter gained his first two majors his first two times out, won Best of Breed over Best in Show Specials, and, needing only one point, completed his title with a four-point major. Owned by Myra Moldawsky, Tempe, Arizona, in co-ownership with the breeder, Jeff Pepper.

Specials, and, needing only one point, completed his championship with a four-point major. Already he has young pointed progeny to his credit, including one who, following in his footsteps, has taken a Best of Breed over Specials from the classes.

Five-week-old Ashwel pups. Myra Moldawsky, owner.

Champion Ashwel's Gold-Rush Logan is a daughter of American, Canadian, and Bermudian Champion Cummings' Gold-Rush Charlie from Wellesley's Lady Ashley, C.D. She has now retired from the show ring, settling into motherhood. She has young puppies by Peter, while older ones she has produced are pointed, also with top wins from the classes.

Also at this kennel, Ashwel's Loganberry Wine (Champion Stone's Gold-Rush Shiloh ex Logan) will soon be starting out. And there are Glen-de-Fir's Myra's Wellesley, C.D.X., and Wellesley's Lady Ashley, C.D., as well.

Ashwel's Loganberry Wine, by Ch. Stone's Gold-Rush Shiloh ex Ch. Ashwel's Gold-Rush Logan. Myra Moldawsky, owner, Tempe, Arizona.

Wellsley's Lady Ashley, C.D., owned by Myra Moldawsky.

Am., Can. Ch. Amberac's Beausoliel, C.D., by Am., Can. Ch. Duckdown's Unpredictable, C.D., W.C., ex Amberac's Reeva Rustelle. Owned by Mary Wuestenberg and Bruce Wylie, Waukesha, Wisconsin.

Ch. Amberac's Aristocrat, by Ch. Gold Coast Here Comes the Sun, C.D., ex Amberac's Sunburst Sunbrave, W.C. Owned by Mary Wuestenberg, Asterling Goldens, Waukesha, Wisconsin.

Asterling

Asterling Goldens belong to Mary Wuestenberg of Waukesha, Wisconsin, and although comparatively new as a Golden kennel, this is one that has made a striking impact by way of show ring successes.

Mrs. Wuestenberg's first two champions were American and Canadian Champion Amberac's Beausoliel, C.D., and Champion Amberac's Aristocrat. These boys, four years old and three years old respectively at the time this is written, have both done well by her, with Aristocrat being a multiple Group winner.

It is her third champion, however, whom Mrs. Wuestenberg considers to be the true foundation bitch of the Asterling breeding program. This is American and Canadian Champion Amberac's

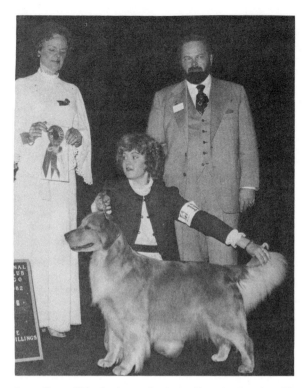

Am., Can. Ch. Amberac's Asterling Aruba, by Ch. Gold Coast Here Comes the Sun, C.D., ex Sunhaven's Amberac's Aruba. This bitch was Best of Breed at the 1982 Westminster show, the first *owner-handled* Golden bitch to accomplish this, and only the third bitch of her breed to gain the distinction in the 106 year history of the Westminster Kennel Club. Mary Wuestenberg, owner, Asterling Goldens. Aruba is pictured here winning the Sporting Group at the Chicago International in April 1982.

Asterling Aruba, a magnificent Golden who finished owner-handled from the Puppy Class with three majors, after which she was sensibly temporarily retired from the ring to grow up and to have her first litter. During 1982, she returned to competition with highly spectacular results, her career as a Special having started with four Group seconds and two Group firsts, the latter including the big Chicago-International. Among her other wins during early 1982 was Best of Breed at Westminster, where she thus became the third Golden bitch, and the first of them owner-handled, to take top breed honors in Goldens at this most prestigious of all American dog shows! Then came Best of Breed at the Greater Cincinnati Golden Retriever Club's Independent Specialty, again handled, as always, by her owner.

During the summer of 1982 came even greater success to this popular team, and Mrs. Wuestenberg has now added another first, a second, and a

fourth in Group and a Best in Show to the exciting record which she and Aruba are piling up. This makes American and Canadian Champion Amberac's Asterling Aruba the first Show Dog Hall of Fame *and* Best in Show winning bitch owner-handled, and Mrs. Wuestenberg's happiness at the accomplishment is surely most understandable.

Ch. Asterling's Tahiti Sweetie, by Ch. Gold-rush's Judgement Day ex Am., Can. Ch. Amberac's Asterling Aruba, going Best Sporting Puppy at the Metropolitan Kennel Club in Canada in February 1981. Owned by Sylvia Donahey and Mary Wuestenberg, Waukesha, Wisconsin.

Proud as she is of Aruba's record, Mrs. Wuestenberg is also very thrilled at the successes of Aruba's daughter, Champion Asterling's Tahiti Sweetie, owned by Sylvia Donahey, co-owned by and bred at Asterling. She, too, finished from the Puppy Classes, with five- five- four- and three-point majors at ten months of age. Brought out as a Special at Detroit, she gained Best of Breed there. In April 1982, at eleven months of age, she became the youngest Golden bitch, according to her owner, to ever win a Sporting Group, which she did at Saginaw Valley on April 10th 1982. Sweetie received a few more Group placements prior to her first birthday, and at thirteen months of age had accumulated a total of a first, a second, a third, and a fourth in Group.

Prior to Aruba, only two bitches had ever reached Golden Retriever Club of America Hall of Fame status. With Aruba now having done so and Sweetie getting closer every weekend, it goes without saying that Mrs. Wuestenberg is looking forward to the day when *both* these girls of hers will be included.

Sweetie, as already mentioned, is Aruba's daughter. She was sired by Champion Gold-Rush's Judgement Day. Aruba is by Champion Gold Coast Here Comes the Sun, C.D., ex Sunhaven's Amberac's Aruba.

Birnam Wood's Mountin' Ash, major pointed at age seven months, is a young hopeful owned by Mary Wuestenberg.

Bargello

Bargello Goldens, at Katonah, New York, were established by Barbara S. Tinker "for the purpose of breeding sound, working retrievers." Of course, conformation is of great importance here, too, and Ms. Tinker is concerned with producing the true tri-purpose Golden, one that can compete and win on the bench, in the field, and in obedience. To do so successfully the dog must have good conformation, temperament, intelligence, and innate retrieving ability.

Behind Bargello Goldens are the High Farms bloodlines developed by Ruth Worrest, on which Bargello was founded. High Farms Goldens were true tri-purpose dogs, and their traits have carried through to Barbara Tinker's bloodlines.

The dog with which Bargello started was a male, the original stud dog there, American and Canadian Champion High Farms Jantze of Curacao, C.D.X., T.D., W.C., Canadian C.D., T.D.X. Sired by Champion High Farms Beau Teak ex Champion High Farms Botacita, he was bred by Ruth Worrest Soule and born in August 1969. "Curry," as he is known, was Barbara Tinker's first dog, and it was she personally who put all of his impressive list of titles on him, thoroughly enjoying every step of the way. "Curry," as we write this, is thirteen years old and still his happy, handsome, clowning self.

Am., Can. Ch. High Farms Jantze of Curacao, C.D.X., T.D., W.C., Can. C.D., T.D.X., at the Garden State Golden Retriever Club Specialty Show in October 1979, where he won first in Veteran Obedience, scoring 195½. Trained by Barbara Tinker who owns and handles this outstanding Golden. Bargello Kennels, Katonah, New York.

Ch. Bargello's Ribbon Candy, by Ch. Moreland's Major Sam, C.D., ex Bargello's Tiffany Tulip, C.D., W.C., was bred by Barbara Tinker who co-owns with Mary K. Ruppero of Mahopac, New York. Here taking Best of Winners at Carolina Kennel Club 1980. Judge, Glen Sommers; handler, Kathy Kirk.

Two of Curry's daughters were kept as foundation bitches for this kennel. One, Bargello's Tiffany Tulip, American and Canadian C.D., W.C., was not herself a champion but produced Ms. Tinker's first homebred champion, Bargello's Ribbon Candy. The other, American and Canadian Champion Ambertrail's Bargello Stitch, U.D.T., W.C.X., Canadian U.D.T.X., W.C., has get that are still young since she spent more time working in the field than in the whelping box.

Am., Can. Ch. Ambertrail's Bargello Stitch, U.D.T., W.C.X., Can. U.D.T.X., W.C., taking a Sporting Group placement.

"Curry" has produced ten or more Utility Dogs, three qualified Open All Age dogs, and several champions in both Canada and the United States.

The Bargello breeding program is based mainly on line-breeding with an occasional outcross to English stock, which seems to combine well with the original lines.

Barbara Tinker's most outstanding Golden to date is Stitch, American and Canadian Champion Ambertrail's Bargello Stitch, U.D.T., W.C.X., Canadian U.D.T.X., W.C., with ten points towards her obedience trial championship. To date she is the most titled Golden bitch in the United States, her owner tells us, and when she gets her T.D.X. in America and her W.C.X. in Canada, possibly before the end of 1982, she will be the first Golden to have all sixteen of the presently available American and Canadian titles. This is truly a fantastic bitch with tremendous intelligence, desire to please, and enthusiasm for work. Stitch is a daughter of Curry ex Canadian Champion Val's Dolly, U.D., W.C.*** (Champion Sir Lancelot of Hawthorne, C.D., ex Katrina of London).

Bargello's Lollipop Tree II at the Golden Retriever Club of America Eastern Regional in 1981. Barbara Tinker, owner.

Beaumaris

Beaumaris Goldens, owned by John and Anne Bissette of Conifer, Colorado, were begun in 1967.

Mrs. Bissette, having been born and raised in England, is partial to the English-type Golden, commenting that "actually it always surprises me that in all the breeds of dog exported from Great Britain I think that only the Golden Retriever is readily identified as being English- or American-bred. Some years ago it was mainly the color being lighter there than here, but now it is length and abundance of coat plus the head type."

Ch. Beaumaris Brilliant, by Ch. Leygore Munster Monarch, U.D., W.C., ex Goldenloe's Glory Be. Here taking Best of Breed at Colorado Springs in 1971 under judge Frank Haze Burch. John and Anne Bissette, breeders, Beaumaris Goldens.

Ch. Leygore Munster Monarch, U.D. *, an Irish import by Woodhaven Sunset (son of Ch. Deerflite Headline) ex Leugh Dahon Beauty of Leygore. Breeder, Mrs. Lang. Owners, John and Anne Bissette, Conifer, Colorado.

The Bissettes' first male at Beaumaris, and also the first Golden that John Bissette trained, was imported from Ireland in 1966. This dog became Champion Leygore Munster Monarch, U.D., W.C. After starting with John Bissette in obedience and field work, by two-and-a-half years of age Monarch had gained his Utility Degree and Working Certificate, so it was decided to try him in conformation competition next.

Although he was blonder than the majority of Goldens being shown in the United States at the time, he gained his championship in short order.

By now Mr. Bissette had become a real devotee of the Golden breed, so an adult bitch purchased in Colorado, from Elisia Enloe of Goldenloe Kennels, was bred to Monarch. Since the Bissettes were not yet known in the Golden world, they had no alternative but to let the puppies be sold as pets. As the litter matured, they saw that the puppies had good looks and were exceedingly trainable, so they repeated the breeding and this time kept co-ownership on the puppy bitch who became Champion Beaumaris Brilliant. Mrs. Bissette is now training a great-grandson of this bitch. Although the Bissettes' Goldenloe bitch did not finish her championship and was bred only twice, she became an Outstanding Dam, Goldenloe's Glory Be, and had five champion littermates.

Next the Bissettes imported a puppy from the Deerflite Kennels in Oxford, England. Of this Mrs. Bissette says,

> Pure luck, really, we consider her the best purchase we ever made. Elizabeth Borrow sent her hoping we would like her and added the price was $100.00. We will always appreciate her trust and confidence in us. The bitch became Champion Deerflite Sunset, C.D.X., Outstanding Dam. Unfortunately, she only had two litters, then had to be spayed. We still consider her the best bitch we have had. She was also a High in Trial dog.

All of the Goldens at Beaumaris now have some Deerflite in their pedigrees.

Ch. Beaumaris Gabrielle, C.D., by Am., Can. Ch. Golden Pine's Courvoisier, C.D.X., W.C., ex Ch. Beaumaris Brilliant, was bred by Mr. and Mrs. John F. Bissette, Conifer, Colorado.

The Bissettes imported another Deerflite bitch, Selina, who is also an Outstanding Dam.

In 1970, a male of Boltby breeding, Bellemount Formula, was imported and they also were well pleased with him. At his first A.K.C. show, in May 1971 when he was just a year old, Formula was judged by Mrs. William Harvey who, although the Bissettes were not aware of this fact at the time, was the daughter of pioneer Golden breeders Mr. and Mrs. Theodore A. Rehm. Mrs. Harvey selected Sunset for Winners

Ch. Deerflite Sunset, C.D.X., an English import by Raynesgold Rainaway ex Deerflite Highlite. Bred by Elizabeth Borrow, Oxford, England. Owned by John and Anne Bissette.

Bitch, then awarded Best of Breed and later first in the Sporting Group to the young dog, making it a never-to-be-forgotten occasion for the Bissettes. It is sad that this lovely dog, who had fourteen points, including two five-point majors, developed cataracts when he was eighteen months old, after he had been used at stud just once. The Bissettes gave him as a pet to friends, but they do wish that he had gained that one little point he needed to finish!

Only two litters are bred annually at Beaumaris, and the Bisettes do not travel a great distance for shows. John Bissette came down with MS in 1978, so Anne now does all the showing; and her full-time job does not leave much opportunity to travel, much as she would like to do so. She notes that it was ten years before they again won a Sporting Group, this time with Formula's great-granddaughter, also from the classes, which again was a very thrilling occasion.

The Bissettes have bred a total of fifteen American champions and three Canadian champions to date, plus a number of C.D., C.D.X., W.C., and/or W.C.X. dogs.

Anne Bissette feels especially grateful to the English breeder Elizabeth Borrow for the help she gave them with their foundation breeding program and describes her as possessing "a vast amount of dog knowledge and a great love for the Golden Retriever breed."

Beaumaris Kingpin, by Consul of Yeo, C.D.X., from Ch. Beaumaris Bide De Fair, is a typical Golden puppy from the Beaumaris Kennels of Mr. and Mrs. John F. Bissette.

Bellemount Formula, by Boltby Nimble ex Contoul Cherokee. This English import has fourteen points including two five-point majors. Owned by Mr. and Mrs. John Bissette.

Beckwith's Misty Meadow

Beckwith's Misty Meadow Goldens, as they are listed on Mrs. Beckwith's stationery, have been in existence for approximately twenty-five years, owned by Ludell L. Beckwith and her husband, R.E. Beckwith. The latter is now an American Kennel Club approved judge for the Sporting Group and Best in Show, while Mrs. Beckwith is approved to judge all retrievers and four of the spaniels, so their lives are now focusing on the judging aspect of the fancy. Their daughter, Lynn Marie Beckwith, at fourteen years of age, is an avid Junior Showmanship competitor and personally handled her own Golden to its championship.

As judges, the Beckwiths have been kept extremely busy and are building up a highly respectful following by officiating at numerous important Specialty shows as well as prestigious all-breed events.

As breeders of Goldens, these fanciers have bred 106 American and Canadian champions of record, including eight Goldens who have won Best in Show! One of these Best in Show Goldens earned the honor on sixteen occasions and also has ninety-eight Group placements and 115 Bests of Breed, all amateur-handled. The Beckwiths have also bred three Goldens who have won Best of Breed at the National Specialty, two obedience trial champions, fourteen dogs who have earned Working Certificates, and many Goldens who have earned High in Trial Awards, plus obedience titles in all degrees obtainable. They are breeders of five Goldens in the Golden Retriever Show Dog Hall of Fame and owned the Top Winning Breeder-Owner-Handled Golden in the United States, 1962-1966. This is a truly remarkable list of achievements. The Beckwiths also are proud to have Goldens from their breeding program used as Leader Dogs for the Blind and as Search and Rescue dogs.

Two of the Beckwiths' most accomplished homebred bitches are the only mother-daughter in the breed to have earned both American and Canadian championships and U.D.T. degrees in the United States. The dam is American and Canadian Champion Beckwith Malagold Cherub, U.D.T., Canadian C.D.X., and the daughter is American and Canadian Champion Beckwith's Apricot Brandy, U.D.T., Canadian C.D.X. These bitches are also Golden Retriever Club of America Outstanding Producers.

Am., Can. Ch. Beckwith's Malagold Cherub, U.D.T., Can. C.D.X., the dam of eight champions. By Ch. Malagold Beckwith Big Buff ex Am., Can. Ch. Beckwith's Frolic of Yeo, C.D.X. Bred and owned by Mr. and Mrs. R.E. Beckwith, Snohomish, Washington.

Am., Can. Ch. Beckwith's Apricot Brandy, by Am., Can., Mex. Ch. Beckwith's Copper Ingot ex Am., Can. Ch. Beckwith's Malagold Cherub, U.D.T., Can. C.D.X. A Golden Retriever Club of America Outstanding Dam with five champions. Bred and owned by Mr. and Mrs. R.E. Beckwith.

The Beckwiths have owned many memorable champions during their history in this breed, but undoubtedly the most memorable of all was American, Canadian, Mexican, Bermudian, and Colombian Champion Beckwith's Copper Coin, who breeder-owner-handled won the Silver Anniversary Show of the Golden Retriever Club of America in 1964. After this exciting success, he was campaigned in the United States and Canada and then went on to win titles in five countries of the world, plus Best in Show in three of these countries and first in the Sporting Group in all five of them. Mrs. Beckwith tells us the most thrilling period in his career was in 1967, when in just forty-four days he won *six all-breed Bests in Show in three countries, plus seven consecutive Sporting Group firsts out of seven successive shows!* In this series, two of the Bests in Show were in Mexico City, two in Winnipeg, Canada, and three Sporting Group firsts with two Bests in Show in the United States. This dog was 1966 Top Producer of Champions in the United States, was a Golden Retriever Club of America Outstanding Sire, and was Top Winning Breeder-Owner-Handled Golden in the United States, 1962-1966.

Am., Can., Bda., Mex. Col. Ch. Beckwith's Copper Coin winning one of his sixteen All-Breed Bests in Show, this one under judge Edith Hellerman at Lake Minnetonka, June 1967. Copper Coin was among the Top Ten Goldens in the U.S. 1962-67, Phillips System, ranking third to seventh during that period.

Am., Can. Ch. Beckwith's Frolic of Yeo, C.D.X., by Ch. Orlando of Yeo (English import, sire of three champions) ex Jessica of Yeo. Imported as a puppy, this beautiful bitch became the Top Producing Golden Bitch in history. Mr. and Mrs. R.E. Beckwith, owners.

Am., Can., Mex. Ch. Beckwith's Copper Ingot, Golden Retriever Club of America Outstanding Sire of twenty-seven champions in the U.S.

Champion Beckwith's Copper Coin became a cornerstone in the Beckwiths' breeding program, but two other Goldens were also highly influential members of the founding stock. One of these was a lovely bitch imported from England, American and Canadian Champion Beckwith's Frolic of Yeo, C.D.X., who became and still is the Number Two Producing Dam of Champions in Golden history. She was 1971 Top Producer, *Kennel Review* System. Her record includes twelve American champions plus two Canadian champions.

The other Golden that became an integral part of the Beckwiths' breeding program was American, Canadian, and Mexican Champion Beckwith's Copper Ingot, a son of Copper Coin. Ingot became a Golden Retriever Club of

Am., Can. Ch. Beckwith's Viking for Dasu, Am. and Can. C.D. Mr. and Mrs. R.E. Beckwith, owners.

Merry Christmas at the Beckwiths'.

This lovely photo (taken in September 1971) of four generations presents, left to right: lying down, the Beckwith's first Golden, Beckwith's Golden Blaze, C.D., at fourteen years of age; left sitting, Golden Blaze's son, twelve years old at that time, Am., Can., Bda., Mex. Col. Ch. Beckwith's Copper Coin; third from left, Copper Coin's son, Am., Can., Mex. Ch. Beckwith's Copper Ingot; fourth from left, Ingot's son, Am., Can. Ch. Beckwith's Malagold Flash, Am. and Can. U.D.T., W.C.; and on the right, Ingot's son, Am., Can. Ch. Beckwith's Malagold Ojibway. A striking depiction of the magnificent quality of Beckwith Goldens, owned by Mr. and Mrs. R.E. Beckwith, Snohomish, Washington.

A current star at Beckwith Kennels, Am., Can. Ch. Beckwith's Chianti, Am. and Can. C.D. Bred, owned, and usually handled by Mr. and Mrs. R.E. Beckwith, the handler here is Bob Hastings. This multiple Best of Breed and Group-winning bitch has twenty-one points toward the Golden Retriever Club of America Show Dog Hall of Fame and is a Best Puppy in Show-winner in Canada.

America Outstanding Sire with twenty-seven American champions, who also subsequently produced Best in Show and obedience producers. Ingot was the 1971 Dog Top Producer by the *Kennel Review* System.

In total, the Beckwiths have raised eight Golden Retriever Club of America Outstanding Dams and three Golden Retriever Club of America Outstanding Sires.

The basic intent of the Beckwiths' breeding program has been to produce not only a good-looking example of the Golden Retriever breed but also a trainable dog with tractable temperament that has sound body structure. The Beckwiths now have a bitch who they have been showing sparingly, via non-professional handlers, and they are proud to say that she has just earned a place in the Golden Retriever Club of America Show Dog Hall of Fame, which only five bitches in history have ever accomplished, so far as the Beckwiths are aware. This is

American and Canadian Champion Beckwith's Chianti, American and Canadian C.D., the latest bitch at time of writing to have achieved Hall of Fame status. She was also among the Top Ten Goldens in 1979 and a Group winner and a Best Puppy in Show winner in Canada. She is a great-great-granddaughter of the Beckwiths' very famous and outstanding winner, American, Canadian, Bermudian, Mexican, Colombian Champion Beckwith's Copper Coin, the fifth generation of the Beckwiths' breeding program. Many Golden *dogs* have achieved this status in the Hall of Fame, but so few bitches have accomplished it that the Beckwiths' pride is well merited.

Copper Coin shows up in most of the Beckwiths' breeding stock and in that of many other breeders, and the Beckwiths plan on continuing their breeding program on a limited scale, delighting in ownership of this marvelous, versatile breed.

Briarmoor

Briarmoor Goldens were established around 1967 by Pat Leakey, now of Hortonville, Wisconsin, and daughter Nancy, at South Bend, Indiana. Based on the Sundance lines, the Leakeys' breeding program began with two beautiful foundation bitches, Champion Sundance's Melody C.D.X., and Champion Sundance's Chorus Girl, C.D. These bitches, in addition to their individual successes, gained considerable acclaim shown as a brace, having won Best Brace in Show and Best Sporting Brace honors on more than one occasion.

This attractive brace, winning first in the Sporting Brace Group at Lake Shore Kennel Club in 1970, consists of Ch. Sundance's Chorus Girl, C.D., and Ch. Sundance's Melody, C.D.X., the foundation bitches at Briarmoor Kennels owned by Pat Leakey, Hortonville, Wisconsin. They have won many honors as a brace, including that of Best Brace in Show.

Champion Sundance's Melody, C.D.X., when bred to her half-brother, produced Champion Briarmoor's Fancy Stepper, C.D.X. Melody became a Top Producer. Fancy Stepper, bred to Ch. Misty Morn's Sunset, Top Producer of champions in Goldens, produced Champion Briarmoor's Gold Drummer who finished with three majors (including one at Chicago-International) and gained two Group placements although not campaigned as a Special.

Mrs. Leakey has maintained a small breeding program and has produced good all-around Goldens including a number of hunting dogs being enjoyed by their owners. During the past few years she has leaned more towards field work than the show ring, but it is hoped that Drummer's three-year-old son will become a third generation show champion for this kennel. In addition to the Goldens, Chesapeake Bay Retrievers are also raised at Briarmoor.

Above: Ch. Briarmoor's Fancy Stepper, C.D.X., belongs to the Briarmoor Goldens. **Below:** Ch. Briarmoor's Gold Drummer on the way to the title. Owned by Briarmoor Kennels.

Am., Can. Ch. Cal-Vo's Starfarm Fleck of Gold, C.D., by Ch. Cal-Vo's Happy Ambassador ex Cragmount's Annabelle. Owned by Bridlewold Goldens, Kathy and Gary Uhrman, Medford, New Jersey.

Bridlewold

Bridlewold Golden Retrievers are located at Medford, New Jersey, and are owned by Kathy and Gary Uhrman, who have both been active in breeding and showing (and Kathy in training) Goldens since about 1971. The Uhrmans take great pleasure in the very fine collection of Goldens which they own.

At this kennel are to be found Champion Wochica's Golden Pumpkin (American, Canadian, and Bermudian Champion Cummings' Gold-Rush Charlie ex Champion Wochica's Sandpiper), American and Canadian Champion Cal-Vo Starform Fleck of Gold, C.D. (Champion Cal-Vo's Happy Ambassador, C.D., ex Cragmount's Annabelle), Champion Starform Colleen O'Wingfield (Champion Wochica's Okeechobee Jake ex Starform Donnegal), Champion Starfarm Wingfield Sunburst (American, Canadian, and Bermudian Champion Cummings' Gold-Rush Charlie ex Starfarm Donnegal), and Sunshine Serenity Sunny (American, Canadian, and Bermudian Champion Cummings' Gold-Rush Charlie ex Legacy's Kentucky Babe) with ten points at this time.

Ch. Starfarm Colleen O'Wingfield, by Ch. Wochica's Okeechobee Jake ex Starfarm Donnegal, finishing at the Ladies Kennel Association Dog Show in May 1979. Bridlewold Goldens.

Ch. Starfarm Wingfield Sunburst, by Am., Can., Bda. Ch. Cummings' Gold-Rush Charlie ex Starfarm Donnegal, is owned by Bridlewold Golden Retrievers, Kathy and Gary Uhrman.

Above: Sunshine Serenity Sunny, by Am., Can., Bda. Ch. Cummings' Gold-Rush Charlie ex Legacy's Kentucky Babe, taking Best of Winners at Somerset Hills in 1980 for owner Kathy Uhrman. **Right:** Bridlewold's Golden Heather is the dam of Talli, the remarkable Golden who guards the Statue of Liberty in New York Harbor. Kathy Uhrman, owner, Bridlewold Goldens. **Below:** Bridlewold's Irish Mist, by Ch. Footprint of Yeo, C.D., ex Bridlewold's Golden Heather, owned by Bridlewold Goldens.

There is also Gold-Rush Irish Legacy (Champior Copper Lee Gold-Rush Apollo ex Champion Goldwings Tiffany), Bridlewold's Gold-Rush Dancer (Champion Copper Lee Gold Dust Apollo ex Champion Wochica's Golden Pumpkin), and Bridlewold's Fascinatin' Rhythm (Champion Copper Lee Gold-Rush Apollo ex Champion Wochica's Golden Pumpkin).

All of the Bridlewold Goldens present a formidable array of outstanding individual quality, plus just about the finest breeding with which one could possibly work.

Champion Wochica's Golden Pumpkin was Winners Bitch at the 100th Anniversary Dog Show of the Westminster Kennel Club. Champion Starfarm Wingfield Sunburst finished at the Hudson Valley Golden Retriever Club Specialty in October 1981. Bridlewold Kennels is also the home of Bridlewold's Irish Mist (Champion Footprint of Yeo, C.D., ex Bridle-

wold's Golden Heather). "Blu," as she is called, was Winners Bitch and Best of Winners in April 1977 at the Potomac Valley Golden Retriever Club Specialty over 151 Goldens. She has twelve points and is a half-sister to Bridlewold's Alchemist, or "Talli," the famous "Lady That Protects the Lady," the latter being the Statue of Liberty in New York Harbor.

Kathy Uhrman is currently engaged in the very interesting work of training dogs for explosive detection and narcotic detection for police department work. Kelly's Honey of Bridlewold, C.D., the grandmother of "Talli," at eleven years of age learned narcotic detection because she saw all the other narcotic dogs working and decided that it looked like fun. This is very typical of a Golden. This training, along with showing all of her Bridlewold foundation stock's promising youngsters, keeps Kathy busily occupied on a full-time basis.

Am., Can. Ch. Country Sun's Ms. Cricket, Outstanding Dam in the Golden Retriever Club of America Hall of Fame, is owned by John and Edie Shields, Parker, Colorado. A daughter of Am., Can., Bda. Ch. Cummings' Gold-Rush Charlie ex Ch. Bookout's Country Sunshine (by Ch. Goldenwire's Gay Cadet).

Bugaboo

Bugaboo Kennels, owned by John and Edie Shields of Parker, Colorado, began in Canada in the early 1970s, getting off to a disappointing start as the Shields' first four Goldens turned out to be dysplastic. They were not discouraged, however, in their love of the breed; and they eventually acquired their first Champion Cummings' Gold-Rush Charlie daughter, Champion Country Sun's Ms. Cricket, since which time they have been moving steadily forward.

All of the present Bugaboo Goldens are descended from Cricket, whose owners quite rightfully consider her to be a great producer. She is now retired except as her owners' companion and as "tender of the flock."

The Shields are basically line-breeding and building their bloodlines primarily on two dogs, Champion Cummings' Gold-Rush Charlie and Champion Misty Morn's Sunset, C.D., T.D. Selections are being made with the Golden Retriever standard and the working retriever in mind, placing particular emphasis on true Golden type. A bit of English blood has been infused with the American strains, as the Shields feel that the English Goldens "have superior fronts and an overall better head, although tending to be too short in muzzle." Otherwise, they prefer the American type of temperament, coat, movement, elegance, and so on.

Above: Am., Can. Ch. Bugaboo's Apache Doll, by Am., Can. Ch. Krishna's Klassic Kachina ex Am., Can. Ch. Country Sun's Ms. Cricket, is owned by Bugaboo Kennels, John and Edie Shields. **Below:** Am., Can. Ch. Bugaboo's Apache Thunder, multiple Group and Best of Breed winner, by Am., Can. Ch. Krishna's Klassic Kachina (Ch. Autumn Lodge's Mr. Zap ** C.D., ex Ch. Lark Hill Genevive, C.D.) ex Am., Can. Ch. Country Sun's Ms. Cricket, O.D. (Am., Can., Bda. Ch. Cummings' Gold-Rush Charlie ex Ch. Bookout's Country Sunshine, C.D.). Owned by John and Edie Shields.

Am., Can. Ch. Chebaco's Brandywine at eight years of age. By Am., Can. Ch. Uthingo Thembalisha Hlope ex Fox Rock's Black Eyed Suzan. Brandywine is a Dam of Merit, and at the age of eleven she went Best of Opposite Sex from the Veterans Class at the Hudson Valley Specialty. Owned by Jeffrey and Judith Gowing, Rowley, Massachusetts.

Chebaco

The Chebaco Goldens, owned by Mr. and Mrs. Jeffrey Gowing, are located at Rowley, Massachusetts. Although Jeffrey Gowing grew up with Goldens, his wife Judith and he didn't buy their first jointly owned Golden until the late sixties after several years of looking at Goldens and discussing them with various breeders. Their final choice was a puppy from the kennels of Orlando and Mary Merchant, Fox Rock Kennels, in Manchester, Massachusetts. The Gowings feel this was one of the best decisions they have ever made, as the Merchants have been extremely helpful to them over the years, guiding them through their first litters, helping them at their first match show, and introducing them to the sport of showing dogs.

That first puppy soon was joined by another. She turned out to be the rock on which Chebaco's breeding program was founded, American and Canadian Champion Chebaco's Brandywine, sired by American and Canadian Champion Uthingo Thembalisha Hlope from Fox Rock's Black Eyed Suzan. The Gowings' one regret is that they did not know enough about showing, specialing a dog, and so on, to realize that she should have been campaigned earlier and much more extensively than she was. A Dam of Merit, she still is being shown in Veterans Class; and in 1981, at the age of eleven, she went Best of Opposite Sex from Veterans to the delight of her proud owners.

It was a very subtle progression for the Gowings from being dog owners to dog fanciers. In those early years, they were working at Ledyard Farm in Wenham, Massachusetts, caring for a stable of hunters and the Foxhound Kennels at the Myopia Hunt Club. Their interest in showing grew with each addition to their Golden pack until, in 1978, they purchased what is now Chebaco Kennels, a full-service boarding and grooming kennel in Rowley, Massachusetts.

Above: Am., Can., Bda. Ch. Chebaco's Mooselook-meguntic, champagne glass between his paws, celebrates his completion of his American title at the Eastern Dog Club with a five-point major.
Below: Am., Can., Bda. Ch. Chebaco Mooselook-meguntic, by Ch. Imvubu Thembalisha, C.D., ex Ch. Chebaco's Brandywine, at nine-and-a-half years of age. Owned by Mr. and Mrs. Jeffrey Gowing.

A puppy kept from "Brandy's" first litter was named Chebaco Mooselookmeguntic, sired by Champion Imvubu Thembalisha, C.D. He turned out, like his dam, to be an exceptional Golden, earning his championship in the United States, Canada, and Bermuda with many Best of Breed wins during a limited career as a Specials dog. Jeffrey Gowing comments:

> I think that the fact that two of our first three Goldens were real good ones probably sustained our interest throughout the first few years when we were just starting out. So many people seem to get discouraged early in the game, blaming the judges, professional handlers, etc., for their initial lack of success. Here, again, in addition to having excellent dogs to learn with, we also had the invaluable help and guidance of the Merchants.

"Moose" is retired now, although he is still shown occasionally as a veteran.

Ch. Chebaco's Christmas Star finishing the title at Eastern Dog Club, 1980. This dog's littermate, Ch. Chebaco's Jacks Or Better, finished the following day, making it a red-letter weekend for handlers Linda and Bob Stebbins.

The breeding program at Chebaco has, by choice, been a very limited one and, with one or two exceptions, confined to the Fox Rock and Thembalisha lines. One exception was a breeding of Brandy to Champion Misty Morn's Sunset. This litter produced several nice pups, the most notable of which were Champion Chebaco's Jacks Or Better (Gowing) and Champion Chebaco's Christmas Star (Clark). That particular litter was whelped on Christmas Day at six in the morning at the foot of the Gowings' water bed.

Some of the famous names to be found in almost all of the Chebaco pedigrees include Lyle Ring's noted dog, Champion Star Spray's Marias Rayo Del Sol, and the two famous Cragmount dogs, Champion Peter and Champion Hi-Lo, plus some of the Celloyd line of Lloyd Case's Goldens.

The plan at Chebaco is to have not more than a litter or two each year, aiming to produce the truly sound old-time Golden. The Gowings find the breed trend toward oversize distressing.

There are several promising young dogs coming along at Chebaco, keeping hopes high for the future. The most promising of these is Chebaco's Grand Gesture, who won the 12-18 month Puppy Class at the 1981 National and went Reserve Winners Dog at Hudson Valley, also from the 12-18 month Puppy Class.

Chebaco's Grand Gesture at eighteen months of age, winning his class under Michele Billings at the Golden Retriever Club of America Specialty. Jeffrey and Judith Gowing, owners, Chebaco Kennels, Rowley, Massachusetts.

Ch. Cragmount's Hi Lo in September 1965, a short time after he had won Best of Breed at the Golden Retriever Club of America National Specialty in that year. Mrs. Charles W. Engelhard, owner, Cragmount, Far Hills, New Jersey.

Ch. Cheyenne Golden's King John, a famous winner and Best of Breed at the National Specialty in 1966, was sired by Champion Cheyenne Golden's King. King John was a homebred from the Cheyenne Goldens owned by William and Marian Herbert, Wichita, Kansas, and was handled by Mrs. Herbert.

Cheyenne Golden

The Cheyenne Golden Kennels were established by William and Marian Herbert of Wichita, Kansas, back in the 1940s. Although they had owned purebred dogs of other breeds prior to that time, both having been interested in dogs since childhood, it was not until then that they became involved with the breed with which they were to become primarily associated.

The Herberts' first Golden was selected principally due to the breed's proficiency at hunting, as both Mr. and Mrs. Herbert hunted a lot in their younger days. They lived at that time in western Kansas on the edge of the Cheyenne Bottoms, which was a great refuge for wildlife and where pheasant and duck hunting were excellent. When the decision was reached that they would raise Goldens, they named their kennel after the Cheyenne Bottoms.

For some time the Herberts used their dogs solely for hunting purposes, not only in their personal hunting but also in running them in field trials. From this their interest extended to the obedience rings and to conformation competition with the result that, as with so many other fanciers, once the show bug had bitten them, they were permanently "hooked."

The Cheyenne Golden foundation bitch came from Squawkie Hill Kennels, well known at that time in the East, with some excellent bloodlines. This bitch was bred to Champion Golden Knoll's Shur Shot, in his own day a big winner for his owners Dorothy and Russell Peterson, then of Waterloo, Iowa. The lines blended perfectly, and the Herberts with Cheyenne Golden Kennels were on their way! Subsequently they raised a good number of Goldens, finishing a number of them, mostly homebreds.

It is a matter of record that several of these Golden Retrievers made it into the Golden Retriever Hall of Fame, and we are honored to be able to include some of their photographs among our illustrations. Those which gained particular fame were Champion Cheyenne Golden's King, winner of the Golden Retriever Club of America National Specialty in 1962; Champion Cheyenne Golden's King John, who did likewise in 1966; and Champion Cheyenne Golden's Son of James, who gained this coveted award in 1973. It is also worthy of special note that although at times the Herberts' dogs were professionally handled, the above wins were gained owner-handled by Marian Herbert.

These three Goldens were in a direct line of descent. King John was a son of Champion Cheyenne Golden's King, and Son of James was a grandson of King John. Both King and King John were homebreds. Son of James was not a homebred, since the Herberts did not own his dam, but they did own his sire; thus they always personally considered him a homebred since the breeding had been their idea. Son of James is undoubtedly the top owner-handled Golden Retriever of all time, almost all of his wins having been made owner-handled and he was retired with a total of 110 Sporting Group firsts (*the record in Goldens*), thirteen Bests in Show, plus more than three hundred Bests of Breed.

Mr. and Mrs. Herbert are now semi-retired and enjoy travelling a great deal of the time; thus they no longer are campaigning Goldens. However, they still own or co-own some, and they will always have tremendous fondness for the breed. Goldens gave them enormous pleasure, and this enthusiastic couple most definitely contributed an inestimable amount to the progress of a breed, which when they first became interested in it was not too well known.

Ch. Cloverdale's Sweet Sadie handled by Bob Stebbins for Richard and Jane Zimmerman,

Cloverdale

Cloverdale Goldens were established in 1971 when Richard and Jane Zimmerman of Tolland, Connecticut, purchased their first Golden bitch from Ruth Worrest, High Farms Kennels. This was High Farms Beau Brittany, who became a Golden Retriever Club of America Outstanding Dam by producing Champion Cloverdale's Sweet Sadie, American and Canadian Champion Cloverdale's Ringold Tobey, and Champion Cloverdale's Bright Promise, C.D., the latter owned by Tom and Pat Martin of New Mexico. Sadie and Tobey had outstanding careers. Sadie, at thirteen months of age, took Winners Bitch at the 1975 Golden Retriever Club of America Specialty and completed her championship at fifteen months of age with three majors. She had seven Bests of Breed before she was twenty months old, at a period when Golden bitches rarely if ever won breeds. Tobey finished well before he was two years old with four majors, is a Best in Show winner in the United States, and is a multi-Group winner in Canada. He is a member of the Golden Retriever Club of America Hall of Fame and is owned by Nancy Fenn of Westport Point, Massachusetts, daughter of the now retired judge and former Golden breeder Lyle Ring.

Sadie was bred to Champion Wochica's Okeechobee Jake for her first litter, and this pro-

Am., Can. Ch. Cloverdale's Ringold Tobey owned by Richard and Jane Zimmerman, Cloverdale Goldens. Handled by Bob Stebbins.

Above: Cloverdale Sabrina at thirteen months of age. She is the dam of the Best in Show bitch Ch. Cloverdale Twin-Beau-D Joy. Owned by Richard and Jane Zimmerman. **Below:** Ch. Cloverdale Pistol of Windsor, owned by Mr. and Mrs. Carl Furniss, is a littermate to Ch. Cloverdale Twin-Beau-D Joy, bred by the Zimmermans at Cloverdale Kennels.

duced the multiple Group winner Champion Cloverdale's Golden Jake, owned by hound judge (and famous breeder of Norwegian Elkhounds) Robert Indeglia, M.D., and his son Vincent. Champion Cloverdale's Foxy Lady Katie, owned by Connie Harris, also finished easily, at the Westminster Kennel Club. Soon after, another bitch, Champion Cloverdale's Bittersweet Sue, owned by Ed and Edith Bryant,

finished to make Sadie's listing as a Golden Retriever Club of America Outstanding Dam, second generation, and to make her a *Kennel Review* Top Producer, 1979. Sadie's second litter was by the Zimmermans' own American and Canadian Champion Cloverdale Bunker Hill Seth, and this produced still another bitch to finish, Champion Cloverdale's Tera of Tamarron, owned by Jan Adams. A littermate to Tera whom the Zimmermans kept, Cloverdale Sabrina, had five points when it was decided to breed her to Champion Sutter Creek Goldrush Flyboy; the litter produced the first bitch in twenty-seven years to take Best in Show, Champion Cloverdale Twin-Beau-D Joy, owned by the Dallaires, now also a Hall of Famer. Joy's littermate, Champion Cloverdale Pistol of Windsor, owned by Mr. and Mrs. Carl Furniss, was sold as a pet but was "rediscovered" at two years of age and finished in six weeks at seven shows with three majors! He finished taking Best of Winners at the 1981 Hudson Valley Golden Retriever Club Specialty. It is expected that Sabrina will soon become the Zimmermans' third generation homebred Top Producing Dam.

In 1976, the Zimmermans purchased, as a puppy, their American and Canadian Champion Cloverdale Bunker Hill Seth, by Champion Misty Morn's Sunset, C.D., T.D., W.C., ex Sutter Creek Gamboge Haze, from Nancy Hughes. He finished at sixteen months and became a Golden Retriever Club of America Outstanding Sire at just four years of age. He is the sire of seven champions including three Group winners.

Am., Can. Ch. Cloverdale Bunker Hill Seth, a fine sire and show winner.

Am., Can. Ch. October Cloverdale Frost is co-owned by Mrs. Robert V. Clark, Jr., Springfield Farms, and Richard and Jane Zimmerman, Cloverdale Goldens.

The Zimmermans have also owned and finished Champion Cloverdale Fox Rock Misty, dam of Champion Cloverdale Pied Piper owned by themselves and Annette Spencer.

Twenty champions have been bred or owned at Cloverdale, including two Best in Show winners, many Group winners, and several Golden Retriever Club of America Outstanding Producers.

Above: Am., Can. Ch. Sutter Creek Cloverdale Erin, co-owned by Susan Breakell and the Richard Zimmermans. **Below:** Ch. October Cloverdale Frost winning the Sporting Group at Holyoke Kennel Club in 1982 for Mrs. Robert V. Clark, Jr., and J. and R. Zimmerman. Handled by William Trainor.

Many more of his get are close to finishing as this is written. His daughter, the Zimmermans' American and Canadian Champion Sutter Creek Cloverdale Erin, co-owned with Susan Breakell, was Number One Bitch (based on Goldens defeated) for 1980. Erin was Best of Opposite Sex at the 1981 National Specialty, handled by Jane Zimmerman, and has as well three other Specialty Best of Opposite Sex awards.

In 1979, the Zimmermans purchased a puppy who grew up to become their newest champion, American and Canadian Champion October Cloverdale Frost. "Frosty" was undefeated in the Puppy Classes and major-pointed at eight months of age. He finished at fifteen months of age with four majors, a Best of Breed and a second in Group over top Specials, and is now being specialed. "Frosty" has become a multiple Group winner and is co-owned with Mrs. Robert V. Clark, Jr., Springfield Farm, in Virginia. This dog was bred by Sharon C. Smith and Carol Vogel and is by Champion Sir Duncan of Woodbury ex Champion Cal-Vo's Nickel Nedi.

Cummings'

Cummings' Golden Retrievers belong to Mrs. Mary W. Cummings of Stillwater, New Jersey, who purchased her first of the breed, Bierly's Golden Sky, when he was eleven months old. Sky came from Ruanme, Des Lac's, and Golden Knolls lines. Then it was decided to get a good bitch, and one from the Cragmount line was purchased from Arnold Veerkamp who was the Engelhards' estate superintendent at Cragmount. The Cummings' first litter turned out very well, and one puppy in particular, Princess (who became American and Canadian Champion Cummings' Golden Princess), attracted so much favorable comment that it was decided to show her, obviously successfully. Mary Cummings handled all of the first Cummings' champions personally, and the first three were Princess, Penny (Champion Cummings' Copper Penny), and Midas (American and Canadian Champion Cummings' King Midas). When Midas was finished, Mrs. Cummings' husband campaigned him as a Special, and the Cummings

Am., Can. Ch. Cummings' Golden Princess winning the Brood Bitch Class at the Garden State Golden Retriever Club Specialty October 9th 1972. Left to right: Am., Can., Bda. Ch. Cummings' Gold-Rush Charlie, Ch. Russo's Cummings' Elsa, and Princess. Mrs. Mary W. Cummings, Stillwater, New Jersey.

The first Golden Retriever owned by Mrs. Mary W. Cummings, Bierly's Golden Sky.

are proud to note that this dog was the top home-bred, owner-handled Golden in the United States for two years early in the 1970s. Additionally, he was the first recipient of the Champion Freshfield Storm King Award, later gained by many Cummings-line Goldens.

Am., Can. Ch. Cummings' King Midas, first holder of the Freshfield Storm King Trophy. Born December 2nd 1966, this dog is by Bierly's Golden Sky ex Am., Can. Ch. Cummings' Golden Princess. Mrs. Mary W. Cummings, owner, Cummings' Goldens.

April 1981. Linda and Midas at Cummings' Golden Kennels, Stillwater, New Jersey.

Left to right: Ch. Cummings' Golden Princess, Ch. Cummings' Copper Penny, Thunder Cloud of Stillwater (thirteen points) and Ch. Cummings' King Midas from the Cummings' Goldens, Mrs. Mary W. Cummings.

Ch. Cummings' Golden Sunshine, first generation champion from Am., Can. Ch. Cummings' Golden Princess, this one by Ch. Sunset's Happy Duke. Born in January 1968. Mrs. Mary W. Cummings, breeder-owner.

The Cummings' most outstanding breeding to date has been that of American and Canadian Champion Cummings' Golden Princess to Champion Sunset's Happy Duke. The first time they were bred, this combination produced Champion Cummings' Golden Sunshine and Champion Cummings' Golden Sunset. Their second breeding produced American, Canadian, and Bermudian Champion Cummings' Gold-Rush Charlie, the Top Winning Golden of All Time. He was the foundation of the Johnsons' Gold-Rush Kennels. Also from this breeding came Champion Russo's Cummings' Elsa, Mercer Russo Ervin's foundation bitch. The third time around, Princess and Duke produced Champion Sunset's Happy Duke II and Champion Cummings' Dame Pepperhill.

After more than fifteen years of breeding Goldens, Mary Cummings' standard is still the same: classic, well-proportioned, sturdy Golden Retrievers with intelligent, mellow temperaments, broad muzzles and skulls, large dark

Am., Can., Bda. Ch. Cummings' Gold-Rush Charlie, born October 13th 1970, handled by Bill Trainor for Mrs. Robert V. Clark, Jr., and Larry Johnson. By Ch. Sunset's Happy Duke ex Am., Can. Ch. Cummings' Golden Princess. Bred by Mrs. Mary W. Cummings.

Mercer Russo Ervin handles her Ch. Russo's Cummings' Elsa, litter-sister to Ch. Cummings' Gold-Rush Charlie, to Best of Opposite Sex at Wallkill, July 1973. By Ch. Sunset's Happy Duke ex Am., Can. Ch. Cummings' Golden Princess.

eyes, and good pigmentation. This is obvious when one looks at the fourth and fifth generations descended from that outstanding Duke-Princess breeding combination. The fourth generation male, Champion Cummings' Alexander The Great, took Best of Winners at the Westminster Kennel Club Dog Show in 1982. The fifth generation male, Champion Cummings' Chip of Gold, finished with a Group first at twenty-two months of age.

Above: Ch. Cummings' Alexander the Great, shown by his breeder-owner Mrs. Mary W. Cummings, Stillwater, New Jersey, for Best of Winners at South Jersey Kennel Club, October 1981. **Below:** Ch. Cummings' Chip of Gold, fifth generation champion from Am., Can. Ch. Cummings' Golden Princess, by Ch. Cummings' Alexander the Great ex Chucklebrook Jingle. Handled by Joy Quallenberg to Best of Winners at Trenton Kennel Club in 1982. Mrs. Mary W. Cummings, owner.

Above: Cummings' Goldenrod, by Ch. Sunset's Happy Duke ex Am., Can. Ch. Cummings' Golden Princess, taking Best of Winners at Bryn Mawr K.C. Handled by Bob Forsyth for owner Mrs. Mary Cummings. Goldenrod was born January 1968. **Below:** Ch. Cummings' Lizette, by Cummings' Goldenrod ex Ch. Cummings' Copper Penny, taking Best of Opposite Sex at Westminster 1977. Bred by Mrs. Mary W. Cummings.

J.D. Wacker with Can. Ch. Amberac's D.J.'s Dixie Darlin in Open Junior Class, West Bend Kennel Club, July 1981. Dixie has been J.D.'s Top Junior Showmanship dog. Together they have earned a Top Junior Handling Award from Badger Golden Retriever Club in 1979, 1980, and 1981. J.D. is now thirteen years old. Together he and Dixie won Best Junior Handler first time out in Open Junior Class in Iowa.

D.J.'s Goldens

D.J.'s Golden Kennels are a family project, belonging to professional photographer Dave Wacker, who also teaches high school biology and photography; his wife Jean; and their son J.D., also a budding young photographer winning many statewide photo contests. J.D., at age thirteen, has been recognized as one of Wisconsin's Badger Golden Retriever Club's top junior handlers for the past three years. He excels in Junior Showmanship, with conformation and obedience competition a close second. He has trained and handled one of his dogs to a bench champion title, trained and handled another to a C.D. title, and is presently working with another in C.D. training.

The Wackers are interested and involved with all phases of Golden ownership. Among their winners are the lovely bitch Canadian Champion Amberac's D.J.'s Dixie Darlin, an outstandingly fine producer and J.D.'s principal Junior Showmanship dog. Together they have earned a Top Junior Handling Award from Badger Golden Retriever Club in 1979, 1980, and 1981; and together they won the Open Junior Class the first time they competed in it, in Iowa.

Dixie is the dam of some very handsome progeny sired by Mary Wuestenberg's Champion Amberac's Aristocrat.

Socialization time—and a pause for new film in the camera. D.J. Goldens owned by Dave, Jean, and J.D. Wacker.

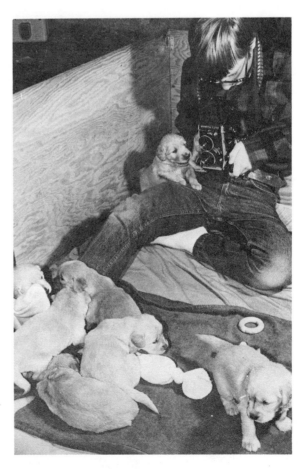

Head study of D.J.'s Gingerbread Crackers, C.D. "Cookie" was trained and handled by J.D. Wacker to a C.D. in three shows when J.D. was nine years old. D.J.'s Golden Kennels, Grafton, Wisconsin.

D.J.'s Stormy Thunderbolt, American and Canadian C.D.X., is by American and Canadian Champion Hobby Horse's Timberdoodle, C.D., from Canadian Champion Amberac's D.J.'s Dixie Darlin.

Amberac's Sungria De Ora, C.D., is the dam of many obedience champions and granddam of champions. Additionally, she is an exceptionally fine hunting dog, greatly enjoyed for this purpose by the Wacker family.

The young dog "Monty," D.J.'s Montana Kid's X-Rated, C.D., represents five generations of the Wackers' breeding program. In his background are to be found, among others, American and Canadian Champion Topbrass Durango Brave, C.D.X., W.C., Canadian C.D.; Amberac's Reeva Rustelle; D.J.'s Dusty Colorado Day Rocky; with Beckwith, Rockgold and Gunnerman lines. The Wackers take great pride in this youngster, who earned his C.D. in three straight shows with J.D.'s father as trainer-

D.J.'s Montana Kid's X-Rated, C.D., will soon be campaigned for his championship.

handler. "Monty's" hunting ability improves with each hunting season, and he has already reached number one among D.J.'s hunting male Goldens.

All of the photos of D.J.'s Goldens which appear in this book were taken either by Dave or J.D. The Wackers are members of the Badger Golden Retriever Club and of the Golden Retriever Club of America.

It isn't *every* one that can carry four balls in his mouth all at once! This talented fellow belongs to D.J.'s Golden Kennel.

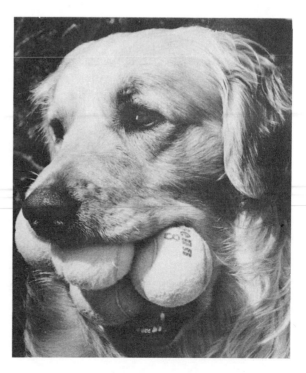

Dasu

Dasu Goldens are owned by Dave and Suzi Bluford and are located at Carmel, California. They really "hit the jackpot" with their foundation bitch, Wendy VIII, U.D., W.C.X., a Golden Retriever Club of America Outstanding Dam, who was bred to only two studs but out of twelve pups gave her owners nine Goldens who have earned bench and obedience titles!

Wendy's sire was Leo of Los Altos, by Royal Golden of Park Lane ex Golden Marideal of Los Altos, by Champion Jason of Gold Anno Nuo from a Champion Oakwin Junior daughter. Her dam was Amanda of Lynn D'Or, by Tradewind Clipper of Gold from Beckwith's Promise of Dalka, C.D.X.*, who was by Colombian, American, Canadian, Bermudian, and Mexican Champion Beckwith's Copper Coin from a daughter of Champion Mel Bachs Curley, C.D.X., ex Beckwith's Flavia, C.D.

Golden baby, photographed by Buffie Collins, at Dasu Goldens, the Dave Blufords, Carmel, California.

Wendy's daughter, Champion Dasu's Champagne Edition, C.D.X., finished entirely in the state of California, earning all of her points from the Bred-by-Exhibitor Class, including a Best of Breed over Specials. She is the only Golden bitch to the Blufords' knowledge who has done this. Her Specials career began in 1982 with Best of Opposite Sex at both the Golden Gate Kennel Club and Santa Clara Kennel Club shows with very large Golden entries; unfortunately, she died in early March of 1982. She produced one litter of pups sired by American and Canadian

Ch. Dasu's Champagne Edition, "Rabbit," by Ch. Sabahka's Alexander of Cal-Vo (Ch. Footprint of Yeo, C.D., ex Ch. Beckwith's Malagold Starfarm) from Ch. Wendy VIII, U.D., W.C.X. (Leo of Los Altos ex Amanda of Lynn D'Or). Breeder-owners, Dave and Suzi Bluford.

Champion and Obedience Trial Champion Sunstreak of Culynwood, T.D., W.C.X., Canadian C.D.; and although the pups are quite young, they look very promising for both breed and obedience competition. "Rabbit," as Champagne Edition was known, had scores in both Novice and Open which qualified her for entry in the Gaines Obedience competitions, and she was training for Utility at the time of her death.

American, Canadian Champion and Obedience Trial Champion Sunstreak of Culynwood, T.D., W.C.X., Canadian C.D., or "Streaker," as he was known informally, also had his home at Desu. His coming to Desu Kennels was the result of Suzi Bluford's having heard about a litter of Goldens, which was expected at another kennel, in which she felt she would be interested. The dam was Champion Tangelo's End of the Rainbow, C.D., and the sire was Champion Sabahka's Alexander of Cal-Vo, C.D.; the breeders were Lynn and Pat Fletcher. The litter had been almost completely reserved for other interested purchasers, and Suzi's name was added to the bottom of the list. When the litter was born, there turned out to be just one puppy—a male. Under these circumstances, Suzi never expected to get that one lone puppy; but the Fletchers figured, quite rightly, that if she had him, Suzi would do well by him,

and that is how "Streaker" joined the Goldens at Dasu Kennels. Since this was right at the time of Suzi's birthday, Dave Bluford and the Fletchers decided on a surprise for her—a long ribbon to be followed through the house, which brought her eventually to a box inside of which was "Streaker."

In the spring of 1975, "Streaker" started out in obedience, earning his C.D. in three shows (at Fresno, Tulare, and Bakersfield). His C.D.X. followed in four shows during the summer; and before a year had passed, he had earned his Utility Dog title in only three more shows.

This is the great "Streaker," Am., Can. Ch. and O.T. Ch. Sunstreak of Culynwood, T.D., W.C.X., Can. C.D., born in Menlo Park, California, bred by Lynn and Patricia Fletcher, and owned by Mr. and Mrs. David Bluford, Carmel, California. Sired by Ch. Sabahka's Alexander of Cal-Vo, C.D., ex Ch. Tangelo's End of the Rainbow, C.D., W.C. "Streaker" holds a unique position in Golden history for his accomplishments and in the heart of the Golden Fancy for his beauty, intelligence, and capability. His death, at far too young an age, just before this book went to press, is mourned by Golden admirers everywhere.

The style of a winner. Am., Can. Ch. and O.T. Ch. Sunstreak of Culynwood, T.D., W.C.X., Can. C.D., or "Streaker," as he was best known to his admirers. Dave and Suzi Bluford, owners, Dasu Goldens, Carmel, California.

"Streaker" was High in Trial at the Golden Retriever Club of America National Specialty in 1977 and at the Golden Retriever Club of America Western Regional Specialties in 1977, 1978, and 1979. He won the Gaines Regional Super Dog in 1977. He is a member of the Golden Retriever Club of America Hall of Fame. His 1978 accomplishments, already listed, made him Top Obedience Dog in the United States that year, for which he received the Quaker Oats' Ken-L-Ration Award, presented to him in New York at the annual awards dinner held on the eve of Westminster each February at the Waldorf Astoria Hotel. He still is in second place for lifetime obedience trial championship points. In 1979, "Streaker" was not only High in Trial and High Combined in the Golden Retriever Club of America Western Regional, held in conjunction with the Tacoma Kennel Club all-breed dog show, but he was also Best of Breed in the Specialty and went on to win the Sporting Group there. The day before, at the Evergreen Independent Specialty, he had been High in Trial and High Combined. "Streaker" passed his first tracking test to earn his Tracking Dog degree and in the fall of 1981 he passed his Working Certificate Excellent test.

Entered in fifty-three shows during 1978, "Streaker" placed forty-nine times, won High Combined twenty-six times, and gained High in Trial nineteen times. Although it was Suzi who always handled "Streaker," Dave took the great dog in when Suzi was once ill, and twice he took High in Trial with him despite not being the handler to whom "Streaker" was accustomed. Additionally, "Streaker" was shown in breed competition at probably two-thirds of the shows where he competed in obedience, and he took Best of Breed four or five times plus a Group placement. Almost all of the shows were in California with the exception of an Oregon circuit and once the Arizona circuit.

Among "Streaker's" total accomplishments were the earning of his C.D., C.D.X., and U.D. in less than one year at under two years of age. He was only the third dog in the United States to win the obedience trial championship and the second champion and obedience trial champion (but the first male to gain this accomplishment). He had a total of thirty-four High in Trials in the United States and three perfect scores of 200, one from the Utility Class and two from the Open B Class. He was not mature until three years old and then finished his championship easily, as mentioned above, winning a Best of Breed and Group fourth along the way.

"Streaker," Am., Can. Ch. and O.T. Ch. Sunstreak of Culynwood, T.D., W.C.X., Can. C.D., at the Tacoma Kennel Club Dog Show in 1979. At this event, "Streaker" won Best of Breed in the Golden Retriever Club of America Regional Specialty, first in the Sporting Group, High in Trial, and High Combined (Open B and Utility) for a truly red-letter day in Golden history. Dave and Suzi Bluford, owners.

In 1981, "Streaker" visited Canada, and here again his appearances were triumphant. He earned his championship in his first three shows there and won the Novice B Class all three days, gaining his Canadian C.D. He was High in Trial all three days and then was pulled by his owners from further competition in fairness to the other exhibitors. His son, Viking, was High in Trial at one of these latter events.

The Blufords have hardly recovered from the tragedy of "Streaker's" untimely death, and that of "Rabbit," in the spring of 1982. This marvelous dog was right in the prime of his life, and to lose him so unexpectedly must have been a heartbreaking experience for his owners. He is mourned by the entire Golden Fancy, as his had been a career which had brought enormous pride to the breed.

The Blufords' hope that "Streaker" will become an Outstanding Sire in 1982 seems entirely likely. His progeny which so far have gained fame include Canadian Champion Beckwith's Zesty Gal; Canadian Champion Beckwith's Zhivago of Oriana, Canadian C.D.; Beckwith's Zanzibar Kid (with points in Canada); Beckwith's Zwierig Sun Shader, C.D. (pointed); Pekay's Jesse James (pointed); Honeywood's Howdy Rebel, C.D.X., W.C.X.; Chaparral's Freelander (with major points); Chaparral's Sundowner Surfer, C.D.X. (started in Utility); Reddigold's Good Bye Girl (expected to finish in 1982); and Beckwith's Kvamme Vogue (with both majors from Bred-by-Exhibitor Class). Among these are included a U.D. son with obedience trial championship points, many with High in Trial scores to their credit, and one of the youngest Goldens ever to have passed the Working Certificate Excellent tests. One of Streaker's proudest achievements was his siring one litter for Guide Dogs for the Blind, and all of the bitches from that litter are brood bitches for Guide Dogs.

Perhaps his son, American and Canadian Champion Beckwith's Viking for Dasu, C.D., Canadian C.D., may follow in the pawprints of his illustrious sire. He is co-owned by Ludell Beckwith and Dave and Suzi Bluford, and hopes are high for him. His dam is American and Canadian Champion Beckwith's Nutmeg, C.D.X., Canadian C.D., who is a Golden Retriever Club of America Outstanding Dam.

Viking completed his American championship with a Best of Breed from the classes over

Above: The great "Streaker" at seven weeks old. Dave and Suzi Bluford, owners. **Below:** An action shot of a Golden puppy belonging to Dave and Suzi Bluford, Dasu Goldens. Photo by Buffie Collins.

Specials and the Winners Dog and Best of Winners awards from the Evergreen Specialty. In Canada he earned his championship with three straight five-point wins including a Best of Breed and Group placement. He earned his first High in Trial in Canada, and his scores in Novice in the United States averaged 195. Viking possesses many of his sire's qualities, including the outgoing personality and willingness to please. Because he is such a handsome dog, large, powerful, heavily coated, and excelling in angulation and movement, an exciting obedience and show career are anticipated for this young dog.

Duckpond

Duckpond Goldens are owned by Bruce and Donna Mittelstaedt of Slinger, Wisconsin. A small kennel up until this time, founded in 1979-80, it is a combined project of Bruce, his wife, and their daughters—brought about by Bruce's desire for a hunting dog. When he broke the news to Donna that he wanted to get one, her reply was, "Well, if you're going to get one, let's get one of those pretty ones with the long golden hair." And that is how Duckpond Kennels began.

Duckpond's Big Fellow, a six-month-old "hopeful" belonging to Bruce and Donna Mittelstaedt, Duckpond Kennels, Slinger, Wisconsin.

Duckpond's Graham Cracker finished retrieving a boat pumper during training. Bruce and Donna Mittelstaedt, owners.

At the proper time, "Sunny" went off for two months of training, with regular visits from his family, of course. At one class the trainer suggested the dog be entered in a field trial and told of a coming one in the area where the Mittelstaedts could visit and learn what it was all about. They did, and after watching the action they started to feel that their dog very definitely could perform as those they had observed had done that day. So at the next sanctioned trial "Sunny" was entered in the Derby Stake and came home with a Judges Award of Merit. Need we add that the Mittelstaedts were "hooked," immediately succumbing to "field trial fever." Of course, meeting nice people and seeing the comradeship shared by them and the teamwork of working together helps, as Bruce put it, "to set the hook."

It is true that one Golden leads to another, and so interest grew. Bruce and Donna joined the Badger Golden Retriever Club (of which he is now President) and started adding to their knowledge. Today in their kennel they are working to breed a combination of proven field lines with show lines, striving for the truly *balanced* Golden Retriever. Bruce comments:

> I love this breed and the versatility it offers. My only personal fear is that not enough effort is being made to keep the retrieving ability alive. I see a real minority of Goldens out in the field, and this is a definite shame because there is no sight more beautiful to see than the grace, elegance, and pride of a Golden bringing back the game.

101

Farview

Farview Golden Retrievers, established in 1966, are owned by Anne M. Plusch and Herman A. Plusch, Jr., at Wrightstown, Pennsylvania. Their first two bitches, the foundation of the kennel, became champions, and Champion Walkir Lafayette Burgandy, C.D., also earned her Working Certificate from the Golden Retriever Club of America. She is in the Golden Retriever Club of America Hall of Fame, having produced seven champions by three different sires.

During their first twelve years, Farview produced eleven American champions and eight Canadian champions. Their stock also includes three Utility Dogs, quite a few C.D.X. dogs, and many C.D. titleholders. Mrs. Plusch comments, with pride, that all of the dogs from their breeding who have ever gone for a Working Certificate have received it.

The aim at Farview is to produce and maintain the triple-purpose dog. In breeding, field lines are crossed with show lines and then back again. All of the Farview dogs are used in the field, and many splendid hunting dogs have resulted.

Mr. and Mrs. Plusch hold their breeding program to between one and three litters annually. The kennel presently (late 1982) consists of twenty-two adult dogs.

The Farview dogs are socialized from three weeks on. By eight weeks they are paper-trained and will retrieve by hand. Obviously they are greatly enjoyed by their owners, who breed to the standard, being well aware of its aims and purposes.

Some of the Farview Goldens owned by Anne and Herman Plusch, Jr., of Wrightstown, New Jersey, enjoying their handsome, well-planned kennel.

Frontier

Frontier Kennels, owned by Henry and Michelle Arszman of Sheridan, Indiana, have been breeding Goldens for about fifteen years, during which time they have had several Golden champions which have done well by them. The most exciting Golden is Champion Tempo's Frontier Bronco who, right from the first,

Above: Number One Golden Retriever for 1981, Ch. Tempo's Frontier Bronco, handled by Dick Cooper for Gandalf Kennels, Dr. George and Vivian Wright, Amelia, Ohio. Bronco was purchased as a youngster by Frontier Kennels, who showed him to championship and now co-own him with the Wrights. Here he is pictured winning one of his four All-Breed Bests in Show, at Evansville Kennel Club in 1981. **Below:** Best of Breed at the Golden Retriever Club of America National Specialty in October 1981, Ch. Tempo's Frontier Bronco, handled by Dick Cooper.

possessed "that special quality which we felt would make a Number One Golden." This dog was bred by Peter and Sheila Huser of Tempo Kennels in Sheridan, Indiana, and was purchased by the Arszmans as a young puppy. The Arszmans finished Bronco to his championship and then in February of 1981 decided to lease him to George and Vivian Wright (of Amelia, Ohio), Gandalf Kennels, to co-own and campaign him. Bronco was then sent out with professional handler Dick Cooper, and the rest is history! By the Arszmans' count, Bronco finished 1981 as the Number One Golden in the Country, having won the 1981 Golden Retriever Club of America National Specialty, the 1981

Kids and Goldens are the best of friends—as one can see from this pair, snapped informally by Michelle and Hank Arszman of the Frontier Kennels.

Golden Retriever Club of America Regional Specialty, and the 1981 Indiana State Golden Retriever Specialty. At the time of this writing, he also has won four Bests in Show (the largest over 2,500 dogs), fourteen Sporting Group firsts, and twenty-nine Group placements.

While standing at limited stud, Bronco has sired several litters. So far, four championships have been gained by his progeny. Bronco is a Number One Golden sired by a Number One Golden, Champion Sun Dance's Rarue, who attained the honor in 1976. His dam, Champion Tempo's Nassau Miss, also was a successful winner when shown.

Ch. Cummings' Gold-Rush Charlie winning a Stud Dog Class with two of his progeny. Handled by William Trainor for Mrs. Robert V. Clark, Jr., and Larry Johnson.

The first homebred to be shown by Gold Dust Kennels, Gold Dust Dashing Daniel, by Am., Can., Bda. Ch. Cummings' Gold-Rush Charlie ex Cummings' Gold Dust Dolly. Marilyn Plantholt of Katonah, New York, owner.

Gold Dust

Gold Dust Goldens, at Katonah, New York, are owned by Marilyn A. Plantholt whose hobby as a Golden breeder started in 1975 with the purchase of a lovely, intelligent bitch from Cummings' Goldens at Stillwater, New Jersey. This was Cummings' Gold Dust Dolly, who at the age of two-and-a-half years was bred to American, Canadian, and Bermudian Champion Cummings' Gold-Rush Charlie. The resulting offspring were the beginning of Gold Dust's future in the breed.

Gold Dust Dashing Daniel, a male retained from this litter, is major-pointed and a Reserve Winner from a National Specialty, won at ten months of age.

Annie Hall III, also from this litter, is the dam of the Plantholts' first champion, American and Canadian Champion Gold Dust Max-A-Million, who was sired by Susan Breakell's Champion Sutter Creek Goldrush Flyboy, an outcrossed dog by Champion Gold-Rush's Great Teddy Bear ex Champion Goldrush Birch of Bearwood. This line-breeding incorporated new genes for Gold Dust, and the result is a beautiful dog well within the Golden Retriever standard.

Max's show career started at the age of six months at the Long Island Golden Retriever Club Specialty in April 1980. He placed in both Sweeps and Regular Classes. He also was Best Sporting Puppy at Taconic Hills Kennel Club match show that same year and Best Sporting Adult in match there the following year. Later, with a professional handler (Bob Stebbins), Max went to Canada for the Barrie Circuit, where he attained his Canadian championship in three straight days of showing. In the United States, he started out owner-handled in June 1981 and

Am., Can. Ch. Sutter Creek Goldrush Flyboy, Susan Breakell, owner-handler, Sutter Creek Kennels.

At the start of his show career, then one year old, Am., Can. Ch. Gold Dust Max-A-Million. Owner, Marilyn Plantholt.

had attained four points prior to his Canadian trip. During five weeks in the autumn of 1981 he finished his American championship, and his victories included Best of Winners at the Eastern Dog Club in Boston. This was an exciting experience for his owner and the culmination of a carefully planned breeding program.

Max is siring very handsome puppies. A line-breeding to Gold-Rush Palimino Pony, U.D., W.C., owned by Susan Jaffee of Bronxville, New York, has produced beautiful puppies, some being field-trained and at only three months of age already retrieving birds. Champion Westmont's Queen Jess, Winners Bitch from the 1981 Golden Retriever Club National Specialty, is currently expecting a litter by Max, due in late 1982.

A repeat breeding of the producers of Max has resulted in Gold Dust Chrystal Clear, Best Junior Puppy at a recent Specialty match as well as Best Sporting Puppy at an all-breed match. Hopes are high for this one's future.

Am., Can. Ch. Gold Dust Max-A-Million, a grandson of Ch. Cummings' Gold-Rush Charlie, takes Best of Winners at Farmington Valley in 1981. Handled by Bob Stebbins under judge Peter Thomson for proud owner Marilyn Plantholt.

A Gold Dust puppy waits patiently in the Plantholts' mail box for the postman's arrival. Marilyn Plantholt, owner.

Winning the Stud Dog Class at the 1978 National Specialty, Ch. Cummings' Gold-Rush Charlie with Ch. Gold-Rush's Great Teddy Bear, Best of Breed at this same show, and Ch. Russo's Pepperhill Poppy, Top Winning Golden Bitch of all time.

Gold-Rush

Gold-Rush Golden Retrievers were established in the early 1970s by Dr. and Mrs. L.C. (Larry and Ann) Johnson at Princeton, New Jersey, with the acquisition of the puppy who grew up to become American, Canadian, and Bermudian Champion Cummings' Gold-Rush Charlie, the Top Winning Golden in the history of the breed. Sired by Champion Sunset's Happy Duke ex American and Canadian Champion Cummings' Golden Princess, Charlie had a remarkable show career with forty-two All-Breed Bests in Show (a record for the breed which still stands in 1982), 105 Sporting Group firsts, sixty-seven other Group placements, and seven Golden Retriever Specialties. In 1974 alone, he defeated more than 34,000 dogs, ranking him fifth among the all-time top Sporting dogs and fifteenth among the all-time top winners all breeds. It was early in 1975 that he broke the breed record for Bests in Show (one which had stood for more than twenty years), adding over half as many more to that previous record.

The great Ch. Cummings' Gold-Rush Charlie, with his handler Bill Trainor, winning one of his numerous Bests in Show, this time under judge Henry Stoecker.

In the show ring, Charlie was a dog who seemed to electrify the gallery. Under Bill Trainor's flawless handling, Charlie's appearance was greeted by an enthusiastic following wherever he went. He is a true personality dog and has taken his place as an outstanding producer. During much of his show career, Charlie was owned by Mrs. Robert V. Clark, Jr., of Springfield Farm, but now he is retired and is again thoroughly enjoying life as a member of the Johnson household.

Charlie was Top Golden in 1973, 1974, and 1975. In 1976 and 1977, this honor went to another Johnson Golden, Champion Gold-Rush's Great Teddy Bear, who defeated more Goldens than any other owner-breeder handled Golden. 1978 and 1979 saw Champion Stone's Gold-Rush Shiloh take over as Top Golden. And the 1980's highlight for this kennel was when the all-breed Best in Show dog, Champion Gold-Rush Copper Lee, won the National Specialty, as had Charlie and Teddy before him.

Ch. Gold-Rush's Great Teddy Bear has won Best of Breed at seven Golden Specialties, is the sire of fifty champions, and is the *Kennel Review* Number One sire for 1981.

Ch. Gold-Rush Copper Lee, a Best in Show winner and a National Specialty Best of Breed winner (1980), owned by Ann and Larry Johnson.

Above: Larry Johnson with two young Goldens sired by Ch. Gold-Rush's Great Teddy Bear. They are Ch. Gold-Rush's Lightnin' and Gold-Rush's Russo's Ciara at a very early age. **Below:** Ch. Jung Olds Gold-Rush Hope, a lovely representative of the Gold-Rush Goldens.

Several more of the Gold-Rush stud dogs distinguished themselves during 1981, and some of their famous offspring include the Top Winning Golden Bitch in U.S. history, Champion Russo's Pepperhill Poppy; the first bench show and obedience champion of any breed, Champion and Obedience Trial Champion Russo's Gold-Rush Joshua Sensation, U.D.; and the Hall of Fame members Champion Laurell's

Above: Ch. Gold-Rush Lightnin', Best of Breed at the Long Island Golden Retriever Club Specialty, was shown for a year on the West Coast, too. Pictured winning the breed at Del Monte in May 1981. **Below:** A handsome head profile of Ch. Gold-Rush Lightnin'.

Ch. Cummings' Gold-Rush Charlie in the field. Gold-Rush Goldens, Ann and Larry Johnson.

York, Champion Gold-wing's True Bear, Champion Southern's Gold-Rush Traveler, Champion Golden Kelby Dustin, Champion Gold-Rush Joshua of Cameron, Champion Kachina's Kamiakin O'Darnley, and numerous others.

Ann Johnson estimates that as of mid-1982 more than 150 champions have been sired at Gold-Rush.

Champion Copper Lee Gold-Rush Apollo is a current winner from this kennel. Co-owned with Judy Beuer of Copper Lee Kennels, Apollo is three times descended from Charlie. He is full brother to Copper; and his mother, Gold-Rush Sara Lee, is littermate to three greats: Champion Gold-Rush Lightnin', Champion Gold-Rush Joshua of Cameron, and Champion Gold-Rush Masterpiece. Apollo's sire, Champion Gold-Rush Skyrocket, is a son of Charlie. With four generations of Gold-Rush winners behind him, he is the brightest star among the youngsters at Gold-Rush and he seems destined to carry on in the family tradition.

The great and famous Ch. Cummings' Gold-Rush Charlie pictured at home in Princeton, New Jersey. Photo courtesy of his owner, R. Ann Johnson.

A group of friends. The Goldens are Ch. Copper Kettle's Headliner, W.C., on the left, and Ch. Copper Kettle's Glory's Gobler, W.C., standing in the background. From Golden Glo Kennels, Don and Marilyn Sturz, Huntington, New York.

Golden Glo

Golden Glo Goldens, owned by Marilyn and Don Sturz at Huntington, New York, began late in the 1960s when the Sturzes purchased a pet for their three-year-old daughter, who was terrified of dogs. The dog's name was Betandray's Nottingham Sherrif, and he fulfilled his job well, being wonderful for the little girl and becoming her constant companion.

Through the breeder of Sherrif, Mr. and Mrs. Sturz met some other Golden owners and were quickly drawn into the fun of getting involved in showing a dog. Six months after their pet purchase, they bought their first show bitch. One year after that, a dog and a bitch (littermates) joined the family. The first bitch became Champion Copper Kettle's Glory's Gobler, and the next two did equally well, becoming Champion Copper Kettle's Headliner and Champion Copper Kettle's Society Page. The Sturzes now were active participants in the dog world, showing their Goldens in breed and working them in obedience and in the field.

The first bitch, Champion Copper Kettle's Glory's Gobler, received a C.D. in obedience and a Working Certificate in the field. She was a natural worker at the field trials, placing in every Gun Dog Stake in which she was entered. She had little training, all of it done by her amateur field-trainer, Don Sturz. She was a triple-purpose dog, the first generation of a three-generation line of top winning Goldens.

Gobler had two puppies in her first litter, a dog and a bitch. The bitch became the Sturzes' first homebred champion, American and Canadian Champion Golden Glo's Valentine. Her show record brought fame and prestige to the kennel. Valentine was the first dog to carry the Golden Glo prefix, and she did so with a flair! She finished her championship at eighteen months of age after just four months of limited showing. Valentine had many Bests of Breed and Bests of Opposite Sex. She competed as a Special when Champion Wochica's Okeechobee Jake and Champion Cummings' Gold-Rush Charlie did their big winning. This was a period during which it was extremely difficult to get a bitch through to the top against their competition, and for that reason the Sturzes take particular pride in the record she attained. She went Best of Opposite Sex at innumerable Specialties, the most exciting of which was the Golden Retriever Club of America National in 1977 in California, when she won over two hundred bitches. She has retired the Long Island Golden Retriever Club Best of Opposite Sex Challenge Trophy by winning it three times in a row. Another trophy was donated in her name and it is still to be won. There are more Golden Glo names on the trophy than any other kennel prefix.

Valentine retired at the National Specialty, coming out to compete as a Veteran Bitch at the Long Island Specialty in 1980. Not only did she handily win that class, but she also went on to become Mrs. Ann Stevenson's choice for Best of Opposite Sex over a large class of Special bitches. This win made her the Long Island Golden Retriever Club Top Show Dog of that year. Valentine was noted and admired for her soundness, movement, and showmanship. The Sturzes feel that it is she who "broke the ice" for future bitches in Specials competition, as, prior to her time, it was rare for Golden bitches to take Best of Breed. Now it is not so uncommon, and Valentine is thought to have had a lot to do with this trend. Valentine was Number One Golden Bitch in the United States in 1978, and Number Five overall, Golden Retriever Club of America ratings.

Am., Can. Ch. Golden Glo's Valentine, Best of Opposite Sex at the Golden Retriever Club of America National Specialty in 1977, handled here and throughout her career as a Special by Donald Sturz. Dr. Bernard McGivern is the judge and Rachel Page Elliot is presenting the trophy.

Ch. Copper Kettle's Glory's Gobler, C.D., W.C., is the dam of the great bitches Ch. Golden Glo's Valentine and Ch. Golden Glo's Margo.

The following year Champion Copper Kettle's Glory's Gobler produced her second litter, eight puppies, including future Champion Golden Glo's Margo. Again they had a great bitch, as Margo's wins soon made her record comparable to that of Valentine, with numerous Best of Breed and Best of Opposite Sex successes. She also won the Golden Retriever Club of Long Island Best of Opposite Sex trophy, and she was Number One Golden Bitch in the United States in 1979 and Number Three overall. Margo also placed Number Seven during another year. She was admired and known for her soft expression, movement, and showmanship. She also proved herself as a producer, being the dam of Champion Golden Glo's Casey Up To Bat and Champion Golden Glo's Novella.

Ch. Copper Glo's Casey's Up To Bat, with owner Don Sturz, gaining points at Boardwalk Kennel Club in 1978.

Both of these bitches were used by the Sturz youngsters, Donald and Janet, for Junior Showmanship. The discipline and stamina required of a dog to compete in Juniors far surpasses the breed ring, and these two never gave up for the children, even on the frequent occasions when they went into the breed ring immediately following or preceding the Junior competition. They always love the ring.

Donald and Janet Sturz were very successful Junior competitors. They developed their skill by using all the dogs in the kennel, not just one favorite dog. Donald's awards included being among *Kennel Review's* Top Ten Junior Handlers every year that he competed, 1971-1977; Top Junior Handler, *Kennel Review*, 1975; *Dog World* Award, 1974 and 1976; Metropolitan Area Top Junior Trophy; and Owner-Handler's Association Junior Trophy. He also

Ch. Golden Glo's Margo is handled here by Don Sturz to Best of Breed at Trenton in 1978 under judge John Lawreck. Don Sturz handling for himself and Marilyn Sturz.

qualified to show at Westminster every year of competition, reaching the finals twice. Janet's awards included being among *Kennel Review's* Top Ten Junior Handlers every year she competed, 1974-1979; Top Junior Handler, *Kennel Review*, 1976; and Metropolitan Area Top Junior Trophy twice. She also qualified to show at Westminster every year of competition, reaching the finals once and placing second.

Donald was a columnist for *Kennel Review* magazine for two years, on the subject of Junior Showmanship. Donald's and Janet's success in Junior Showmanship with Goldens has encouraged many other young Golden owners to compete with their dogs.

The first stud dog owned by Don and Marilyn Sturz was Champion Copper Kettle's Headliner, W.C. He was a breed winner with Group placements to his credit. He lacked the flair to make a top Special but more than made up for

Ch. Shorona's Ben Hur, by Ch. Copper Kettle's Headliner, W.C., a Group winner owned by Don and Marilyn Sturz.

Ch. Copper Kettle's Headliner, W.C., handled by Don Sturz. Owners, Don and Marilyn Sturz, Golden Glo Kennels.

113

Ch. Shorona's Clyde, another Group-winning son of Ch. Copper Kettle's Headliner, W.C., taking a Group first at Plainfield Kennel Club for Don and Marilyn Sturz.

that, proving his worth as a sire by producing two Group-winning Goldens and numerous other pointed get. His two champions are Champion Shorona's Ben Hur and Champion Shorona's Clyde. They were sound dogs of admirable substance. Headliner used to attend school with Marilyn who is a teacher and he became the mascot of that school, visiting all thirty classrooms throughout the day, rolling on the floor to let the kindergarten youngsters cuddle him, stealing lunches from the older children's desks, and sleeping by the principal's air conditioner. His temperament was superb.

Champion Copper Kettle's Society Page, W.C., was Headliner's littermate. Her biggest show victory was going Winners Bitch at the Golden Retriever Club Eastern Regional Specialty in 1972. She was handled by Marilyn to her championship; and when "Bonnie," as

she was called, retired from the show ring, so did Marilyn, to take over backstage management as there were just too many handlers in the family at that time.

The Golden Glo dogs have been used in magazine ads, TV commercials, and some books and magazines. Goldens respond very well to all the attention they receive doing these kinds of things.

Don Sturz became a professional handler in 1975. He started by handling Goldens and now handles dogs in the Sporting, Hound, and Working Groups.

Donald and Janet were the founders of the Long Island Junior Handlers Club, along with two other Juniors from that area.

The Sturzes' Golden Retrievers became a total family activity, the children travelling with their parents almost every weekend. They met many different people and they still correspond with a number of their Junior friends. It opened up many opportunites for the family, and it certainly affected all of them. Donald's recognition by the Dog Writer's Association, a Certificate of Merit for his column in *Kennel Review*, encouraged him to develop his writing talents, which have helped him in his college career. Don had been a detective for the Nassau County Police Department, but he retired to pursue his interests in the Golden world. Thus the Golden Retrievers provided an alternate career for him! Without realizing how it happened, the Sturz family has found that their lives have become entwined with their Goldens, and they feel that they have gained a great deal from this experience.

Golden Pine (East Coast)

Golden Pine came about in what owner, Mary Luise Semans of Chesapeake, Virginia, describes as a very inauspicious way, although we feel that the circumstances were rather prophetic.

Jo Semans won the Daily Double at Saratoga Race Track one day in August 1949, and gave Mary Luise fifty dollars, with which they purchased their first Golden Retriever. One-and-a-half years later this dog, Duke of Rochester II ("Rusty" to his friends), was Best of Breed and placed in the Sporting Group at Westminster, only his third dog show, and *from the classes*. So, who knows? Perhaps it was the "lucky money" gained by the track win that put Golden Pine off

The first of the Golden Pine Goldens, Duke of Rochester II, winning Best of Breed at Westminster, on his way to third in the Sporting Group from the classes on only his third appearance in the show ring, February 1951. The judge is Mrs. Beatrice Hopkins Godsol; the handler is Lloyd M. Case for owner Mary Lu Semans.

to so exciting a start! Lloyd M. Case handled "Rusty" through to Best of Winners and the Group win that day, but he had to turn him over to Charles Crane for the Best of Breed competition as he was already committed to handle Champion Prince Alexander, another famous Golden of the period. The judge was Mrs. Beatrice Hopkins Godsol. Mary Luise Semans comments, "and all this came about because a Golden breeder who is also a neighbor said 'you ought to show that dog.' "

"Rusty's" first stud service, to Wessala Tawny, produced Champion Wessala Pride of Golden Pine, who in turn was bred to Champion Little Joe of Tigathoe***, owned by Mrs. George H. (Torch) Flinn. Pride and Joe produced seven champions and the start of the Golden Pine line.

Ch. Golden Pine's Brown Bear taking Best in Show at Green Mountain Dog Club, 1958.

Ch. Wessala Pride of Golden Pine, Outstanding Dam, owned by Mary Luise Semans, Chesapeake, Virginia, on June 5th 1958 with her handler Lloyd M. Case.

Ch. Golden Pine's Easy Ace winning the Sporting Group at Wallkill Kennel Club, July 10th 1960. Lloyd M. Case is handling, and Miss Laura F. Delano is the judge. Owned by Mary Luise Semans, Golden Pine Kennels.

Ch. Goldwing True Bear, owned by Mrs. William B. Long and Leslie Dove, making a good Sporting Group win. Photo courtesy of William J. Trainor.

Seven generations later, with Golden Pine on both sides, there is Best in Show-winning Champion Goldwing True Bear, bred, owned, and handled by Leslie Dove, Number Four Golden Retriever for 1981. Golden Pine can indeed take justifiable pride in what they started and in the fact that their dogs have accomplished and contributed to the progress of their breed.

There have been many field trial wins, obedience titles, High in Trials, Bests in Show, and Group wins, along with Group placements too numerous to count. Golden Pine has been fortunate over the years to have champions in all sections of the United States and in Canada.

Mrs. Semans gives special credit to those who have purchased promising young puppies from Golden Pine and were sufficiently interested to show them. Special credit also goes to those who have handled for her: the late Lloyd Case, Robert J. Walgate, and Eric Thomee during the early years, and Bobby B. Barlow for the present.

Above: Ch. Golden Pine's Bambi's Lady, Outstanding Dam, with her handler Eric Thomee winning at Framingham in 1957 under judge Alva Rosenberg. Mary Luise Semans, owner, Golden Pine Kennels. **Below:** Ch. Golden Pine's Glorybe, Outstanding Dam, taking Reserve Winners Bitch at the 1971 Golden Retriever Club of America National Specialty. Judge, Lee Murray. Owner, Mary Luise Semans.

Ch. Golden Pine's Punkin Pi, C.D., Outstanding Dam, handled by Susan Slade for owner Mary Luise Semans. The judge is James Duncan.

Ch. Golden Pine's Brown Bear at Champlain Valley, July 13th 1958, with handler Lloyd M. Case, on the way to Best in Show. Mary Luise Semans, owner.

Some of the outstanding Goldens (there have been Dachshunds, too, and a Shetland Sheepdog champion, but it is with the Goldens that we are concerned here) which have represented the Semans so successfully in the show ring have included, among many others, Champion Duke of Rochester II, C.D., Champion Wessala Pride of Golden Pine, Champion Golden Pine's Beau Tigathoe, Champion Golden Pine's Brown Bear, Champion Golden Pine's Bambi's Lady, Champion Golden Pine's Easy Ace, W.C., Champion Golden Pine's Punkin Pi, C.D., Champion Golden Pine's Glorybe, Champion Golden Pine's Down Payment, Champion Golden Pine's Full House, C.D., Champion Golden Pine's Heavenly Days, U.D., Champion Golden Pine's Ace's Hi, Champion Golden Pine's High Farms Fez, Champion Golden Pine's Gradene's J.D., C.D.X., W.C., Champion Golden Pine's Courvoisier, C.D.X., W.C., Champion Golden Pine Glorybe's Angel, Champion Golden Pine's Just-A-Minute, and Champion Golden Pine Angel Seraphim.

Along the way, Mr. and Mrs. Semans have involved themselves with a wide variety of activities pertaining to Goldens. Mr. Semans was President of the Golden Retriever Club of America for two years, 1957-1959, and Mrs. Semans was President of the Potomac Valley Golden Retriever Club three different times.

Ch. Golden Pine Angel's Seraphim, daughter of Ch. Cummings' Gold-Rush Charlie ex Ch. Golden Pine Glorybe's Angel (litter-sister to Ch. Gold-Rush's Great Teddy Bear) finishes her championship by winning this Sporting Group from the classes. Bobby B. Barlow, handler. Gordon Parham, judge. Mary Luise Semans, owner, Golden Pine Kennels.

Am., Can. Ch. Golden Pine's Courvoisier, Am. and Can. C.D.X. and W.C.. Am. W.C.X.

Golden Pine (West Coast)

The West Coast branch of Golden Pine Kennels is owned by Nancy Kelly Belsaas who was active in the kennel with Mary Luise Semans some years back. When Nancy was ready to begin breeding Goldens again, after having graduated from college and beginning a career in the airline industry, she contacted her old friend Mary Lu Semans, whom she had known for more than thirteen years at that point and with whom she had kept in close contact. As Nancy says, "I liked her lines, which not only had my old stuff behind them, but also Tigathoe (field and conformation) and I had known Torchy Flinn (owner of Tigathoe) from Greenwich, Connecticut, for years." Nancy had hoped to buy an "older Golden," but she was not able to

find what suited her. Mary Luise Semans had a repeat breeding of Champion Misty Morn's Sunset, C.D.T., W.C., to Champion Golden Pine's Punkin Pi, C.D. (the first breeding had produced a spectacular litter) and Nancy Belsaas had the option for third choice male. She figured that was great, as the people with the first and second choice had a concept of an outstanding dog which was different from hers; if there were to be enough males to go around, she was sure there would be no problem. The litter had nine males and one female, so all was well! Out of that litter came Nancy's third choice puppy, American and Canadian Champion Golden Pine's Courvoisier, American and Canadian C.D.X. and W.C., American W.C.X. Also in this litter were Champion Golden Pine's Full House, C.D., Champion Golden Pine's Gradene's J.D., C.D.X., plus several others who performed well in obedience.

Am., Can. Ch. Golden Pine's Courvoisier, Am. and Can. C.D.X. and W.C.X., Am. W.C.X. Best of Breed at Del Monte, at seven years of age. Nancy Kelly Belsaas, owner.

Courvoisier, or "Cognac" as he is known, finished his championship in the United States with four majors, including two Bests of Breed from the classes by the time he was twenty months old. He finished his Canadian championship with all majors which included two Canadian Specialty wins. He completed his obedience titles of C.D. and C.D.X. in both countries with awards for outstanding performance. He completed his W.C. title in the United States in Illinois at a Golden Retriever Club of America National Specialty and his W.C. Canadian title in Toronto at the Golden Retriever Club of Canada National Specialty. When the W.C.X. title was initiated he was nine years old and he achieved that title. He twice won Best Conformation Field Dog at the Canadian National Specialty in Toronto. As a Veteran Dog he also excelled with numerous wins, the most outstanding of which was winning Best of Breed from the Veteran Dog Class and Sporting Group second, this in 1980 when he was eight years old; and in 1981, when he was nine, at the Golden Gate Kennel Club, over 110 Goldens, he also was victorious. In 1982, two weeks prior to his eleventh birthday, he won Best of Breed at Del Monte.

"Cognac" is an Outstanding Sire not only with conformation champions to his credit but also two top-performing obedience champions. "Cognac's" sire was Champion Misty Morn's Sunset, the top producing Golden sire in history. "Cognac's" dam was a top producing bitch, and it's through her side that the lineage goes back to Nancy Belsaas' old line.

Best in Show at Staten Island in 1973, Ch. Misty Morn's Sunset, C.D., T.D., handled by Bob Stebins for Peter and Rose Lewesky.

Am., Can. Ch. Golden Pine's Remy Martin, Am. and Can. C.D. Owned by Nancy Kelly Belsaas and Janis Teichman, San Mateo, California.

Nancy Belsaas has owned and finished some other lovely Goldens, too. Champion Brandy's Golden Ghost was a Group winner and the dog who helped her win Best Junior Showmanship contender at Westminster in 1955. American and Canadian Champion Golden Pine's Remy Martin, American and Canadian C.D., was a Specialty winner. Champion Golden Pine's O'Luv Amaretto, American W.C., was a Specialty winner. Champion Golden Pine's Benedictine is at this kennel also. Now, Champion Pepperhill Golden Pine Irish, a beautiful and already successful Best of Breed-winning bitch, has joined Nancy and Dean Belsaas in San Mateo, California.

Ch. Golden Pine's O'Luv Amaretto, W.C., pictured as an eleven-month-old puppy. Nancy Kelly Belsaas, owner.

Ch. Golden Pine's Benedictine, owned by Nancy Kelly Belsaas, Gail Cortesia, and Margaret A. Flynn.

Ch. Pepperhill Golden Pine Irish in April 1982 at twenty-two months of age. Owned by Nancy Kelly Belsaas, Gail Cortesia, Margaret Flynn, and Pepperhill Farm Kennels.

A bucket filled with Golden babies! These two are owned by Mrs. Jay S. Cox, Annapolis, Maryland.

Golden babies playing tug o' war. Owned by Mrs. Nancy Cox.

A pensive Golden puppy from Goldencharm Kennels, owned by Mrs. Nancy Cox.

Goldencharm

Goldencharm Golden Retrievers, owned by Mrs. Jay S. (Nancy) Cox of Annapolis, Maryland, are famous as the home of American and Canadian Champion Goldenquest's Lucky Charm, their foundation bitch, sired by American and Canadian Champion Cal-Vo's Happy Ambassador, C.D. (Champion Footprint of Yeo, C.D., ex Champion Beckwith's Malagold Starfarm) from Canadian Champion Deegoljay's Amorous Aspasia, C.D. (American and Canadian Champion Beckwith's Malagold Flash, U.D.T., ex Beckwith's Allegro of Sand).

Charm became the Number One Golden Bitch in the United States, Phillips System, and in Canada for 1976. She gained her American title in four shows, all majors undefeated in the classes with four times Best of Winners, one Best of Opposite Sex, two Bests of Breed (in entries of sixty-eight and twenty-one Goldens), and a Group first over 302 sporting dogs. She has produced a Canadian Best in Show-winning son and two American Champions along with numerous others who are pointed and headed toward their titles. The Best in Show son is Goldenquest the Entertainer, currently the Number Three Golden in Canada.

Charm is nine years old and continues to bring great pleasure to her owners.

Goldust Kennels' Stilrovin Disco Dusty, owned and bred by Pam German, sired by Malagold Captain Misty Max ex Miss Goldust Molly, is successful in upland game bird field work and in the obedience classes at dog shows.

James Carson with Stilrovin Disco Dusty, left, and Brian German with Goldust English Frost doing some homework prior to competing in a 4-H dog show. Nephew and son of Mrs. Pam German, breeder-owner of the Goldens.

Goldust

Mrs. Pam German, owner of the Goldust Goldens at Belvidere, Illinois, obtained her first of the breed, an excellent gun dog and wonderful companion, in 1967. Five years later she purchased Miss Goldust Molly, now retired, who is the dam of the Goldens now being trained and shown by Mrs. German and her son Brian. Both of these first acquisitions are granddaughters of the famous Field and American Field Champion Beautywood's Tamarack and the famous Field Champion Stilrovin Nitro Express.

The sire of the youngsters at Goldust is Mrs. German's Malagold Captain Misty, a son of Champion Malagold Summer Chant, Connie Gerstner's famed winner.

Mrs. German has been exhibiting her Goldens since about 1977, when friends convinced her that her bitch, Molly, was good enough to compete in conformation classes. She has come to love doing so, encouraged by Molly's successes, so some well-known winners should be part of the future at Goldust.

Goldust English Frost at seven months of age. Bred and owned by Mrs. Pam German, this Golden is currently winning in 4-H Obedience Classes and Novice Obedience.

Above: Goldust Kennels' Miss Goldspike Express photographed while hunting pheasant. An excellent worker, she is used for all upland game birds, along with being shown throughout the Midwest in the Bred-by-Exhibitor Classes by her breeder-owner-handler Pam German, Belvidere, Illinois. **Below:** Miss Goldspike Express winning a big American-bred Class at the 1980 Golden Retriever Club Central Regional Specialty for proud owners Mrs. Pam German and Brian German, Goldust Kennels.

Above: December 1981. Pam German's homebred eight-month-old Goldust Captain Nero is doing well in obedience competition. **Below:** Good form at a match show. Miss Goldspike Express is winning Best of Breed here, breeder-owner-handled by Pam German.

Harambee

Harambee Goldens officially became a kennel in 1978. Art and Caroline Baihly of Kassan, Minnesota, surely started out on the right foot with their first winner, the handsome and well-known Champion Valhalla's Dogo Dancer. A son of Champion Cummings' Gold-Rush Charlie ex Champion Valhalla's Amber Kate,

Above: Bill Trainor handling Ch. Cummings' Gold-Rush Charlie, sire of Dogo Dancer, to one of his many Bests in Show for Mrs. Robert V. Clark, Jr., and Larry Johnson at Monmouth County in 1974. **Below:** Ch. Valhalla's Amber Kate, C.D., dam of Dogo Dancer, at fourteen months of age. By Am., Can. Ch. Beckwith's Malagold Flash, C.D., W.C., ex Beckwith's Chickasaw Jingle. Kathy Liebler, owner, Carmel, New York.

Above: Ch. Valhalla's Dogo Dancer, C.D.T., taking Best in Show at Grand Island Kennel Club, November 1977. The judge is Herman Cox, the handler Delores Burkholder. Owners, Harambee Kennels, Art and Caroline Baihly, Kasson, Minnesota. **Below:** Ch. Valhalla's Dogo Dancer, C.D.T., at the Key City Kennel Club Dog show in 1978.

Two handsome Goldens, Pepperhill's Harambee Megan and Harambee's Good Time Charlie, belonging to Art and Caroline Baihly.

Right, upper photo: Harambee's Dance At Dawn getting in some early training with owner Art Baihly. **Right, lower photo:** Harambee's Dance At Dawn is all set to go.

Harambee's Dance At Dawn, drying off after a swim. Owned by Art and Caroline Baihly.

Dogo gained his bench show title in April 1977, finishing twelfth (ranked on the number of dogs defeated that year). He won Best in Show at the Grand Island Kennel Club, November 25th, 1977, and was admitted to the Golden Retriever Club of America Show Dog Hall of Fame in 1978. Dogo earned his T.D. in 1980 and his C.D. in 1981.

Presently the Baihlys are in the process of acquiring a foundation bitch on which to base their breeding program. They intend to concentrate on the bloodlines of American and Canadian Champion Cummings' Gold-Rush Charlie and American and Canadian Champion Russo's Pepperhill Poppy. Their breeding philosophy holds that the background of the dam is equal to or even exceeds in importance the background of the stud, and they are hoping for some lovely youngsters to prove this theory.

Ch. Cupid's Beau of Ladykirk, C.D., W.C., is a member of the Golden Retriever Club of America Show Dog Hall of Fame, the Top Winning Golden for 1981, Best of Breed at the Western Regional Specialty that year, and a multiple Group-winner. Bred by Toni Stovall, owned by R. Steve Andrews, and handled by Betty R. Andrews. The Andrews own High Timber Kennels at Colorado Springs, Colorado.

High Timbers

Located at beautiful Colorado Springs, Colorado, High Timbers is a comparatively new kennel in the Golden Retriever world, but it is certainly off to a flying start. Owned by R. Steve and Betty R. Andrews, High Timbers was established in 1979 when Mr. Andrews selected and purchased the dog that became Champion Cupid's Beau of Ladykirk, C.D., W.C. This dog was, as Mrs. Andrews tells us, "selected with the help of information gleaned from just such breed publications as your future book." To begin with so outstanding a representative of the breed has certainly been exciting and rewarding!

Beau was bred by Toni Stovall and is handled by Betty Andrews. A multiple Group-winner, he has earned a position in the Golden Retriever Club of America Hall of Fame. He was the Top Winning Golden in 1981, when his victories included that of Best of Breed at the Western Regional Specialty show.

Although his owners are really just beginning with their breeding program, Beau is already making his presence felt as a stud dog, with pointed progeny in the show ring and at least one obedience C.D. holder to his credit. We are certain that High Timbers has a bright future to which the Andrews look forward.

Hillside

Hillside Golden Retrievers, at Marthasville, Missouri, are owned by Sharon Rosenkoetter, who, over a period of six years, has been breeder or co-breeder of fourteen litters. Principally she has worked with the Sun Dance lines, which she admires tremendously, but she has also been successfully involved with Goldens from Beckwith Kennels, Gay Haven, High Farms, Rusticana, and Topbrass. Many of her homebreds are pointed, are obedience titled, and have earned field placements.

Mrs. Rosenkoetter has also been involved with The Seeing Eye, telling us proudly that within two years Hillside had four successful guide dogs.

Top dog at Hillside is Champion Meadowpond Trojan's Pride, C.D., by Champion Sun Dance's Alexander ex American and Canadian Champion Meadowpond Dazzle's Sparkle, C.D. Pride belongs to Sharon and Carl Rosenkoetter,

Ch. Sun Dance's Alexander, a Group winner and Number Three Golden for 1978. Sire of two Group-winning sons prior to his death. Owned by Shirley and William Worley and bred by Lisa Schultz, Algonquin, Illinois.

Hillside's Vanilla Fudge, by Ch. Meadowpond Trojan's Pride, C.D., ex Hillside's Gold Nugget, at Edwardsville Kennel Club, June 1982, taking Best of Winners under judge Roy Ayers for owners M'Linde Tomey and Sharon Rosenkoetter. Ruth Stiefferman, handling.

and he finished his championship with four majors and two Bests of Breed from the classes. He now has multiple Group placements, including a Group first. His obedience title was won in a spectacular manner, too, having been obtained in three placements.

Hillside's Rock 'n' Roll, C.D., is another fine Golden belonging to the Rosenkoetters. By Champion Sun Dance's Bootleg Whiskey, U.D., ex Orion's Sunjoy Zesta, "Rocky" has fourteen points toward championship as this is written, including one five-point major, and he has five Bests of Breed from the classes. His C.D. degree was obtained in three straight shows.

Mrs. Rosenkoetter co-owns, with M'Linde Tomey, a very exciting puppy who at eight months of age is pointed from the Puppy Class. This is Hillside's Vanilla Fudge, by Champion Meadowpond Trojan's Pride, C.D., ex Hillside's Gold Nugget, who is now well on the way to achieving championship status.

Other Goldens to be found at Hillside, all of whom show great promise, include Hillside's Echo of Lynel, Hillside's Chantilly Lace, Hillside's Take A Chance, and Hillside's Raspberrie Annie. The Rosenkoetters are primarily concerned with conformation and obedience, although they have done a bit of field work with their dogs, too.

These five-week-old puppies are Hillside's Echo of Lynel, Hillside's Adonis at Harmony, and Hillside's Chantilly Lace, bred by Sharon and Carl Rosenkoetter, sired by Ch. Meadowpond Trojan's Pride, C.D., ex Faera's Hillside's Sparkle.

Hillside's Rock 'n' Roll, C.D., taking Best of Breed at Edwardsville Kennel Club, May 1980, for owners Sharon and Carl Rosenkoetter, Marthasville, Missouri. Handled by Ruth Stiefferman.

Jolly

Jolly Kennels, owned by John and Lynne Lounsbury and now located on a twenty-two-acre wooded hilltop at La Grange, New York, was founded in 1969, but survived many disappointments in the dog show arena prior to really hitting its stride in the Golden Fancy. The first three Goldens purchased all had to be spayed and placed as pets due to hip problems, cataracts, and poor conformation. Thus it was that although they had purchased their first Golden, a male pup bred by Dr. Merle and Esther Long of Indian Knolls Kennels, West Chicago, Illinois (the Lounsburys were living in the Chicago area at that time) back in 1964, it was not until some five years later, and after a whirl in Vizslas, that their actual start in Goldens took place.

Lynne decided that Chrystie, their Golden, needed canine companionship, so a German Shorthaired Pointer was purchased. During the next two years the Lounsburys joined the Mid-Hudson Kennel Club, becoming involved with

Ch. Indanda Thembalisha, ten months old. Breeder, Rev. Edward French. Owners, John and Lynne Lounsbury, Jolly Goldens, Billings, New York.

Ch. Sir Duncan of Woodbury at six years of age. Breeder, Mrs. Robert Krause. Owner, Lynne Lounsbury, Jolly Kennels.

the running of sanctioned matches and A.K.C. licensed dog shows. Companion Dog degrees were earned by both their Golden and their Shorthair, with occasional entries being made for breed competition as well. By 1967, the Lounsburys had commenced the search for a show-quality Golden bitch puppy.

Between 1968 and 1972, three little Lounsburys arrived, Richard, Karen, and Thomas, making life exciting for the family; but these were not very progressive years so far as dog activities were concerned. A superb male Vizsla was struck by a car and killed when six months old. To help compensate for this devastating loss a second male Vizsla was purchased but feil far short of the quality of the first. Two Vizsla bitch puppies purchased for show and breeding were spayed and placed as pets due to lack of quality. In 1972, things started looking up. A Vizsla bitch was purchased, Jolly Classy Brass Barat, who gave the Lounsburys their first homebred champion, Jolly Aranyos Vadasz, C.D.; and it was in that same year that the foundation Golden bitch was purchased, a seven-week-old puppy from Rev. Edward French of Ipswich, Massachusetts, who grew up to become Champion Indanda Thembalisha, the Lounsbury's first Golden champion and the dam of seven champions. In 1972, a year-old bitch was purchased, Autumn Lodge's Indian Sunset, who never finished her championship and never produced a single puppy but who nonetheless was of great value at Jolly Kennels; it was through her that the magnificent stud dog, Champion Sir Duncan of Woodbury, came to the Lounsburys.

Duncan, a littermate to Indian Sunset, had been a house pet until nearly six years old when, in the spring of 1977, he became homeless owing to a divorce in his family and the absence of anyone wanting him. George and Betsy Dartt, also Golden owners who lived at Huntington, New York, temporarily took Duncan into their home, but they could not permanently keep him owing to the fact that their own adult male resented the newcomer. The Dartts met with a series of disappointments as they showed Duncan to fellow fanciers they felt might be interested; but Duncan, despite being a littermate to Champion Autumn Lodge's Mr. Zap, a Golden Retriever Club of America Show Dog Hall of Fame member and an Outstanding Sire, simply did not look the part. A small (23") refined dog with small bone, he weighed seventy pounds in his then neglected and overweight condition, and he was quite gray in the face and had gray hair generously distributed through his body coat. In short, there was little about him to generate confidence in his future as a show or stud dog, and everyone suggested that he be placed as a pet.

Then the Dartts thought of the Lounsburys, knowing they owned a pointed littermate of Duncan, and a phone call was made. Indeed, the Lounsburys *would* be interested in taking Duncan, and this decision became one of the wisest moves in their Golden career.

Duncan came to Jolly Kennels in mid April 1977. By July, he was well conditioned and ready for the show ring. Bob Stebbins and he started out during the beginning of August, and within twenty-four days Duncan was a champion. In October 1977, Duncan's first litter was whelped, and as of August 1982, he has sired thirty-eight litters; so far twenty-four championships have been gained by the produce of these litters.

Duncan was shown very little as a Special when he was seven years old, handled by his good friend Patty McCoy; he won Best of Breed eight times, Best of Opposite Sex on four occasions, and a second in Group. Duncan climaxed his show career when nearly eight, taking Best of Breed at Westminster over the largest Golden entry ever shown at this prestigious event. It certainly is a heartwarming and thought-provoking

Ch. Sir Duncan of Woodbury, at eight years and ten months of age, winning the Veterans Dog Class at the Long Island Golden Retriever Club Specialty Show in April 1980. Bred by Mrs. Robert Krause and owned by Lynne Lounsbury, Jolly Kennels. Duncan is a son of Ch. Misty Morn's Sunset, C.D.*, ex Autumn Lodge's Li'l Indian (Ch. Aureal Wood's Okemo * ex Ch. Lorelei Fez-Ti Zu-Zu).

Ch. HGL's Golden West Coquette completing her title in November 1977, at nineteen months of age. Bred by John and Nancy Garcia and owned by Vicki Beran and John and Lynne Lounsbury.

Ch. Sir Dindiago of Woodside, at fifteen months of age, taking the points at Riverhead in March 1979. Bred by Robert and Sheila Humphreys, co-owned by them with John and Lynne Lounsbury, Jolly Kennels.

story that an unwanted, unproven six-year-old dog could go on to become one of the great producers in the history of his breed! How fortunate for the breed that Duncan had good friends in the Dartts and that the Lounsburys had the eye to recognize his quality and potential.

The Lounsburys take a real interest in all phases of Golden ownership. They have done tracking with their dogs, under the guidance of Marian Schuler, and field training with the Westchester Retriever Club under the tutelage of the famous retriever-trainer Jack MacIntosh. Many hours were spent receiving breed-handling instructions at classes run by the Mid-Hudson Kennel Club and the Top Dog Training School at Newburgh, New York. John Lounsbury, especially, became quite involved with obedience training, holding classes for which he was instructor, at first with the Mid-Hudson Kennel Club and then later at Jolly Kennels as well. By the late 1970s, the amount of time consumed by the children had increased, so the time available for other interests was cut back to the Jolly Kennels breeding program and breed ring competition.

Am., Can. Ch. Jolly October's Chevalier, bred by John Lounsbury and Peter Lewesky and owned by Lynne Lounsbury and Sharon Smith.

Above: Ch. Misty Morn's Sunset, C.D., T.D., W.C., owned by Rose Lewesky, on the left. His double grandson, Am., Can. Ch. Jolly Jack Daniels, owned by John and Lynne Lounsbury, on the right. **Below left:** Am., Can. Ch. Jolly Jack Daniels, bred by Dr. John Lounsbury and Tina Lewesky and owned by John and Lynne Lounsbury, is a double grandson of Ch. Misty Morn's Sunset, being by Ch. Golden Pine's Gradene's J.D., C.D.X., W.C. (Sunset ex Ch. Golden Pine's Punkin Pi, C.D.) from Ch. Indanda Thembalisha (Sunset ex Kletha Thembalisha, she by Ch. Cragmount's Hi-Lo). **Below right:** An informal head study of the lovely and famous dog Am., Can. Ch. Jolly Jack Daniels.

Jolly Kennels has developed on the foundation bitch Champion Indanda Thembalisha, a daughter of the Top Producing Stud Dog in the History of the Breed, Champion Misty Morn's Sunset, C.D., T.D., W.C., whose pedigree is strong in Mrs. Engelhard's Cragmount breeding. "Dandy" was bred to Champion Golden Pine's Bradene's JD, C.D.X., W.C., owned by Bill Dean. Four champions resulted, one of which, American and Canadian Champion Jolly Jack Daniels, remains at Jolly Kennels, strongly contributing to the development of their breeding program.

The most important stud dog to date at Jolly has been Champion Sir Duncan of Woodbury, also a Misty Morn's Sunset son. Duncan not only has contributed to the Jolly Kennels linebreeding on Sunset, but he also has brought in strong influences from Aureal Wood lines, Lorelei, Nerrissida, and High Farms. The significant influence that Duncan has had on the breed is very evident at the many dog shows throughout the country where his progeny and their descendants are in competition.

During the most recent years, there has been an incorporation of other lines into the Jolly Kennels equation. The most important contributions have come from Yeo of England through the Cal-Vo Kennel of Carol Vogel. Particularly important has been the influence of American, Canadian, and Mexican Champion Cal-Vo's Happy Ambassador, C.D., owned by Joan Young. Most of the young bitches with which Jolly Kennels looks to the future are Duncan and Jack daughters out of Happy Ambassador daughters. Other recent incorporations to Jolly have come from Cloverdale Kennels, Four K's Goldens, and Valhalla Kennels.

Rusticana's Princess Teena at the Central Ohio Kennel Club in November 1966. The judge is Maurice Baker and Laura Ellis (now Laura Ellis Kling) is handling. This was the occasion of the first point she ever put on a dog. Teena was Laura's first champion and the foundation bitch for Laurell Kennels.

Ch. Indanda Thembalisha, twenty-six months old, bred by Rev. Edward French and owned by John and Lynne Lounsbury, Jolly Goldens.

Laurell

Laurell Goldens are among the most famous and excellent ever produced in this country and are to be found behind many greats from other kennels as well as their own. Thomas C. Kling and Laura Ellis Kling own Laurell, which is located in Cincinnati, Ohio, and which was founded back in the mid-1960s by Mrs. Kling when she was still Laura Ellis.

As it turned out, the foundation bitch for Laurell Kennels was Champion Rusticana's Princess Teena, American and Canadian C.D., to whom Laura Ellis gave a home before she had ever reached the show ring, as this bitch was in the unfortunate situation of being starved and mistreated. Mrs. Kling's kindness and consideration for this Golden surely brought back many rewards, as Teena was the first dog on which Mrs. Kling ever put a point, her first champion, and, as already mentioned, her foundation bitch. After gaining this first point at Central Ohio Kennel Club in 1966 under judge Maurice Baker, Teena completed her championship and also her C.D.

135

Above left: Am., Can. Ch. Laurell's Allspice, C.D., from the first Laurell litter and first Laurell champion. Owned by Laura Ellis Kling and Thomas C. Kling, Cincinnati, Ohio. **Above right:** Ch. Laurell's Extra Extra, C.D.X., W.C., by Ch. Major Gregory of High Farms ex Ch. Laurell's Amiable Caboose. Owned by Bob and Jerri Danenhauer.

Below left: Ch. Laurell's Amiable Caboose at South Shore Kennel Club August 10th 1969. From the first Laurell litter and the second Laurell champion. Owned by Thomas C. Kling and Laura Ellis Kling, Laurell Goldens. **Below right:** Ch. Laurell's Edited Edition, by Ch. Major Gregory of High Farms ex Ch. Laurell's Amiable Caboose. Owned by Thomas C. Kling and Laura Ellis Kling.

The first litter raised at Laurell included the kennels' first two homebred champions, American and Canadian Champion Laurell's Allspice, C.D., and Champion Laurell's Amiable Caboose. Teena, the foundation bitch, was the dam of the litter, which was sired by the multiple Group winner Champion High Farms Sutter's Gold.

Amiable Caboose became a highly successful producer in her own right and, bred to Champion Major Gregory of High Farms, her progeny included such Goldens as American and Canadian Champion Laurell's Especial Jason★, American and Canadian U.D.T., a member of the Golden Retriever Club of America Show Dog Hall of Fame; Champion Laurell's Extra Extra, C.D.X., W.C.; Champion Laurell's Edited Edition; and Laurell's Etago Catawba who had six points including one major.

A brother-sister team which came to Laurell Kennels had a tremendous impact as producers. The dog was American and Canadian Champion Duckdown's Unpredictable, C.D.*, and the bitch was Champion Duckdown's Veronica Laker, C.D., both by Champion Sun Dance's Moonlight Gambler, C.D.X. (Champion Sun Dance's Sir Ivan, C.D.X., ex Sun Dance's Gold Ingot, C.D.) out of Champion Sprucewood's Harvest Sugar, C.D. (Champion Furore Harvest Gold ex American and Canadian Champion Sprucewood's Chinki). Unpredictable sired a long list of famous Goldens, including American and Canadian Champion Bardfield Boomer, American and Canadian U.D.T.*, Cherie Burger's famous first and only Golden Retriever to win every show and every obedience title offered by the American Kennel Club and the Canadian Kennel Club; Champion Amberac's Royal Rufus, C.D., W.C.; and very many others of importance to the breed.

Ch. Amberac's Royal Rufus, C.D., W.C., son of Ch. Duckdown's Unpredictable, C.D., W.C., is owned by Thomas C. Kling and Laura Ellis Kling.

Am., Can. Ch. Duckdown's Unpredictable, C.D., W.C., known informally as "Peter," is behind many of the great Goldens winning today. Here he is taking Best of Breed at the Michigan Specialty in 1972.

Ch. Duckdown's Veronica Laker, C.D., figured in the background of some very famous Laurell champions. Photo courtesy of Laura Ellis Kling.

Veronica Laker produced among others, Champion Laurell's Honey 'n' Spice, Champion Laurell's Heather of the Moor, U.D., and Champion Laurell's Happy Go Lucky, all sired by Champion Laurell's Allspice, C.D.; and Laurell's Gadabout Grandee and Laurell's Honor's Gibson Girl, C.D.X., both by Champion Honor's Grandeur, C.D.X.* (Beckwith's Copper Ingot ex Champion Honor's Charade).

One of the most valuable bitches ever owned at Laurell Kennels is Champion Laurell's Kilimanjaro, daughter of another noted Outstanding Dam, Champion Little Bit of Laurell. "Killer," as she is known, was sired by a well-known winner of the early 1970s, Champion Vagabond's Cougar Bill, C.D.

Bred to Champion Gold-Rush Lightnin', "Killer" produced one of the current "stars" at Laurell, the handsome young dog Champion Laurell's York, who is making his presence strongly felt in Sporting Group competition at prestigious shows. This combination also produced Champion Yats of Luck, another highly successful stud and show dog; Champion Laurell's Yellow Jacket, Best of Breed at the Fort Detroit Golden Retriever Club Specialty,

November 1979; Judy Glasgow's Champion Laurell's Yasmine of Jonesi; Champion Laurell's Yolanda, also owned by Judy Glasgow; and Champion Laurell's Yours Truly, owned by Vicki Siegel and Laura Kling. Bred to Champion Southern's Gold Rush Travler, "Killer's" offspring include Champion Laurell's Travlin' Alone, Champion Laurell's Travlin' in Style, Champion Laurell's Travlin' My Way, C.D., and Champion Laurell's Travlin' Too Far, owned by John Freed.

As is the case with the majority of leading Golden breeders, the Klings are involved with all phases of breed ownership. Champion Laurell's York was Number Two among show Goldens in 1980 and 1981 and Number One breeder-owned. Numerous Laurell dogs are constantly distinguishing themselves in all levels of obedience competition, and Caernaco's Troyman Trang ***, W.C., W.C.X., Open All Age Qualified Dog won the Golden Retriever Club of America Field Trial Dog Class at the National in 1981.

Ch. Laurell's Kilimanjaro, dam of many champions, owned by Thomas C. Kling and Laura Ellis Kling, Cincinnati, Ohio.

Rusticana Masterpiece, U.D., taking one of the jumps in the good form that helped win him his title. Owned by Linda Smith of Loudon, Tennessee.

Lindale

Lindale Kennel, in existence since 1963 and owned by Linda G. Smith, Loudon, Tennessee, registered its first Golden, Rusticana Masterpiece, a son of Champion Misty Morn's Sunset, C.D., T.D., W.C., in 1974. "Master" was bred by Mr. and Mrs. Al Munneke. He is a Utility Dog, is trained in tracking, needs one major for his breed championship, and in the winter of 1981 retrieved seventeen doves and one duck. Because of family problems, Ms. Smith retired "Master" from obedience competition at six years of age—but not before he had acquired three High in Trials, had gained several obedience trial championship points (obedience trials had just been instituted shortly before his retirement), and had successfully competed in a Gaines Regional Competition and the National Competition in St. Louis. Most important, "Master" is a sweet-tempered, well-mannered, eager-to-please, enthusiastic but sensible friend who has done well everything that has been asked of him.

In 1977, at three-and-a-half-years of age, Rusticana Ms. Trace came to live at Lindale. Before her untimely death from a massive infection, she raised one litter of eleven. One pup died at birth, one when three-and-a-half months old and one as an adult. The book on the remaining ones is not nearly complete yet, but as of July 1982, there are four dogs with C.D. degrees, three with C.D.X., two High in Trials, and two dogs who have several points each in breed. One male owned by Lindale has just been to his first two breed shows and will be shown both in breed and obedience beginning in the fall of 1982.

The philosophy of Lindale Kennels is two-fold. First, it is firmly believed that dogs are not livestock like cattle and horses, to be bred purely for financial gain. In the same vein, the belief at Lindale is that no breeder has stock good enough to justify making multiple breedings in any year's time. Lindale believes that no one has the

Rusticana Masterpiece after three seagulls nearly broke up the show flying over the Geodesic Dome in Charleston, South Carolina, where he was waiting to receive his just-won obedience trophies. Linda Smith, owner.

right to breed or raise or own dogs in such quantities that each dog does not have daily attention, training, and "sense of relationship" with the person special to him. Ms. Smith recognizes the fact that dogs have very different emotional needs and sensitivities than cattle and horses and deserve to be treated differently.

Second, Lindale believes that the Golden Retriever should be first a tractable, sensible, intelligent dog who can do many things with style and enthusiasm, but not a hyper, wild dog who is emotionally incapable of lying quietly by the fire on a winter night without making everyone else in the room miserable.

Lindale wishes to raise handsome dogs who are competitive in the breed ring, who are enthusiastic, capable but tractable, sensible, and natural (without years of training) and who are good, stylish obedience dogs who want to please and are capable of being high scorers even with novice handlers. No Lindale stud has ever bred a bitch who did not have normal hips and eyes. None ever will. Nor will any bitch be bred who does not have normal hips and eyes.

Rusticana Masterpiece, U.D., taking Best of Winners under judge Raphael Schulte for Linda Smith. Houston Clark is handling.

Malagold

Malagold Kennels, located at De Forest, Wisconsin, belong to Connie Gerstner whose interest in showing and training dogs dates back to 4-H obedience work in 1957. Malagold became a reality in 1964 when Mrs. Gerstner and her husband bred several litters of Goldens, mostly as pets. Malagold was so named because Mrs. Gerstner's interest is divided between the Goldens and some very fine Alaskan Malamutes which she also breeds and enjoys. Later, on her own, Mrs. Gerstner developed a desire to improve the Golden breed; and as her expertise in handling dogs became greater, she turned to experienced breeders for advice and a foundation dog on which to base her own strain.

The dog selected was Champion Malagold Beckwith Big Buff, C.D., whelped December 5th 1966, bred by Mr. and Mrs. R.E. Beckwith. Connie describes Buff as a "once in a lifetime dog" who taught her a great deal. She handled him to three all-breed Best in Show victories, two Specialty Bests of Breed including the National in 1970, and numerous Group firsts and other Group placements. Buff had the Beckwith proven bloodlines, correct coat, sound movement, and a lovely head—all of which Mrs. Gerstner tries to preserve. Buff eventually became a Golden Retriever Club of America Show Dog Hall of Fame member and a Top Producer.

Above: Lindale A Trace of Sparkle at seven-and-a-half months of age. Linda Smith, owner. **Below:** Rusticana Masterpiece, U.D., relaxing with his friend, Ruby. Owned by Linda Smith.

Ch. Malagold Beckwith Big Buff, C.D., winning Best in Show at Land O'Lakes Kennel Club in 1971 for owner-handler Connie Gerstner, De Forest, Wisconsin.

One of the first outstanding litters sired by Buff, from Beckwith's Chickasaw Jingle in 1968, contained Malagold Beckwith Bootes. Although a very finishable bitch, Bootes was never shown. Her claim to fame is the production of eleven champions for Malagold, truly a foundation bitch of the very best kind! It is interesting that her littermate, Champion Beckwith Malagold Starfarm, became the foundation for Cal-Vo Kennels and became another Top Producer.

A very influential dog in the Malagold kennel history was Champion Apollo of Yeo, an English import owned by Mrs. Mary Strange of BraeLea Kennels. This dog was the sire of Bootes' first two litters, whelped in 1972 and in

Ch. Malagold Summer Chant, a multiple Group-winner by Ch. Hunt's Finnegan ex Ch. Malagold Svea, is a member of the Golden Retriever Show Dog Hall of Fame. Bred and owned by Connie Gerstner, Malagold Kennels.

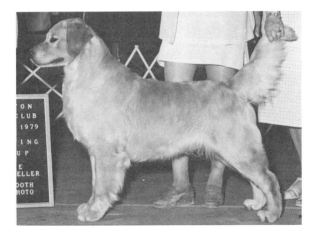

1973, in which a total of six champions were included, among them Mrs. Gerstner's Champion Malagold Svea. This bitch became a second generation Top Producer, with six champions so far from her first two litters both sired by Champion Hunt's Finnegan. Among the most famous Goldens from these two litters are multiple Group winner Champion Malagold Summer Chant, Champion Malagold Summer Encore (a multiple Best in Show winner in 1982), and Champion Malagold Nikki. Chant has sired two champions thus far, with many more to follow. Both he and Encore are Show Dog Hall of Fame members. Nikki, meanwhile, is following her mother's pawprints towards being a Top Producer, one daughter having already finished while two others have major points.

Malagold Beckwith Bootes, the foundation bitch at Connie Gerstner's Malagold Kennels, was never shown, although she obviously was a bitch who could easily have finished. A daughter of Ch. Malagold Beckwith Big Buff, C.D., ex Beckwith's Chickasaw Puzzle, she produced eleven champions for Malagold. Bootes was born in 1968.

Out of another Bootes litter, this one sired by Champion Misty Morn's Sunset, C.D., T.D., W.C., came two champions with a third lacking just one major. Champion Malagold's Ring of Fire and Champion Malagold's Wing Song have produced several champions and producers of champions.

The handsome Ch. Malagold High Voltage, with his breeder-owner-handler Connie Gerstner, following a Best in Show at Sandemac Kennel Club.

Mrs. Gerstner's first homebred Best in Show-winner was a son of Bootes, Champion Malagold High Voltage, sired by Champion Malagold Beckwith O.K. Ivan, C.D. On the Top Ten list of Goldens for 1978, High Voltage has produced several champions for Pat Haines and Oncore Kennels.

In general, Malagold bloodlines have been developed from Beckwith, Rockgold, and High Farms roots. Over the years Mrs. Gerstner has worked to hold the consistent qualities in head, substance, toplines, and proper coat length, which combine for an instantly recognizable Golden type. Currently she has several young offspring of Chant, High Voltage, and Nikki who are carrying on the Malagold tradition with distinction. Champion Summer Encore, in the Top Five Goldens for 1982, adds to the Malagold record with each passing week.

Eight-week-old Malagold puppies owned by Connie Gerstner, De Forest, Wisconsin.

Meadowpond

Meadowpond Golden Retrievers are indeed a distinguished group owned by Mrs. Cherie Berger at Romeo, Michigan. This kennel is operated on the ideal of producing all-around Goldens, dogs that can and do win in both breed and obedience rings, while at the same time serving as family companions and hunting partners.

Mrs. Berger started out by selecting outstanding stock on which to base her breeding program. The dogs involved include such greats in the breed as American and Canadian Champion Bardfield Boomer, American U.D.T., W.C., Canadian U.D., T.D.X., who was the first Golden Retriever to attain every available bench show and obedience title offered in the United States and Canada, and American and Canadian Champion Laurell's Especial Jason, W.C., American and Canadian U.D.T. Boomer, sired by American and Canadian Champion Duckdown's Unpredictable, C.D., W.C., ex Sandia's Flaxen Babe, C.D., was whelped in October 1968. He is the all-time top producer of obedience trial champions *all breeds*, numbering among his progeny Obedience Trial Champion and Champion Meadowpond Dust Commander, U.D., who was Top Obedience Dog, all breeds, in 1979, 1980, and 1981; Obedience Trial Champion Meadowpond Fem de Fortune, U.D., W.C., winner of the 1981 Gaines Super Dog Classic Tournament; Obedience Trial Champion Meadowpond Happy Valentine, U.D., W.C.; Obedience Trial Champion Meadowpond Christopher, U.D.; Obedience Trial Champion Meadowpond Angelic Abbey, T.D., W.C.X.; Obedience Trial Champion Windy's the Forecast, U.D.; Obedience Trial Champion Karagold's Magic Marker, U.D.; and Obedience Trial Champion Beckwith's Indian Summer, U.D.T. Boomer's other progeny include Champion Meadowpond Fetch; Champion Beckwith's I Tianna; American and Canadian Champion Rusty of Golden Shores (a Best in Show winner); American and Canadian Champion Meadowpond Cain Raiser, C.D.X., W.C.X.; Champion Meadowpond Shanner Hunt, C.D.; Champion Jagersbo Meadowpond Melody, C.D.; Champion Meadowpond Crowd Pleaser, C.D.; Meadowpond Tackle, U.D. (with ninety-seven obedience trial championship points in April 1982); Meadowpond Strut, U.D. (with obedience trial championship points); Nordlin's Rocket Fire, U.D., W.C. (obedience trial cham-

Am., Can. Ch. Bardfield Boomer, Am. U.D.T., W.C. and Can. U.D., T.D.X. Born in October 1968, sired by Am., Can. Ch. Duckdown's Unpredictable, C.D., W.C., ex Sandia's Flaxen Babe, C.D. Owned by Cherie Berger, Meadowpond Goldens, Romeo, Michigan.

pionship points); Windy's Flaxen Taffy, U.D.; Meadowpond Goldnugget, U.D.; Meadowpond Attaboy Kilroy, U.D.T., W.C.; Cherie of Brookshire, U.D., W.C.; Bluehaven's Teressa of Troy, U.D.T., W.C.; Brook's Lord Cholmodly, U.D.T., W.C.; and Meadowpark Shana Maidel, U.D. Many High in Trial awards have been gained by Boomer's progeny, and the Leader Dog School for the Blind in Rochester, Michigan, have used him extensively in their breeding program.

Boomer himself was a multiple High in Trial winner, plus a bench champion in two countries—truly a remarkable dog.

American and Canadian Champion Laurell's Especial Jason, W.C., American and Canadian U.D.T., was sired by Champion Major Gregory of High Farms ex Champion Laurell's Amiable

Caboose. He too made an inestimable contribution towards putting Meadowpond off to a proper start in the Golden world. Jason was honored by the Golden Retriever Club of America as a member of the Show Champion Hall of Fame for multiple Group placements, and during 1973 and 1974 he was on the listings of Top Ten Show Dogs. He completed all of his obedience titles prior to reaching twenty-eight months of age. He has two High in Trial awards, plus several High Combined in Trial wins. He earned his American Kennel Club and Canadian Kennel Club Tracking Dog titles at his first tests, and he was awarded a trophy for Best Tracking Dog of the Day competing in Canada. He earned the Golden Retriever Club of America Working Certificate for retrieving birds on land and ducks in water, and he has other honors too numerous

Above: Am., Can. Ch. Laurell's Especial Jason, Am. U.D.T., W.C., Can. U.D.T., a member of the Golden Retriever Hall of Fame and the Golden Retriever Outstanding Sire Award roster. Born in 1971, Jason was one of the earliest Goldens at Mrs. Cherie Berger's Meadowpond Kennels.
Below: Ch. Chafa Honeybun of Jungold, C.D.X., T.D., Ch. Meadowpond Glo of Cherrywood, C.D. (seven weeks old), and Ch. Laurell's Especial Jason, U.D.T., are three of the splendid Goldens from Cherie Berger's Meadowpond Kennels at Romeo, Michigan.

to mention. As a Golden Retriever Club of America Outstanding Sire, Jason's progeny include champions, High in Trial winners, Group winners, tracking titleholders, Leader Dogs for the Blind, plus dogs running in field events. Jason completed the combined titles of champion-Utility Dog Tracking at a younger age than any Golden Retriever before him. He was the seventeenth Golden Retriever champion-U.D.T. in the United States and the fourth in Canada.

Other foundation dogs at Meadowpond include American and Canadian Champion Cimaron's Dazzle Dust, C.D.X., T.C., W.C.; Laurell's Jaunty Jinn Jinn, C.D.X.; American and Canadian Champion Meadowpond's Dazzle's Sparkle, C.D.; and American and Canadian Champion Chafa Honeybun of Jungold, C.D.X., T.D., W.C. All of these dogs, in addition to Boomer and Jason, were honored by the Golden Retriever Club of America as being Outstanding Producers.

One of the most notable dogs to carry the Meadowpond name is Champion and Obedience Trial Champion Meadowpond Dust Commander who was the Top Obedience Dog *all breeds* 1979-1981. He is the all-time top winner of obedience trial championship points. Another outstanding homebred dog here is American and Canadian Champion Meadowpond David the Bold, American and Canadian C.D., who is in the Golden Retriever Hall of Fame as a consistent Group-placing dog.

Ch. Russo's Wildwood Flower taking points en route to her title. Mercer Russo Ervin, owner, Patterson, New York.

Mercer's

Mercer's Golden Retrievers, which formerly used the kennel prefix "Russo's," are owned by Mercer Russo Ervin and are situated at Patterson, New York.

Ms. Erwin has been "in dogs" all of her life, her parents having bred and shown English Bulldogs. She was born in Chicago and then moved with her family to the San Francisco area of California where she was raised. By the time she came East in 1970, Ms. Ervin had done a three-year study on the various breeds of dog in order to decide which one would best suit her. Goldens became her choice, after which more study-time went into the decision regarding which bloodlines she wanted. The decision was Mary Cummings' line, from which she picked future Champion Russo's Cummings' Elsa, litter-sister to Champion Cummings' Gold-Rush Charlie. Elsa was owner-handled (as are all of Ms. Ervins' Goldens) to her title and then bred to her half-brother, Champion Misty Morn's Sunset, which produced the wonderful bitch "Daisy," more formally known as Russo's Wildwood Flower. "Daisy," with her title completed by way of four majors within one month, was well on the way to becoming one of the nation's top bitches when, at only three years of age and after two litters, she developed bone cancer—truly a tragic loss to her owner and to the breed.

Ch. Russo's Gold-Rush Sensation, C.D., C.D.X., an obedience trial champion, is one of the fine Goldens bred by Mercer Russo Ervin.

Ch. Russo's Cummings' Elsa in 1972. By Ch. Sunset's Happy Duke ex Am., Can. Ch. Cummings' Golden Princess, Elsa is a full sister to Ch. Cummings' Gold-Rush Charlie and is owned by Mercer Russo Ervin.

From Daisy bred back to Champion Cummings' Gold-Rush Charlie came some magnificent Goldens, among them American and Canadian Champion Russo's Pepperhill Poppy, who came from the second Charlie ex "Daisy" litter and who became the Top Golden Bitch in the Hall of Fame in twenty-two years. From the earlier litter, there was Champion Russo's Gold-Rush Sensation, C.D.X., U.D., Obedience Trial Champion, who became the first Golden in breed history to earn both a bench championship and an obedience trial championship in the same year. "Daisy" really set the type for a lot of breeders through her offspring, as Ms. Ervin points out.

Above left: Ch. Mercer's Sweet William (Am., Can., Bda. Ch. Cummings' Gold-Rush Charlie ex Valhalla's Autumn Mist), owned by Mercer Russo Ervin. **Above right:** Ch. Mercer's Morning Glory, by Ch. Gold-Rush's Great Teddy Bear ex Ch. Russo's Cummings' Elsa, completing title at Westchester in 1980. Mercer Russo Ervin, owner. **Below:** Teakwood Farms Russo's Troy taking Best in Match, Bronx County, 1980, for owner Mercer Russo Ervin.

After "Daisy's" death, Ms. Ervin went to another line, puchasing a five-year-old bitch from Kathy Liebler. There was a span of three years when she did only limited showing, due to a divorce, at which time she switched her kennel name from Russo's to Mercer's Goldens, which is the prefix her dogs are known by now. The new bitch was Valhalla's Return Mist, and she was bred to Gold-Rush Charlie, to keep the line Ms. Ervin had so much wanted. From this she produced a litter of three pups which included her first male, Champion Mercer's Sweet William, better known as "Huckleberry." At the same time, Champion Russo's Cummings' Elsa was bred back to Champion Gold-Rush's Great Teddy Bear. There were only three puppies in this litter, one being Champion Mercer's Morning Glory, who is herself well on the way to becoming an Outstanding Dam. Thus, quality has made up for whatever might have been lacking in quantity.

Around 1980, Ms. Ervin was fortunate enough to get back Poppy's litter-brother, Teakwood Farms Russo's Troy. Ch. Mercer's Morning Glory and Troy were bred twice in succession and produced some of the finest Goldens around; the get are now (mid-1982) fourteen months and eight months old respectively, and almost all of them are already in the winner's circle.

With the exception of Elsa, all of Ms. Ervin's dogs are named after flowers or plants. Elsa, by the way, is still in good health and going strong at the age of twelve years, having produced her final litter when she was ten—a remarkable bitch who has certainly contributed well to her breed!

Misty Morn

Misty Morn Kennels, owned by Peter and Rose Lewesky, are among the most famous in the world of purebred dogs, being the home of the magnificent Champion Misty Morn's Sunset, C.D., T.D.

"Sunny" distinguished himself in the show ring with many exciting victories, including Best of Breed in 1968, 1969, and 1970 at the Garden State Golden Retriever Club Specialty and Best of Breed at the 1972 Eastern Regional of the Golden Retriever Club of America National at Reston, Virginia.

Most important and impressive of all, however, is the fact that "Sunny" has had an almost incredible impact on this breed as a sire, with about 150 champions to his credit, including many of the breed's most famous and successful dogs. He is far and away the all-time record holder as a sire of Goldens, and he is, of course, a member of the Hall of Fame as an Outstanding Sire.

Ch. Wochica's Sandpiper, W.C., by Ch. Misty Morn's Sunset, C.D., T.D., W.C., ex Champagne Lady of Wochica. This champion daughter from Sunset's first litter was also the first bitch bred to Ch. Cummings' Gold-Rush Charlie, a mating which produced four champions. Janet L. Bunce, owner, Wochica Goldens, Smithtown, New York.

Ch. Misty Morn's Sunset, C.D., T.D., owned by Peter and Rose Lewesky, handled here by Bob Stebbins. This is the Top Golden Sire in History, with get still winning and finishing. Always handled by Terry Correll or Bob Stebbins.

Morning Sun Lochan Ora E.M.A. is a double grand-daughter of Ch. Misty Morn's Sunset, C.D., T.D., W.C. Owned by Elizabeth M. Anderson, Connie A. Harris, and Christine Jones; bred by Connie Harris.

Sired by Champion Sunset's Happy Duke (Champion Cragmount's Peter ex Glen Willow's Happy Talk) ex Amber Lady of Tercor Farm (Champion Cragmount's Double Eagle ex Champion Golden Wallis), "Sunny" was bred by the Reverend Edward French. His bloodlines carry those of the outstanding dogs owned several decades back by Mrs. Charles Englehard which were so very influential in the breed in their day.

Rose Lewesky is now living in Ohio, although formerly this was an Eastern kennel. At present she owns and is campaigning a very fine Toy Manchester Terrier, but we feel certain that she retains every bit of her love of the Golden breed, along with continuously renewed happy memories of "Sunny" as she sees successive generations of his descendants making their impact on the breed. Champion Misty Morn's Sunset, C.D., T.D., is truly a dog never to be forgotten!

Moreland

Moreland Golden Retrievers started in 1968 with the acquisition by William C. Prentiss, New Britain, Pennsylvania, of Moreland's Golden Randy, C.D., as a family pet.

Obedience work with Randy led to shows and the desire to exhibit in breed competition; thus arrangements were made to obtain a Golden puppy with show potential. After three in a row had to be put down because of crippling hip dysplasia, the Prentiss family resolved that their own breeding program would have a reduction in the incidence of hip dysplasia as one of its prime objectives.

A daughter of Champion Misty Morn's Sunset, C.D., T.D., became the first O.F.A. normal in the Moreland Kennel. She was Darlington Del-Beth Rochelle, who was bred to Champion Major Gregory of High Farms, also O.F.A. normal. In her first litter she produced nine "normals," including three champions: Champion Moreland's Major Sam, C.D., T.D.; Champion Amber Tory of Moreland, and Champion Moreland's Golden Bonnie. Subsequently, any dogs which did not have clear hips and clear eyes which were born at Moreland Kennels were placed as pets, with an agreement that they not be bred. Bill Prentiss comments,

Ch. Misty Morn's Sunset, C.D., T.D., winning Veterans during the latter part of his show career. Peter and Rose Lewesky, owners.

Ch. Moreland's Major Sam, C.D., going Best in Show under judge Suzanne Rowe at Southern Adirondacks Dog Club in 1974, Bobby Fisher handling for owner Bill Prentiss, New Britain, Pennsylvania.

"Because of the complex genetics of hip dysplasia it may not be possible to completely eliminate it, but we are trying, while still breeding to standard and maintaining those qualities which make the Golden Retriever the all-around dog." Currently, Moreland Goldens have from three to five generations of hip and eye clearance behind them.

Champion Moreland's Major Sam, C.D., began his show career in 1972. Handled by Terry Correll, he accumulated ten points in three shows, two majors, and a Best of Breed from the classes at the prestigious Trenton Kennel Club event in May 1972, where he defeated eight Specials. He completed his championship easily that year. The following year his owner sparingly showed him as a Special while he matured and learned obedience for his C.D. ti-

tle. In 1974, under Roy Holloway's guidance, Major Sam became Number Two Golden, with a Best in Show contributing to that distinction. Major Sam was in the Top Ten Show Golden list in both 1975 and 1976 as well. His total record includes one Best in Show, thirteen Group firsts, fourteen Group seconds, eight Group thirds, and seven Group fourths—a record which put him in the Golden Retriever Club of America Hall of Fame. An uncle to the first obedience trial champion, Moreland's Golden Tonka, Major Sam has produced both obedience and bench champions in sufficient number to be given an Award of Merit as an Outstanding Sire by the Golden Retriever Club of America.

The accomplishments of Obedience Trial Champion Moreland's Golden Tonka are the sort which bring pride and pleasure to all dog breeders and dog owners. This remarkable bitch was whelped in 1972, sired by Champion Misty Morn's Sunset, C.D., T.D., ex Champion Moreland's Golden Bonnie. Ross Klipple purchased her, his second Moreland dog, principally for obedience trial work; his first Moreland dog was Moreland's Golden Lancer, C.D.X. Tonka's obedience training started early in life, and she took to it readily. By the time she was sixteen months old, she had completed her C.D. with three firsts in Novice B, three firsts in Open B, and three firsts in Utility. Mr. Klipple continued to campaign her in obedience trials, making her the Number One Obedience Golden Retriever in 1974, 1975, and 1976. She was, as we have mentioned previously, the first United States obedience trial champion of any breed, having completed all requirements in 1977.

An amusing anecdote told to us by Mr. Prentiss is about another of his dogs, Champion Moreland's Amber Tory. This dog readily completed his championship at an early age, almost always as Winners Dog or Reserve while in the classes. Mr. and Mrs. Prentiss said of him that he "never failed to bring home lunch money." Tory was the particular favorite of Mrs. Prentiss, who thought him a better dog than Major Sam; and Mr. Prentiss, too, agrees that the dog had a lot of merit, having won five Bests of Breed and a second in Group. But it did not seem appropriate to campaign both of them at the same time, and Mr. Prentiss preferred Sam. Anyway, he did agree to enter both at a local show if Mrs. Prentiss would handle one, and as it turned out she took Major Sam while Mr. Prentiss had the lead on Tory. Since they were the only Specials in competition, John Laytham, the judge, took his time in reaching his decision, finally pointing to Tory as Best of Breed. Mrs. Prentiss immediately jumped to her feet cheering, thus prompting a ringsider to ask her, in obvious wonderment, "Whassa matter, lady, you *like* to lose?" In this case, that was certainly true!

Ch. Moreland's Major Sam, C.D., winning Group first under judge Gerhardt Plaga. Roy Holloway, handling. Owned by William C. Prentiss, Moreland Kennels, Pennsylvania.

Morningsage

Morningsage Goldens started out with the purchase, by Joanne A. and Laddie C. Lastoka of Worthington, Minnesota, of a puppy in 1965. After having attended obedience classes, the Lastokas were introduced to licensed breed and obedience competition in 1967, and they have been consistently active exhibitors ever since. They are Charter Members of the Greater Twin Cities Golden Retriever Club (since 1967) and have been members of the Golden Retriever Club of America since 1969.

The first litter at Morningsage was whelped in 1970, giving the Lastokas their first homebred owner-handled Champion of Record, American and Canadian Champion Little Big Man. This handsome Golden became a Sporting Group winner in both the United States and Canada with multiple Group placements in both countries, and he was a recipient of the Greater Twin Cities Golden Retriever Club's Show Dog of the Year award, for the years 1974 and 1975, as well as having earned entrance into the Golden Retriever Club of America's Show Dog Hall of Fame. He was sired by the Lastokas' first champion, Duck Pass Noble Impulse, American and Canadian C.D. (also an owner-handled Group winner and Group placing dog) out of the first of the Lastokas' Goldens, Laddie's Golden Tassel, C.D.

The foundation brood bitch for the Lastokas has been Morningsage Malagold Honey, by Champion Malagold Beckwith's Om K Ivan,

Morningsage Malagold Honey appears in the 1982 *Yearbook* of the Golden Retriever Club of America as an Outstanding Dam. Owner, Joanne A. Lastoka, Worthington, Minnesota.

Ch. Morningsage Some Punkin winning the third major in April 1981. Bred, owned, and handled by Joanne A. Lastoka. By Ch. Gold Coast Here Comes The Sun, C.D., ex Ch. Morningsage Sandpebble, C.D.

C.D., ex Champion Dangret Emerald of Yeo. To date, Honey has produced four Champions of Record, as well as several High in Trial winners in both the United States and Canada who have competed in the Gaines Obedience Classics in the Novice and Open divisions. Her daughter, Morningsage Cinnamon Toast, C.D.X., owned by Brian Gensmer, placed seventh in the Open division at the 1981 Obedience Classic held in Texas. Honey is pointed in both the United States and Canada; and although she never completed her title, she has made her mark on the breed and has been named an Outstanding Dam by the Golden Retriever Club of America. She has won the Brood Bitch Classes at licensed Specialty shows in the United States and Canada. Another Honey daughter in whose accomplishments the Lastokas take special pride is Champion Morningsage Sandpebble, C.D., who also has distinguished herself as an Outstanding Dam and, along with her daughter, Champion Morningsage Some Punkin, was awarded Best Brace in Show at the Rapid City Kennel Club, October 1980.

151

Am., Can. Ch. Morningsage Last Tango, winning a Group under judge Mrs. Kitty Drury.

American and Canadian Champion Morningsage Last Tango (by Champion Honor's Let 'Em Have It ex Morningsage Malagold Honey, thus a full brother to Champion Morningsage Sandpebble, C.D.) is another breeder-owner-handled Group-winning Special in Canada, with numerous Group placements there and in the United States. Tango was the 1981 recipient of the Greater Twin Cities Golden Retriever Club's Show Dog of the Year award and was the Best of Breed winner at the Golden Retriever Club of Manitoba's licensed Specialty show held in Winnipeg, Canada, in May 1981.

The Lastokas started their breeding program with proven bench, field, and obedience lines and have basically held with the Beckwith and Honor background, as well as the "of Yeo" English line. The cornerstone is now in place, and the goal of producing a true Morningsage line of competitive Goldens in all phases is slowly becoming a reality.

The well-known Goldens which have carried the Morningsage banner to victory thus far, in addition to those already mentioned, include Champion Duck Pass Noble Impulse, American and Canadian C.D., by Champion King Chocki

Above: An informal head study of the lovely Ch. Morningsage Bouquet. **Above right:** A more formal view of Ch. Morningsage Bouquet, by Am., Can. Ch. Crackerjack of Keesus, C.D.X., ex Morningsage Malagold Honey. Bred, owned, and titled by Joanne A. Lastoka, Morningsage Goldens.

Below: Ch. Morningsage Sunrio Sandman belongs to Sue and Rick Deckert and Joanne A. Lastoka. **Below right:** Ch. Morningsage Sandpebble, C.D., by Ch. Honor's Let 'Em Have It, C.D., W.C., ex Morningsage Malagold Honey, is an Outstanding Dam. bred, owned, and handled to the title by Joanne A. Lastoka.

of Hilltop ex Pam's Khaki, with Group wins and placements, who was born in 1967; Canadian Champion Morningsage Flankerback, by American and Canadian Champion Topbrass Durango Brave, C.D.X., W.C., ex Morningsage Malagold Honey; Champion Sweetbay Morningsage Cajun, C.D., by Champion Rockgold Chug's Ric O' Shay ex Champion Starfarm's Carolina Ginger, C.D., a Group winner with additional Group placements in the United States, owner-handled; Champion Morningsage Bouquet, by American and Canadian Champion Crackerjack of Keesus, C.D.X., from Morningsage Malagold Honey; Champion Morningsage Little Big Shot, C.D., co-owned by Joanne Lastoka and Sheri DeVries, by Champion Sweetbay Morningsage Cajun, C.D., ex Champion Morningsage Sandpebble, C.D.; Champion Morningsage Some Punkin, Champion Morningsage Sunrio Sandman (co-owned with Sue and Rick Deckart), and Champion Morningsage Here Comes Linus, C.D. (owned by Mike and Kathy Inge), by Here Comes the Son ex Sandpebble.

Okeechobee

Susan Taylor, of New York City, was the owner of one of history's truly great Goldens, Champion Wochica's Okeechobee Jake. Sired by Champion Misty Morn's Sunset (by Champion Sunset's Happy Duke who was in turn a son of Champion Cragmount's Peter) from Little Dawn of Chickasaw (Champion Golden Pines High Fez ex High Farms Chickasaw's Gale), Jake has had considerable impact on this breed, both as a show dog and as a sire.

During his show career, Jake's accomplishments included being the only Golden in history ever to win the National three times, which he did in 1972, 1975, and 1977, on the third occasion from the Veterans Class at eight-and-a-half years of age! He was also the only

Ch. Wochica's Okeechobee Jake with his owner Susan Taylor in August 1977.

Bob Stebbins with Ch. Wochica's Okeechobee Jake. A handsome photo of a marvelous dog who contributed inestimably to Goldens in the United States.

Golden to date ever to have taken Best of Breed in Goldens at Westminster on three occasions. He was a multiple Best in Show winner, with seventy-three Group placements to his credit, and he was a member of the Golden Retriever Club of America Show Dog Hall of Fame. He earned a Certificate of Merit for having won the three National Specialties and a Certificate of Merit for the Bench in 1973 and 1974.

As a son of the breed's outstanding producer, Jake has certainly carried on in the family tradition! Susan Taylor tells us that he is second only to his sire in this regard, and it is impressive to consider the total of famed winners produced by one or the other of these two magnificent dogs!

Jake is, of course, in the Hall of Fame as an Outstanding Sire. He has also been honored by receiving the Gold Certificate of Distinction Award from Irene Schlintz (the Phillips System) as a Top Producer.

Susan Taylor's first bitch, who became an Outstanding Dam, was Beckwith's Beta of Spindrift, by Champion Beckwith's Tally Ho, C.D.X., Canadian C.D., from Champion Beckwith's Malagold Omega (a daughter of American, Canadian, and Mexican Champion Beckwith's Copper Ingot from American and Canadian Champion Beckwith's Frolic of Yeo, C.D.X.).

Needless to say, the loss of Jake was a very sad one. Susan Taylor has three handsome young sons of his with which she is carrying on the line and which are just getting started in their show careers. We wish her great success with them.

Above left: Susan Taylor's favorite photo of her great Golden, Ch. Wochica's Okeechobee Jake, showing all the beauty of a truly magnificent member of this breed. **Above:** Ch. Wochica's Okeechobee Jake winning one of his Bests in Show. Bob Stebbins handling. **Below:** Okeechobee's Blue Skye's Brian, son of Ch. Wochica's Okeechobee Jake, is owned by Susan Taylor.

Two very famous Golden Retrievers owned by Pekay Kennels, Pat Klausman and Kitty Cathey, Alpharetta, Georgia. In the foreground, O. T. Ch. Pekay's Charm Temptress, U.D.T., W.C., and behind her, Ch. Pekay's Deliverance, U.D.T., W.C.X. An excellent combination of brains and beauty is seen in these two splendid members of the breed.

Pekay

Goldens like to show their affection, as these two owned by Pat Klausman are doing.

Pekay Golden Retrievers are owned by Pat Klausman and Kitty Cathey of Alpharetta, Georgia. The aim here is to breed multi-purpose dogs, both owners agreeing that they want dogs with which to compete and which excel in all areas (conformation, obedience, field, and tracking). Temperament, ability, and soundness are all major factors in the breeding program here.

It is a source of pride and satisfaction at Pekay to have produced such multi-purpose Goldens as Champion Pekay's Crescendo of Ghinge, U.D., W.C.X., belonging to Ginger Gotcher; Obedience Trial Champion Pekay's Magic Moment, U.D., belonging to Ken Miller; Obedience Trial Champion Pekay's Charm Temptress, U.D.T., W.C., belonging to Jeannie Brown; and Champion Pekay's Deliverance, U.D.T., W.C.X., belonging to Nancy Patton and Kitty Cathey.

O. T. Ch. Beckwith's Eta of Spindrift, U.D.T., W.C.X., owned by Pat Klausman, Pekay Golden Retrievers.

Pekay is the home of Champion Honor's Kickback, U.D.T., W.C.X., the *first* in the breed to gain this particular combination of titles, who belongs to Kitty Cathey. The noted Obedience Trial Champion Beckwith's Eta of Spindrift, U.D.T., W.C.X., is owned by Pat Klausman; Champion Beaumaris Pekay's Kilowatt is owned by Kitty Cathey and Pat Klausman; Obedience Trial Champion Pekay's Charm Temptress, U.D.T., W.C., belongs to Jeannie Brown and Pat Klausman; and Champion Pekay's Deliverance, U.D.T., W.C.X., the fourth Champion U.D.T., W.C.X., who so far has sixty-six obedience trial championship points, belongs to Nancy Patton and Kitty Cathey.

At the time of this writing, Pekay dogs hold four obedience trial championships, eight Tracking Dog titles, twenty-four Companion Dog Excellent degrees, forty-two Companion Dog titles, nine Utility Dog titles, fourteen Working Certificates, four Working Certificate Excellents, and nineteen show championships.

Ch. Beaumaris Pekay's Kilowatt, "Killer," is owned by Kitty Cathey and Pat Klausman, Pekay Goldens.

Pepperhill

Pepperhill Golden Retrievers were established in 1969 when Barbara and Jeffrey Pepper of Putnam Valley, New York, purchased a well-bred pet from a local breeder and then two years later started training the dog for the obedience ring. While they were showing him there, many people asked if he was also entered in conformation classes, so, after protesting a few times that he had been purchased only as a pet, Mr. Pepper decided that he would give conformation competition a try with the dog, choosing as his first point show the National Specialty. The dog placed that day and went on to complete his championship a year later with four majors. This dog, Champion Sir Richard of Fleetwood, C.D., is still alive and with the Peppers today.

Above: Ch. Sir Richard of Fleetwood, C.D., photographed in the yard at Pepperhill Farms. Owned by Barbara and Jeffrey Pepper, Putnam Valley, New York. **Below:** Ch. Sir Richard of Fleetwood, C.D., in a more formal moment at a dog show. Handled here by Gerlinda Hockla.

Ch. Cummings' Dame Pepperhill, foundation bitch at Pepperhill Kennels owned by Barbara and Jeffrey Pepper, is by Ch. Sunset's Happy Duke ex Am., Can. Ch. Cummings' Golden Princess.

The first Golden purchased by the Peppers as a show dog was Champion Cummings' Dame Pepperhill, their foundation bitch, a daughter of Champion Sunset's Happy Duke (Champion Cragmount's Peter ex Glen Willow's Happy Talk) from American and Canadian Champion Cummings' Golden Princess (Champion Cragmount's Double Eagle ex Cragmount's Easy Lady). By eighteen months of age she had acquired both her majors and an aversion to dog shows; so she was retired and bred four times. In one of her litters, sired by Champion Gold-Rush's Great Teddy Bear (a son of American, Canadian, and Bermudian Champion Cummings' Gold-Rush Charlie ex Champion Golden Pines Glorybe's Angel), she produced four champions. "DeDe" (Dame Pepperhill) was named a Golden Retriever Club of America Outstanding Dam and *Kennel Review's* Outstanding Producer in 1978. She has several other pointed get as well. At just under six years of age, "DeDe" returned to the ring, handled by Elliot More, and completed her championship with another major. She died in July 1981.

Best known of the Goldens at Pepperhill, as this is written, is American and Canadian Champion Russo's Pepperhill Poppy, purchased as a puppy from Mercer Russo. In terms of dogs defeated, Poppy is the top winning bitch in breed history. Her record includes six Group firsts with seventeen other Group placements.

She was Best of Breed at the 1979 National Specialty, one of only four bitches ever to have won this honor, and Best of Breed at the 1981 Long Island Specialty. Poppy has fifty-one Bests of Breed to her credit and has been Best of Opposite Sex on more than ninety occasions, including the 1978 National, both the 1977 and the 1978 Garden State Specialty, the 1979 Central Regional Specialty, the 1981 Eastern Regional Specialty, and the 1981 Potomac Specialty. She was also Best of Breed at Westminster in 1980, perhaps the only Golden bitch to have won that show until this time and certainly the first for over twenty-five years (the point to which the Peppers have been able to check back).

The Peppers take great pride in the fact that Poppy is only the third bitch in history to have achieved inclusion in the Golden Retriever Club of America Hall of Fame, which she did in 1979. This honor is based on wins at Group and Best in Show levels. The first bitch to attain it was American and Canadian Champion Des Lac's Lassie, C.D., in 1949, and the second, American and Canadian Champion Chee Chee of Sprucewood, in 1953.

Am., Can. Ch. Russo's Pepperhill Poppy snapped informally at Pepperhill Farms.

Am., Can. Ch. Russo's Pepperhill Poppy taking Best of Breed at Delaware Water Gap. Handled by Elliot More for Jeffrey and Barbara Pepper.

Although proud of these achievements by Poppy, the Peppers are even more elated by the fact that Poppy has been named a Golden Retriever Club of America Outstanding Dam, presently having eight champions to her credit, four of which finished within thirty days. All of these are from three litters sired by Champion Pepperhill's Basically Bear, who has now been named an Outstanding Sire. There are also five Companion Dog titleholders from this breeding, two of them having *Dog World* awards; and one of the sons, Champion Pepperhill's Travelin' Bear, American and Canadian C.D., is also a Specialty Best of Breed dog, having won the Hudson Valley Specialty in 1981.

Ch. Pepperhill's Basically Bear, handled by Jeffrey Pepper, going Best of Breed at Central New York, April 1978. Barbara and Jeffrey Pepper, owners.

The third outstanding dam of the Peppers' kennel is Champion Pepperhill's Return Ticket, who has to her credit three champions from one litter, among them American and Canadian Champion Pepperhill's Lady Ruston who was Winners Bitch at the 1981 Long Island Specialty and has several breed and Canadian Group placements to her credit, while a second bitch from this litter, Champion Pepperhill East Point Airily, won the Group at Hartford in 1982.

Pepperhill, which takes its name from that of the owners combined with the topography of where they live, is a small kennel that has raised only eighteen litters (including one of Whippets) since 1970. Two litters are planned for 1982, one from Poppy who is already pregnant and one out of Return Ticket who will be bred to

Ch. Pepperhill's Return Ticket, another fine Golden from Pepperhill Farms, Barbara and Jeffrey Pepper, Putnam Valley, New York. Jeffrey Pepper handling.

Am., Can. Ch. Pepperhill Lady Ruston winning the Puppy Group at United Kennel Club in Canada, judged by Mrs. Virginia Hampton and handled by Jeffrey Pepper. Co-owned by Andrew Montgomery and Pepperhill Farms.

Jeffrey Pepper with Ch. Pepperhill's Ticket Taker.

Above: Ch. Pepperhill's Peter Principle, owned by Myra Moldawsky and Jeffrey Pepper. **Below:** Ch. Pepperhill's Allison Charlen at Greenwich in 1980. Jeffrey Pepper handling for Barbara Pepper and Charles Ingher.

Pepperhill's Triple Play taking Best of Winners at Mohawk Valley. Handled by Barbara Pepper who is co-owner with Jeffrey Pepper.

Travelin' Bear. Despite holding down puppy production to this extent, the Peppers have produced nineteen American champions, four Canadian champions, and at least eleven Companion Dog titlists in Goldens. The Peppers have worked hard to retain the outstanding movement that helped Poppy to do so well and feel that they have succeeded in this goal. They plan to continue their breeding operations on the same limited schedule as in the past.

The bloodlines on which the Peppers have worked are closely related. The foundation bitch, Champion Cummings' Dame Pepperhill, is a full sister to American, Canadian, and Bermudian Champion Cummings' Gold-Rush Charlie. Poppy is a Charlie daughter out of a bitch whose dam is a Charlie sister. Basically Bear and his littermates are out of Champion Cummings' Dame Pepperhill and sired by Champion Gold-Rush's Great Teddy Bear, a Charlie son. Travelin' Bear and his littermates are out of Basically Bear and Poppy. In other words, the Peppers have been line-breeding on the producers of Charlie and his descendants— with outstanding results.

Southern

Southern Goldens are located at Spartanburg, South Carolina, where they are owned by Clark and Colleen Williams, both keenly devoted to the breed. The kennel has been active since 1973, although Mrs. Williams herself has been "in" dogs for about nineteen years.

At present the Williams own two very exciting Goldens. They are both Outstanding Sires, both Golden Retriever Club of America Hall of Fame dogs, and both come from an equally distinguished background. These are American and Canadian Champion Goldrush's Contender, U.D., a Best in Show winner and the *fourth* Golden in breed history to have *both* Best in Show honors and a Utility Dog Degree in obedience, and American and Canadian Champion Southern Gold-Rush Traveler, a multiple Group-winner, a Specialty winner, and the Number Two Group-winning Golden in 1978-79.

Am., Can. Ch. Southern's Gold-Rush Traveler, at nineteen months of age, on the day he completed his title. Owners, Colleen and Clark Williams.

Among the promising youngsters at this kennel are a daughter of Traveler who was Winners Bitch and Best of Winners at the 1981 National Specialty and a son of his who won the Bred-by-Exhibitor Class at that same Specialty.

Mrs. Williams comments that their great show dog, Traveler, is also used for hunting in the fall and is very proficient. The kennel strives to produce all-purpose Goldens who can win in the show ring, obtain obedience titles, and hunt. To the delight of their owners, both of the Southern males are producing these qualities in their progeny. The Williams have four living Golden champions at the time of this writing—and co-own a young Norwegian Elkhound who is pointed from the Puppy Class!

A handsome photo of Am., Can. Ch. Goldrush's Contender, U.D., winning one of his Bests in Show for his owners.

Am., Can. Ch. Goldrush's Contender, U.D., owned by Southern Goldens, Clark and Colleen Williams, South Carolina. A most excellent head!

Michelle Metz winning first place in Junior Showmanship Class with Faera Rain Dance, owned by Wanda Metz, De Kalb, Illinois. In this picture Michelle was thirteen years old, "Goldy" twenty-two months old.

Starkin's

Starkin's Kennel is a young one in the Golden Retriever world, owned by Wanda and Phil Metz and their family at DeKalb, Illinois. Their first Golden was a gift from a business client. Beaumaris Fraser, "Aesop," came to them with a large yellow bow around his neck and was the start of many valued, lasting friendships. Through this dog the Metzes soon found themselves involved with conformation and obedience rings, which later led them to television appearances, schools, old age homes, and homes for the handicapped, all visited with their lovable Golden clown who made friends for himself and his breed wherever he appeared.

A friend of the Metzes also acquired a Golden which she had planned to breed to "Aesop," but being involved with a divorce changed her plans; as a result she gave the bitch, Faera Rain Dance, To Mrs. Metz, feeling the latter was in better position to do justice to this lovely Golden. Mrs. Metz did all the proper things for her, including eye examinations and hip x-rays and then bred her to Champion Cummings' Gold-Rush Charlie. There was a litter of four in which future Champion Starkin's Dan-D-Dazzler was included.

The serious illness of the Metzes' son caused the family to temporarily give up their activities with the Goldens, but Dan-D-Dazzler eventually came back to them from the home in which he had been placed during this emergency and went on the road with professional handler Tom Glassford, with whom he gained his championship with major wins in four shows. The Metzes permitted Mr. and Mrs. Thomas Sallen, Rottweiler owners from Florida, who were also clients of Mr. Glassford's, to lease Dan, and under their "ownership" Dan made the Golden Retriever Club of America's Top Ten List for 1981. The Sallens also took the bitch, Kelly, from this same litter, and put a championship on her. Mrs. Metz comments,

> Starkin's Kennel is a young starter but has found and made a lifetime of friends through the dogs. It isn't just the success of the kennel but the people it has brought together that makes it so very worthwhile. The precious gift of "Aesop," our original Golden, and the trust of our friends, along with the care of Mr. and Mrs. Sallen, are what have given Dan and Kelly their stories.

Chalfant's Lady Kelly at eight-and-a-half weeks of age. Owned by Wanda Metz, Starkin's Kennels.

Sun Dance

Sun Dance Goldens, now owned by Lisa Schultz of Algonquin, Illinois, was founded in 1954 by her stepfather, William Worley. The family is still actively breeding dogs, but Lisa does more of the showing as Bill is busy tending to his farm and cattle. Lisa now lives in the Chicago area and works for professional handler Dick Cooper, but all of her own Golden breedings and those of her parents are still based on the Sun Dance dogs, descendants of the original winners.

Bill Worley's first Golden was Champion Indian Knoll's Roc-Cloud, U.D. From this dog came the magnificent Champion Sun Dance's Bronze, two-time winner of the National Specialty during the mid-1960s. Since that time, dogs carrying the Sun Dance prefix have won the National four times, and Sun Dance proudly claims as its present total more than 160 champions of record.

Among those bringing fame to the Worleys' kennel have been Champion Sun Dance's Esquire, C.D., great-grandson of Bronze, who was campaigned in the late 1960s. A multi-Group winner and many time Specialty winner, Esquire took Best of Breed at Westminster as well. An Outstanding Sire, his progeny included Utility Dogs and Group winners. He has been listed as both a Golden Retriever Club Outstanding Sire and as a *Kennel Review* System Top Producer.

Ch. Sun Dance's Esquire, C.D., a great-grandson of Ch. Sun Dance's Bronze, was campaigned in the late 1960s. A multiple Group-winner and many times Specialty winner, he was also Best of Breed at Westminster. As an Outstanding Sire, his progeny include U.D. and Group winners. Owned by Sun Dance Kennels, Bill and Shirley Worley, Westfield, Indiana.

Above: Golden Retriever Club of America National Specialty in 1965 was won under Mrs. R. Gilman Smith by Ch. Sun Dance's Bronze, who gained the Best of Breed honors twice at National Specialties along with being a Group winner and Outstanding Sire. Photo courtesy of Lisa Schultz, Sun Dance Kennels. **Below:** Ch. Sun Dance's Contessa, one of the greatest Golden bitches in breed history, with her owner-handler, Bill Worley, of the famed Sun Dance Goldens. This bitch will long be remembered as a great producer, a great winner, and the constant companion and beloved friend of Mr. Worley's step-daughter Lisa Schultz.

Perhaps the most famous of all the Sun Dance winners was Esquire's fantastic daughter, Champion Sun Dance's Contessa. This was the top winning Golden bitch since the time of the great Champion Chee Chee of Sprucewood, in 1953, until the recent advent of Champion Russo's Pepperhill Poppy. Contessa was bred only twice, these two breedings resulting in a total of twelve puppies. The first litter, sired by Champion Kyrie Deamon, C.D.X., produced three pups. One became a champion-U.D., while the other two became champions. The second litter, sired by Champion Wochica's Okeechobee Jake, produced nine pups. Eight are finished, three are Group winners and Top Ten Goldens, six have Group placements, and one is a champion, U.D., W.C., T.D. From both litters there is a total of three Outstanding Sires, one Outstanding Dam, one with another champion to go, and one an Obedience Hall of Fame Golden and a *Kennel Review* Top Producer.

Contessa was twice Best of Opposite Sex at the National Specialty and Westminster and she also

Sun Dance's My Special Beau at fifteen months of age. This Jake-Contessa son was halfway to his title when his owners divorced, ending his show career. He was owned by the Cohns and bred by Sun Dance Kennels.

had two Group firsts, many placements, and an Independent Specialty win. Her record as a great producer and show dog will stand for many years to come, but Lisa Schultz comments that "most of all, she was my best friend and constant companion." Contessa was campaigned by Bill Worley throughout her career.

Champion Sun Dance's Rarue, Number One Golden in 1976, and National Specialty winner

Ch. Tempo's Frontier Bronco, owned by Vivian Wright and Hank Arszman, is handled here by Dick Cooper to another strong Group victory.

that same year, has distinguished himself well as a stud, being both an Outstanding Sire and the sire of the Number One Golden for 1981, Champion Sun Dance's Frontier Bronco, co-owned by the Wrights and Lisa Schultz's brother-in-law, Hank Arszman, who selected him as a puppy and campaigned him to the title.

Champion Sun Dance's Alexander and Champion Sun Dance's Rainmaker, the latter co-owned by Lisa Schultz and T. D'Alessandro, are both from the Jake-Contessa litter. Alex was a

Ch. Sun Dance's Rainmaker, Best of Breed at the Golden Retriever Club of America Eastern Regional and an all-breed Best in Show-winner. Handled by Bob Stebbins. Pictured winning the Specialty under judge Maxwell Riddle.

Brigdton's Cedar Sun Dance, C.D.X. **, owned by Lisa Schultz and Nancy Ferguson, is a daughter of Ch. Sun Dance's Rainmaker and is within one major of her championship at the time of this writing.

Group winner, the Number Three Golden for 1978, and an Outstanding Sire (two of his sons are Group winners). Rainmaker was Number Two Golden for 1979 and Best of Opposite Sex at the National Specialty that same year. Sire of one Group-winning son and two ** field trial dogs, he is a Golden Retriever Club of America Outstanding Sire. A Best in Show winner, he also has Best of Breed at the Eastern Regional and the Mid-West Regional to his credit.

Brigdton's Cedar Sun Dance, C.D.X. **, a daughter of Rainmaker, is within one major of her show championship and one leg away from being a Utility Dog—a good representative of the multi-purpose Golden!

The only one from the Jake-Contessa litter not to finish, Sun Dance's My Special Beau, was halfway to the title when his owners, to whom the Worleys had sold him, were divorced and his show career ended.

Sun Dance has been a kennel of inestimable importance in the Golden world since the early 1950s, and it will undoubtedly continue to be just as important for many more years to come.

Sunapee

Sunapee Golden Retrievers (and Gordon Setters) are located in Parma, Michigan, and are owned by Linda and Doug Walker. Although they have been in Goldens for more than ten years (since the early 1970s), the Walkers' first litter was not born until the later 1970s, having been co-bred with Sylvia Donahey, thus carrying her Birnam Wood Kennel name. At this time the litter is doing well, with Champion Birnam Wood's Foolish Pleasure recently finished as an American champion and on the way to Canadian titular honors, already having five points there. She is owned by Sally Sklar. Birnam Wood's Fire-N-Brimstone, owned by Virginia Wilson and Linda Walker, has eleven points including both majors. Birnam Wood's Sunapee Full Tilt gained points from the Puppy Class, and Birnam Wood's Four Leaf Clover is currently being shown. The litter was sired by Champion Gold Coast Here Comes The Sun, C.D., ex Birnam Wood's Best Seller.

The current top Golden at Sunapee Kennels is Champion Birnam Wood's Rita D Riot Act, probably by now also a C.D., as she was working on this title as this was written. Rita is line-bred on two excellent breedings between Champion

Ch. Birnam Wood's Rita D Riot Act, owned by Linda Walker, Parma, Michigan, taking Best of Opposite Sex at Ingham County Kennel Club in 1979. By Ch. Decoy's Buckingham Grover, C.D.X., Am. and Can. W.C., ex Spannen's Winged Victory. Breeder, Sylvia Donahey.

Golden Knoll's King Alphonzo and Champion Chee Chee of Sprucewood, the latter a multiple Best in Show winner and the dam of seventeen champions, several of which are Best in Show winners and Top Producers, too.

Rita finished her championship entirely amateur owner-handled, with a five-point major from the Puppy Class and two other majors.

Sunapee is based on Duckdown, Beckwith, and Gayhaven-Kirie-Ocoee lines, and the Walkers have just introduced some English lines through breeding Rita to Beaumaris Good As Gold, a dog bred by Anne Bissette.

Sutter Creek

Sutter Creek Goldens were established at Norton, Massachusetts, in 1967 with the purchase of two Golden Retrievers given by Susan and Larry Breakell to each other as wedding gifts. Windrock Russet Copper produced two litters; however, due to various complications, the line was dropped from the breeding program, and "Windy" was placed as a pet in a good home. Fox Rock's Watchful Harold (1967-1981) became a permanent family member; and although he was never bred, he helped the Breakells to establish the sound, typey, standard line they have today.

During their first decade in dogs, the Breakells were primarily concerned with breeding sound Goldens for their own future breeding purposes. Those not retained for breeding and showing were, and still are, sold as pets to homes in non-breeding situations. Susan admits that the "re-

Ch. Golden Horizon's Cupid in 1968. Owner-handler, Susan Breakell, Sutter Creek Kennels.

jects" outnumbered the "keepers" by at least twenty-five to one! During that time, the Breakells ran into numerous problems as they sought sound dogs of a type that appealed to them. Finally they turned to Rachel Page Elliott, a long-time Golden breeder, who was tremendously helpful and guided them to England to find lines with which to start over.

The imports, Charade, Fanfare, and Cognac proved to be the *real* foundation at Sutter Creek, and they are carried on in the bloodlines there today. These three carried the background of the older Ulvin, Weyland, Ambria, and Camrose.

The second decade at Sutter Creek has been spent in crossing these lovely, sound, typey working lines with older lines from Sun Dance, Sprucewood, Cragmount, and Beckwith; and the results have brought about sound, top winning Goldens now being used in top breeding programs throughout the United States.

The Breakells believe in line-breeding, looking to fourth and fifth generations for suitable combinations, with very occasional light inbreeding to compound certain traits that, once developed, might be useful to retain for future generations. In other words, the aim is to breed good sound dogs today for *better* sound dogs in the future.

Champion Golden Horizon's Cupid, acquired as a three-year-old in 1969, became the Breakells' first champion. Owner-handled, he became a multiple Best of Breed winner. He sired two litters, after which he was placed as a pet in a new home.

Sutter Creek Goldens enjoying the snow in Norton, Massachusetts.

Ch. Alstone Sutter Creek Charade, U.D.*, at ten-and-a-half years of age. Owner-handled by Susan Breakell, Sutter Creek Kennels, Norton, Massachusetts.

Ch. Tanya's Sunburst Kemo Sabi, C.D.X., by Ch. Alstone Sutter Creek Charade, U.D.*, ex Robin's Lady Tanya. Breeder-owner, Rita Di Salvio. Handler, Susan Breakell.

Champion Alstone Sutter Creek Charade, U.D.* (1969-1981), imported from England when he was seven years old, brought with him important working lines. Charade became a Golden Retriever Club of America Outstanding Sire and among his get were Champion Toryglen Idling Jerome, U.D.***; Champion Goldenrod Lark of Trowsnest, U.D.*; Champion Tanya's Sunburst Kemo Sabi, T.D.; and Kyle Karakan of Sutter Creek, American, Canadian, and Bermudian U.D.T. Kyle Karakan was on the list of Top Ten Obedience Dogs for three years, Number One Golden in the *Front and Finish* ratings for 1972, and a member of the Golden Retriever Club of America Obedience Hall of Fame, where he has been joined by several of his own top obedience get.

Charade, bred to Featherquest Golden Diana, produced the foundation bitches for Libra Kennels and for Englewood Kennels.

Teecon Sutter Creek Cognac, C.D. (1970-1981), by English Show Champion Gamebird Debonair of Teecon ex English Show Champion Peatling Stella of Teecon, the second import to Sutter Creek, brought primarily Ambria and Camrose lines to the kennel. Cognac was a multiple Best in Match and High Scoring in Trial dog and the sire of several U.D. dogs. Unhappy as a kennel dog, he was placed in a home when he was around five years old, with breeding rights retained by the Breakells. He was instrumental in the establishment of several young kennels in the New England area.

Teecon Sutter Creek Fanfare, C.D., born in 1971, full sister to Cognac, was the foundation bitch at Sutter Creek and a multiple High in Trial winner. She was not shown in breed com-

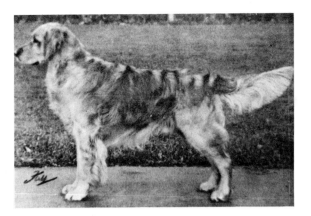

Above: English Show Ch. Gamebird Debonair of Teecon. **Below:** English Show Ch. Peatling Stella of Teecon. Photos courtesy of Susan Breakell, Sutter Creek.

Featherquest Sutter Creek K.C., by Ch. Alstone Sutter Creek Charade ex Ch. Featherquest Morning Sunray, at ten months of age. Bred by Rachel Page Elliott and owned by Susan Breakell.

petition due to corrective eye surgery for a nonhereditary problem, and she was the dam of several pointed get. Bred to Charade, she produced Sutter Creek's Tararu Allegro, U.D.T.X.*. Bred to Fox Rock's Bwana, she produced Sutter Creek Gamboge Haze, dam of American and Canadian Champion Cloverdale Bunkerhill Seth, foundation stud for Cloverdale Kennels.

Featherquest Sutter Creek K.C. was a multiple Best in Match puppy; but unfortunately, he died before he was started on his show career. He did leave several litters behind him, which included some excellent youngsters.

Canadian Champion Goldenquest Sutter Creek Lyric, American and Canadian C.D., was born in 1974, by Champion Misty Morn's Sunset, C.D., T.D.*, ex Canadian Champion Deegojay's Amorous Aspasia, C.D. She was imported from Canada due to her Misty Morn's Sunset line-bred Beckwith pedigree. She became Sutter Creek's first Golden Retriever Club of America Outstanding Dam. On loan to Pamela

Can. Ch. Goldenquest Sutter Creek Lyric, Am. and Can. C.D., a Golden Retriever Club of America Outstanding Dam, was imported by Susan Breakell and is co-owned with Pamela Tillotson. Handler, Kimberly Tillotson.

Tillotson (Tessahoc Goldens) for show purposes, this bitch was put into co-ownership and retained by Pamela's family as a house dog. "Tweeter," as she was called, was shown by Pam to all of her titles. She returned twice to Sutter Creek for two litters, the first by Champion Cloverdale Bunker Hill Seth. This breeding produced American and Canadian Champion Sutter Creek Cloverdale Erin, owned by Cloverdale Kennels; Erin was later, in co-ownership, breeder-owner-handled by Susan Breakell to multiple Group firsts, making her one of the top winning bitches in breed history. "Tweeter's" second breeding, to Champion Sutter Creek Goldrush Flyboy, produced Champion Westmont's Sutter Creek Aria and Champion Sutter Creek Tessahoc Wiloby. A third litter produced lovely puppies just now starting out.

American and Canadian Champion Fox Rock Sutter Creek Ulanda is one of the favorites at this kennel and has been influential in directing the Breakells to introduce more of the Cragmount line, as the heavy concentration of it in her pedigree when bred to Charade and Flyboy has produced some promising youngsters.

Above: Multiple Group-winner, Am., Can. Ch. Sutter Creek Cloverdale Erin, handled by co-breeder and co-owner Susan Breakell. Co-breeder, Pamela Tillotson. Co-owners, Richard and Jane Zimmerman. Winning the Group at Tidewater, March 1980, under judge Virginia Hampton. **Below:** Am., Can. Ch. Fox Rock Sutter Creek Ulanda, bred by Mary Merchant, at seven-and-a-half months of age wins Best Puppy in Show. Owner-handler Susan Breckell, Sutter Creek Kennels.

Ch. Sutter Creek's Libra Bearhug at two-and-a-half years of age. Owner-handler, Susan Breakell.

Champion Sutter Creek's Libra Bearhug, C.D., is by Champion Goldrush's Contender, U.D., ex Champion Libra Lady Carioca, C.D., and was purchased at the age of ten months from his breeder, Cheryl Blair of Libra Kennels; Ms. Blair's foundation bitch, Sutter Creek Serendipity, C.D.X., a multiple pointed High in Trial winning Charade daughter, had been raised by the Breakells. It is expected that Bearhug, an exuberant Specialty winner, will prove most valuable to Sutter Creek in unifying the bloodlines for the future. This dog has become one of the house dogs at Sutter Creek, and the Breakells are watching his progeny with satisfaction as they are already showing exciting potential for the future.

American and Canadian Champion Sutter Creek Goldrush Flyboy, born in 1976, was third choice puppy male from the exceptional litter by champion Gold-Rush's Great Teddy

Ch. Sutter Creek Goldrush Flyboy, owner-handled by Susan Breakell, taking Best of Breed and on to Group placement, Windham County, 1980.

Bear ex Champion Goldrush's Birch of Bearwood, C.D., bred by D. Jean Baird. "Junior." as he is called, was purchased with the idea in mind that the Sun Dance type crossed into the Cragmount pedigrees was exactly what the Breakells were seeking, and they were evidently correct, as Flyboy has become the dog they consider to be their greatest asset. Owner-handled to earn a place in the Golden Retriever Club of America Show Dog Hall of Fame at twenty-two-and-a-half months of age and becoming an Outstanding Sire of nine champions despite extremely limited stud use by July 1982 (the latter owing to travelling commitments), he is now in heavy demand for stud work as the public becomes aware of the soundness and exceptional quality of his progeny. His list of noted winners includes Champion Cloverdale Twin-Beau-D Joy (Golden Retriever Club of America Hall of Fame member, who in 1981 became the first bitch in thirty-eight years to win Best in Show), Champion Laurell's Golden Oaks Nashua (numerous Group placements), Champion Cloverdale Pistol of Windsor (Specialty winner), and Champion Sutter Creek Tessahoc Wiloby (Sutter Creek's newest homebred champion, gained his title owner-handled from the Bred-by-

Sutter Creek Tessahoc Trilby, bred and owned by Susan Breakell and Pamela Tillotson.

Exhibitor Class and then, three weeks after finishing, became Sutter Creek's third Group winner).

Other Goldens contributing to the Sutter Creek breeding program include Sutter Creek Tessahoc Trilby (litter-sister to Wiloby), Cloverdale Sutter Creek Tik'L, Sutter Creek Laurell Ruffian, Sutter Creek's Ruby Red Dress, Sutter Creek's Simply Smashing, and Canadian Champion Sutter Creek's Crispy Critter.

After fifteen years of carefully breeding sound, selectively chosen dogs, the Breakells now feel that they have established the Sutter Creek line of winning Goldens that are so invaluable an asset to any breeding program.

Cloverdale Sutter Creek Tik'L, owner-handled by Susan Breakell. Breeder, Jane Zimmerman.

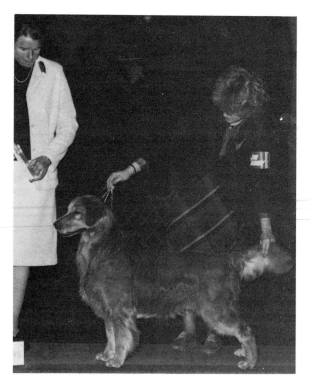

Ch. Laurell's Golden Oaks Nashua at eighteen months of age. By Am., Can. Ch. Sutter Creek Goldrush Flyboy ex Ch. Laurell's Yats of Luck. Terri Weaver, owner.

Thistledue

Thistledue Goldens are highly respected in the world of dog shows and have enjoyed some distinguished show ring records through the achievements of their dogs. Located at Liberty, Missouri, the kennel is owned by Mr. Carter Foss, whose association with Goldens began in 1962, with the purchase of Shawn of Fox Lake Hills, who lived to the ripe old age of fifteen. Now Mr. Foss has bred five champions and a Show Dog Hall of Fame winner, Champion Thistledue's Shining Star.

Thistledue was selected by Carter and Diana Foss as their kennel identification in honor of their outstanding dam, Champion Goldenquest's Thistledue, mother of Shining Star, who traces her ancestry back to, among her great-grandparents, Champion Sunset's Happy Duke and American and Canadian Champion Beckwith's Malagold Flash, American and Canadian U.D.T. and W.C. Thistledue's crowning achievement to date has been Star, a great dog with some very noteworthy accomplishments to his credit.

Ch. Goldenquest's Thistledue became a champion at seventeen months of age. A Group-placing bitch, she has also won the Brood Bitch Class at the National in 1978, 1980, and 1981. Carter F. Foss, owner-handler.

Above: This is the very first Golden Retriever owned by Mr. and Mrs. Carter F. Foss at Thistledue Kennels, Shawn of Fox Lake Hills, born June 10th 1962 and died August 15th 1977. **Below:** Ch. Thistledue's Shining Star winning Best of Breed at the Evergreen Golden Retriever Specialty, Monroe, Washington, May 1981. Bred, owned, and handled by Carter F. Foss, Liberty, Missouri.

Ch. Thistledue's Shining Star winning the Sporting Group under Haworth Hoch, Topeka Kennel Club, September 1981. Breeder-owner-handler, Carter F. Foss.

Born in October 1976, Star is a son of Champion Wochica's Okeechobee Jake (by Champion Misty Morn's Sunset, C.D., T.D., W.C., ex Little Dawn of Chickasaw) from Champion Goldenquest's Thistledue (Champion Misty Morn's Sunset ex Canadian Champion Deegojay's Amorous Aspasia, C.D.). Shown ten times as a puppy, including the 1977 National Specialty, Star made a clean sweep, undefeated, of the Puppy Classes in which he was entered. He finished his championship at thirteen months of age with back-to-back majors at shows seven hundred miles apart. He has been handled exclusively by his breeder-owner-handler, Carter Foss, throughout his career in the show ring.

During the years 1978 through 1981, Star was the Number One breeder-owner-handled Golden Retriever in the United States, and he currently leads that category for 1982, as of June 10th, with wins which have included two Bests in Show. He has been, as this is written, in the Top Ten listing (all systems) for three consecutive years. In 1981, he won Best of Breed twenty-five times and placed in the Sporting Group on twenty-three of these occasions. As of June 1982, Star's total show record consists of 110 times Best of Breed, seventy-three Group placements (of which twenty-five were firsts), three all-breed Bests in Show, and two Specialty

Show Bests of Breed, earning him a position in the Golden Retriever Club of America's Show Dog Hall of Fame. In 1981, Star retired the trophy for breeder-owner-handler offered through the Golden Retriever Club of America. Mr. Foss will replace the trophy with a similar one for future competition.

Not only has Star "made it on his own" as a single contender in the show ring but, as part of a brace, he has also met with success, as he and Champion Thistledue's Chance have won Best Brace in Show at several National Specialties and at all-breed dog shows.

Mr. Foss has given generously of his time to club activities through the years. In 1964 and 1965, he served on the Board of Directors of the Golden Retriever Club of Illinois. He joined the Golden Retriever Club of America in 1963 and served as Nominating Chairman 1975-1976. He also was the founder and first President of the Kansas City Golden Retriever Club, 1975 to the present.

As an aside while speaking of his first Golden acquired in 1962, Mr. Foss comments that there were approximately eighteen hundred Goldens registered with the American Kennel Club in 1962, but now the A.K.C. is registering more than fifty thousand Goldens annually.

Ch. Thistledue's Shining Star winning Best in Show under Mrs. Maxine Beam in February 1982. Handled, as always, by breeder-owner, Carter F. Foss.

Tigathoe

Tigathoe Goldens, at Greenwich, Connecticut, have been active in the Golden Fancy since the mid-1940s. Their owner is Mrs. George H. ("Torch") Flinn, a lady of energy and talent who, at the age of seventy, still does all her own puppy raising, kennel clean-up, training for field, and so on—in other words, a truly dedicated fancier who enjoys her dogs and finds pleasure in personally working with them.

Mrs. Flinn has long since lost track of the number of bench champions she has bred; they came fast and easily in the late 1940s and mid-1950s. It was then that she became interested in what these Goldens are intended to be: hunting dogs, competitive trial dogs, who were still attractive in appearance—this she found much more exciting and challenging, and much tougher!

During the eight years (1947-1955) she showed in conformation, Mrs. Flinn recalls finishing about fifteen bench champions. During the ensuing twenty-seven years, she *knows* that she owned five field champions, amateur field champions, and a dual champion and that she bred four field champion-amateur field champions, one dual champion-amateur field champion, one amateur field champion, and three Canadian field champion-amateur field champions. To

quote Mrs. Flinn, "No breeder, no professional, no owner—Labrador or Golden (and in our trials there are sixty Labs to three Goldens *in each stake*)—has ever even come close to this record." Needless to say, she is justifiably very proud of her accomplishments with the breed!

More successes are obviously in the future for the Tigathoes, as Mrs. Flinn speaks with enthusiasm of a brilliant youngster she is preparing for the trials. May it carry on in the tradition of those who have preceded it from this prestigious kennel!

Topbrass

Topbrass Golden Retrievers belong to Mrs. Joseph Mertens of Elgin, Illinois. The foundation bitch here, Valentine Torch of Topbrass, a full sister to Champion Rockgold Ric's Cookie and Beckwith's Topbrass Regent (who had thirteen points and a *Dog World* award at time of death), had the misfortune to lose a leg when she was one year old. She was, however, still able to become the mother of eight bench champions and two obedience champions as her excellent contribution to the breed. Sired by Champions Rockgold's Chug's Ric O Shay ex Champion Goldenloe's Bronze Lustra, Torch had done some nice winning herself from the Puppy Classes prior to the loss of her leg.

Valentine Torch of Topbrass is behind all of the present winners from this well-known kennel. When she was one year old, Torch lost a leg; she had been shown as a puppy and was started toward championship when this misfortune occurred. Topbrass Kennels, and Torch, owned by Mrs. Joseph Mertens, Elgin, Illinois.

Ch. Topbrass Ad-lib's Bangor, one of Torch's famous offspring, winning more honors for owner Mrs. Joseph Mertens.

Noteworthy dogs produced by Topbrass Kennels include the following, all from Valentine Torch of Topbrass: Champion Topbrass Durango Brave, C.D.X., W.C.; Champion Topbrass Ad-Lib's Bangor, C.D.; Champion Topbrass Topeka of Sunstream, C.D., W.C.; Champion Topbrass San Francisco Flame; Champion Topbrass Ad-Lib's Dynamite; Champion Topbrass Lucky Streak O' Slade; Champion Topbrass Thunderwater Totum; Champion Topbrass Delta Dawn, C.D.; Obedience Trial Champion Topbrass Cisco Kid; Obedience Trial Champion Topbrass Stubblesfield Pippa; and Topbrass Sea of Joy, U.D.

Also noteworthy are Obedience Trial Champion Topbrass Rocky Mountain High; Obedience Trial Champion Topbrass Ric O Shay Barty; Topbrass Ad-Lib's Rip Off, U.D.; Topbrass Degis Ven, U.D.; Topbrass Zephyr, U.D.; Champion Topbrass Dazzlin Daisy Slade; Champion Topbrass It's My Lucky Day; Champion Rockgold's Ric's Cookie; Champion Topbrass Sterlingold Dynamo, W.C.; and Canadian Champion Topbrass Target of Ambertrail.

Above: Ch. Topbrass San Francisco Flame, who finished her title in six shows and is a Golden Retriever Club of America Outstanding Dam, is owned by Mrs. Joseph Mertens, Topbrass Kennels, Elgin, Illinois. **Below:** O. T. Ch. Topbrass Stubblesfield Pippa, owned by Kay Gutzself, is a winner of the Gaines Classic.

Ch. Sunstream Gypsy of Topbrass taking the points at Southeastern Iowa Kennel Club in 1977. Owned by Topbrass Goldens, Mrs. Joseph Mertens.

All of the Topbrass dogs are descended from Valentine Torch of Topbrass, W.C. The recent field trial breedings have been out of Champion Sunstream Gypsy of Topbrass, who finished with four majors and is by Field Trial Champion-Amateur Field Champion Tigathoe's Kiowa II ex Champion Topbrass Topeka of Sunstream, thus a Torch granddaughter. Gypsy was bred to Amateur Field Champion Holway Barty, producing two field champion and amateur field champion titleholders and many obedience degree winners.

F.C., A.F.C. Topbrass Mandy, one of the outstanding Goldens belonging to Mrs. Joseph Mertens, Topbrass Kennels.

Particular pride is taken in the accomplishments of Field Champion and Amateur Field Champion Topbrass Mandy, with twenty-three Derby points and fifty-seven all-age points. She is one of only two living field champion Golden *bitches* in the United States who qualified for the 1980 and 1981 National Amateur and 1980 National Open. Pride is also taken in Field Champion and Amateur Field Champion Topbrass Cotton, who has forty-six Derby points in nineteen trials, an amateur field champion at three years of age and a field champion prior to four years of age. Cotton was the only Golden qualified in 1981 for the 1981 National Open and was the youngest dog to win the Open.

Then there are the exciting accomplishments of Champion Topbrass Ad-Lib's Bangor, qualified open all-age bitch, one of only three which are also bench champions in the United States. Bangor is, additionally, an obedience C.D. titleholder and a Golden Retriever Club of America Outstanding Dam.

F.C., A.F.C. Topbrass Cotton, another fine representative of the Goldens bred at Topbrass Kennels owned by Mrs. Joseph Mertens.

The Mertens have worked hard to achieve a functional Golden who can truly compete in all phases of activity—field, obedience, and show. They have been notably successful in this endeavor, with many champions in all three areas.

The beautiful owner-handled Golden, Ch. Cloverdale Twin-Beau-D Joy, with her family the Robert Dallaires of Warren, Rhode Island, immediately following her victory over 1700 dogs at Riverhead Kennel Club, March 1981.

Twin-Beau-D

Twin-Beau-D Goldens belong to Nancy and Robert Dallaire, Warren, Rhode Island, who have owned the breed since about 1977. They started out with a pet bitch who was very sound but would never finish her championship, so the Dallaires bought another Golden, a dog this time, and he became their first owner-handled (as are all of the Dallaires' dogs) champion. This was Champion Englewood's Rough N Ready, known to his friends as "Beau." Next the Dallaires received from her breeders, J. and R. Zimmerman, the bitch who became Champion Cloverdale's Twin-Beau-D Joy. Nancy had done some handling for the Zimmermans and this bitch was her payment—one which surely worked out to become *very* satisfactory!

Ch. Cloverdale Twin-Beau-D Joy earning a Group placement at Dayton Kennel Club in 1982. Sired by Ch. Sutter Creek Goldrush Flyboy ex Cloverdale Sabrina.

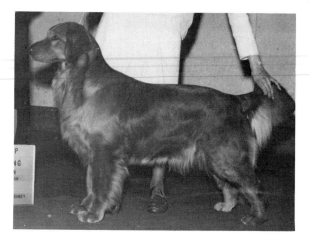

Ch. Twin-Beau-D's JJ is the sire of this typical puppy with owner Nancy Dallaire.

Ch. Twin-Beau-D's JJ, by Ch. Gold-Rush's Great Teddy Bear ex Englewood Cleo's Starshine, C.D., is one of the fine Goldens owned by Nancy and Robert Dallaire.

Ch. Twin-Beau-D's Blue Nun, the fourth champion belonging to Robert and Nancy Dallaire, Twin-Beau-D Goldens.

From the very moment Joy joined the Dallaires as a member of their family, she was a delight in every way. Owner-handled all the way, Joy finished her championship and won Best in Show, all on the same day, at Riverhead in March 1981. She was the first Best in Show Golden bitch in twenty-eight years (following American and Canadian Champion Chee Chee of Sprucewood) and the first *ever* owner-handled. In 1981, she was the Number One Golden Bitch in the United States. Joy was retired from the show ring in June 1982, when she became a member of the Golden Retriever Club of America Show Dog Hall of Fame (status by Group placements only), the first owner-handled Golden bitch to attain this honor. The Dallaires plan to breed Joy in the autumn of 1982.

The Dallaires also own another good dog in Champion Twin-Beau-D's JJ. He was out of their first bitch and finished his title at the National Specialty under Michele Billings over 146 dogs. He produced a new young bitch, Champion Twin-Beau-D's Blue Nun, who gained her championship, owner-handled, in June 1982. In three months of showing she won five majors, one of these being the Eastern Regional Specialty, to complete her title at sixteen months of age. She has just been bred to Cloverdale Frost Fire, a young male belonging to Jane Zimmerman.

The Dallaires keep only hip- and eye-clear Goldens who have sound movement and can win. Hopes are high right now for three youngsters coming along at Twin-Beau-D and expected out in 1983.

Valhalla

Valhalla Farms, owned by Kathy Liebler and located at Carmel, New York, is an important kennel in Eastern Golden circles. Goldens from this kennel are both outstanding bench show winners and very successful obedience dogs, and the kennel is well known in both areas of competition.

Foundation bitch at this kennel, or at least the one behind the current leading winners, is Beckwith's Chickasaw Jingle, winner of an Award of Merit from *Dog World* magazine as a Dam of Distinction, with five champions to her credit including the outstanding brother-sister pair, both also *Dog World* Award of Distinction winners in their own right, American and Canadian

Ch. Valhalla's Amber Waves winning Best of Breed at Farmington Valley Kennel Club, July 1975. Kathleen M. Liebler, owner, Valhalla Farms, Carmel, New York.

Beckwith's Chickasaw Jingle, Outstanding Dam, owned by Kathy and Larry Liebler, Valhalla Farms.

Am., Can. Ch. Valhalla's Cedar Wood Son, by Am., Can. Ch. Valhalla's Amber Waves ex Valhalla's Autumn Mist, winning at Boise, Idaho. Owned by the Lieblers, Valhalla Farms.

Champion Valhalla's Amber Waves and Champion Valhalla's Amber Kate, C.D. (both by American and Canadian Champion Beckwith's Malagold Flash, C.D.). Others helping their dam gain the award, in 1974, included Champion Beckwith's Viceroy to Newton, Champion Beckwith's Malagold Starfarm, and Champion Valhalla's Trowsnest Folly, C.D.X., W.C.

Amber Waves and Amber Kate both were honored by *Dog World* in 1979, he for five champions and she for three. Amber Waves sired Clark's Totoket Betsy Ross, Ropahi's Valhalla Jingle Too, Russo's Alderbrooke Valhalla, Valhalla's Cedar Wood Sam, and Jolly Oahu Cougar, all of whom have earned titles. Amber Kate won with her three champion get: Valhalla's Dogo Dancer, Valhalla's Amber Velvet, and Valhalla's Shawn's Golden Lance. Kate is also the dam of a very distinguished obedience dog, Valhalla's After Dinner Licker, C.D.X., W.C.X.

Valhalla's Professor Higgins, by Deremac Ameche Liberator ex Ch. Valhalla's Amber Kate, C.D., owned by Kathy Liebler.

Ch. Valhalla's Dogo Dancer at thirteen months of age, winning the Sporting Group at the Sands Motel, Stillwater, Minnesota, in February 1976. By Ch. Cummings' Gold-Rush Charlie ex Ch. Valhalla's Amber Kate, C.D. Kathleen Liebler, owner.

Above: An exciting day for Valhalla Kennels at the National in 1974, where judge Mrs. Winifred Heckman selected Valhalla's Amber Waves, now a champion, as Best of Winners and Ch. Valhalla's Amber Kate, C.D., as Best of Opposite Sex to Best of Breed. **Below:** Westley Valhalla Noah, C.D., one of the handsome Goldens from Valhalla Farms, owned by the Liebers.

Amber Waves and Amber Kate have accounted for some extremely exciting show days for Kathy Liebler. One such day was in 1974, when Winifred Heckman adjudged them Best of Winners and Best of Opposite Sex to Best of Breed respectively at the National; another exciting day was when Amber Waves took Best of Breed at Westminster in 1977—to mention just two of many! The day when Kate's daughter by Champion Cummings' Gold-Rush Charlie, Champion Valhalla's Dogo Dancer, at only thirteen months of age won the Sporting Group at Stillwater, Minnesota, was another occasion which we are sure will not be soon forgotten. Also to be recalled is the day when Valhalla's After Dinner Licker, C.D.X., W.C.X., won Highest Scoring in Obedience at Monticello.

Over the years, Valhalla Goldens have added to their breeding program by importing some noted English bloodlines, principally Westley, Nortonwood, and Camrose. Westley Valhalla Noah, C.D., is a recent one of these, and we understand that he has already gained a *Dog World* award for his excellence in obedience competition.

Westbrook

Westbrook Goldens are among the newer kennels which seem to show particularly bright promise of a "golden" future. The owners, Ted and Beth Greenfield of Chittenango, New York, are very enthusiastic breeders and exhibitors of Goldens.

The Greenfields have started out well with their bitch, American and Canadian Champion October's Cal-Vo Spirit, which they purchased in February 1979 from her breeder, Sharon Smith, from October Kennels in Cornwallville, New York. Starting out with some nice wins as a puppy, Spirit has matured into a very handsome Golden and is already making her presence felt in Sporting Group competition, following time out for a litter sired by American and Canadian Champion Cloverdale's Bunker Hill. The puppies are now just starting show careers (so far one is pointed in Canada), while Spirit herself is preparing to enter obedience competition as well as conformation classes.

Spirit taking second in Group under Ralph Del Deo at Onandaga Kennel Association.

Her first time out as a Special and owner-handled, Am., Can. Ch. October's Cal-Vo Spirit takes Best of Opposite Sex at Westminster 1981, under judge William Geisenhafer. Ted and Beth Greenfield, owners, Westbrook Goldens.

Wingsong

Wingsong Golden Retrievers are owned by Susan and John Heinl of Medway, Ohio, and were established in 1971 with a Golden which Mrs. Heinl received as a gift. As it turned out, even though he became Sue Heinl's best friend and a very successful contender in obedience competition where he earned a C.D.X., T.D., and W.C., this Golden could not be shown in breed conformation classes, so a bitch who could be shown was purchased from Connie and Jim Lee who owned Rockgold Kennels.

This bitch was Rockgold's Fanfare of Brass, by Champion Rockgold Chug's Ric-O-Shay (Group placing grandson of American and Cana-dian Champion Star Spray Maria's Rayo Del Sol and Champion Rockgold's Frolicking Gypsy) ex Champion Rockgold's Lysistrata (Champion Hunt's Copperfield Daemon, W.C., ex Champion Ryden's Charisma), and she was shown to eight points, including a five-point major in a Specialty and Reserve in several other major entries before being bred to Champion Goldrush's Contender, U.D. From this litter came the fantastic young dog Champion Wingsong Maker's Mark with which Mrs. Heinl is rapidly making history in the show ring.

Mark became a champion in the autumn of 1981 with Best of Breed over Best in Show Specials. Since then he has gained nineteen Bests of Breed, a Specialty Best in Show (Cincinnati

Ch. Wingsong Maker's Mark, with his breeder-owner-handler Susan Heinl, winning the Greater Cincinnati Golden Retriever Club Specialty Show, May 1982. This handsome son of Ch. Goldrush's Contender, U.D., ex Rockgold's Fanfare of Brass (Ch. Rockgold Chug's Ric-O-Shay ex Ch. Rockgold's Lysistrata) is also the winner of two Bests in Show (all-breed) and has fourteen Group placements as of June 1982.

Golden Retriever Club, 1982), two all-breed Bests in Show (Cincinnati Kennel Club, May 30th 1982, and Columbiana Kennel Club, June 12th 1982), plus four Sporting Group firsts, seven Group seconds, two thirds, and one fourth. His Group placements have already earned him a position in the Golden Retriever Club of America Show Dog Hall of Fame.

Champion Goldrush's Contender, U.D., Mark's sire, who is in the Golden Retriever Club of America Outstanding Sire listings, is by the famed Champion Misty Morn's Sunset, C.D., T.D., W.C. (an Outstanding Sire and member of the Show Dog Hall of Fame) from Champion Goldrush's Birch of Briarwood, American and Canadian C.D., W.C., and an Outstanding Dam. Based on Mark's performance in the ring thus far, it seems safe to predict that he will be a dog long remembered and one who will make important contributions to his breed.

Wochica

Wochica Goldens, at Smithtown, New York, belong to Janet L. Bunce who "as a breeder and handler of a couple of Irish Setters" started handling dogs professionally in 1947. Her Golden Retriever kennel was established in 1965 with her two foundation dogs, Champion Pathfinder of Lazy Pines, C.D., W.C., and Little Dawn of Chickasaw, the latter purchased at the age of five years, campaigned toward her championship but retired (with fourteen points) for breeding purposes. Many champions have descended from these two beautiful and even-tempered Goldens.

Little Dawn of Chickasaw is a Golden Retriever Club of America Outstanding Dam for having produced, in the same litter by Champion Misty Morn's Sunset, C.D., T.D., W.C., Champion Wochica's Okeechobee Jake (multiple Best in Show winner), Champion Wochica's Wind Song (multiple Specialty Best of Opposite Sex winner), Champion Wochica's M.J. Protege, C.D., W.C. (Westminster Best of Breed and a third in Group winner), and Champion Jib of Cedarmoor.

This same bitch was foster mother to Ringling Brothers-Barnum and Bailey Circus' tiger cubs, which certainly is another proof of the versatility of a Golden! Additionally, she has produced a number of other noted Golden champions.

Above: Little Dawn of Chickasaw, dam of many winning Golden champions, in 1971 took over the rearing of two one-day-old three-pound tiger cubs. Dawn is owned by Janet L. Bunce, Wochica Goldens, Smithtown, New York. **Below:** Ch. Wochica's M.J. Protege, C.D.*, owned by John and Jean Lavin and bred by Janet Bunce, was a winner of Best of Breed and a Group third at Westminster.

185

Ch. Jib of Cedarmoor with Janet L. Bunce, Wochica Goldens, Smithtown, New York.

Champion Wochica's Sandpiper, W.C., is another highly successful producing bitch at Wochica. This Golden Retriever Club of America Outstanding Dam is from the first litter sired by Champion Misty Morn's Sunset, C.D., T.D., W.C., and was the first bitch to be bred to Champion Cummings' Gold-Rush Charlie, to produce Champion Wochica's Gold-Rush Bonanza, Champion Wochica's Hickory Whisper, Champion Highgate's Puff of Wochica, and Champion Wyngate's Kristi.

Sandpiper also produced Champion Wochica's Gold-Rush Banner, Champion Sandy Hills Wochica's Jenny, Champion Wochica's Golden Pumpkin, and Champion Wochica's Symphony (by Champion Gold-Rush's Great Teddy Bear). Additionally she is a great worker in the field.

Even though she is a handler of all Sporting breeds, Janet Bunce has derived her greatest joy as a participant in developing Goldens for field, show, and obedience and seeing their offspring go on to win Best in Show awards.

Ch. Wochica's Hickory Whisper with Janet Bunce.

Ch. Wochica's Gold-Rush Banner, a multiple Best of Breed and Sporting Group winner and one of the many champion get from Ch. Wochica's Sandpiper, W.C. Photo courtesy of Janet Bunce.

Wylwind

Wylwind Kennels at West Bloomfield, Michigan, were founded about 1977 by two very enthusiastic Golden fanciers, Bruce and Ruth Wylie, who had the good fortune to obtain some very excellent quality dogs on whom to base their planned breeding program.

The bloodlines represented here include some of the finest to be found in Midwestern Goldens. For example, American and Canadian Champion Sugarbear's Wylwind Tobey, American and Canadian C.D., is a son of American and Canadian Champion Meadowpond Dustin Sugarbear (Champion Jungold Legend of Golden Pine ex American and Canadian Champion Cimaron's Dazzle Dust) from Topbrass Ruffian's Heide (Champion Malagold Beckwith Om K. Ivan, C.D., ex Topbrass Fiery Saffron, C.D.X.). Another of the Wylies' well-known winners, American and Canadian Champion Amberac's Beausoliel, C.D., co-owned with Mary Wuestenberg of Asterling Goldens, is by American and Canadian Champion Duckdown's Unpredictable, C.D., W.C. (Champion Sundance's Moonlight Gambler, C.D.X., W.C., ex Champion Sprucewood's Harvest Sugar, C.D.) ex Amberac's Reeva Rustelle (Laurell's Etego Catawba, C.D., ex Zeurcher's Tawneika Lass). Another lovely Golden at Wylwind is Meadowpond Secret Desire, C.D., by American and Canadian Champion Laurell's Especial Jason, American and Canadian U.D.T., ex Champion Chafa Honeybun of Jungold.

The Wylies' limited breeding program has already produced some very fine homebreds, including offspring of these dogs, obedience and tracking titled Goldens, promising future show dogs, and numerous all-around loving and loved family members.

Am., Can. Ch. Amberac's Beausoliel, C.D., by Am., Can. Ch. Duckdown's Unpredictable, C.D., ex Amberac's Reeva Rustelle, is co-owned by Bruce and Ruth Wylie, Wylwind Goldens, and Mary Wuestenberg of the Asterling Goldens.

Head study of the late Ch. Jake's Hanalei Valley Jem, a Jake son and double Sammy grandson and the only Golden twice to have won the Golden Retriever Club of Hawaii Specialty. Owned by Joan Luria, Kailua, Hawaii.

CHAPTER FOUR

Golden Retrievers In Hawaii

Ch. Echowoode's Okeechobee Idyll, owned by Joan Luria and Susan Taylor, Kailua, Hawaii. This is the first breeder-owner-handled Golden bitch to finish in Hawaii. She is a daughter of Ch. Wochica's Okeechobee Jake and a double grand-daughter of Ch. Misty Morn's Sunset, C.D., T.D.

Joan Luria, of Echowoode Goldens, has sent us a most interesting description of breed activity in Hawaii, mentioning the importation of fine breeding stock from the Top Producers in America and England.

As we are all aware, Hawaii is part of the United States and is therefore governed by the same American Kennel Club rules and regulations as exist on the Mainland. It is interesting to note, however, that for Goldens there are only eight opportunities a year for exhibitors to put points on their dogs, and not all of these shows take place on the same island. There are three all-breed clubs which each hold two shows annually, in addition to the Golden Retriever Club of Hawaii, Inc., which conducts two independent Specialties each year. While the point schedules there are considerably lower than those on the Mainland, it is no easy feat growing and keeping coat twelve months of the year, when the fleas are as happy with Hawaii as are the tourists and there is less than one show held each month (none take place during November and December).

One of the obstacles facing serious breeders in Hawaii is "the heartbreaking custom of some Mainland breeders to send inferior stock to Hawaii figuring we won't know the difference," to quote Mrs. Luria, who in her capacity as columnist from Hawaii for the *Golden Retriever*

News (the newsletter of the Golden Retriever Club of America) has spent six years trying to put the Golden Retriever Club of Hawaii, Inc. on the map, so to speak, in the minds of the Mainland breeders and to make them aware that Hawaiian owners and breeders have very high standards regarding the breed. The time and money spent by the Hawaiian Golden Fancy are considerable, especially when one considers the weeks involved in quarantine when a dog is brought in, the hazards of air shipping, and the amount it costs (several hundred dollars for one dog) for the four-month quarantine period. Although a few Hawaiian Golden owners have been "burned," the majority are getting really nice Goldens from the Mainland and these are proving of great value in breeding programs. A few years ago, the greater portion of entries at the Hawaiian Specialties were Mainland imports. Now they point with pride to the fact that as many as nineteen of twenty-six entries are "home-grown," and several specimens are as competitive as those to be seen on the Mainland itself, proving that the Hawaiian breeders are using good imports to best advantage.

The Golden Retriever Club of Hawaii, Inc., has been a member of the Golden Retriever Club of America, Inc., since 1972. When Joan Luria moved to Hawaii from New York in 1975, the club was at the "B" Match level and by

June 1979 Specialty of the Golden Retriever Club of Hawaii, R. Beckwith judging, was the scene of this fine class of Goldens (left to right): Ch. Jake's Hanalei Valley Jem, Best of Breed; Ch. Liberator Matt Dillon; Ch. Beckwith's Jetnoise Jasper; Ch. Maui Boy's Kula Girl, C.D., Best of Opposite Sex; Okeechobee's Sunset Song, C.D., Best of Winners; and Ch. Jolly Jennifer of Goldenway, the latter two now also champions. Photo courtesy of Joan Luria, Kailua, Hawaii.

Above: Ch. Jake's Hanalei Valley Jem belongs to Mark and Joan Luria, Echowoode Kennels, Kailua, Hawaii. **Below:** Ch. Smith Ridge d'Okeechobee, a Jake son and Golden Retriever Club of Hawaii Specialty winner, owned by Joan Luria.

January 1978, it was holding its first Specialty. On Sunday, July 4th 1982, the Hawaiian club put on its tenth Independent Specialty show. Joan Luria is President of this club, having served at different times as Vice-President and Director, too. The membership remains between twenty-five and thirty persons, with a steady turnover due to military transfers. The officers of the Golden Retriever Club of Hawaii, Inc., are all permanent residents of the islands.

Joan Luria introduced the Champion Wochica's Okeechobee Jake line to Hawaii when she brought down her first son of Jake, who reached Hawaii at six months of age and finished his title when he was three-and-a-half years old. This was Champion Jake's Hanalei Valley Jem, who has the distinction of being one of only two Goldens to have won the Golden Retriever Club of Hawaii Specialty show on two occasions. Jem did this for the first time from the Open Class over Specials and the second time as a Special himself over five Specials. The other double Best of Breed winner is also a Jake son and is also owned by Mrs. Luria, Champion Smith Ridge d'Okeechobee, by Jake from American and Canadian Champion Beckwith's Autumn Wind, C.D., bred by Ronald F. and Darlene J. Smith. This dog took the Specialty Best of Breed in January 1982 at the club's ninth Specialty Show and again in July 1982 at the tenth.

In the first nine Specialty shows, five of the Best of Winners awards were gained by Jake progeny (four dogs and one bitch), three of the dogs and the bitch belonging to Mrs. Luria who bred the bitch and the fourth dog who are littermates. The bitch is the first breeder-owner-handled Golden bitch to have finished in Hawaii, and she is co-owned by Mrs. Luria with Susan Taylor of New York. At the tenth Specialty, it was a Jake granddaughter, Echowoode Whispered Wishes, bred and owned by Joan Luria, by Jake's Hanalei Valley Jem, who took Best of Winners. Whispered Wishes and the Winners Dog, Echowoode Okeechobee Poetry (Jake ex Jermac's Autumn Mist), bred by Joan Luria but owned by Kenneth Robbins, also finished their championships at the July Specialty, making their dam, the foundation bitch at Echowoode, an Outstanding Dam subject to Golden Retriever Club of America approval. This gives Mrs. Luria her first Outstanding Producer and Hawaii its first Golden so honored. This bitch, Jermac's Autumn Mist, is a daughter of Champion Misty Morn's Sunset, C.D., T.D., W.C., the top producing sire in U.S. Golden history.

Echowoode Kennels have now finished five of Jake's progeny: Champion Jake's Hanalei Valley Jem, Champion Okeechobee's Sunset Song, C.D., Champion Smith Ridge d'Okeechobee (these three dogs have champion littermates on the Mainland), and littermates Champion Echowoode Okeechobee Idyll and Champion Echowoode Okeechobee Poetry.

Joan Luria, who owns the Echowoode Goldens at Kailua, raised her first litter in 1978 when Susan Taylor sent her five-and-a-half-year-old Jermac's Autumn Mist, in whelp to Jake; both sire and dam of the expected litter were sired by Champion Misty Morn's Sunset. The puppies were whelped during Mist's four-month quarantine period and were released to Mrs. Luria when they were three weeks old. That litter, you will note, produced several of the champions previously mentioned.

A year later, Autumn Mist was bred to Jem, the Jake son, and another litter of outstanding quality was produced.

The Jake-Sunset line is being emphasized in Mrs. Luria's breeding program and exciting young stock from the combination is appearing.

The Hawaiian Goldens, on the whole, represent a cross section of many different bloodlines from geographical locations scattered around the globe.

G.R.C.A. Hall of Fame Outstanding Dam, Jermac's Autumn Mist, carrying on a family tradition as the daughter of the all-time Top Producing Golden Sire, Ch. Misty Morn's Sunset, C.D. Joan Luria and Susan Taylor, owners.

Ch. Okeechobee's Sunset Song, C.D., a son of Ch. Wochica's Okeechobee Jake, owned by Joan Luria.

Ch. Nordlys Australis making a fine retrieve. This Australian-bred dog is by Aust. Ch. Calrossie of Westley (United Kingdom import) ex Aust. Ch. Camrose Antanya (United Kingdom import) and was bred by Mr. and Mrs. W.F. Mitchell, from whom he was imported to Hawaii by Karl and Lei Taft, Volcano, Hawaii.

Mrs. Lei Taft of Volcano, Hawaii, has some beautiful stock of English descent that she acquired by way of Australia. One of her dogs, Champion Nordlys Australis, is believed unofficially to be the only Australian-bred Golden to have attained an American championship as of the date of this writing. He is line-bred on the Camrose and Westley lines from England, being by Australian Champion Calrossie of Westley (United Kingdom import to Australia) ex Australian Champion Camrose Antanya (United Kingdom import), and he was bred by Mr. and Mrs. W.F. Mitchell.

Sunrunner Goldens are owned by Karl and Lei Taft. Their first Golden, now a spayed and well-loved family pet, was Kakulakoa's Mellie, who is pointed. Mellie was bred by Margsretha Doughty and was sired by Champion Liberator Matt Dillon, C.D.X., from Pengalli Golden Promise (United Kingdom import).

Kakulakoa's Mellie, owned by Karl and Lei Taft, with their son Kaleo. This Golden, the first owned by the Tafts, is now a spayed family pet.

Also at this kennel are two Australian imported littermates, bred by Mr. R.G. Betteridge. They are Semperidem Sunrunner and Semperidem Sunflower, the former within a couple of points of championship and the latter also pointed. They are by Australian Champion Deremar Duke (United Kingdom import) ex Australian Champion Chantesuta Arabella.

Mrs. Taft and her husband Karl are highly enthusiastic Golden owners who deeply appreciate the breed's marvelous temperament and the attitude with which these dogs approach life. They are thoroughly enjoying their dogs and take pleasure in the splendid records they are making. They are anticipating a litter due by their Champion Nordlys Australis from Semperidem Sunflower, who is a line-bred combination of the best English bloodlines, "Flower" being related to "Aussie" on his dam's side.

Kenneth P. and Joyce R. Wicks, also breeders of Goldens in Hawaii, own a handsome dog bred by the Richard Beckwiths in Snohomish, Washington. This is Champion Beckwith's Jet Noise, by Champion Krishna's Klassic Kachina ex Champion Beckwith's Apricot Brandy, U.D.T.

A bitch from the Lounsburys' Jolly kennel in New York has done well in Hawaii, too, and there is a champion dog from the Liberator kennel in Massachusetts that has had a worthy Hawaiian show career for still another owner, who has two promising puppies from the Synergold Kennels in Massachusetts.

Am., Can. Ch. Pepperhill's Basically Bear, by Ch. Gold-Rush's Great Teddy Bear ex Ch. Cummings' Dame Pepperhill, homebred from Pepperhill Kennels, Barbara and Jeffrey Pepper.

Above: Ch. Mercer's Sweet William and Ch. Mercer's Morning Glory are homebreds owned by Mercer Russo Ervin, Mercer's Goldens.

Facing page, top: Am., Can. Ch. Southern Gold-Rush Traveler at almost six years of age. Southern Goldens, owners, Colleen and Clark Williams. **Facing page, bottom:** Ch. Rockhill's Fancy Free taking Best of Winners at the 1978 Eastern Regional Specialty. Owned by Claire Firestone, Rockhill Goldens, Ridgefield, Connecticut.

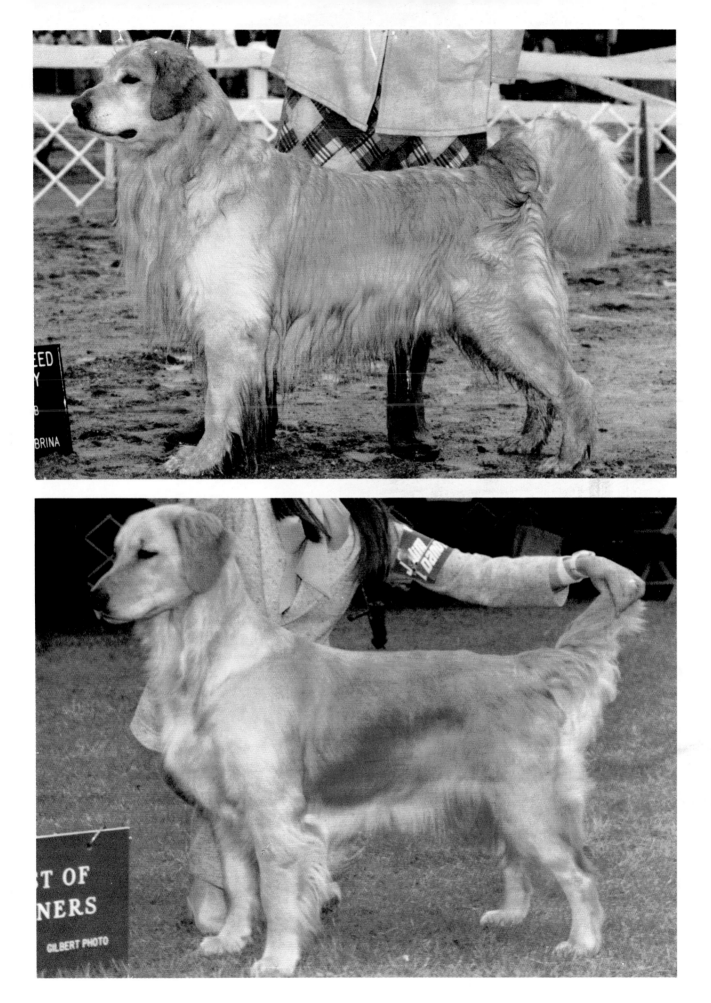

Left: Ch. Thistledue's Shining Star, bred, owned, and handled by Carter F. Foss, is a son of Ch. Wochica's Okeechobee Jake ex Ch. Goldenquest's Thistledue. A Best in Show winner, a Specialty winner, a Golden of true quality! **Below:** A head study of Ch. Morningsage Bouquet, owned by Joanne A. and Laddie C. Lastoka, Morningsage Kennels. **Facing page, top:** Am., Can. Ch. Valhalla's Amber Waves dons glasses to read what it says on the ribbon he has just won as first in the Veterans Class, June 1980. Kathy Liebler, owner. **Facing page, bottom:** Myra Moldawsky with, sitting left to right, Ch. Pepperhill's Peter Principle and Wellesley's Lady Ashley, C.D., and, lying down left to right, Glen-de-Fir's Myra's Wellesley, C.D.X., and Ch. Ashwel's Gold-Rush Logan.

Above: Sunswept's Renaissance, handled by Bob Stebbins for Sunswept Goldens, Bradley and Schofield, Wilton, Connecticut.

Facing page, top: Ch. Starkin's Dan-D-Dan Chieftain, bred by Wanda Metz. **Facing page, bottom:** Ch. Thistledue's Chance and Ch. Thistledue's Shining Star winning Best Brace in Show at Mid-Continent Kennel Club, November 1981. Owned by Carter F. Foss.

BEST OF BREED
OR VARIETY

OKALOOSA
KENNEL CLUB
FEBRUARY 1981

PHOTO BY *Graham*

L CLUB
MA

SHOW

MAN JR

Above: Ch. Westmont's Sutter Creek Aria, owned by Howard and Carol Falberg, Westmont's Goldens, Westport, Connecticut, and handled by Linda Stebbins to take the points at Carroll Kennel Club in 1981.

Facing page: Ch. Sutter Creek Tessahoc Wiloby, Best of Winners from the Bred-by-Exhibitor Class at supported entry, Burlington County Kennel Club, 1982. Handled by co-breeder and co-owner Susan Breakell.

T OF
NERS

ON COUNTY
EL CLUB
KERNAN

RS

HAM PHOTO

Above: Ch. Cummings' Gold-Rush Charlie with handler Bill Trainor winning the Sporting Group at Cheshire Kennel Club in 1975 under judge Joe Faigel for Mrs. Robert V. Clark, Jr., and Larry Johnson.

Facing page: Ch. Sutter Creek Goldrush Flyboy finishing his title, at eighteen months of age. Susan Breakell, owner-handler.

Above: This magnificent Golden is the great winning bitch Am., Can. Ch. Russo's Pepperhill Poppy, owned by Pepperhill Kennels, Barbara and Jeffrey Pepper.

Facing page: A famous Canadian Golden Retriever, Am., Can. Ch. Gauldyn Benn of Shaynedoro, taking Winners Dog at the Garden State Golden Retriever Club Specialty to finish in the U.S.A. One of the many top winners handled by Bob Stebbins.

WINNERS
DOG

207

Can., Am. Ch. Nanno Chryshaefen Son of Skye, C.D., by Can., Bda. Ch. Skylon Lancelot ex Ch. Candace of Nanno, C.D., is owned by Jennifer and Ian McAuley of Canada.

CHAPTER FIVE

Golden Retrievers In Canada

The very beautiful Can., Bda. Ch. Skylon Lancelot, by Skylon Figaro ex Ch. Chrys-haefen Spring Entity, owned by Judy Taylor, Kitchener, Ontario, Canada.

Without a doubt, Canada's premier breeders and exhibitors of Golden Retrievers are the twin sisters, Judy Taylor and Jennifer McAuley, who started their breeding program back in 1965 under the prefix "Chrys-haefen," based on American bloodlines. Soon a change of heart took place regarding their preference in breed type; and in 1968, Judy and Jennifer began their breeding program in earnest with an English import, Champion Drexholme Ling, by Champion Beauchasse Nous ex Drexholme Oakwear Honey. In her first litter, by Champion Beckwith Chrys-haefen Hamlet (Canadian and American Champion Gayhaven Lldeil, Canadian and American C.D.X., ex Canadian and American Champion Beckwith's Frolic of Yeo, C.D.), Ling produced Champion Chrys-haefen Spring Entity, who has been one of the most influential dams in the McAuley-Taylor breeding program so far.

During 1969, Judy and her husband Brian Taylor had the opportunity to purchase the Skylon Goldens from John McNicol, including all his breeding stock. To quote Judy, "John McNicol had a great influence on my knowledge of the breed and the destiny of this kennel." Jennifer chose to continue her breeding program using "Chrys-haefen" as her kennel name, and the two kennels started working side by side. At the present time, Chrys-haefen Kennels is run by Jennifer and Ian McAuley. Skylon Kennels was run by Judy and Brian Taylor until 1981, and is now being carried on by Judy Taylor.

The first Skylon breeding under Brian and Judy Taylor's name joined two English imports from Mrs. Harrison's Janville kennel, Champion Janville Delegate (International Champion Cabus Cadet ex Champion Janville Renown) and Janville Jillian (Alresford Illustrious ex Janville Diadem) to produce Champion Skylon Fontaine and his brother Skylon Figaro. In 1970, Champion Chrys-haefen Spring Entity was bred to Skylon Figaro and in the autumn of that year Canadian and American Champion Skylon Lancelot was whelped. "Skye," we understand, was a most insignificant puppy, and he was sold to Peter and Greta Nixon as a pet. It was not until he had reached a year's age that any suggestion of his beauty and excellence started to surface. After the Nixons had been persuaded that they had a show dog, "Skye" gained his title with a little difficulty, being, to quote Judy, "one of the most spirited dogs to control." Judy additionally remarks, "I will always remember well-known American judge Howard Tyler commenting that 'if I didn't fool around with him so much, I had quite a nice dog'—this after a circuit of eight shows in the heat of summer." It was at this period, however, that Judy began to feel that if "Skye" continued to develop, she just might have her special dog for the future.

"Skye" did, indeed, continue to develop and as Canadian and American Champion Skylon Lancelot he made breed history in Canada. With six all-breed Bests in Show to his credit, he was the Top Canadian Golden in 1973, 1974, and 1975, and he was also in the Top Three Sporting Dogs for those years. Always a show dog once he had developed the "feel" for it, this great Golden never gave up. On one particularly hot day, and after competing in a Group, "Skye" collapsed from heat prostration the minute he stepped out of the ring. Although he was revived

successfully, the Taylors realized that they had to be wary of his exuberance, for it could cover a real problem.

"Skye's" untimely death in 1976 left a terrible void in the breeding program and in the hearts of his owners. Fortunately, he left behind a young son, Canadian and Bermudian Champion Nanno Chrys-haefen Son of Skye, owned by the McAuleys and bred by Nancy Freeman, who was beginning to make his impact felt on the show scene. "Junior," as he was called, became Top Golden in Canada for the years 1976, 1977, and 1978, making it to Number One Sporting Dog in 1978. Thus, he even surpassed his sire's record, again making breed history in Canada.

Can., Bda. Ch. Nanno Chrys-haefen Son of Skye, C.D., winning Best Stud Dog at the Golden Retriever Club of Canada Specialty for his owner, Judy Taylor, Kitchener, Ontario, Canada. The progeny, right to left, are Ch. Chrys-haefen Thor's Fury, Ch. Chrys-haefen Foolish Pride, Can., Am. Ch. Chrys-haefen Fox Fire, C.D., and Ch. Chrys-haefen Chorus o'the Dawn.

Ch. Chrys-haefen Foolish Pride winning a Best in Show at Woodstock. Chrys-haefen Goldens, Jennifer McAuley, Tottenham, Ontario, Canada.

During this period, the McAuleys combined a litter-sister of "Skye's," Skylon Lydia, with "Junior" and produced such dogs as Champion Chrys-heafen Thor's Fury, Canadian and American Champion Chrys-heafen Foxfire, Champion Chrys-heafen Foolish Pride, and Champion Chrys-heafen Ace of Trumps. This aunt-nephew breeding between the sister and the son of Champion Skylon Lancelot proved so successful that it was repeated five times, producing an impressive number of Best in Show and Specialty winners.

Mention must be made of various English dogs who were imported by both Skylon and Chrys-haefen Kennels and who proved extremely influential in their breeding programs. The imports included Champion Tugwood Cavalier

Can., Am. Ch. Chrys-haefen Fox Fire, C.D., by Can., Bda. Ch. Nanno Chrys-haefen Son of Skye, C.D., ex Skylon Lydia, is owned by Jennifer and Ian McAuley.

Skylon Lydia winning the Brood Bitch Class at the Canadian Golden Retriever Specialty with, right to left, Ch. Chrys-haefen's Thor's Fury, Ch. Chrys-haefen Foolish Pride, Can., Am. Ch. Chrys-haefen Fox Fire, and Ch. Chrys-haefen Chorus o' the Dawn. Jennifer and Ian McAuley, owners.

This handsome Golden is an import, Ch. Tugwood Cavalier, owned by Judy Taylor. He is a son of Ch. Cossack of Rachenco ex Tugwood Cilla of Milo.

(by Champion Cossack of Rachenco ex Tugwood Cilla of Milo), Champion Glennessa Uppity (by Chinnordale Saxon of Rachenco ex Glenessa Raynesgold Rita), and Westley Lisbeth; Champion Skylon Clyde, Champion Skylon Star, and Skylon Bonnie were bred in England but whelped in Canada.

Champion Styal Squire of Nortonwood, W.C., by Champion Nortonwood Faunus (Champion Camrose Cabus Christopher ex Nortonwood Fantasy of Milo) from Champion Styal Susila (Champion Camrose Cabus Christopher ex Champion Styall Sibella) was imported by Peter and Greta Nixon when Greta Nixon and Judy Taylor travelled to England and fell in love with him at Crufts.

Chrys-haefen Goldens and Skylon Goldens have been successful in either owning or producing the top Goldens in Canada since 1973, and in some years their dogs held the top three spots! They have exported to various countries, including the United States, France, and Singapore, and are proud of the reputation with which they stand behind their dogs. Judy Taylor and Jennifer McAuley have held correct type foremost in their minds, which includes temperament and soundness, because without all three of these ingredients a Golden is certainly not typical of the breed.

Line-breeding is credited with having been the principal ingredient of success by these breeders.

When it becomes necessary to introduce new blood, care is taken in choosing a dog similar in type to what they already have and whose bloodlines run back into the same lines as theirs. Judy says,

> We have often been criticized for our 'light' Goldens, and wish that people would get past the colour prejudice and appreciate the pigmentation and eye colour as well as the conformation. Colour can be changed in one generation, but we have always been concerned with too many other qualities to be concerned with the shade of gold.

Winning Best in Show at the Golden Retriever Club of Canada's 1977 Specialty, Ch. Skylon Paracelsus, by Ch. Skylon Fontaine ex Ch. Chrys-haefen Spring Entity. Judy Taylor, owner.

Can., Am. Ch. Skylon Vagabond, by Ch. Tugwood Cavalier ex Ch. Candace of Nanno, C.D., one of the exciting winners owned by Judy Taylor.

Ch. Tugwood Cavalier with an Irish Setter friend. Cavalier is by Ch. Cossack of Rachenco ex Tugwood Cilla of Milo. Judy Taylor, owner.

A stern aunt inspects the puppies. Ch. Chryshaefen Cargill Emma, C.D., belongs to the Matglo Kennels of M.D. Wilson, Renfrew, Ontario, Canada, as do the puppies.

Am., Can. Ch. Gauldyn Benn of Shaynedoro, C.D., waiting for lunch at M.D. Wilson's Matglo Kennels.

Ch. Brador-Chryshaefen Bionic Gal looks for the bottom of a swamp. Matglo Kennels.

This adorable group of Golden puppies is by Am., Can. Ch. Gauldyn Benn of Shaynedoro, C.D., ex Ch. Brador-Chryshaefen Bionic Gal and are owned by the Matglo Kennels of M.D. Wilson.

Can. Ch. Mandalaro Sunrise Cynosure, at seven months one week old, completing title under judge Peter Smith, breeder-owner-handled. This lovely bitch is by Am., Can. Ch. Goldwing True Bear ex Ch. Beaumaris Genevieve and belongs to Lee and Wendy Lepper, Sharon, Ontario. "Magic" became a champion in three straight shows from the Bred-by-Exhibitor Class, then her first time out as a Special took Best of Opposite Sex and Best Puppy at the 1982 Golden Retriever Club of Canada National Specialty, where 140 Goldens competed; she is the youngest bitch ever to gain Best of Opposite Sex at this event. "Magic" is the Top Winning Female (all ages) in the Golden Retriever Club tabulations for 1982, as well as Top Puppy (both sexes) for this year.

What possibly could be more appealing than a Golden puppy? This charmer is from Amberac Kennels, Ellen Manke.

CHAPTER SIX

Selection of a Golden

What nicer way to be greeted on Christmas morning than with this quartet of baby Goldens? Owned by D.J.'s Golden Kennel, Dave, Jean, and J.D. Wacker.

Once you have made the decision that the Golden Retriever is the breed of dog you wish to own, the next important step for you is to determine the right Golden to best satisfy your needs. Do you prefer to start out with a puppy, with an adult dog, or with one partially mature? Do you prefer a male or a female? What type of dog do you wish—one for show or for competition in field trials or obedience? Are you looking for a Golden for breeding, possibly as the foundation for a kennel? Do you simply want one for companionship, to be a family pet, with perhaps occasional, informal trips to the field for hunting?

A decision should be reached about these matters prior to your contacting breeders; then you can accurately describe your requirements and the breeder can offer you the most suitable dog for your purposes. Remember that with any breed of dog, as with any other major purchase, the more care and forethought you invest when planning, the greater the pleasure and satisfaction likely to result.

Referring to a dog as a "major investment" may possibly seem strange to you; however, it is an accurate description. Generally speaking, a sizable sum of money is involved, and you are assuming responsibility for a living creature, taking on all the moral obligations this involves.

Assuming that everything goes well, your Golden will be a member of your family for a dozen or more years, sharing your home, your daily routine, and your interests. The happiness and success of these years depend largely on the knowledge and intelligence with which you start the relationship.

Certain ground rules apply to the purchase of a dog, regardless of your intentions for its future. Foremost among these is the fact that no matter what you will be doing with the dog, the best and most acceptable place at which to purchase a Golden Retriever is a kennel specializing in that breed. Even though pet shops occasionally have Golden Retriever puppies for sale, they are primarily concerned with *pet* stock, puppies without pedigrees. When you buy from a breeder you are getting a dog that has been the result of parents very carefully selected as individuals and as to pedigree and ancestry. For such a breeding, a dog and a bitch are chosen from whom the breeder hopes to achieve show type dogs that upgrade both his own kennel's quality and that of the breed generally. Much thought has been given to the conformation and temperament likely to result from the combination of parents and bloodlines involved, for the breeder wants to produce sound, outstanding dogs that will further the respect with which he is regarded in the Golden Retriever world. A specialist of this sort is interested in raising *better* dogs. Since it is seldom possible to keep all the puppies from every litter, fine young stock becomes available for sale. These puppies have flaws so slight in appearance as to be unrecognizable as such by other than the trained eye of a judge or a specialist on Goldens. These flaws in no way affect the strength or future good health of these Goldens; they simply preclude success in the show ring. The conscientious breeder will point them out to you when explaining why the puppy is being offered for sale at "pet price." When you buy a Golden like this, from a knowledgeable, reliable breeder, you get all the advantages of good bloodlines with proper temperament, careful rearing, and the happy, well-adjusted environment needed by puppies who are to become satisfactory, enjoyable adults. Although you are not buying a show dog or show prospect, puppies raised in the same manner have all the odds in their favor to become dogs of excellence in the home and in the field.

Above: Coda and Dollar, adorable baby Goldens from Ellen Manke's Amberac Kennels. **Below:** Ch. Southern's Goldrush Flair, C.D., at eight weeks of age (left) and Am., Can. Ch. Southern's Gold-Rush Traveler at eleven weeks of age (right). Owned by Southern Goldens, Colleen and Clark Williams.

Who could resist a puppy like this one? A D.J. puppy owned by Dave, Jean, and J.D. Wacker.

An eight-week-old puppy line-bred on Am., Can., Bda. Ch. Cummings' Gold-Rush Charlie, Top Breed Winner in Golden History, ex Am., Can. Ch. Southern's Goldrush Flair, C.D. Bred by Southern Goldens, Colleen and Clark Williams.

Ch. Twin-Beau-D's JJ at six weeks of age, with a littermate. Nancy Dallaire, owner, holding these lovely examples of the Goldens raised at Twin-Beau-D Kennels.

If you are looking for a show dog, obviously everything I have said about buying only from a specialized Golden breeder applies with even greater emphasis. Show-type dogs are bred from show-type dogs of proven producing lines and are the result of serious study, thought, and planning. They do *not* just happen.

Throughout the pages of this book are the names and locations of dozens of reliable Golden breeders. Should it so happen that no one has puppies or young stock available to go at the moment you inquire, it would be far wiser to place your name on the waiting list and see what happens when the next litter is born than to rush off and buy a puppy from some less desirable source. After all, you do not want to repent at leisure.

Another source of information regarding recognized Golden breeders is the American Kennel Club, 51 Madison Avenue, New York, NY 10010. A note or phone call will bring you a list of breeders in your area.

Another source of information is a professional handler. They have many contacts and might be able to put you in touch with a breeder and/or help you choose a dog.

A group of Sun Dance Goldens. These three lovely puppies are by the famous Jake ex Ch. Sun Dance's Contessa, and all grew up to become champions. Lisa Schultz, owner, Sun Dance Kennels.

Ch. Pepperhill's Peter Principle as a promising puppy. Pepperhill Farms.

Seven-week-old puppy bitch from Goldust Kennels, bred and owned by Pam German.

Beckwith's Golden Ginger at ten weeks of age. Mr. and Mrs. R.E. Beckwith, owners.

The moment you even start to think about purchasing a Golden, it makes sense to look at, observe, and study as many members of the breed as possible prior to taking the step. Acquaint yourself with correct type, soundness, and beauty before making any commitments. Since you are reading this book, you have already started on that route. Now add to your learning by visiting some dog shows if you can. Even if you are not looking for a show dog, it never hurts to become aware of how such a dog appears and behaves. Perhaps at the shows you will meet some breeders from your area with whom you can discuss the breed and who you can visit.

If you wish your Golden to be a family dog, the most satisfactory choice often is a female. Females make gentle, delightful companions and usually are quieter and more inclined not to roam than males. Often, too, they make neater house dogs, being easier to train. And they are of at least equal intelligence to the males, in both the home and the field. In the eyes of many pet owners, the principal objection to having a bitch

This Golden Retriever puppy was photographed at six months of age and grew up to become Ch. Dasu's Champagne Edition, a bitch who finished entirely in the Bred-by-Exhibitor Class in the state of California, on the way taking a Best of Breed from the classes over Specials, the only Golden bitch to her owner's knowledge to have done this. She had qualified to enter the Gaines Obedience Competitions at the time of her death. A "Streaker" daughter ex Ch. Wendy VIII. Bred and owned by Dave and Suzi Bluford, Dasu Goldens.

is the periodic "coming in season." Sprays and chlorophyll tablets that can help to cut down on the nuisance of visiting canine swains stampeding your front door are available; and, of course, I advocate spaying bitches who will not be used for show or breeding, with even the bitches who are shown or bred being spayed when their careers in competition or in the whelping box have come to a close. Bitches who have been spayed, preferably before four years old, remain in better health later on in life, because spaying almost entirely eliminates the dangers of breast cancer. Spaying also eliminates the messiness of spotting on rugs and furniture, which can be considerable during her periods with a member of a medium-sized or large breed and which is annoying in a household companion.

To many, however, a dog (male) is preferable. The males do seem to be more strongly endowed with true breed character. But do consider the advantages and disadvantages of both males and females prior to deciding which to purchase.

Mercer's Dusty Miller taking Best Puppy in Match, Lenape Golden Retriever Club Specialty Match, March 1982. A future star by Teakwood Farms Russo's Troy ex Ch. Mercer's Morning Glory, breeder-owner-handled by Mercer Russo Ervin.

If you are buying your Golden as a pet, a puppy is usually preferable, as you can teach it right from the beginning the ways of your household and your own schedule. Two months is an ideal age at which to introduce the puppy into your home. Older puppies may already have established habits of which you will not approve and which you may find difficult to change. Besides, puppies are such fun that it is great to share and enjoy every possible moment of their process of growing up.

When you are ready to buy, make appointments with as many Golden breeders as you have been able to locate in your area for the purpose of seeing what they have available and discussing the breed with them. This is a marvelous learning experience, and you will find the majority of breeders are willing and happy to spend time with you, provided that you have arranged the visit in advance. Kennel owners are busy folks with full schedules, so do be considerate about this courtesy and call on the telephone before you appear.

If you have a choice of more than one kennel where you can go to see the dogs, take advantage of that opportunity instead of just settling for and buying the first puppy you see. You may return to your first choice in the long run, but you will do so with greater satisfaction and authority if you have seen the others before making the selection. When you look at puppies, be aware that the one you buy should look sturdy and big-boned, bright-eyed and alert, with an inquisitive, friendly attitude. The puppy's coat

Halloween is an exciting occasion for such young "trick or treaters" as these most handsome baby Goldens owned by the Wackers, D.J.'s Goldens.

Sun Dance's My Special Beau at three months of age. A quality puppy bred by Sun Dance Kennels.

Burfie Collins caught this Golden baby smiling so nicely at Dave and Suzi Bluford's Dasu Kennels.

Note the beautiful head on this Beckwith Golden puppy owned by Mr. and Mrs. R.E. Beckwith.

should look clean and glossy. Do not buy a puppy that seems listless or dull, is strangely hyperactive, or looks half sick. The condition of the premises where the puppies are raised is also important as you want your puppy to be free of parasites; don't buy a puppy whose surroundings are dirty and ill kept.

One of the advantages of buying at a kennel you can visit is that you are thereby afforded the opportunity of seeing the dam of the puppies and possibly also the sire, if he, too, belongs to the breeder. Sometimes you can even see one or more of the grandparents. Be sure to note the temperament of these Goldens as well as their conformation.

If there are no Golden breeders within your travelling range, or if you have not liked what you have seen at those you've visited, do not hesitate to contact other breeders who are recommended to you even if their kennels are at a distance and to purchase from one of them if you are favorably impressed with what is offered. Shipping dogs is done with regularity nowadays and is reasonably safe, so this should not present a problem. If you are contacting a well-known, recognized breeder, the puppy should be fairly described and represented to you. Breeders of this caliber want you to be satisfied, both for the puppy's sake and for yours. They take pride in

Gosling's Yeoman of Bedford at seven weeks of age. Owned by Mrs. Bryan Gosling of New York.

These adorable Golden babies are from the Goldust Kennels owned by Mrs. Pam German.

An informal study of a beautiful Celloyd Golden Retriever.

their kennel's reputation, and they make every effort to see that their customers are pleased. In this way you are deprived of the opportunity of seeing your dog's parents, but even so you can buy with confidence when dealing with a specialized breeder.

Every word about careful selection of your pet puppy and where it should be purchased applies twofold when you set out to select a show dog or the foundation stock for a breeding kennel of your own. You look for all the things already mentioned but on a far more sophisticated level, with many more factors to be taken into consideration. The standard of the Golden Retriever must now become your guide, and it is essential that you know and understand not only the words of this standard but also their application to actual dogs before you are in a position to make a wise selection. Even then, if this is your first venture with a show-type Golden, listen well and heed the advice of the breeder. If you have clearly and honestly stated your ambitions and plans for the dog, you will find that the breeders will cooperate by offering you something with which you will be successful.

A promising Malagold youngster from Malagold Kennels, Connie Gerstner.

A dog of championship quality is easier to find and less expensive, although it still will bring a good price. The least difficult to obtain is a fair show dog that may pick up some points here and there but will mostly remain in class placements. Incidentally, one of the reasons that breeders are sometimes reluctant to part with a truly excellent show prospect is that in the past people have bought this type of dog with the promise it will be shown, but then the buyer has changed his mind after owning the dog awhile, and thus the dog becomes lost to the breed. It is really not fair to a breeder to buy a dog with the understanding that it will be shown and then renege on the agreement. Please, if you select a dog that is available only to a show home, think it over carefully prior to making a decision; then buy the dog only if you will be willing to give it the opportunity to prove itself in the show ring as the breeder expects.

Pepperhill's Serendipity at seven months of age. Bred at Pepperhill, Barbara and Jeffrey Pepper.

There are several different degrees of show dog quality. There are dogs that should become top flight winners which can be campaigned for Specials (Best of Breed competition) and with which you can hope to attain Sporting Group placements and possibly even hit the heights with a Best in Show win. There are dogs of championship quality which should gain their titles for you but are lacking in that "extra something" to make them potential Specials. There are dogs that perhaps may never finish their championships but which should do a bit of winning for you in the classes: a blue ribbon here and there, perhaps Winners or Reserve occasionally, but probably nothing truly spectacular. Obviously the hardest to obtain, and the most expensive, are dogs in the first category, the truly top-grade dogs. These are never plentiful as they are what most breeders are working to produce for their own kennels and personal enjoyment and with which they are loathe to part.

If you want a show dog, obviously you are a person in the habit of attending dog shows. Now this becomes a form of schooling rather than just a pleasant pastime. Much can be learned at the Golden ringside if one truly concentrates on what one sees. Become acquainted with the various winning exhibitors. Thoughtfully watch the judging. Try to understand what it is that causes some dogs to win and others to lose. Note well the attributes of the dogs, deciding for yourself which ones you like, giving full attention to attitude and temperament as well as conformation. Close your ears to the ringside "know-it-alls" who have only derogatory remarks to make about each animal in the ring and all that takes place there. You need to develop independent thinking at this stage and should not be influenced by the often entirely uneducated comment of the ringside spoilsports. Especially make careful note of which exhibitors are campaigning winning homebreds—not just an occasional "star" but a series of consistent quality dogs. All this takes time and patience. This is the period to "make haste slowly;" mistakes can be expensive, and the more you have studied the breed, the better equipped you will be to avoid them.

Above: October's Bargello Diamond, owned by Barbara Tinker and S. Smith, at nine weeks of age. **Below:** Golden puppies owned by Don Sturz, Golden Glo Kennels.

Above: Merry Christmas from Topbrass! **Below:** Another one of the typical Golden puppies belonging to Mrs. Joseph Mertens.

As you make inquiries among various breeders regarding the purchase of a show dog or a show prospect, keep these things in mind. Show-prospect puppies are less expensive than fully mature show dogs. The reason for this is that with a puppy there is the element of chance, for one never can be absolutely certain exactly how the puppy will develop, while the mature dog stands before you as the finished product— "what you see is what you get"—all set to step out and win.

There is always the risk factor involved with the purchase of a show-type puppy. Sometimes all goes well and that is great. But many a swan has turned into an ugly duckling as time passes, and it is far less likely that the opposite will occur. So weigh this well and balance all the odds before you decide whether a puppy or a mature dog would be your better buy. There are times, of course, when one actually has no choice in the matter; no mature show dogs may be available for sale. Then one must either wait awhile or gamble on a puppy, but please *be aware that gambling is what you are doing.*

If you do take a show-prospect puppy, be guided by the breeder's advice when choosing from among what is offered. The person used to working with a bloodline has the best chance of predicting how the puppies will develop. Do not trust your own guess on this; rely on the experience of the breeder. For your own protection, it is best to buy puppies whose parents' eyes have been certified clear and who have been O.F.A.-certified free of hip dysplasia.

An appealing Golden puppy owned by Ginny Boyle, Charms Goldens, Joppa, Maryland.

This adorable Golden puppy playing in the snow is a daughter of Ch. Gold-Rush's Great Teddy Bear. Larry and Ann Johnson, owners, Gold-Rush Goldens.

This is "Streaker," future Am., Can. Ch. and O.T. Ch. Sunstreak of Culynwood, T.D., W.C.X., Can. C.D., at five weeks of age. Owned by Dave and Suzi Bluford.

Am., Can. Ch. October's Cal-Vo Spirit at eight-and-a-half weeks of age, February 1979. Ted Greenfield, owner, Westbrook Goldens.

Although initially more expensive, a grown show dog in the long run often proves to be the far better bargain. His appearance is unlikely to change beyond weight and condition, which depend on the care you give him. Also to your advantage, if you are a novice about to become an exhibitor, is that a grown dog of show quality almost certainly will have been trained for the ring; thus, an inexperienced handler will find such a dog easier to present properly and in winning form in the ring.

If you plan to have your dog campaigned by a professional handler, have the handler help you locate and select a future winner. Through their numerous clients, handlers usually have access to a variety of interesting show dogs; and the usual arrangement is that the handler buys the dog, resells it to you for the price he paid, and at the same time makes a contract with you that the dog shall be campaigned by this handler throughout the dog's career.

If the foundation of a future kennel is what you have in mind as you contemplate the purchase of a Golden, concentrate on one or two really excellent bitches, not necessarily top show bitches but those representing the finest producing Golden Retriever lines. A proven matron who has already produced show type puppies is, of course, the ideal answer here, but, as with a mature show dog, a proven matron is more difficult to obtain and more expensive since no one really wants to part with so valuable an asset. You just might strike it lucky, though, in which case you will be off to a flying start. If you do not find such a matron available, do the next best thing and select a young bitch of outstanding background representing a noted producing strain, one that is herself of excellent type and free of glaring faults.

Great attention should be paid to the background of the bitch from whom you intend to breed. If the information is not already known to

A handsome eleven-month-old youngster bred by Sun Dance Kennels. My Special Beau had a brief but highly successful career in the show ring.

Wochica's Gold-Rush Bonanza at seven weeks of age Photo courtesy of Janet Bunce.

Ch. October's Foxy Lady, C.D., the founder of Gosling's Goldens at Voorheesville, New York. By Ch. Sir Duncan of Woodbury ex Ch. Cal-Vo's Nickel Nehi.

Above: Golden Retriever puppy from Morningsage Goldens, owned, bred, and photographed by Joanne A. Lastoka. **Below:** Charms Two Toots n Hollar as a puppy. Ginny Boyle, owner, Charms Goldens.

Ashley, at ten weeks of age, playing with a twig. Promising youngster owned by Myra Moldawsky.

you, find out all you can about the temperament, character, field ability, and conformation of the sire and dam, plus eye and hip rating. A person just starting in dogs is wise to concentrate on a fine collection of bitches and to raise a few litters sired by leading *producing* studs. The practice of buying a stud dog and then breeding everything you have to that dog does not always work out. It is better to take advantage of the availability of splendid stud dogs for your first few litters.

In summation, if you want a family dog, buy it young and raise it to the habits of your household. If you are buying a show dog, the more mature it is the more certain you can be of the future. If you are buying foundation stock for a breeding program, bitches are better than dogs, but they must be from the finest *producing* bloodlines.

Regarding price, you should expect to pay up to a few hundred dollars for a healthy pet Golden puppy and more than that for a show-type puppy with the price rising accordingly as the dog gets older. A grown show dog can run well into four figures if of finest quality, and a proven brood matron will be priced according to

230

Six-week-old puppies sired by Ch. Misty Morn's Sunset. Owned by Peter and Rose Lewesky.

"Dugan," one of the beautiful Cummings' Goldens from Stillwater, New Jersey.

the owner's valuation and can also run into four figures.

When you buy a purebred Golden Retriever dog or puppy that you are told is eligible for registration with the American Kennel Club, you are entitled to receive, from the seller, an application form that will enable you to register your dog. If the seller cannot give you the application, you should demand and receive an identification of your dog consisting of the breed, the registered names and numbers of the sire and dam, the name of the breeder, and the dog's date of birth. If the litter of which your Golden is part has been recorded with the American Kennel Club, then the litter number is sufficient identification.

Do not accept a verbal promise that registration papers will be mailed to you. Demand a registration application form or proper identification. If neither is supplied, do not buy the dog. These words are to be especially heeded if you are buying show dogs or breeding stock.

231

The best chess players start at an early age. Golden puppy owned by Dave, Jean, and J.D. Wac

CHAPTER SEVEN

Caring for a Golden Puppy

Beaumaris Noble Promise, by Brae Lea Diplomat, C.D., ex Ch. Beaumaris Gabrielle, C.D., obviously loves kids, as do most Goldens. Bred by Mr. and Mrs. John F. Bissette, Beaumaris Goldens.

Ownership of a dog entails a great deal of responsibility. You must be willing and prepared to provide your pet with shelter, food, training, and affection. With proper attention and care, your pet will become a loving member of the family and a sociable companion to be enjoyed for many years to come.

Advance Preparation

The moment you decide to become the owner of a Golden Retriever puppy is not one second too soon to start planning for the new family member in order to make the transition period more pleasant for yourself, your household, and the puppy.

The first step in preparation is a bed for that puppy and a place where you can pen him up for rest periods. I am a firm believer that every dog should have a crate of its own right from the very beginning. This will fill both of the previously mentioned requirements, and the puppy will come to know and love this crate as his special haven. Crates are ideal, for when you want the puppy to be free, the crate door stays open. At other times, you securely latch it and know that the puppy is safe from harm, comfortable, and out of mischief. If you plan to travel with your dog, his crate comes along in the car;

and, of course, to travel by plane, the dog must be put in a crate. If you show your dog, or take him to obedience or field trials, what better place to keep him when you are not working with him than in his crate? No matter how you look at it, a crate is a very sensible, sound investment in your puppy's comfort, well-being, and safety—not to mention your own peace of mind.

The crates we prefer are the sturdy wooden ones with removable side panels. These wooden crates are excellent for cold weather, with the panels in place, and they work equally well for hot weather when the solid panels are removed, leaving just the wire sides for better ventilation. Crates made entirely of wire are all right in the summer, but they provide no protection from drafts or winter chills. I intensely dislike solid aluminum crates due to the manner in which aluminum reflects surrounding temperatures. If it is cold, so is the metal of the crate. If it is hot, that too is reflected, sometimes to the point that one's fingers can be burnt when handling it. For this reason I consider them unsuitable.

When you choose the puppy's crate, be certain that it is roomy enough not to be outgrown as your Golden matures. He should have sufficient height in which to stand up comfortably and sufficient area to stretch out full length when relaxed.

Amberac puppies owned by Ellen Manke.

When the puppy is young, give him shredded newspapers as his first bed. In time, the newspapers can be replaced with a mat or turkish towels. Carpet remnants are great for the bottom of the crate as they are inexpensive and in case of accidents can be easily replaced. Once the dog has matured past the chewing stage, a pillow or a blanket for something soft and comfortable is an appreciated luxury in the crate.

Sharing importance with the crate is a safe area where the puppy can exercise and play. If you have a yard of your own, then the fenced area in which he can stay outdoors safely should be ready and waiting upon his arrival. It does not need to be a vast area, but it should have shade and be secure. Do have the fenced area planned and installed *before* bringing the puppy home if you possibly can do so; this is far more sensible than putting it off until a tragedy occurs. As an

Winter's scene at Valhalla Farms, owned by Larry and Kathy Liebler.

234

"What tree?" wonders an inquisitive puppy, with littermate, at Gosling's Goldens.

absolute guarantee that a dog cannot dig his way out under the fence, an edging of cinder blocks tight against the inside bottom of it is very practical protection. If there is an outside gate, a key and padlock are a *must* and should be *used at all times*. You do not want to have the puppy or dog set free in your absence either purposely or through carelessness. I have seen people go through a fence and then just leave the gate ajar. So for safety's sake, keep the gate locked so that only someone responsible has access to its opening.

The ultimate convenience, of course, is if there is a door in your house situated so that the fence can be installed around it, thereby doing away with the necessity for an outside gate. This arrangement is ideal, because then you need never be worried about the gate being left unlatched. This arrangement will be particularly appreciated during bad weather when, instead of escorting the dog to wherever his fenced yard is, you simply open the house door and he exits

Cummings' Sunset O' Gold, bred by Mrs. Mary W. Cummings.

directly into his safe yard. In planning the fenced area, do give serious thought to the use of stockade fencing for it, as it really does work out well.

When you go to pick up your Golden, you should take a collar and lead with you. Both of these should be appropriate for the breed and age of the dog, and the collar should be one that fits him now, not one he has to grow into. Your new Golden also needs a water dish (or two, one for the house and one for outside) and a food dish. These should preferably be made from an unbreakable material. You will have fun shopping at your local pet shop for these things, and I am sure you will be tempted to add some luxury items of which you will find a fascinating array. For chew things, either Nylabone or real beef bones (leg or knuckle cut to an appropriate size, the latter found as soup bones at most butcher shops or supermarkets) are safe and provide many hours of happy entertainment, at the same time being great exercise during the teething period. Rawhide chews can be safe, too, if made under the proper conditions. There was a problem, however, several years back owing to the chemicals with which some of the rawhide chew products had been treated, so in order to take no chances, avoid them. Also avoid plastic and rubber toys, *particularly* toys with squeakers. If you

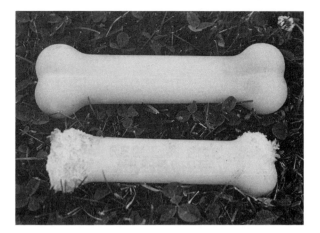

Nylabone® is the perfect chewing pacifier for young dogs in their teething stage and even for older dogs to help satisfy that occasional urge to chew. Unlike many other dog bones on the market today, Nylabone® does not splinter or fall apart; it will last indefinitely and as it is used it frills, becoming a doggie toothbrush that cleans teeth and massages gums.

Left and below: On the beach at Atlantic City, Ch. Russo's Pepperhill's Poppy and Elliot More enjoy a game of ball as a short break from show business at Boardwalk Kennel Club. Poppy is one of the stars from Pepperhill Kennels, Barbara and Jeffrey Pepper.

want to play ball with your Golden, select a ball that has been made of very tough construction; Goldens have strong jaws. Even then do not leave the ball with the puppy alone; take it with you when you finish the game. There are also some nice "tug of war" toys which are fun when you play with the dog. But again, do not go off and leave them to be chewed in privacy.

Too many changes all at once can be difficult for a puppy. Therefore, no matter how you eventually wind up doing it, for the first few days keep him as nearly as you can on the routine to which he is accustomed. Find out what brand of food the breeder used, how frequently and when the puppies were fed, and start out by doing it that way yourself, gradually over a period of a week or two making whatever changes suit you better.

Of utmost precedence in planning for your puppy is the selection of a good veterinarian whom you feel you can trust. Make an appointment to bring the puppy in to be checked over on your way home from the breeder's. Be sure to obtain the puppy's health certificate from the breeder, along with information regarding worming, shots, and so on.

With all of these things in order, you should be nicely prepared for a smooth, happy start when your puppy actually joins the family.

Larry and Susan Breakell with Fox Rock's Watchful Harold and Alstone Sutter Creek Charade, U.D.*. Little did the Breakells know back then that the new pool would soon be taken over by Charade and Harold!

Goldens and kids go very well together! The photograph of this handsome pair courtesy of Don and Marilyn Sturz.

Joining the Family

Remember that as exciting and happy as the occasion may be for you, the puppy's move from his place of birth to your home can be a traumatic experience for him. His mother and littermates will be missed. He will perhaps be slightly frightened or awed by the change of surroundings. The person he trusted and depended on will be gone. Everything, thus, should be planned to make the move easy for him, to give him confidence, to make him realize that yours is a pretty nice place to be after all.

Never bring a puppy home on a holiday. There just is too much going on, with people and gifts and excitement. If he is honoring "an occasion" (a birthday, for example), work it out so that his arrival will be a few days before or, better still, a few days after the big occasion. Then he will be greeted by a normal routine and will have your undivided attention. Try not to bring the puppy home during the evening. Early morning is the ideal time, as then he has the opportunity of getting acquainted, and the first strangeness wears off before bedtime. You will find it a more peaceful night that way, I am sure. Allow the puppy to investigate his surroundings under your watchful eye. If you already have a pet in the household, carefully watch that things are going smoothly between them, so that the relationship gets off to a friendly start; otherwise, you may quickly have a lasting problem.

At home at Pepperhill Farms, everyone the best of friends. Barbara and Jeffrey Pepper.

Be careful not to let your older pet become jealous by paying more attention to the newcomer than to him. You want a friendly start. Much of the future attitude of each toward the other depends on what takes place that first day.

If you have children, again, it is important that the relationship start out well. Should the puppy be their first pet, it is assumed that you have prepared them for it with a firm explanation that puppies are living creatures to be treated with gentle consideration, not playthings to be abused and hurt. One of my friends raised her children with the household rule that should a dog or puppy belonging to one of the children bite one of the children, the child would be punished, not the dog, as Mother would know that the child had in some way hurt the dog. I must say that this strategy worked out very well, as no child was ever bitten in that household and both daughters grew up to remain great animal lovers. Anyway, on whatever terms you do it, please bring your children up not only to *love* but also to *respect* their pet, with the realization that dogs have rights, too. These same ground rules should also apply to visiting children. I have seen youngsters who are fine with their own pets unmercifully tease and harass pets belonging to other people. Children do not always realize how rough is too rough, and without intending to, they may inflict considerable pain or injury if permitted to ride herd on a puppy.

Ch. Nordlys Australis with Taylor the cat, both owned by Karl and Lei Taft, Hawaii.

If you start out by spoiling your new puppy, your puppy will expect and even demand that you continue to spoil it in the future. So think it out carefully before you invite the puppy to come spend its first night at your home in bed with you, unless you wish to continue the practice. What you had considered to be a one-night stand may be accepted as just great and expected for the future. It is better not to start what you may consider to be bad habits which you may find difficult to overcome later. Of course, a lovely Golden Retriever is not all that bad on the bed, particularly on a chilly night, but be sure you will like it that way before you introduce the puppy to the idea!

Socialization of puppies is most important to the development of their personalities. These are at Gosling's Goldens.

Above: "Goldens get along with *everyone*," as this photo clearly illustrates! Amico of Maine, W.C.X., C.D., on the right, with friend Amanda, the African Pygmy Goat, on the left. Jennifer Kesner, owner. **Below:** Goldens and Whippets enjoy one another's company. Here they are relaxing after a busy day at Barbara and Jeff Pepper's Pepperhill Farms.

Socialization and Training

Socialization and training of your new baby Golden actually starts the second you walk in the door with him, for every move you make should be geared toward teaching the puppy what is expected of him and, at the same time, building up his confidence and feeling of being at home.

The first step is to teach the puppy his name and to come when called by it. No matter how flowery or long or impressive the actual registered name may be, the puppy should also have a short, easily understood "call name" which can be learned quickly and to which he will respond. Start using this call name immediately, and use it in exactly the same way each time that you address the puppy, refraining from the temptation to alternate various forms of endearment, pet names, or substitutes which will only be confusing to him.

Using his name clearly, call the puppy over to you when you see him awake and looking about for something to do. Just a few times of this, with a lot of praise over what a "good dog" he is when he responds, and you will have taught him to come to you when he hears his name; he knows that he will be warmly greeted, petted, and possibly even be given a small snack.

"Let's see now—how *does* this thing open?" wonders the inquiring Gosling Golden puppy pictured here. Mrs. Bryan Gosling, owner.

This adorable baby Golden, playing with a toy, is from the Topbrass Kennels, Mrs. Joseph Mertens.

As soon as the puppy has spent a few hours getting acquainted with his new surroundings, you can put a light collar on the puppy's neck, so that he will become accustomed to having it on. He may hardly notice it, or he may make a great fuss at first, rolling over, struggling, and trying to rub it off. Have a tasty tidbit or two on hand with which to divert his attention at this period, or try to divert his attention by playing with him. Soon he no longer will be concerned about that strange new thing around his neck.

The next step in training is to have the puppy become accustomed to the lead. Use a light-weight lead, attached to the collar. Carry him outdoors where there will be things of interest to investigate; then set him down and see what happens. Again, he may appear hardly to notice the lead dangling behind him, or he may make a fuss about it. If the latter occurs, repeat the diversion attempts with food or a toy. As soon as the pup-

"Getting into the closet" describes what has just taken place as six-month-old Goldust English Frost looks extremely pensive. Owned by Mrs. Pam German, Goldust Golden Retrievers.

Golden puppies sniffing the flowers. These adorable youngsters are from D.J.'s Golden Kennels.

"Let's see—what'll we build *this* time?" is what these young Goldens evidently are considering. From Dave, Jean, and J.D. Wacker's D.J.'s Kennel.

py has accepted the presence of the lead, pick up the end of it and follow after him. He may react by trying to free himself, struggling to slip his head through the collar, or trying to bite at the lead. Coax him, if you can, with kind words and petting. In a few moments, curiosity regarding his surroundings and an interesting smell or two should start diverting him. When this takes place, do not try at first to pull on him or guide his direction. Just be glad that he is walking with the lead on and let him decide where to go. When he no longer seems to resent the lead, try gently to direct him with short little tugs in the direction you would like him to travel. Never jerk him roughly, as then he will become frightened and fight harder; and never pull steadily or attempt to drag him, as this immediately triggers a battle of wills with each of you pulling in an opposite direction. The best method is a short, quick, gentle jerk, which, repeated a few times, should get him started off with you. Of course, continue to talk encouragingly to him and offer him "goodies" until he gets started. Repetition of the command "Come" should accompany all of this.

Once this step has been mastered and walks are taken on the lead pleasantly and companionably, the next step is to teach him to remain on your left-hand side. Use the same process as you used to teach him to respond correctly while on the lead, this time repeating the word "Heel." Of course, all of this is not accomplished in one day; it should be done gradually, with short work periods each time, letting the puppy know when he pleases you. The exact length of time required for each puppy varies and depends on the aptitude of each individual puppy.

Housebreaking a puppy is more easily accomplished by the prevention method than by the cure. Try to avoid "accidents" whenever you can rather than punishing the puppy once they have occurred. Common sense helps a great deal. A puppy will need to be taken out at regularly spaced intervals: first thing in the morning directly from his bed, immediately after meals, after he has napped, or whenever you notice that he is "looking for a spot." Choose roughly the same place outdoors each time that you take the puppy out for this purpose, so that a pattern will be established. If he does not go immediately, do not just return him to the house as chances are that he will go the moment he is back inside. Try to be patient and remain out with him until you get results; then praise him

Ch. Cloverdale Twin-Beau-D Joy moving along with her owner Nancy Dallaire.

enthusiastically and both of you can return indoors. If you catch the puppy having an "accident," pick him up firmly, sharply say, "No!" and rush him outside. If you do not see the accident occur, there is little point of doing anything beyond cleaning it up, as once it has happened and been forgotten, the puppy will likely not even realize why you are angry with him.

Your Golden puppy should form the habit of spending a certain amount of time each day in his crate, even when you are home. Sometimes the puppy will do this voluntarily, but if not, he should be taught to do so. Lead the puppy by the collar over to the crate, and then gently push him inside firmly saying "Down" or "Stay" as you fasten the door. Whatever command you use, always make it the same word for each act every time. Repetition is the big thing in training, and the dog must learn to associate a specific word or phrase with each different thing he is expected to do. When you mean "Sit," always say exactly that. "Stay" should mean that the dog should remain where he was when you gave the command. "Down" means something else again. Do not confuse the dog by shuffling the commands, as you will create confusion for him and a problem for yourself by having done so.

As soon as he has received his immunization shots, take your Golden puppy with you wherever and whenever possible. Nothing else can equal this close association for building up self-confidence and stability in a young dog. It is extremely important that you spend the time necessary for socialization, particularly if you are planning on the puppy becoming a show dog.

Alert and at attention. "Cookie" belongs to Jolly Goldens.

Ashwel pups owned by Myra Moldawsky.

Left: Am., Can. Ch. Ambertrail's Bargello Stitch, U.D.T., W.C.X., Can. U.D.T.X., W.C., here is "sitting." **Above:** Stitch "standing." Owned by Barbara Tinker, Bargello Goldens.

Take your Golden in the car, so that he will learn to enjoy riding without becoming carsick, as can happen to a dog unused to the car's motion. Take him everywhere you go, provided you are certain he will not be unwelcome or create any difficulties by his presence: visiting friends and relatives (if they like dogs and do not have house pets of their own who will consider your puppy an intruder), to busy shopping centers (always keeping him on his lead), or just walking around the streets of your town. If someone admires him, as always seems to happen under these circumstances, encourage that person to pet or talk with him; becoming accustomed to people in this manner always seems especially beneficial in instilling self-confidence. You want your puppy to develop a relaxed, happy canine personality and like the world and its inhabitants. The most debilitating thing for a puppy's self-confidence is excessive sheltering and pampering. Keeping a growing puppy always away from strange people and strange dogs may well turn him into a nervous, neurotic dog— surely the last thing anyone can enjoy as a pet.

Make obedience training a game with your puppy while he is extremely young. Try to teach him the meaning of and expected responses to the basic terms such as "Come," "Stay," "Sit," "Down," and "Heel," along with the meaning of "No" even while he is still too young for formal training, and you will be pleased and proud of the good manners that he will exhibit.

"We're both waiting." The Lounsburys send this photo of two young pals, taken at Jolly Goldens.

Feeding

There was a time when providing good, nourishing food for our dogs involved a far more complicated routine and time-consuming process than people now feel is necessary. The old belief was that the daily rations should consist of fresh beef, vegetables, cereal, egg yolks, and cottage cheese as basics, with such additions as brewer's yeast and other vitamin supplements.

During recent years, however, many attitudes have been changed regarding the necessity, or even the desirability, of this procedure. We still give eggs, cottage cheese, and supplements to the diet, but the basic methods of feeding dogs have changed; and the changes are definitely for the better in the opinion of many an authority. The school of thought now is that you are doing your dogs a definite service when you feed them some of the fine commercially prepared dog foods in preference to your own home-cooked concoctions.

The reasoning behind this new outlook is easy to understand. The production of dog food has grown to be a major industry, participated in by some of the best known, most highly respected names in the dog fancy. These trusted firms do turn out excellent products. People are feeding their dogs these preparations with confidence, and the dogs are thriving, prospering, and keeping in top condition. What more could we want or ask?

There are at least a half dozen absolutely splendid dry foods which can be mixed with water or broth and served to your dog, either "as is" or with the addition of fresh or canned meat. There is a variety of canned meat preparations for your dog, either 100% meat to be mixed with kibble or complete prepared dinners, a combination of both meat and cereal. There are several kinds of "convenience foods," these in packets which you open and dump out into the dog's dish. It is just that simple. The "convenience foods" are neat and easy for you when travelling, but generally speaking we prefer to feed a dry food mixed with hot water, to which we usually add canned meat (although leftover meat scraps or ground beef are sometimes added instead of the canned meat). Actually we feel that the canned meat, with its added fortifiers, is more beneficial to the dogs than the fresh meat. However, the two can be used alternately or, if you prefer and your dogs do well on it, by all means use ground beef.

"Lunch time." Six hungry Golden babies at the Gosling Kennels.

"Mmmm *good*" would seem to be the comment on the rations at Gosling's Goldens, as mealtime is enjoyed by some of the puppies.

Dogs enjoy variety in the meat part of their diet, which is easy to provide with the canned meat. The canned meats available include all sorts of beef (chunk, ground, stewed, and so on), lamb, chicken, liver, and numerous concoctions of several of these blended together.

There also is prepared food geared to every age bracket of your dog's life, from puppyhood on through old age, with special additions or modifications to make it especially nourishing and beneficial. The dogs of yesteryear never had it so good during the canine dinner hour because these foods are tasty and geared to meet the dog's gastronomical approval.

Additionally, contents and nutritional values are clearly listed on the labels, and careful instructions for feeding exactly the right amount for the size and weight of each dog are also given.

With the great choice of dog foods available today, we do not feel that the addition of vitamins is necessary; but if you do, there are several highly satisfactory vitamin products available at pet shops. These products serve as tasty treats along with being beneficial.

Of course there is no reason not to cook up something for your Golden's dinner if you would feel happier doing so, but it seems to us superfluous when such truly satisfying rations are available at so much less expense and trouble.

How often you feed is a matter of how a schedule works out best for you and for your dog or dogs. Many owners prefer to feed their dogs once a day. Others feel that twice daily is better for the digestion and more satisfying to the dog, particularly if he is a family member who stands around and watches the preparation of family meals. The important thing is that you *do not overfeed*, as overfeeding can bring on many canine problems.

Until they are about twelve weeks old, fully weaned puppies should be fed four times daily. Each morning and evening, a Golden pup needs a meal of kibble soaked in hot water, broth, or soup to which either canned or fresh raw beef has been added. At noontime and bedtime, condensed milk mixed with an equal amount of water to which a bit of dry kibble has been added can be given. The amounts should be adjusted to the individual puppy's weight and appetite.

As the pup grows older, from three to six months of age, cut back to three meals, increasing the size of each. At six months of age, the pup should be fed twice daily, and at twelve months, if you wish, you may cut back to one daily feeding with a biscuit or two morning and evening. If you do feed just once daily, it should be given by early afternoon.

Remember that fresh, cool water should always be available to your dog. This is of utmost importance to his good health throughout his lifetime.

Naptime—and we think that this picture, courtesy of Jennifer Kesner, speaks for itself!

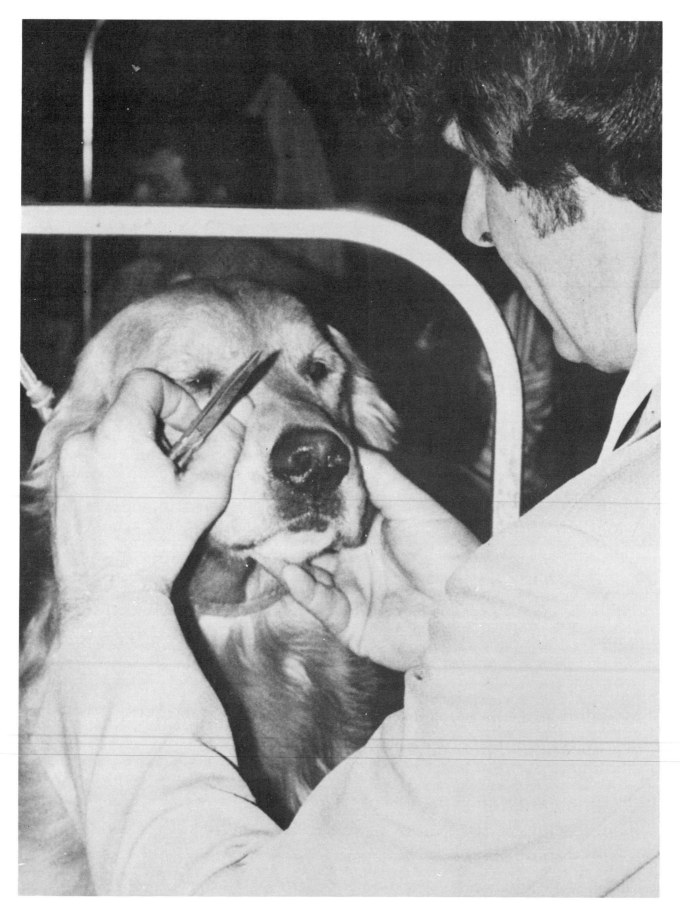

Ch. Willow Lane's Sunswept Luke being readied for the show ring. Mr. and Mrs. Charles Bradley, owners, Wilton, Connecticut.

CHAPTER EIGHT

Coat Care and Grooming

by Robert Stebbins

Getting acquainted with how it looks to be a duck. One of the puppies from D.J.'s Goldens, Dave, Jean, and J.D. Wacker.

Grooming is an important responsibility of every Golden owner. If a Golden is combed weekly, has trimmed nails, and is bathed at least every three weeks, he or she should live a healthy and happy life and not be an embrassment to family and friends. The following procedures deal with maintaining Goldens in top condition for showing and will give any pet the polished look that the finer and treasured things in life possess.

The nose of the Golden is black, but during the winter months the pigmentation may turn to a shade of pink. This is referred to as a "snow-nose." The use of kelp tablets will, in some instances, help keep this pigment from fading. We have found that dogs kept in basements or other locations without a lot of sunlight usually lack a good dark nose pigment, and changing their living facilities to a well sunlit area will help. If the dog's nose is dry, a thin layer of vaseline will help moisten it; vaseline also gives the nose a healthy, shiny look for showing. Removal of the whiskers is optional.

Occasionally the eyes will develop a discharge. Use a clean tissue to remove any excess mucus from the eyes. A pus discharge should be checked by a veterinarian who will recommend proper treatment. Some dogs have a tendency to tear and a tear stain will result under the eyes. Repeated use of a commercial eye stain remover, which contains a safe bleaching action, will eliminate the stain and can also be used effectively for discoloration on elbows or areas that have been licked.

Teeth should be cleaned at least once a month with a dental scraper. This will remove all tartar and help preserve a healthy mouth and gums. Removal of any yellow discoloration can be accomplished by brushing the teeth with a toothbrush and a dental powder or a commercial product prepared for this purpose.

The ears on any dog are very important and are very sensitive. Any neglect of them could result in serious problems which could be extremely painful to your pet. The area going into the ear canal should be trimmed very closely. The use of curve-tipped scissors is recommended to avoid any injury. Use a Q-tip moistened with mineral oil or one of several commercial ear cleansers available at your local pet shop. Slowly insert the Q-tip into the ear and swab gently. Continue to swab with clean, moistened Q-tips until the ear canal is clean. If the canal is filled with a thin liquid discharge, a medicated powder will help to dry the area. A dark brownish black accumulation with a few white specks is usually an indication of mite infestation and can be eliminated with a medication from the veterinarian. Any discharge of thick pus should be immediately cultured by your vet who will recommend proper medication.

Almost all puppies, and many adult dogs, have lots of soft thick hair around and under the ears. There is usually a path of this soft hair beginning at the top back side of the ear and continuing around and down under the ear onto the neck. This area is a prime "hot spot" because this hair mats easily and the thickness often prevents the skin from breathing; neglect in this area can also result in skin irritations. Keep the soft hair out by pulling it with your fingers. With practice, you will find that this does not hurt the dog at all. If hair on your dog will come out with gentle pulling, it does not belong there and is usually dead. The use of a steel comb or a wide-toothed terrier knife will also help in removing this unwanted hair. If the hair is extremely thick, you may use single-edge thinning shears to thin the hair. Take the shears against and under the grain of the hair, and then only cut lightly in any given area. This takes practice;

Puppies should become accustomed to grooming at an early age, as this handsome youngster is doing at D.J.'s Golden Kennel owned by Dave, Jean, and J.D. Wacker. Jean Wacker grooming this one.

and care must be exercised in darker colored dogs, for a color change will occur if you remove too much of the outer hair and leave the lighter undercoat. Never trim the edge of the ears with straight scissors. The removal of this soft cotton-like hair may be a continual process with some dogs. The argument that this removal will make a Golden seem setter-like in appearance can only be warranted when the degree of removal affects the overall appearance of the dog. Remember that only a moderate amount should be removed. *Never* use an electric clipper in this or any other area on a Golden.

Hair removal on the outside flap of the ear very much depends on the individual head type of the dog and how much ear covering he carries. Excessive amounts of hair, especially on the upper portion of the ear, will often make the rest of the head appear smaller or the ear set too high. The thinning and pulling process previously described will be effective if used with discretion. The amount of hair on the flap varies tremendously from dog to dog, and the effect of removing or leaving it on varies accordingly for each individual. One guideline is to learn your dog's attributes or faults in this area and then proceed slowly in complementing or correcting them.

The beautiful headpiece which was so widely admired during the show career of Ch. Cummings' Gold-Rush Charlie. Ann and Larry Johnson, owners.

Ashwel's Battle of Jericho, at five weeks of age, sitting on the table. Myra Moldawsky, owner.

Most Golden Retrievers have a natural thick mane that will vary in degrees of thickness and length from dog to dog. The amount of hair in this area, more often than not, will create an optical illusion; the neck will appear considerably shorter than it is in actuality. Some dogs have a naturally curly or wavy coat all over; but if your dog's hair is curly only in that area, it is usually due to the adult coat being forced to grow up and away from the body because the puppy coat was left in too long. If you keep the puppy coat combed and use a wide-toothed knife to remove the puppy coat as it is ready to come out, there will not be a tendency toward curliness later on. Depending on the degree of thickness, this area can become a health problem if not combed regularly. If you elect to thin this area with thinning shears, the thinning should take place several weeks prior to showing because of the degrees of color change that may take place as a result.

The body coat should be combed and brushed at least every other week, weekly if you show your dog. When your dog is starting to lose its

A handsome Golden headed for the show ring receives finishing touches. Owned by Dave, Jean, and J.D. Wacker.

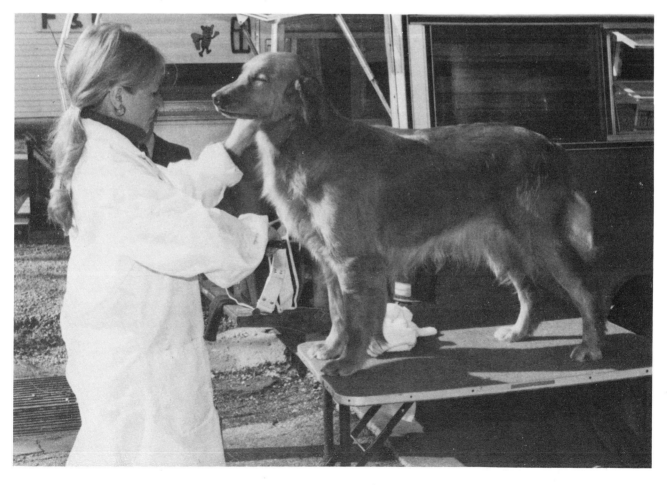

coat, don't try to leave it in. Immediate removal of the dead hair will encourage the new hair to grow back in much more quickly. If the top coat is falling out by the roots whenever it is gently rubbed or pulled, the dog is probably wormy; your vet should immediately be given a sample of your dog's stool to examine and then proper treatment can be initiated. Another indication of worms is a dry, wiry feel to the coat (this hair should be removed so the new healthy hair has a chance to grow).

The tail should be combed weekly. Use the terrier knife on the top side for the removal of unwanted undercoat. If the tail is excessively long, extending below the hocks, round it off with thinning shears, cutting sideways. Do not cut in a straight line but rather maintain the natural curve that a dog with less length of tail has. In other words, avoid a setter look of a straight cut off the end of the tail. Thin hair and trim as closely as required at the anal area and below the base of the tail. Keeping the hair short in this area will help maintain cleanliness.

In summer months, the belly and genital area may be trimmed closely with thinning shears. This will keep the dog cooler and, in the case of males, cleaner. Since Goldens should never appear tucked up, the removal of belly hair depends on the amount of flank hair. If the amount of hair on the flank is ample, removal of the belly hair will not be noticeable.

Feathering, or furnishings, should never be trimmed or thinned. Use a steel comb and a pin brush in these areas. Do *not* use a slicker brush which is meant for removal of coat. Use a pin brush and begin either at the bottom or front of the longer hair areas. Use one hand to push the hair in the opposite direction from that in which you are brushing. Gradually slide your hand away from the brushed area, maintaining a part. This ensures brushing completely to the skin. Tangled or matted areas should be pulled apart with your fingers. You may use a metal comb to separate these areas, but do not pull so hard on the hair as to remove the hair unnecessarily. The use of oily conditioners on featherings will help prevent breakage and matting from weeds, brambles, and hardened snow.

Use sharp straight scissors with rounded tips for cutting hair between the pads of the feet. This helps to prevent things getting caught between the pads and toes and causing sore feet or fungus infections. The outside of the foot should be trimmed so it appears round and not rabbit-shaped. Hair may be trimmed close to the toe exposing part of the toenail. Thinning shears should be used on the top of the foot only to remove thick, stray tufts of hair. Do not cut the hair from in between the individual toes as this will give the foot a splayed look. Trim the toenails a minimum of once a month. The weekly use of a nail grinder creates the appearance of a tighter foot for show purposes. Long nails are uncomfortable for your dog.

On the hock hair use single-edged thinning shears, and even off only to the natural line of the individual dog.

Grooming your Golden is not complete unless you bathe him. He should be bathed at least once a month if he is a pet dog and weekly if he is shown. Never let him go without a bath for extended lengths of time as this will surely cause skin problems. Pet shops carry many different shampoos and conditioners specially formulated for dogs, and you can experiment with several different brands to see which is best for your dog's particular coat. If your dog develops dandruff, a good dandruff shampoo can be safely used to help control the problem. There are several good dog shampoos on the market that are effective in controlling fleas and ticks if you are in an area that is bothered by these pests.

We recommend always using warm water for the bath as it cuts through dirt and oils better than cold water. Soak the dog and then thoroughly work the shampoo into all parts of the coat, gently massaging the skin with your fingers. Thoroughly rinse and repeat. It is very important to rinse all of the shampoo out of the

Pepperhill's Wochica V.I.P. stands on the grooming table and takes a big yawn. Barbara and Jeffrey Pepper.

coat as any left in the hair can cause irritations. Conditioner should be applied and left on for about five minutes and then may be rinsed with cool water. A small residue of conditioner may be left in and will help the coat feel full and rich (certain brands of conditioner, however, will make the coat feel greasy if not fully rinsed). If your dog should develop skin problems or hair loss right after a bath, discontinue the use of that product. Dogs who have sensitive skin do not tolerate all products.

Unless you have the time to stand with your dog and blow-dry him with an electric hairdryer to ensure that the coat is completely dry and lying correctly, you can use a full-size bath towel. Fold over one end of the towel so that the towel covers the dog from the top of his neck to the base of his tail. Make sure that the coat has been combed flat underneath it and pin the towel with horse blanket pins or large safety pins under the throat, belly, and base of the tail. You may leave the dog to dry naturally this way or to dry the furnishings and then remove the towel to touch up the slightly damp top coat.

This handsome head study is of Ch. Golden Pine's Easy Ace, a fine representative of the Golden Pine Kennels owned by Mary Luise Semans.

Left and below: How to bathe a Golden, demonstrated at the Wackers' D.J.'s Golden Kennel.

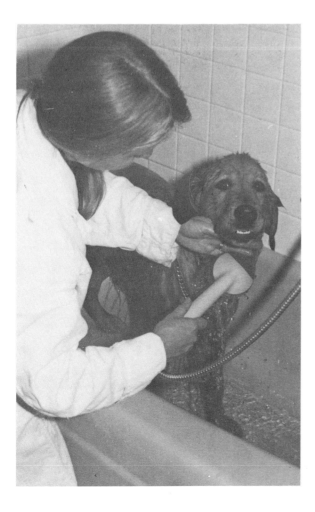

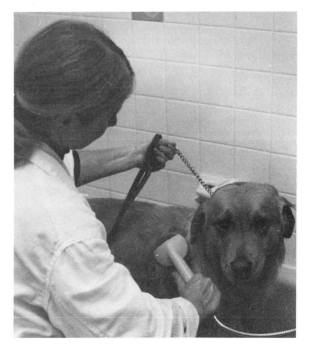

J.D. Wacker and D.J.'s Montana Kid's X-Rated, C.D.

CHAPTER NINE

Specialty Clubs, Honors, and Awards

Ch. Wochica's Okeechobee Jake is the only Golden to have won the National three times, the third time at nine years of age. He is also the second Top Producer in Goldens and has received the Irene Schlintz Gold Certificate of Distinction Award as a Top Producer. Owned by Susan Taylor and handled by Bob Stebbins.

Everyone who owns a purebred dog really owes it to himself, and to his or her dog, to join a Specialty club devoted to that breed. Descriptions of only three of the many Golden Specialty clubs are given here: the National organization, a member club of long establishment, and a new club which has accomplished important advances within a short period of time. We strongly urge everyone interested in Goldens to apply for membership in the National and, if there is a local Golden club in your area (the breeder of your dog or puppy will probably know of one), ask to join that, too. There are many benefits to be derived from such a membership, including the opportunity to make friends with people who share your mutual interest, to broaden your education about the breed, to attend meetings, to participate in such club activities as match shows, Specialty shows, and training classes, and to win the honors and awards bestowed by the clubs.

Specialty Clubs

Golden Retriever Club of America, Inc.

The parent club for Goldens in the United States is the Golden Retriever Club of America, Incorporated (G.R.C.A.). "Parent club" means

that this is the American Kennel Club Member Club for the breed and that smaller Golden clubs either are affiliated with this one or operate with its permission. The parent club does what a good parent does for its children: guards their welfare, always bearing in mind what is most beneficial to the breed in all of its many facets.

The Golden Retriever Club of America was organized in 1938 with the first officers as follows: President, S.S. Magoffin; First Vice-president, H.R. Ward; Second Vice-president, E.F. Rivings, Jr.; and Secretary-Treasurer, W.F. Gregg. John C. Gibbons was the first Delegate to the American Kennel Club from the G.R.C.A., serving from 1940 to 1944.

When the club was founded, Goldens were a little-known breed. Nowadays, A.K.C. registrations of Goldens annually run close to fifty thousand, and this club has a total membership of nearly four thousand persons.

The Golden Retriever Club of America, Incorporated, is the only parent club that over the years has always held its National as an independent, the first of which, a combined show and field trial, took place in Thiensville, Wisconsin, on May 13th and 14th 1940, with forty-five entries. In 1982, the National Specialty to be held on the 22nd through the 26th of September will be the forty-third annual Specialty show, the thirty-third annual national Specialty Obedience Trial, the forty-third annual National Specialty Field Trial, the seventeenth annual National Specialty Tracking Test, the third annual National Specialty Tracking Excellent Test, the nineteenth annual National Specialty Working Certificate Test, and the third annual National Specialty Working Certificate Excellent Test.

The Golden Retriever Club of America is the only parent club that demands that all the phases of its most versatile breed must be held at the National Specialty, including the Working Certificate and the Working Certificate Excellent Tests, which are G.R.C.A.-governed tests. With the popularity of the breed exploding as it did in the late 1970s, the National Specialty now draws between six hundred and eight hundred Goldens from the United States and Canada. In addition to the previously described events, the five days of continuous activities include educational seminars, judges' workshop, the annual membership meeting, the G.R.C.A. board meeting (open to the membership), and the annual awards banquet. A highlight of the National Specialty is that the exhibitors and field

Wochica's Classic Gift, by Ch. Westmont's Defender ex Ch. Wochica's Wind Song, winning the 9-12 Month Bitch class at the Golden Retriever Club of America Specialty in 1978. Janet L. Bunce, handling.

Ch. Quantock's Double Entry, by Sir Duncan of Woodbury ex Quantock's Ruffian, completing his title with a Best of Winners at the Fort Detroit Golden Retriever Club Specialty in 1981. Owned and bred by Gillian Massemore; handled by Barbara Dismultes. Photo courtesy of Janet Churchill.

trialers enjoy a marvelous opportunity to renew old friendships and start new ones.

The Golden Retriever Club of America also conducts annual Regional Specialties that, like the National, are rotated throughout the regions: Western, Central, and Eastern. The member club hosting a Regional must conduct competitions in conformation and obedience and hold tests for Working Certificate and Working Certificate Excellent, for the National's greatest ambition is to preserve the *retriever* in our Goldens.

In May of each year, the parent club also conducts a licensed *all-breed* field trial. For the past ten years, this all-breed field trial has been held in the Central region, normally in the Wisconsin-Illinois area. With field trial dates at a premium, the G.R.C.A. wishes to hold onto their May date for the field trial circuit and will most likely continue to keep their all-breed field trial in the Central region.

Ch. Cloverdale's Sweet Sadie as a young bitch taking Winners Bitch at the Golden National Specialty. Handled by Bob Stebbins.

Many of the older G.R.C.A. member clubs, such as Fort Detroit Golden Retriever Club, Garden State Golden Retriever Club, Evergreen Golden Retriever Club, and NORCAL Golden Retriever Club, are also licensed by the American Kennel Club to conduct Independent Golden Retriever Specialty shows and obedience trials. During the year, all of these clubs conduct Working Certificate and Working Certificate Excellent Tests, in conjunction with their Independent Specialties, if possible.

One of the worthiest projects of the Golden Retriever Club of America has been its study of the problem of hip dysplasia. The committee formed by G.R.C.A. members to make a study of the subject evolved into a nucleus for the O.F.A., which has certainly performed wonderfully, not only for Goldens but also for all the other breeds with similar problems.

Golden Retriever Club of America Specialty, May 1979. Judge, Dr. Bernard McGivern. Am., Can. Ch. Pepperhill's Basically Bear handled by Jeff Pepper; Ch. Pepperhill's Travelin' Bear, Am. and Can. C.D., handled by Barbara Pepper; and Ch. Pepperhill's Allison Charlen handled by Elliot More. All owned by Pepperhill Farms.

1981 Golden Retriever Club of America National Specialty Veterans Class. Am., Can. Ch. High Farms Jantze of Curacao, C.D.X., T.D., W.C., Can. C.D., T.D.X., owned by Barbara Tinker, is placing second.

Badger Golden Retriever Club, Inc.

The Golden Retriever Club of Wisconsin was the first organized group of Golden Retriever fanciers to affiliate with the Golden Retriever Club of America (Wisconsin was the founding state of the Golden Retriever Club of America) and is the oldest Golden Retriever Club in the country. The Wisconsin club was organized in 1938 and was host to the first Golden Retriever Club of America National Specialty in 1940.

The first newsletter, published on May 7th 1966, was called *Newsletter of the Wisconsin Chapter of the G.R.C.A.* Officers and board members of the club were equally divided among the three phases of bench, obedience, and field, and clinics were held covering all three interests.

In December 1966, work began on a club logo and club patch or pin. In January 1968, the A.K.C. requested all present chapters be converted to member clubs, inasmuch as the Golden Retriever Club of America by-laws did not provide for chapter status. At that time the Wisconsin Club had a membership of seventy-one persons. On May 3rd 1968, as a start on the procedure to affiliate with the national club as a member club, the name of the club was changed to Golden Retriever Club of Wisconsin. In February 1969, the American Kennel Club proposed another name change, having found Golden Retriever Club of Wisconsin unacceptable since it included the state name. In April 1969, the name "Badger Golden Retriever Club" was adopted, and this is the name by which the club is known today.

Best of Breed at the Fort Detroit Golden Retriever Club Specialty, November 1979. Ch. Laurell's Yellow Jacket, by Ch. Gold-Rush Lightnin', was bred by Thomas C. Kling and Laura Ellis Kling and is owned by Joan Stoppleman.

Ch. Wochica's Golden Watersprite, by Ch. Misty Morn's Sunset, C.D., T.D., W.C., ex Wochica's Apple Wine (daughter of Ch. Wochica's Wind Song), was winner of the 1976 Eastern Regional Specialty at only six months of age! Janet L. Bunce handling to a good win for owner John S. Mleczko of Wilton, Connecticut.

A proud moment for breeder Mercer Russo Ervin at the 1981 Garden State Golden Retriever Club Specialty Show as the top three awards in 6-9 Months Puppy Sweepstakes are won by her homebreds. Left to right: Mercer's Jumping Juniper, first; Mercer's Merrygold Sprite, second; and Mercer's Orange Blossom Special, third.

The Badger Golden Retriever Club has been active in all phases of competition since the club's inception in 1938. The club hosted National Specialties, the most recent of which was in 1971, and presently hosts the G.R.C.A. spring all-breed field trial which takes place bi-annually in Wisconsin and the G.R.C.A. Central Regional Specialty. Each year Badger hosts sanctioned field trials, sanctioned A.K.C. matches, health programs such as an eye clinic and a heartworm clinic, and seminars and clinics in obedience, field, and show, and Working Certificate tests.

One of the biggest undertakings for the Badger Golden Retriever Club has been the Guardian Plan, a program instituted to educate the public about our breed and to help individuals purchase a sound, quality puppy or older dog. Advertising is placed in the state-wide edition of the *Milwau-kee Journal* each month, and Club members volunteer to answer phone calls and to mail information to those callers. This program has proved to be very successful, and during the first year of its operation, February 1981 to February 1982, it answered over two hundred inquiries.

Bruce Mittelstaedt is President of Badger, Jean Kaml is Secretary, and Elmer Custer is the Treasurer. This club holds general membership meetings six times each year, usually at a local restaurant for a Friday night fish fry. The program at these meetings includes either a veterinarian's speech on a current topic, movies, or a panel discussion. The club also publishes a very high-quality newspaper six times a year. Additionally, a flier is issued for the purpose of attracting new members. The club is open to people interested in all phases of Golden ownership, including pets.

Golden Retriever Club of St. Louis

Becky Denney, the club's Vice-president, has this to say about the Golden Retriever Club of St. Louis, one of the newest Golden clubs:

Two obviously well-bred Golden Retrievers caught my eye at obedience class one spring evening in 1975. I can still remember my excitement when I met Carol Falberg, her daughter Vicki, and their Goldens, Westmont's Diana and Westmont's Defender (a future champion). Carol and Howard Falberg had been active in a Golden Retriever club while living in California and saw the need for one in their new area. And so a meeting was held in June 1975, temporary officers elected, and plans for the future were formulated.

Many of our ideas and planned events came from information about other clubs and the breed itself as reported in the *Golden Retriever News*. Carol Falberg, as the first President, steered the group toward American Kennel Club recognition to hold licensed obedience trials and conformation shows. Also we had frequent club programs featuring grooming, conformation, and training sessions which helped newcomers and enabled us all to share our experiences with one another. Before that time, Golden owners in St. Louis had only read of eye clinics and Golden Specialty events such as shows and Working Certificate tests, but now we were planning and train-

Working Certificate Tests, recently given by the Badger Golden Retriever Club, were passed by all of these dogs.

ing for them. Thanks to the local newsletter, first edited by Mary Schaub, we not only had a calendar of club events but also a communication link between local Golden exhibitors, a way of dispensing educational information, and an ideal place to discuss controversial issues. Our all-breed eye clinic, first given in February 1976, was so well accepted that we recently have expanded to include a blood clinic; and several other St. Louis clubs are now offering annual eye clinics.

Our first conformation and obedience match was in spring 1975, with Jean Baird Crowley judging conformation and Harvey Konradi, obedience. Our well-run matches are often won by Goldens who later become champions. Champion Starfarm Wingfield Cash, U.D., W.C., owned by Barbara Sheehan, has won Best Adult in Match twice. The only St. Louis-bred champion bitch, Champion Fox Creek's Beginner's Luck, bred and owned by Lyn and Dave Cortright, has won Best Adult of Opposite Sex twice at our match, too. Another Best in Match winner, later amateur-handled to his championship, was LaVerne and Earl Buechting's Champion Reddigold's Diplomat. We are also proud of Best in Match winner Champion Meadowpond Trojan's Pride, C.D., owned by Sharon and Carl Rosenkoetter. Our first "A" match, spring 1982, was well organized by chairman Karen Arbuthnot.

From the beginning, the club offered field sessions with dummies or sometimes with birds and shotguns to train any retriever for hunting, for fun, for W.C. or W.C.X. tests, or for trial work. We were the only St. Louis area retriever club offering field sessions and fun trials. Rumrunner's Handyman, a qualified open all-age dog at two years, now has two points towards his amateur field champion title; he is owned by George Mitchell, one of our club

Mercer's Flowering Quince with breeder-owner Mercer Russo Ervin winning a big class at the Garden State Golden Retriever Club Specialty in October 1980.

members. Our second sanctioned trial in March 1982, as before open to all retriever breeds, had thirty-six Goldens entered out of 102 entries, which was a noticeable increase in Golden activity. Our Golden club trial program is dependent on the two field trial clubs in the area for entries, judges, advice, gunners, and other types of support. We reciprocate by supporting the field clubs with our entries, advice, and so on. About a third of our members gain experience by working in trials and by entering their Goldens in them. We gave our first W.C.-W.C.X. in 1980 but successfully combined the tests with a singles trial in 1981.

Our club has grown so we focus on a variety of issues and events, but our members still do not breed many litters, and they choose the mating with their own ideals in mind, bent not always on winning but on producing all around quality Golden Retrievers. Our members produce puppies they want to own, not simply to sell.

The success of our club has depended on responsible, far-seeing individuals just as the vigor of our breed depends on such individuals.

The Golden Retriever Hall of Fame

Throughout the pages of this book you will note references to the Hall of Fame, Outstanding Sires and Dams, and Certificates of Merit. In order that they be fully understood by all, we have asked the Golden Retriever Club of America for an outline of the requirements of these coveted and prestigious awards; and we are deeply indebted to Hobart S. Arnold, Statistical Secretary, for fulfilling our request. After reading the requirements, it will become apparent why Golden owners so highly prize the distinction of being listed in the various categories in the Hall of Fame, for attaining the honor signifies that your dog's distinguished accomplishments were achieved in a grand manner.

Outstanding Sire. All dogs who have sired two field champions, one field and one show champion, or five champions of any kind (show, field, and/or obedience) are included. A dog holding a Utility Dog or Utility Dog Tracking or Utility Dog and Tracker Excellent title is considered by the National to be an obedience champion.

Outstanding Dam. Requirements are the same as for Outstanding Sire *except* that only three champion progeny of any kind are required.

Ch. Valhalla's Amber Kate, C.D., Outstanding Dam, with her daughter, Valhalla's After Dinner Licker, C.D.X., W.D.X. Both of these very famous and distinguished Goldens are owned by Kathy Liebler.

Ch. Cloverdale Twin-Beau-D Joy, owner-handled by Nancy Dallaire and bred by Jane and Richard Zimmerman, is a member of the Golden Retriever Hall of Fame. Being honored in the Hall of Fame is an outstanding achievement.

Show Champion. Any Golden Retriever who accumulates twenty-five points or more, based on his performance in Sporting Groups or Best in Show or independent Specialty shows (Specialty shows held in conjunction with all-breed shows are specifically excluded) will automatically be honored in the Hall of Fame. Point scales: Best in Show = 10 (plus Group award); Group first = 5; Group second = 3; Group third = 1; Group fourth = ½; National Specialty Best of Breed = 5; Golden Retriever Club of America Regional Specialty = 3; Local Club Specialty = 1.

Field Dogs. Any Golden Retriever who accumulates a total of twenty-five points or more as a field champion and/or amateur field champion in Amateur Stakes or in licensed and/or member field trials will automatically be included in the Hall of Fame. Any Golden Retriever who wins the National Field Trial or National Amateur Field Trial will also be included. *Note*: although a dog may be included simply by virtue of winning either of the Nationals, current rules for eligibility for the Nationals and the level of competition at them make it a virtual impossibility that any dog will get entry to the Hall of Fame simply by this accomplishment.

Obedience Champion. Any Golden Retriever Utility Dog or Obedience Trial Champion who accumulates a total of five Highest Scores in Trial (or ties for highest score) will automatically be honored in the Hall of Fame.

Right: Little Dawn of Chickasaw, foundation bitch at Wochica Kennels, Golden Retriever Club of America Outstanding Dam of (in same litter) Ch. Wochica's Okeechobee Jake (multiple Best in Show dog), Ch. Wochica's Wind Song (multiple Specialty Best of Opposite Sex), Ch. Wochica's M.J. Protege, C.D., W.C. (Westminster Group third) and Ch. JIB of Cedarmoor. This same bitch was foster mother to two tiger cubs from the Ringling Brothers Barnum and Bailey Circus. Mrs. Janet L. Bunce, owner, Wochica Goldens.

Below: Ch. Wochica's Wind Song, by Ch. Misty Morn's Sunset C.D., T.D., W.C., ex Little Dawn of Chickasaw. A multiple Specialty Best of Opposite Sex winner and an Outstanding Dam, this is the bitch who retired the Golden Ghost Challenge Trophy offered through the Golden Retriever Club of America for Best of Opposite Sex won three times by the same owner. Janet L. Bunce, breeder-owner, Wochica Goldens.

Above: Am., Can. Ch. Beckwith's Terra Cotta, C.D., is a G.R.C.A. Outstanding Dam of three U.S.A. champions and three Canadian champions. Owned by Mr. and Mrs. R.E. Beckwith. **Left:** Ch. Sun Dance's Rainmaker, co-owned by T. D'Alessandro and Lisa Schultz, was Number Two Golden for 1979, Best of Opposite Sex at the National Specialty in 1979, sire of one Group-winning son and two ** field trial dogs, a G.R.C.A. Outstanding Sire, winner of both the Eastern Regional and the Mid-West Regional Specialty, and a Best in Show winner.

Am., Can. Ch. Sutter Creek Goldrush Flyboy, bred by Jean Baird and owned and handled by Susan Breakell, is a Golden Retriever Club of America Outstanding Sire and a member of the G.R.C.A. Show Dog Hall of Fame.

Ch. Little Bit of Laurell, owned by Thomas C. Kling and Laura Ellis Kling, is a noted Outstanding Dam, having to her credit the also great producing bitch Ch. Laurell's Kilimanjaro, plus Ch. Laurell's Katie Did or Didn't, Ch. Laurell's Kasey of Ashlyn, Ch. Laurell's Mint Mark Morgen, Ch. Laurell's Merry Performance, C.D.X., W.C., W.C.X., and Ch. Laurell's Xpectations.

Am., Can. Ch. Laurell's Especial Jason, W.C., Am. and Can. U.D.T., sired by Ch. Major Gregory of High Farms ex Ch. Laurell's Amiable Caboose, is owned by Cherie Berger, Meadowpond Golden Retrievers. This dog is in the Golden Retriever Club of America Hall of Fame and is a Golden Retriever Club of America Outstanding Sire.

Above: Lynn Beckwith, in 1979, with Am., Can. Ch. Beckwith's Xciting Fellow, a Golden Retriever Club of America Outstanding Sire of champions.

Left: Amberac's Reeva Rustelle, O.D., bred and owned by Amberac Kennels, Ellen Manke.

Below: Am., Can. Ch. Pepperhill's Basically Bear, an Outstanding Sire, taking Winners Dog en route to his title, handled by co-owner Barbara Pepper, Pepperhill Farms.

Ch. Cummings' Dame Pepperhill in competition in the show ring. Dame Pepperhill is one of the Hall of Fame members owned by Barbara and Jeffrey Pepper, Pepperhill Farms.

Ch. Thistledue's Shining Star winning Best in Show at the Leavenworth Kennel Club's all-breed show on May 10th 1982. Mr. Carter F. Foss is owner-handling his great Hall of Fame dog to this win under Mrs. William Lehnig.

Best in Show winning Am., Can. Ch. Goldrush's Contender, U.D., the fourth Best in Show-Utility Dog Golden in breed history. Owned by Southern Goldens, Colleen and Clark Williams.

O. T. Ch. Topbrass Cisco Kid is the second top obedience trial champion in U.S. history. Owned by Pauline Czameski and bred by Mrs. Joseph Mertens, Topbrass Kennels.

Toryglen Chestnut Heights, U.D.*, by Ch. Alstone Sutter Creek Charade, U.D.*, ex Beckwith's Sparkle Plenty. Breeder, Esther Verrissimo. Owner-trainer, Al Rochefort.

Left, Ch. Alstone Sutter Creek Charade, U.D.*, Golden Retriever Club of America Outstanding Sire of numerous champions and Utility Dogs. Right, Teecon Sutter Creek Cognac, C.D., full brother to Fanfare, sire of exceptional top obedience-titled get, himself a multiple High in Trial winner. Owned, trained, handled, and loved by Susan Breakell.

Ch. Toryglen Idling Jerome, U.D.***, by Ch. Alstone Sutter Creek Charade, U.D.*, ex Beckwith's Sparkle Plenty, C.D. The sire of several multiple titled get. Bred by Esther Verrissimo. Owned by Ed and Susan Brown-Leger.

Ch. Tanya's Sunburst Kemo Sabe, C.D.X., T.D.*, at Cape Cod, January 1976. Breeder-owner, Rita Di Salvio. Handler, Susan Breakell.

Star Champions

The ideal Golden Retriever is a dog who, in addition to his other qualities, can perform creditably in the field, doing a day's work in keeping with the tradition and heritage of the breed. The editors of the Golden Retriever Club of America annual *Yearbook*, therefore, devised and created a "star system" to bestow special honor on and to indicate the fact that a bench show champion Golden has, in addition, successfully competed in field trials. A number of stars are added to the dog's name, and the specific number of stars depends on the importance of that dog's field achievements.

A single star (*) is added to the name of a champion Golden who has also earned a Working Certificate. Two stars (**) indicate that a champion Golden has placed in a licensed field trial or won a Certificate of Merit. Three stars (***) indicate a champion Golden who has qualified for Limited All-Age Stakes. Four stars (****) mean that a champion Golden has also become a dual champion.

The first dual champions in the breed were Stilrovin Rip's Pride and Tonkahof Esther Belle, both owned by Kingswere Kennels. The third was Stilrovin Nitro Express, owned by Ben L. Boalt.

Caernac's Troyman Trang*** W.C., W.C.X., Open All Age Qualified dog owned by Thomas C. Kling and Laura Ellis Kling, Laurell Goldens, winning first, Golden Retriever Club of America Field Trial Dog Class, at the National in 1981.

Specialty Best of Breed Winners

The following is a list of the winners of Best of Breed, and their owners, at the Golden Retriever Club of America's National Specialty, the first of which was held in 1940.

1940—BEAVERTAIL GAY
Beavertail Kennels
1941—CH. BEAVERTAIL BUTCH
Robert Bruce
1942—CH. GOLDWOOD PLUTO
Goldwood Kennels
1943—STILROVIN CHIANG
Lewis E. Thorne
1944—LORD GEOFFREY
Dr. and Mrs. John F. Noble
1945—CH. HIGHLAND CHIEF
Leslie C. Brooks
1946—CH. NORANBY BALOO OF
TARAMAR
Taramar Kennels.
1947—CH. CZAR OF WILDWOOD
Eric S. Johnson
1948—DES LAC'S LASSIE C.D.
Des Lac's Kennels
1949—CH. DES LAC'S LASSIE C.D.
Des Lac's Kennels
1950—CH. GOLDEN KNOLL'S SHUR SHOT
Mrs. Russell S. Peterson
1951—CH. GOLDEN KNOLL'S SHUR SHOT
Mrs. Russell S. Peterson
1952—CH. CHEE-CHEE OF SPRUCEWOOD
Maurine M. Zwang
1953—CH. CHEE-CHEE OF SPRUCEWOOD
Maurine M. Zwang
1954—CH. GOLDEN KNOLL'S KING
ALPHONZO
N. Bruce Ashby
1955—CH. SPRUCEWOOD'S CHORE BOY
Mrs. Henry D. Barbour
1956—CH. RUSINA'S MR. CHIPS
Van Holt Garret, Jr.
1957—CH. SPRUCEWOOD'S CHINKI
Mr. and Mrs. Millard C. Zwang
1958—CH. SPRUCEWOOD'S CHOCKI
Mr. and Mrs. Millard C. Zwang
1959—CH. SUN DANCE'S BRONZE C.D.
Opal Horton
1960—CH. SPRUCEWOOD'S CHORE BOY
Mrs. Henry D. Barbour
1961—CH. PRINCE ROYAL OF LOS ALTOS
Oliver and Janet Wilhelm

Ch. Sprucewood's Chocki, born March 16th 1954, by Am., Can. Ch. Golden Knoll's Alphonzo ex Am., Can. Ch. Chee Chee of Sprucewood, was bred and owned by Mr. and Mrs. M.C. Zwang. Handler, Hollis Wilson. Chocki won the Specialty Best of Breed in 1958.

Above: Ch. Beckwith Copper Coin, owned by Mr. and Mrs. R.E. Beckwith, with Lynn Marie Beckwith, then three-and-a-half months old. Copper Coin won the Specialty Best of Breed in 1964. **Below:** The great winning and producing Golden, Ch. Malagold Beckwith Big Buff, C.D., with his owner-handler Connie Gerstner following Best in Show honors at Wisconsin Kennel Club in 1973. Big Buff won the breed honors at the 1970 Specialty.

1962—CH. CHEYENNE GOLDEN'S KING
Cheyenne Golden Kennels
1963—CH. FIGARO OF YEO
Mrs. Charles W. Engelhard
1964—CH. BECKWITH'S COPPER COIN
Richard E. and Ludell Beckwith
1965—CH. SUN DANCE'S BRONZE C.D.
Opal Horton
1966—CH. CHEYENNE GOLDEN'S KING JOHN
Cheyenne Golden Kennels
1967—CH. LORELEI'S FEZ-TI ZA-ZA
Reinhard M. Bischoff
1968—CH. SUN DANCE'S VAGABOND LOVER
Violet Topmiller and Laura Ellis
1969—BECKWITH'S MALAGOLD FLASH
Marvin and Carole Kvamme
1970—CH. MALAGOLD BECKWITH BIG BUFF
Connie D. Gerstner
1971—CH. COLACOVE COMMANDO DI SHAN
John and June Mastracola
1972—CH. WOCHICA'S OKEECHOBEE JAKE
Susan Taylor
1973—CH. CHEYENNE GOLDEN'S SON OF JAMES
Cheyenne Golden Kennels
1974—CH. CUMMINGS' GOLD-RUSH CHARLIE
Mrs. Robert V. Clark, Jr., and Larry C. Johnson
1975—CH. WOCHICA'S OKEECHOBEE JAKE
Susan Taylor
1976—CH. SUN DANCE'S RARUE
Shirley and William Worley
1977—CH. WOCHICA'S OKEECHOBEE JAKE
Susan Taylor
1978—CH. GOLD-RUSH'S GREAT TEDDY BEAR
Diane Smith and R. Ann Johnson
1979—CH. RUSSO'S PEPPERHILL POPPY
Barbara and Jeffrey Pepper
1980—CH. GOLD-RUSH COPPER LEE
William W. Wingard and R. Ann Johnson
1981—CH. TEMPO'S FRONTIER BRONCO
Hank Arszman and Vivian Wright

Above: Ch. Gold-Rush's Great Teddy Bear was the Specialty Best of Breed winner in 1978. Diane Smith and R. Ann Johnson, owners. Below: Elliot More and Am., Can. Ch. Russo's Pepperhill Poppy in a moment of relaxation. Mr. More has piloted this great bitch to a spectacular record, including Specialty Best of Breed in 1979, for the Jeffrey Peppers, owners.

Above: Ch. Wochica's Okeechobee Jake at the National with his handler Bob Stebbins. One of the greatest of the greats in Golden history! Sue Taylor, owner.

Left: The action of a winner! Ch. Wochica's Okeechobee Jake showing how it's done at the National! This outstanding movement helped make Jake one of the greatest Goldens of all time.

Bob Stebbins' happy reaction immediately after hearing judge Dr. Bernard McGivern announce that Ch. Wochica's Okeechobee Jake had won the 1977 Golden Retriever Club of America National Specialty.

Below: The happiness of Jake's handler, Bob Stebbins, is clearly apparent in this formal photo with judge McGivern holding the rosette. Sue Taylor, the proud owner of this dog, stands behind Bob Stebbins. Ch. Wochica's Okeechobee Jake, at nine years of age, won Best of Breed at the National Specialty from the Veterans Class. Jake was the only Golden to win the National three times (retiring the club trophy for this award, which has now been replaced with the Ch. Wochica's Okeechobee Jake Trophy) and the only Golden to win the breed at Westminster three times.

Ch. Tempo's Frontier Bronco, by Ch. Sun Dance's Rarue ex Ch. Tempo's Nassau Miss, was bred by Peter and Sheila Huser and was purchased and shown to his title by Henry and Michelle Arszman, Frontier Kennels. Later under the co-ownership of George and Vivian Wright of Amelia, Ohio, and Gandalf Kennels, Bronco was put out with handler Dick Cooper. He finished 1981, by his owner's count, Number One Golden in the United States (not yet officially confirmed). Bronco won the 1981 National Specialty, the 1981 Regional Specialty, and the 1981 Indiana State Golden Retriever Specialty. He has also won four Bests in Show (the largest being 2,500 dogs), fourteen Group firsts, and twenty-nine Group placements. At the time of this writing, he has four champions to his credit as a sire.

Facing page: Ch. Sun Dance's Rarue, Number One Golden in 1976 and National Specialty winner that same year, Outstanding Sire, and sire of Ch. Tempo's Frontier Bronco, Number One Golden for 1981. Bred by Patrick Worley and owned by Shirley and William Worley, Sun Dance Kennels. Photo courtesy of Lisa Schultz, Mr. Worley's stepdaughter.

SPORTING GROUP

RUBBER CITY
KENNEL CLUB
JUNE 6 1976
PHOTOS BY D ALVERSON

M-B

RUBBER CITY K.C.
SPORTING

Above: Ch. Malagold Summer Encore, a two-time Best in Show winner so far in 1982, here is gaining the honor at St. Croix Valley Kennel Club. Another Show Dog Hall of Fame member sired by Ch. Hunt's Finnegan ex Ch. Malagold Svea. Connie Gerstner, breeder-owner-handler.

Facing page: Kyle Karakan of Sutter Creek, Am., Can., and Bda. U.D.T., by Ch. Alstone Sutter Creek Charade, U.D.*, ex Rusticana Cloud Nine, U.D., is a member of the Golden Retriever Club of America Obedience Hall of Fame. Bred by Frances Tuck. Owned and trained by Brenda Schofield. Show-handled by Susan Breakell.

Ch. Cheyenne Golden's Son of James, Best of Breed at the Golden Retriever Club of America National Specialty in 1973, owned by William and Marian Herbert, Cheyenne Golden Kennels. Handled by Mrs. Herbert, this grandson of Champion Cheyenne Golden's King John is undoubtedly the top owner-handled Golden in history, having been retired with a total of 110 Sporting Group firsts (the record in Goldens), thirteen Bests in Show, more than three hundred Bests of Breed, and numerous other Group placements, *entirely owner-handled*.

Am., Can. Ch. Goldenquest's Lucky Charm, Number One Golden Retriever Bitch, U.S.A. (Phillips System) and Canada for 1976, by Am., Can., Mex. Ch. Cal-Vo's Happy Ambassador, C.D., ex Can. Ch. Degojay's Amorous Aspasia, C.D., is owned by Mrs. Jay S. Cox, Annapolis, Maryland. Pictured winning a Sporting Group from the late Mrs. Winifred Heckman at Seattle Kennel Club.

Left: Ch. Valhalla's Dogo Dancer, C.D.T., with Art Baihly. A son of Ch. Cummings' Gold-Rush Charlie ex Ch. Valhalla's Amber Kate, Dogo finished in April 1977. A Best in Show winner and a member of the Golden Retriever Club Show Dog Hall of Fame, Dogo earned his T.D. in 1980 and his C.D. in 1981. Art and Caroline Baihly own this handsome Golden. **Below:** Ch. Sir Duncan of Woodbury, shown here at ten years four months of age, is a magnificent stud dog and Hall of Fame member. Jolly Goldens, the Lounsburys.

Am., Can. Ch. Sutter Creek Goldrush Flyboy, a member of the Golden Retriever Club of America Show Dog Hall of Fame, an Outstanding Sire, G.R.C.A. Bred by Jean Baird and owner-handled by Susan Breakell.

Best of Breed at the 1981 Regional National Specialty, Ch. Cupid's Beau of Ladykirk, C.D., W.C., was the Top Winning Golden for that year and is in the Golden Retriever Club of America Show Dog Hall of Fame. Owned by R. Steve Andrews of Colorado Springs, Colorado, Beau was bred by Toni Stovall and is handled by Betty R. Andrews.

Am., Can. Ch. Little Big Man is a member of the Golden Retriever Club of America Show Dog Hall of Fame. By Ch. Duck Pass Noble Impulse, Am. and Can. C.D., ex Laddie's Golden Tassel, C.D., he was born in 1970 and died in 1981. The first homebred breeder-owner-handled champion of record at Morningsage Goldens, Joanne A. Lastoka.

Am., Can. Ch. Russo's Pepperhill Poppy in a most beautiful pose with her handler Elliot More. Barbara and Jeffrey Pepper own this stunning bitch, the third bitch to be included in the Hall of Fame.

Ch. Cummings' Gold-Rush Charlie, Top Golden in 1973, 1974, and 1975, snapped informally at home. This lovely Golden brought many honors to Gold-Rush Kennels, Ann and Larry Johnson, and Springfield Kennels, Mrs. Robert V. Clark, Jr., during a star-studded career in the show ring handled by Bill Trainor.

Left: Susan Taylor with her beloved Jake—Ch. Wochica's Okeechobee Jake, winner of multiple Bests in Show, seventy-three Group placements, and many other honors. Jake is in the Golden Retriever Club of America Hall of Fame both as a Show Dog and as an Outstanding Sire, and he has a Certificate of Merit for winning the National in 1972, 1975, and 1977 and a Certificate of Merit for the Bench in 1973 and 1974. **Below:** Ch. Wingsong Maker's Mark, by Ch. Goldrush Contender, U.D., ex Rockgold's Fanfare of Brass, is a Group winner, a Best in Show dog, and a Specialty Best of Breed winner who appears in the Golden Retriever Club of America Show Dog Hall of Fame. Pictured with his breeder-owner-handler Susan Heinl, Wingsong Goldens. **Facing page:** Ch. Camelot's Noble Fella, owned by M. Zonghetti and Kay Bickford, handled by Bob Stebbins. An unusually outstanding head study of a truly magnificent dog!

Above: The scent hurdle relay racing team at a Golden Retriever Club of America National Specialty. Barbara S. Tinker, Bargello Goldens.

Facing page, top: "Take them around, please." The opening phase of judging a class of Goldens. **Facing page, bottom:** All in line, waiting to be examined by the judge.

Ch. Wochica's Golden Pumpkin, by Am., Can., Bda. Ch. Cummings' Gold-Rush Charlie ex Ch. Wochica's Sand-piper, taking Winners Bitch at the Westminster Kennel Club's 100th Anniversary Dog Show, Madison Square Garden, New York. Kathy and Gary Uhrman, owners, Bridlewold Goldens.

CHAPTER TEN

Standard for Golden Retrievers

Ch. Laurell's York, by Ch. Gold-Rush Lightnin' ex Ch. Laurell's Kilimanjaro, was Number Two Golden in 1980 and 1981 and Number One breeder-owned Golden. Thomas C. Kling and Laura Ellis Kling, Laurell Goldens.

The breed standard is the description of the perfect, or ideal, Golden Retriever. It is used as a guideline for objectively measuring the appearance (and temperament, to a certain extent) of a given specimen of the breed. The degree of excellence of a particular dog is based on how well that dog meets the requirements described in the standard for its breed—how well the dog approaches the ideal.

The following revised standard for Golden Retrievers, submitted to the American Kennel Club by the Golden Retriever Club of America, Inc., was approved for the breed and became effective on January 1st 1982.

GENERAL APPEARANCE. A symmetrical, powerful, active dog, sound and well put together, not clumsy nor long in the leg, displaying a kindly expression and possessing a personality that is eager, alert and self-confident. Primarily a hunting dog, he should be shown in hard working condition. Over-all appearance, balance, gait and purpose to be given more emphasis than any of his component parts.
HEAD. Broad in skull, slightly arched laterally and longitudinally without prominence of frontal bones (forehead) or occipital bones. Stop well defined but not abrupt. Foreface deep and wide, nearly as long as skull. Muzzle

straight in profile, blending smoothly and strongly into skull; when viewed in profile or from above, slightly deeper and wider at stop than at tip. No heaviness in flews. Removal of whiskers is permitted but not preferred.
EYES. Friendly and intelligent in expression, medium large with dark, close-fitting rims, set well apart and reasonably deep in sockets. Color preferably dark brown; medium brown acceptable. Slant eyes and narrow, triangular eyes detract from correct expression and are to be faulted. No white or haw visible when looking straight ahead. Dogs showing evidence of functional abnormality of eyelids or eyelashes (such as, but not limited to, trichiasis, entropian, ectropian, or distichiasis) are to be excused from the ring.
TEETH. Scissors bite, in which the outer side of lower incisors touches the inner side of the upper incisors. Undershot or overshot bite is a disqualification. Misalignment of teeth (irregular placement of incisors) or a level bite (incisors meet each other edge to edge) is undesirable, but not to be confused with undershot or overshot. Full dentition. Obvious gaps are serious faults.
NOSE. Black or brownish black, though fading to a lighter shade in cold weather not serious. Pink nose or one seriously lacking in pigmentation to be faulted.

A truly outstanding puppy head! Beckwith's Cabarnet in January 1980. Bred and owned by Mr. and Mrs. R.E. Beckwith.

EARS.   Rather short with front edge attached well behind and just above the eye and falling close to cheek. When pulled forward, tip of ear should just cover the eye. Low, hound-like ear set to be faulted.

NECK.   Medium long, merging gradually into well laid back shoulders, giving sturdy, muscular appearance. Untrimmed natural ruff. No throatiness.

BODY.   Well-balanced, short coupled, deep through the chest. Chest between forelegs at least as wide as a man's closed hand including thumb, with well-developed forechest.

Brisket extends to elbow. Ribs long and well sprung but not barrel shaped, extending well towards hindquarters. Loin short, muscular, wide and deep, with very little tuck-up. Back line strong and level from withers to slightly sloping croup, whether standing or moving. Slab-sidedness, narrow chest, lack of depth in brisket, sloping back line, roach or sway back, excessive tuck-up, flat or steep croup to be faulted.

FOREQUARTERS.   Muscular, well coordinated with hindquarters and capable of free movement. Shoulder blades long and well laid back with upper tips fairly close together at withers. Upper arms appear about the same length as the blades, setting the elbows back beneath the upper tip of the blades, close to the ribs without looseness. Legs, viewed from the front, straight with good bone, but not to the point of coarseness. Pasterns short and strong, sloping slightly with no suggestion of weakness.

Valhalla's Sally Forth taking Reserve Winners from the Bred-by-Exhibitor Class at Westminster, 1974. Judge, Fred Hunt. Sired by Am., Can. Ch. Beckwith's Malagold Flash, C.D., W.C., ex Beckwith's Chickasaw Jingle, Sally Forth is a litter-sister to Am., Can. Ch. Valhalla's Amber Waves and Ch. Valhalla's Amber Kate. Kathleen Liebler, owner, Valhalla Kennels.

Am., Can. Ch. Valhalla's Amber Waves, C.D., taking Best of Breed at Westminster, 1977. Handled by Kathy Kirk under judge E.W. Tipton for owners Kathy and Larry Liebler, Valhalla Farms.

290

Am., Can. Ch. Pepperhill's Lady Ruston handled by Barbara Pepper to Best of Winners at Westminster 1981. Co-owned by the Peppers with Andrew Montgomery.

In the big Group ring at Madison Square Garden, Am., Can. Ch. Russo's Pepperhill's Poppy with her handler, Elliot More. Westminster's Show Chairman, Chester A. Collier, to the right. Poppy is owned by Barbara and Jeffrey Pepper.

HINDQUARTERS. Broad and strongly muscled. Profile of croup slopes slightly; the pelvic bone slopes at a slightly greater angle (approximately 30 degrees from horizontal). In a natural stance the femur joins the pelvis at approximately a 90 degree angle; stifles well bent; hocks well let down with short, strong rear pasterns. Legs straight when viewed from rear. Cow hocks, spread hocks, and sickle hocks to be faulted.

FEET. Medium size, round, compact, and well knuckled, with thick pads. Excess hair may be trimmed to show natural size and contour. Dewclaws on forelegs may be removed, but are normally left on. Splayed or hare feet to be faulted.

TAIL. Well set on, thick and muscular at the base, following the natural line of the croup. Tail bones extend to, but not below, the point of hock. Carried with merry action, level or with some moderate upward curve; never curled over back nor between legs.

COAT. Dense and water repellent with good undercoat. Outer coat firm and resilient, neither coarse nor silky, lying close to body; may be straight or wavy. Moderate feathering on back of forelegs and on under-body; heavier feathering on front of neck, back of thighs and underside of tail. Coat on head, paws, and front of legs is short and even. Excessive length, open coats, and limp, soft coats are very undesirable. Feet may be trimmed and stray hairs neatened, but the natural appearance of coat or outline should not be altered by cutting or clipping.

Am., Can. Ch. Russo's Pepperhill Poppy winning the Sporting Group at Staten Island in 1979, handled by Elliot More for Barbara and Jeffrey Pepper.

COLOR.   Rich, lustrous golden of various shades. Feathering may be lighter than rest of coat. With the exception of greying or whitening of face or body due to age, any white marking, other than a few white hairs on the chest, should be penalized according to its extent. Allowable light shadings are not to be confused with white markings. Predominant body color which is either extremely pale or extremely dark is undesirable. Some latitude should be given to the light puppy whose coloring shows promise of deepening with maturity. Any noticeable area of black or other off-color hair is a serious fault.

GAIT.   When trotting, gait is free, smooth, powerful, and well co-ordinated, showing good reach. Viewed from any position, legs turn neither in nor out, nor do feet cross or interfere with each other. As speed increases, feet tend to converge toward center line of balance. It is recommended that dogs be shown on a loose lead to reflect true gait.

SIZE.   Males 23-24 inches in height at withers; females 21½-22½ inches. Dogs up to one inch above or below standard size should be proportionately penalized. Deviation in height

The very famous Ch. Laurell's Especial Jason, handled by Bob Stebbins, showing off his excellence of type and quality.

Ch. Sir Duncan of Woodbury, at seven-and-a-half years of age, competing in the Sporting Group at Westminster. Breeder, Mrs. Robert Krause. Owner, Lynne Lounsbury.

Ch. Pepperhill East Point Airily, by Ch. Sir Duncan of Woodbury ex Ch. Pepperhill Return Ticket, winning the Sporting Group at Hartford in February 1982. In four months since this win, this lovely young bitch has earned ten-and-a-half Hall of Fame points, winning nine Bests of Opposite Sex, eleven Bests of Breed, one Group fourth, two Group thirds, one Group second and one Group first. She was bred by Barbara and Jeffrey Pepper, is handled by Linda and Elliot More, and belongs to Helene Geary and Dan Flavin, Wainscott, New York.

Ch. Mercer's Sweet William and Ch. Mercer's Morning Glory at Westminster in 1981, representing the Mercer's Goldens, Mercer Russo Ervin, owner.

of more than one inch from the standard shall disqualify. Length from the breastbone to point of buttocks slightly greater than height at withers in ratio of 12:11. Weight for dogs 65-75 pounds; bitches 55-65 pounds.

TEMPERAMENT. Friendly, reliable, and trustworthy. Quarrelsomeness or hostility towards other dogs or people in normal situations, or an unwarranted show of timidity or nervousness, is not in keeping with Golden Retriever character.

Such actions should be penalized according to their significance.

FAULTS. Any departure from the described ideal shall be considered faulty to the degree to which it interferes with the breed's purpose or is contrary to breed character.

This is the way we like to see a Golden move, with ideal reach and drive. Am., Can. Ch. Russo's Pepperhill Poppy, owned by Barbara and Jeffrey Pepper, with her handler Elliot More.

Ch. Wochica's Golden Jay, by Ch. Sunset's Happy Duke ex Champagne Lady of Wochica (Ch. Pathfinder of Lazy Pines ex Little Dawn of Chickasaw), a multiple Best of Breed-winner with Group placements, with Janet L. Bunce, breeder-owner-handler, Wochica Goldens.

DISQUALIFICATIONS. Deviation in height of more than one inch from standard either way. Undershot or overshot bite.

Ch. Camelot's Noble Fella, C.D.X., on the Florida Circuit in 1981, where he won seven Groups and three Bests in Show, going on to Group second at Westminster. Bob Stebbins, handler. Owners, Kay Bickford and Margaret Zonghetti.

Ch. Camelot's Noble Fella, C.D.X., Number One Golden of 1980, taking Best in Show at Staten Island for owners M. Zonghetti of Bradlyn Goldens and K. Bickford of Bickford Goldens. Handler, Bob Stebbins. Judge, John Stanek, who is presenting the award.

CHAPTER ELEVEN

Judging the Golden Retriever

by Mrs. Ludell L. Beckwith

Best of Breed at the Evergreen Golden Retriever Club Specialty, August 6th 1977, Am., Can. Ch. Beckwith's Nutmeg, Am. C.D.X., Can. C.D. Handled here by Mrs. Ludell L. Beckwith, co-owner with R.E. Beckwith. Nutmeg is a Golden Retriever Club of America Outstanding Dam.

Being a breeder-judge I have been invited to interpret the A.K.C. standard of the Golden Retriever and to offer some helpful suggestions to you who are approved to judge or aspire to judge Golden Retrievers or are breeders and exhibitors. Since our breed has become extremely popular, it is of utmost importance that judges and exhibitors be knowledgeable about our breed if we are to protect its future.

First, let's talk a bit about the word *standard*. The *American College Dictionary* defines the word *standard* as "anything taken by general consent as a basis of comparison: an approved model." When we consider this definition, we see that the A.K.C. standard is an official word picture of a perfect example of an ideal Golden Retriever. It is a target for breeders and judges—a bull's eye to aim for for true breed quality. The interpretation of the standard involves creating a mental image from words and comparing the dogs using this image as the gauge.

Judges should remember that the function of our breed serves as the basis for the breed standard. Our breed is a *retriever*. It is primarily a hunting dog with a definite *purpose of use*! Don't think of the Golden Retriever as merely a glamourous dog. He must be properly assembled if he is to have the stamina for strenuous hunting

in the field, have lasting power for swimming and buoyancy, and have a moderate coat which will not be a hindrance in the field. He must have a tractable, friendly, self-confident temperament to fulfill the duties required for his purpose of use.

Another pertinent word in dog terminology which I feel functions along with the term *standard* is *type*, which means "a group set apart by common characteristics, a general form or plan common to a group of animals." Type, then *is* the standard—the description of the breed based upon the purpose of use. A dog which most closely resembles its standard, both in disposition and appearance, and which is most typical of a specific kind of dog developed for a particular purpose has type.

The dog which is typical of its breed, then, is not exaggerated. He is in such perfect balance that your eye notes a smooth, functional dog whose every part seems proper. He is completely balanced and his purpose of use is maintained. This dog will catch the expert's eye because he embodies the breed's heart and character; he is truly a living example of the ideal Golden.

When judging Golden Retrievers, type should be of paramount importance, so select the most typical Goldens and from these choose the most sound.

Ch. Billaura's Mariah's Ruffian, here taking Best of Winners at Central Florida in 1981, finished shortly thereafter by taking Best of Breed from the classes at Grand Rapids. Handled by Linda Stebbins for owners, John and Midge Jones.

Soundness is another word which we consistently use in speaking about dogs. In dog terminology this means a dog who has all his physical parts in their proper place and who functions as nature intended. This means a dog who moves properly and vigorously and can see, hear, and scent—a dog who wants to do all these things. His disposition should be alert, poised, and cooperative.

The first impression that you receive when Goldens enter a judging ring should be one of confident, symmetrical, powerful dogs that are well balanced and short-coupled with rich lustrous golden coats of various shades. Remember that a Golden Retriever's "over-all appearance, balance, gait and purpose [are] to be given more emphasis than any of his component parts."

As you begin to judge you will note differences in individual features and conformation. Examine these differences point by point. Evaluate the virtues and the faults, determining which dog has more virtues and thus most closely conforms to the ideal standard.

Now, let's consider some specific points of the standard.

Balance is mentioned in the very first paragraph of our standard and is closely related to the size and lines of the dog.

The proportion of the Golden Retriever is very important. The dog's height from the withers to the ground should be 11/12 of the length of the dog from breastbone to the point of the buttocks.

Not only must the Golden Retriever be in correct proportion, but he must also be within specific height limits, as described in detail in the standard. Measure any dog if you question its height.

These size limits have been set to keep the Golden in proper size to perform his work most efficiently and yet large and powerful enough to be used in rough hunting terrain and water. He must be able to carry a heavy duck or pheasant and yet small and agile enough to get into a blind or duck boat.

Lines are important when you observe the profile of the Golden. The dog must exhibit balance between the front and rear assemblies, display adequate reach of neck, and have a head which is in proper proportion to the body. All of these lines must fit together into a balanced, well-proportioned outline.

Ch. Golden Pine's Brown Bear with Lloyd M. Case.

Ch. Peachy's Happy Lady of Charms, C.D., has twelve Bests of Opposite Sex to her brother Am., Can. Ch. Peachy's Technical Knockout. Both belong to Virginia A. Boyle, Charms Goldens, Joppa, Maryland.

The judge approaches to examine Ch. Cummings' Dame Pepperhill, very nicely set up and at attention for her handler, Elliot More. Note all four feet are correctly placed, and a taut lead shows off correct neck and topline. Barbara and Jeffrey Pepper, owners.

The *head*, with its soft, kindly expression and dark eyes, is the hallmark of our lovely breed. As you look at the Golden from the front, check his face and note the wide skull. The muzzle in profile should be nearly as long as the skull and should be straight and slightly deeper and wider at the stop than it is at the tip. There should be a good stop. Level planes are desirable.

The nose and eye rims should be dark brown or black. A lighter nose shade in winter should not be faulted. The eyes should be medium large and should be medium brown or black with a kindly, intelligent, alert expression. Slanted or triangular-shaped eyes should be faulted, and dogs which display evidence of eyelid or eyelash abnormality should be excused from the ring.

When checking the teeth, the judge should look for a scissors bite and full dentition. Several missing teeth, producing an obvious gap, should be faulted.

The short ears can be checked for correct size by pulling the ear forward and seeing if the tip just covers the entire eye.

The *neck* is succinctly described in the standard, and nothing need be added here.

The *body* of the Golden should be judged, at least partially, by using the hands-on method. A judge should not be misled by heavy feathering on the chest but be aware of the real structure underneath. Take your hand and feel back into the coat. Is the sternum adequate? Is the forechest well developed? Does the brisket extend down to the elbow? Is the chest the proper width? It is necessary to use your hands to make certain of each of these properties.

Ch. Cummings' Dame Pepperhill looking her best as the judge approaches from the rear. Elliot More handling for Barbara and Jeffrey Pepper.

The ribs should be "long and well sprung but not barrel shaped, extending well towards hindquarters." The loin should be "short, muscular, wide and deep, with very little tuck-up." Check and see if the back is strong and level from the withers to a slightly sloping croup. The backline should be level whether the dog is standing or moving.

The descriptions of the *forequarters* and *hindquarters* in the standard are very clear and need not be repeated here. Judges should check for angulation in the front quarter assembly; and when the stifle angle is checked, the muscle on the thighs should also be checked to see if the dog is in hard condition.

The *feet* should be medium-sized and should appear to be cat-pawed.

The *tail* should exhibit a "merry action" and be carried level with the back with only a "moderate upward curve." Long feathering on the tail must, at times, be shaped slightly because if the feathering on the tail is much longer than the tail bone (which should reach the point of the hock), the dog will appear to be out of balance.

The judge here is checking the shoulders and withers of Pepperhill's Ticket Taker, well handled by Jeffrey Pepper, co-owner with Barbara Pepper.

Ch. Laurell's Happy Go Lucky, C.D.X., by Ch. Laurell's Allspice ex Ch. Duckdown's Veronica Laker, C.D. Bred by Thomas C. Kling and Laura Ellis Kling and owned by Barbara Kuban.

The *color* is what makes our Goldens so beautiful and appealing to observe. The shades may range from blond or honey-colored to a rich copper; and the feathering under the tail, pants, and belly may be a lighter shade—this makes a very striking combination. Although white markings are certainly not desirable, the color of some Goldens does whiten or become gray due to age; and this whitening or graying is allowable. Judges should be aware, however, that some Goldens gray at an early age, so graying is not necessarily indicative of an elderly dog.

The *coat* should be of moderate length, and a dense, water-repellent undercoat is desirable. It should, however, be noted that the undercoat is sometimes lacking in hot weather as the Golden may shed it in the summer heat; otherwise, the coat should appear as described in the standard.

Gait is a small but very complex and vital word. When judging gait from the side, you should look for smooth transition, animation, angulation, and the working relationship of the body as a whole. From the side, you see the dog's topline, contour of croup, depth of body, and tuck-up—all work together to create a balanced picture. The dog should maintain his longitudinal stability by his head and neck carriage with assistance from his tail movement, general angulation, and musculature; all of these influence the dog's overall reach and extension.

This is how we like a Golden to move. Ch. Sun Dance's Rarue in 1976 competing in a Sporting Group. Handled by his co-owner Bill Worley.

Am., Can., Bda. Ch. Chebaco's Mooselookmeguntic in action in the show ring. Owned by Jeffrey and Judith Gowing.

Am., Can. Ch. Fox Rock Sutter Creek Ulanda, by Ch. Imvubu Thembalisha, C.D., ex Ch. Fox Rock's Brunhilde, was bred by Mary Merchant. Owner-handler, Susan Breakell, Sutter Creek Kennels.

Style and *elegance* are attributes which are desirable but not actually written into the standard. I feel that style is a quality attendant to proper movement. It applies to superior manner and action. It's like the icing on a cake; it indicates a special distinction. Elegance is "presence" in the show ring; it is polish—an expression of harmony and symmetry.

The quality Golden Retriever is one which combines all these attributes: purpose of use, balance and lines, proper temperament, and style and elegance. We see many dogs which have one or two of these attributes, but the goal for breeders and judges is to find the dog that combines them all and is truly a quality Golden Retriever!

The judge or breeder of Goldens does more than influence the breed today. What the judge or breeder selects today will influence the breed tomorrow and for posterity. By our choices, we make a statement about our interpretation of the standard. Broad spectrums or variations appear in the ring because of the breeder's creativity and selection process which in turn may bring out exaggerations of or digressions from the standard.

Breeders and exhibitors must realize that the judge can pass judgment only on what is presented to him in the show ring. You determine which dogs are brought into the ring for critiquing.

Above left: Gosling's Precious Peronele wins a first in Puppy at the Long Island Golden Retriever Club Match, April 4th 1981. Bob Stebbins handled for owner Kay Gosling. Judge, Tom Gately. **Above right:** Ch. Laurell's York, by Ch. Gold-Rush Lightnin' ex Ch. Laurell's Kilimanjaro, winning the Sporting Group at Louisville in 1981. Bobby Barlow handling. Bred and owned by Thomas C. Kling and Laura Ellis Kling. **Below:** Marcia del Cammann is the owner of this Golden, High Farms Autumn Haze, handled here by Ed Larsen to Best of Winners at the Langley Kennel Club Dog Show. Mrs. Janet Churchill, judge.

Above: Ch. Moreland's Major Sam, C.D., taking Best of Breed from the Open Dog Class, Trenton Kennel Club, May 1972. Judge, Raymond Beale. Terry Correll handling for William C. Prentiss. **Left:** Ch. Laurell's Katie Did or Didn't, winning at Agathon Kennel Club, 1978, under judge Ed Bracy. Owned by Thomas C. Kling and Laurell Ellis Kling, Laurell Kennels.

We expect the judge to analyze what is presented to him, to be well informed, and to be able confidently to sort out the dogs which are exaggerated from those which are well within the standard, dogs which are so balanced and harmonious that they provide a living example of the standard, dogs which are so appealing, legitimate, and acceptable that they warrant the comment: "What a quality Golden—so typey, balanced, and sound!"

A very special picture for Nancy Dallaire, taken at Greenwich Kennel Club, 1981, immediately after her Golden bitch, Ch. Cloverdale Twin-Beau-D Joy, had won Best of Breed over sixty-two Goldens, including eleven Specials. Snapped by a ringsider.

CHAPTER TWELVE

Showing Your Golden

Ch. Russo's Cummings' Elsa taking Winners Bitch at Mid-Hudson Kennel Club in 1972. Mercer Russo Ervin, owner.

The groundwork for showing your Golden has been accomplished with your careful selection and purchase of your future show prospect. If it is a puppy, we assume that you have gone through all the proper preliminaries of good care, which actually should be the same whether the puppy is a pet or a future show dog, with a few extra precautions in the case of the latter.

General Considerations

Remember that a winning dog must be kept in trim, top condition. You want him neither too fat nor too thin, so do not spoil his figure and his appearance, or his appetite for proper nourishing food, by allowing family members or guests to be constantly feeding him "goodies." The best "treat" of all is a small wad of ground raw beef or the packaged dog "goodies." To be avoided are ice cream, potato chips, cookies, cake, candy, and other fattening items which will cause the dog to gain weight. A dog in show condition must never be fat, nor must he be painfully thin to the point of his ribs fairly sticking through the skin.

The importance of temperament and showmanship cannot possibly be overemphasized. These two qualities have put many a mediocre dog across, while lack of them can ruin the career of an otherwise outstanding specimen. So, from the day your dog or puppy arrives home, socialize him. Keep him accustomed to being with people and to being handled by people. Encourage your friends and relatives to "go over" him as the judges will in the ring, so that at the shows this will not be a strange, upsetting experience. Practice showing his "bite" (the manner in which his teeth meet) deftly and quickly. It is quite simple to spread the lips apart with your fingers, and the puppy should be accustomed and willing to accept this from you or from the judge, without struggle.

Take your future show dog with you in the car, so that he will love riding and not become carsick when he travels. He should associate going in the car with pleasure and attention. Take him where it is crowded: downtown, shopping malls, or, in fact, anywhere you go where dogs are permitted. Make the expeditions fun for him by frequent petting and words of praise; do not just ignore him as you go about your errands or other business.

Do not overly shelter your future show dog. Instinctively you may want to keep him at home, especially while a young puppy, where he is safe from germs or danger; but this can be foolish on two counts. To begin with, a dog kept away from other dogs or other environments builds up

Golden brothers, owned by Jennifer Kesner, waiting expectantly in the car.

Above: Ch. Pepperhill's Jake O'Richmaur, owned by Maureen Leary, handsomely "set up" as a Golden should be for the judge's eye. **Below:** In the ring at the Golden Retriever Club of America National Specialty in 1975, Mercer Russo Ervin at the head of the line gaits with her Ch. Russo's Wildwood Flower.

no natural immunity against all the things with which he will come in contact at the dog shows. Actually it is wiser to keep him well up-to-date on all protective "shots" and then allow him to become accustomed to being among other dogs and dog owners. Also, a dog who never goes among people, to strange places, or among strange dogs, may grow up with a timidity of spirit that will cause you deep problems when his show career gets under way.

Assuming that you will be handling the dog personally, or even if he will be professionally handled, it is important that a few moments of each day be spent practicing dog show routine. Practice "stacking," or "setting him up," as you have seen the exhibitors do at the shows you've attended, and teach him to hold this position once you have him stacked to your satisfaction. Make the learning pleasant by being firm but lavish in your praise when he behaves correctly. Work in front of a mirror for setting up practice; this enables you to see the dog as the judge does and to learn what corrections need to be made by looking at the dog from that angle.

Teach your Golden to gait at your side at a moderate rate of speed on a loose lead. When you have mastered the basic essentials at home, then look for and join a training class for future work and polishing up your technique. Training classes are sponsored by show-giving clubs in many areas, and their popularity is steadily increasing. If you have no other way of locating

one, perhaps your veterinarian may know of one through some of his clients; but if you are sufficiently aware of the dog show world to want a show dog, you will probably be personally acquainted with other fanciers who will share information of this sort with you.

Accustom your show dog to being in a crate (which you should be doing, even if the dog is to be only a pet). He should be kept in the crate "between times" for his own well-being and safety.

A show dog's teeth must be kept clean and free of tartar. Hard dog biscuits can help toward this. If tartar does accumulate, see that it is removed promptly by your veterinarian. Bones are not suitable for show dogs once they have their second teeth as they tend to damage and wear down the tooth enamel (bones are all right for puppies, as they help with the teething process).

Match Shows

Your Golden Retriever's first experience in show ring procedure should be at match show competition. There are several reasons for this. First of all, this type of event is intended as a learning experience for both the puppies and for the exhibitors; thus you will feel no embarrassment if your puppy misbehaves or if your own handling technique is obviously inept. There will be many others in that same position. So take the puppy and go, and the two of you can learn together what it is like actually to compete against other dogs for the approval of the judge.

Another reason for beginning a show career at match shows is the matter of cost. Entries at the point shows nowadays cost over ten dollars. True, there are many clubs who reduce this fee by a few dollars for the Puppy Classes (but by no means do all of them), but even so it is silly to throw this amount away when you know full well your puppy will not yet have the ring presence to hold its own. For the match shows, on the other hand, the entry fee is usually less than five dollars, so using those shows as a learning ground for you and your puppy certainly makes better sense. Another advantage of match shows is that advance entries for them are

Starkins Fallon, by Ch. Gold Coast Here Comes The Sun ex Faera's Rain Dance, winning Best in Match from the 2-4 Month Class. Owned by Wanda Metz, Starkin's Goldens.

seldom necessary, and even those clubs having them usually will accept additional entries the morning of the show. If you wake up feeling like taking the puppy for an outing, you can go right ahead. The entries at point shows, however, close about two-and-a-half weeks in advance.

Golden Retriever Puppy Kindergarten Class of the Yankee Golden Retriever Club, instructed by Jennifer Kesner. Goldens are started out as early as three months of age for this important phase of puppy training—early lessons in good manners. The first few months are a most important period in the puppy's life and should not be overlooked, and kindergarten training will put your Golden at a decided advantage over those who do not start to learn at this tender baby age.

You will find the judges more willing to discuss your puppy with you at a match show than during the day of a full and hectic point show; one of their functions, when officiating at a match, is to help new exhibitors with comments and suggestions. We might wish that we could do so at the point shows; but, generally speaking, our schedules do not permit this time to be taken. Unless you stay until the judge's working day is ended, it is often difficult to get even a few words with him. The informality of match shows makes it far easier to get a judge's verbal opinion there; and since judges at these events are usually professional handlers or already licensed judges who are working toward applying for additional breeds, the opinions should be knowledgeable and helpful.

As with training classes, information regarding match shows can be obtained from breeders in your area, your local kennel club if there is one, your veterinarian, or, of course, the person in charge of your training class, if you belong to one. The A.K.C. can also furnish this information; and if your local newspaper carries a pet column, announcements of such coming events will almost certainly appear there.

Goldtrak Wayward Gypsy Wind practicing a show stance. Photo courtesy of the Peppers.

Point Shows

Entries for American Kennel Club licensed or member point shows must be made in advance. This must be done on an official entry blank of the show-giving club and then filed either in person or by mail with the show superintendent (or show secretary) in time to reach the latter's office prior to the published closing date and hour or the filling of the advertised quota. These entries should be written out clearly and carefully, signed by the owner of the dog or his agent (your professional handler), and must be accompanied by the entry fee; otherwise they will not be accepted. Remember, it is not when the entry blank leaves your hands or is postmarked that counts but the time that the entry arrives at its destination. If you are relying on the postal system, bear in mind that it is not always reliable, and waiting until the last moment may cause your entry to arrive too late for acceptance. Leave yourself a bit of leeway by mailing *early*.

A dog must be entered at a dog show in the name of the actual owner at the time of entry closing date for that specific show. If a registered dog has been acquired by a new owner, it must be entered in the name of that new owner at any show for which entries close following the date of purchase, regardless of whether or not the new owner has actually received the registration certificate indicating that the dog is registered in the new owner's name. State on the entry form whether or not the transfer application has been mailed to the American Kennel Club, and it goes without saying that the latter should be promptly attended to when you purchase a registered dog.

Valhalla's Dr. Pepperhill at three-and-a-half months of age taking Best Puppy in Show at the Hudson Valley Specialty Match, May 1975, judged by Lyle Ring. By Am., Can. Ch. Cummings' Gold-Rush Charlie ex Ch. Valhalla's Amber Kate, C.D., Dr. Pepperhill was bred and owned by Jeffrey and Barbara Pepper. Handled, and now owned, by Kathy Liebler.

Bargello's Lollipop Tree, II, winning Best Puppy in Show at Le Club Canin Chateauguay Valley Kennel Club in July 1981. Barbara Tinker, owner.

When you fill out your entry blank, be sure to type, print, or write legibly, paying particular attention to the spelling of names, correct registration numbers, and so on. Sign your name as owner *exactly*—not one time as Jane Doe, another as Jane C. Doe, and another as Mrs. John Doe.

Puppy Classes are for dogs or bitches that are six months of age and under twelve months, were whelped in the United States, and are not champions. The age of a puppy is calculated up to and inclusive of the first day of a show you are entering. For example, the first day a dog whelped on January 1st is eligible to compete in a Puppy Class at a show is July 1st of the same year; and he may continue competing in Puppy Classes up to and including a show on December 31st of the same year, but he is *not* eligible to compete in a Puppy Class at a show held on or after January 1st of the following year.

The Puppy Class is the first one in which you should enter your puppy, for several reasons. To begin with, a certain allowance for behavior is made in recognition of the fact that they *are* puppies and lack show experience; a puppy who is immature or displays less than perfect ring manners will not be penalized so heavily as would be the case in an adult class such as Open. It is also quite likely that others in the Puppy Class will

be suffering from the same puppy problems as your own; all of the puppies will be pretty much on equal footing where age and ring assurance are concerned. A puppy shown in the same class with fully matured Goldens who are experienced in the show ring looks all the more young and inexperienced and thus is far less likely to gain the judge's admiration than in a class where it does not seem out of place. There are many good judges who will take a smashing good puppy right from the Puppy Class on through to Winners, but more often than not, this puppy started the day and was "discovered" by the judge right where it belonged, in the Puppy Class. Another bonus of using Puppy Class is the fact that numerous clubs offer a reduced entry fee to those competing in it; this certainly is beneficial because showing dogs is becoming increasingly expensive.

One word of caution on entering the Puppy Class: carefully check the classification, as in some cases it is divided into a 6-9 months old section and a 9-12 months old section; if this is the case you will have to ascertain that your puppy is entered in the correct section for the age he will be on the day of the show.

The Novice Class is for dogs six months of age and over, whelped in the United States or in Canada, who *prior to* the official closing date for

Birnam Woods Les Laurell, with nine points toward championship, is a son of Ch. Duckdown's Unpredictable, C.D., W.C. Owned by Laura Ellis Kling.

Ch. Pepperhill's Sam I Am at a dog show. Owned by Jeffrey and Barbara Pepper.

entries have *not* won three first prizes in the Novice Class, any first prize at all in the Bred-by-Exhibitor, American-bred, or Open Classes, or one or more points toward championship. The provisions for this class are confusing to many people, which is probably the reason it is so infrequently used. A dog may win any number of first prizes in the Puppy Class and still retain his eligibility for Novice. He may place second, third, or fourth not only in Novice on an unlimited number of occasions but also in Bred-by-Exhibitor, American-bred, or Open and still remain eligible for Novice. But he may no longer be shown in Novice when he has won three blue ribbons in that class, when he has won even one blue ribbon in either Bred-by-Exhibitor, American-bred, or Open, or even a single championship point.

In determining whether or not a dog is eligible for the Novice Class, keep in mind the fact that previous wins are calculated according to the official published date for closing of entries, not by the date on which you may actually have made the entry. So if, in the interim, between the time you made the entry and the official closing date, your dog makes a win causing it to become ineligible for Novice, change your class *immediately* to another for which your Golden will be eligible. The Novice Class always seems to have the fewest entries of any class, and therefore it is a splendid "practice ground" for you and your young Golden while you both are getting the "feel" of being in the ring.

Bred-by-Exhibitor Class is for dogs whelped in the United States or, if individually registered in the American Kennel Club Stud Book, for dogs whelped in Canada that are six months of age and over, are not champions, and are owned wholly or in part by the person or the spouse of the person who was the breeder or one of the breeders of record. Dogs entered in this class must be handled *in this class* by an owner or by a member of the immediate family of the owner. Members of an immediate family for this purpose are husband, wife, father, mother, son, daughter, brother, or sister. This is the class which is really the "breeder's showcase," the one which breeders should enter with special pride, to show off their achievements. It is *not necessary* for the winner of Bred-by-Exhibitor to be handled by an owner or a member of the owner's family in the Winners Class, where the dog or bitch *may be handled by whomsoever the exhibitor may choose*, including a professional handler.

The American-bred Class is for all dogs excepting champions, six months of age or older, who were whelped in the United States by reason of a mating which took place in the United States.

Ch. Laurell's Yolanda, by Ch. Gold-Rush Lightnin' ex Ch. Laurell's Kilimanjaro, was bred by Laurell Goldens and belongs to Judy Glasgow. Here taking points en route to the title.

Pepperhill Lochan Ora Sara, bred by Jeff and Barbara Pepper and owned by Betty Anderson, is close to the title. A double granddaughter of Ch. Cummings' Gold-Rush Charlie.

The Open Class is for any dog six months of age or older (this is the only restriction for this class). Dogs with championship points compete in it; dogs who are already champions can do so; dogs who are imported can be entered; and, of course, American-bred dogs compete in it. This class is, for some strange reason, the favorite of exhibitors who are "out to win." They rush to enter their pointed dogs in it, under the false impression that by so doing they assure themselves of greater attention from the judges. This really is not so; and it is my feeling that to enter in one of the less competitive classes, with a better chance of winning it and then getting a second crack at gaining the judge's approval by returning to the ring in the Winners Class, can often be a more effective strategy.

One does not enter for the Winners Class. One earns the right to compete in it by winning first prize in Puppy, Novice, Bred-by-Exhibitor, American-bred, or Open. No dog who has been defeated on the same day in one of these classes is eligible to compete in Winners, and every dog who has been a blue-ribbon winner in one of them and not defeated in any of the others *must* do so. Following the selection of the Winners Dog or the Winners Bitch, the dog or bitch receiving that award leaves the ring. Then the dog or bitch who placed second in the class, unless previously defeated by another dog or bitch at the same show, re-enters the ring to compete against the remaining first-prize winners for Reserve. The latter award means that the dog or bitch receiving it is standing by "in reserve" should the one that received Winners be disallowed through any technicality when the awards are checked at the American Kennel Club. In that case, the one that placed Reserve is moved up to Winners, at the same time receiving the appropriate championship points.

Winners Dog and Winners Bitch are the awards which carry points toward championship with them. The points are based on the number of dogs or bitches actually in competition; and the points are scaled one through five, the latter being the greatest number available to any dog or bitch at any one show. Three-, four-, or five-point wins are considered majors. In order to become a champion, a dog or bitch must win two majors under two different judges, plus at least one point from a third judge, and the additional points necessary to bring the total to fifteen. When your dog has gained fifteen points as described above, a certificate of championship will be issued to you, and your Golden's name will be published in the list of new champions which appears monthly in *Pure-Bred Dogs, American Kennel Gazette*, the official publication of the American Kennel Club.

The scale of championship points for each breed is worked out by the American Kennel Club and reviewed annually, at which time the number required in competition may be either changed (raised or lowered) or remain the same. The scale of points for all breeds is published annually in the May issue of the *Gazette*, and the current ratings for each breed within that area are published in every dog show catalog.

Ch. Gosling's Daystar Dawn, by Ch. Jolly October's Chevalier ex Ch. October's Foxy Lady, C.D., at sixteen months of age, winning a first major. Kay Gosling, owner.

Ch. Toryglen Yankee Trader, U.D.T., at twenty months of age, taking a four-point major at South Shore Kennel Club. By Featherquest Sutter Creek K.C. ex Toryglen Pembroke. Proud owner-handler, Alfred G. Rochefort, Coventry, Rhode Island.

When a dog or a bitch is adjudged Best of Winners, its championship points are, for that show, compiled on the basis of which sex had the greater number of points. If there are two points in dogs and four in bitches and the dog goes Best of Winners, then *both* the dog and the bitch are awarded an equal number of points, in this case four. Should the Winners Dog or the Winners Bitch go on to win Best of Breed, additional points are accorded for the additional Goldens defeated by so doing, provided, of course, that there were entries specifically for Best of Breed competition, or Specials, as these specific entries are generally called. If your dog or bitch takes Best of Opposite Sex after going Winners, points are credited according to the number of the same sex defeated in both the regular classes and Specials competition. Many a one- or two-point class win has grown into a major in this manner.

Above: Ch. Laurell's Whirlaway, by Ch. Sutter Creek Goldrush Flyboy ex Ch. Laurell's Yats of Luck, taking Winners Dog at Kingsport Kennel Club, April 1982. Bred and owned by Thomas C. Kling and Laura Ellis Kling, Laurell Kennels. **Below:** Portici's Whisper O'Wochica, by Ch. Cummings' Gold-Rush Charlie ex Ch. Wochica's Sandpiper, W.C., taking Best of Winners. Steven and Terry Pollard, owners. Photo courtesy of Janet Bunce.

Moving further along, should your Golden win the Sporting Group from the classes (in other words, if it has taken either Winners Dog or Winners Bitch, Best of Winners, and Best of Breed), you then receive points based on the greatest number of points awarded to any breed included within that Group during that show's competition. Should the dog's winning streak also include Best in Show, the same rule of thumb applies, and your Golden receives points equal to the highest number of points awarded to any other dog of any breed at that event.

Best of Breed competition consists of the Winners Dog and the Winners Bitch, who automatically compete on the strength of those awards, in addition to whatever dogs and bitches have been entered specifically for this class for which champions of record are eligible. Goldens who, according to their owner's records, have completed the required number of points for a championship after closing of entries for the show but whose championships are unconfirmed, may be transferred from one of the regular classes to the Best of Breed competition, provided this transfer is made by the show superintendent or show secretary *prior to the start of judging at the show.*

This has proven an extremely popular new rule, as under it a dog can finish on Saturday and then be transferred and compete as a Special on Sunday. It must be emphasized that the change *must* be made a half hour *prior* to the start of the day's judging, which means to the start of *any* judging at the show, not your individual breed.

This lovely Golden taking Winners Bitch belongs to Mrs. Phyllis Whiteside. Handled by William Trainor.

311

Ch. Givemhel Lucy Laurell, sired by Ch. Duckdown's Unpredictable, C.D., W.C., is owned by Stephanie J. Bechfelt, Milford, Ohio. Photo courtesy of Laurell Goldens.

In the United States, Best of Breed winners are entitled to compete in the Variety Group which includes them. This competition is not mandatory; it is a privilege which Golden exhibitors value. The dogs winning *first* in each Variety Group *must* compete for Best in Show.

Non-regular classes are sometimes included at the all-breed shows, and they are almost invariably included at Specialty shows. These include Stud Dog Class and Brood Bitch Class, which are judged on the quality of the offspring (usually two) accompanying the sire or dam. The quality of the latter two is beside the point; it is the youngsters that count, and the qualities of *both* are averaged to decide which sire or dam is the best and most consistent producer. Then there is the Brace Class (which, at all-breed shows, moves along to Best Brace in each Variety Group and then Best Brace in Show), which is

Ch. Sparkle's Plenty of Sun winning Best of Breed at Jacksonville, Florida in 1982. Bob Stebbins handling for Mr. and Mrs. Charles Bradley, Wilton, Connecticut.

Ch. Thistledue's Chance and Ch. Thistledue's Shining Star winning the Brace Class at the 1979 National Specialty, the first of three consecutive times these lovely dogs have taken this award at the National. Carter F. Foss, owner-handler.

Ch. Briarmoor's Gold Drummer finished in three shows and has Group placements to his credit although not campaigned as a Special. Owned by Briarmoor Goldens.

judged on the similarity and evenness of appearance of the two members of the brace. In other words, the Goldens should look like identical twins in size, color, and conformation and should move together almost as a single dog, one person handling with precision and ease. The same applies to the Team competition except that four dogs are involved and, if necessary, two handlers.

The Veterans Class is for the older dog, the minimum age of whom is usually seven years. This class is judged on the quality of the dogs, as the winner competes for Best of Breed and, on a number of occasions, has been known to win it. So the point is *not* to pick the oldest looking dog, as some seem to think, but the best specimen of the breed, exactly as throughout the regular classes.

Then there are Sweepstakes and Futurity Stakes, sponsored by many Specialty clubs, sometimes as part of their shows and sometimes as separate events. The difference between the two is that Sweepstakes entries usually include dogs and bitches from six to eighteen months of age, and entries are made at the usual time as others for the show, while for a Futurity the entries are bitches nominated when bred and the individual puppies entered at or shortly following their birth.

Ch. Thistledue's Shining Star was snapped by a newspaper reporter covering the show for the *Des Moines Free Press* as he was awarded the Sporting Group blue ribbon at the dog show there in September 1981. Owned and handled by Carter F. Foss.

313

Kevin Metz in Junior Showmanship with Dan-D-Dan, by Ch. Starkin's Dan-D-Dan Dazzler, at a Lorain County Match Show in 1979. Wanda Metz, owner.

Below: J.D. Wacker with D.J.'s Montana Kid's X-Rated, C.D., in the summer of 1981. **Right:** J.D. Wacker is a splendid example of the successful young Junior Handler, having trained and handled one of his dogs to a championship title, trained and handled another in obedience to a C.D. title, and is now working with a second one in obedience training.

Junior Showmanship

If there is a youngster in your family between the ages of ten and seventeen, I can suggest no better or more rewarding a hobby than having a Golden to show in Junior Showmanship competition. This is a marvelous activity for young people. It teaches responsibility, good sportsmanship, the fun of competition where one's own skills are the deciding factor of success, proper care of a pet, and how to socialize with other young folks. Any youngster may experience the thrill of emerging from the ring a winner and the satisfaction of a good job done well.

Your Golden is an outstandingly satisfactory breed of dog for Junior Showmanship competition. His amiability and desire to please make him cooperative, and his comparatively simple show preparation make him an easy dog for a youngster to keep looking well to take into the ring.

Goldens and juniors work well together, thus are often to be seen in the winners circle.

Entry in Junior Showmanship is open to any boy or girl who is at least ten years old and under seventeen years old on the day of the show. The Novice Junior Showmanship Class is open to youngsters who have not already won, at the time the entries close, three firsts in this class. Youngsters who have won three firsts in Novice

Ch. Bardfield's Lindsay Laurell owned by Pat Hardy (Haines), pictured winning Best Junior Handler at Westminster, 1970, judged by Frank Sabella. This is a daughter of Ch. Duckdown's Unpredictable, C.D., W.C.

may compete in the Open Junior Showmanship Class. Any junior handler who wins his third first-place award in Novice may participate in the Open Class at the same show, provided that the Open Class has at least one other junior handler entered in it. The Novice and Open Classes may be divided into Junior and Senior Classes. Youngsters between the ages of ten and twelve, inclusively, are eligible for the Junior division; and youngsters between thirteen and seventeen, inclusively, are eligible for the Senior division. Any of the foregoing classes may be separated into individual classes for boys and for girls. If such a division is made, it must be indicated on the premium list. The premium list also indicates the prize for Best Junior Handler, if such a prize is being offered at the show. Any youngster who wins a first in any of the regular classes may enter the competition for this prize, provided the youngster has been undefeated in any class at that show.

Junior Showmanship Classes, unlike regular conformation classes in which the dog's quality is judged, are judged entirely on the skill and ability of the junior handling the dog. Which dog is best is not the point—it is which youngster does the best job with the dog that is under consideration. Eligibility requirements for the dog being shown and other detailed information can be found in *Regulations for Junior Showmanship*, issued by the American Kennel Club.

A junior who has a dog that he or she can enter in both Junior Showmanship and conformation classes has twice the opportunity for success and twice the opportunity to get into the ring and work with the dog. Goldens and juniors work well together, and this combination has often wound up in the winner's circle.

At Westminster 1976, both brother and sister qualified for Junior Showmanship with their Goldens: Donald Sturz with Am., Can. Ch. Golden Glo's Valentine and Janet Sturz with Ch. Golden Glo's Marge.

Ch. Beckwith's Kopper Kavalier, C.D., by Ch. Mala-gold Beckwith Om K Ivan, takes Winners Dog at the Long Island Golden Retriever Club Specialty, April 1975. Owner, Elizabeth Jones. Handler, Susan Breakell.

Barbara Pepper here has Am., Can. Ch. Pepper-hill's Huggy Bear smartly at attention as she is "baited" with a tempting piece of liver or other favorite snack. Barbara and Jeffrey Pepper, owners.

Pre-Show Preparation

Preparation of the things you will need as a Golden exhibitor should not be left until the last moment. They should be planned and arranged for at least several days before the show in order for you to relax and be calm as the countdown starts.

The importance of the crate has already been discussed, and we assume it is already in use. Of equal importance is the grooming table, which we are sure you have already acquired for use at home. You should take it along with you, as your dog will need final touches before entering the ring. If you do not have one yet, folding tables with rubber tops are made specifically for this purpose and can be purchased from the concession booths found at most dog shows. Then you will need a sturdy tack box (also available at the show's concessions) in which to carry your brush, comb, scissors, nail clippers, whatever you use for last minute clean-up jobs, cotton swabs, first-aid equipment, and anything else you are in the habit of using on the dog, such as a leash or two of the type you prefer, some well-cooked and dried-out liver or any of the small packaged "dog treats" your dog likes for use as "bait" in the ring, and a turkish towel.

Take a large thermos or cooler of ice, the biggest one you can accommodate in your vehicle, for use by "man and beast." Take a jug of water (there are lightweight, inexpensive ones available at all sporting goods shops) and a water dish. If you plan to feed the dog at the show, or if you and the dog will be away from home more than one day, bring food from home so that he will have the type to which he is accustomed.

You may or may not have an exercise pen. Personally, I think that one is a *must*, even if you have only one dog. While the shows do provide areas for exercise of the dogs, these are among the best places to come into contact with any ill-nesses that may be going around, and I feel that having a pen of your own for your dog's use is excellent protection. Such a pen can be used in other ways, too, such as a place other than the crate in which to put the dog to relax and a place in which the dog can exercise at rest areas or motels during your travels. A word of caution: never tie a dog to an exercise pen or leave him unattended in it while you wander off, as the pens are not sufficiently secure to keep the dog there should he decide to leave, at least not in most cases. Exercise pens are also available at the

Pepperhill's Repeat of Zagern taking Best of Winners at Wilmington, 1982. Jeffrey Pepper handling for Ann and Robert Hall, Agawam, Massachusetts.

Lochan Ora Ragtime Bear, an owner-handled homebred known as "Bingo," became a Canadian champion in his first three shows, two from the Puppy Class. By Ch. Westben's Dancing Bear ex Lochan Ora Glory-Be, he is a double grandson of Ch. Cummings' Gold-Rush Charlie. Bred by Connie M. Harris. Owned by Elizabeth M. Anderson, Connie M. Harris, and Christine Jones.

dog show concession booths should you not already have yours when you reach the dog's first show. They come in a variety of heights and sizes.

Bring along folding chairs for the members of your party, unless all of you are fond of standing, as these are almost never provided by the show-giving clubs. Have your name stamped on the chairs so there will be no doubt as to whom the chairs belong. Bring whatever you and your family enjoy for drinks or snacks in a picnic basket or cooler, as show food, in general, is expensive and usually not great. You should always have a pair of boots, a raincoat, and a rain hat with you (they should remain permanently in your vehicle if you plan to attend shows regularly), as well as a sweater, a warm coat, and a change of shoes. A smock or big cover-up apron will assure that you remain tidy as you prepare the dog for the ring. Your overnight case should include a small sewing kit for emergency repairs, headache and indigestion remedies, and any personal products or medications you normally use.

In your car you should always carry maps of the area where you are headed and an assortment of motel directories. Generally speaking, we have found that Holiday Inns are the friendliest about taking dogs. Some Ramadas and some Howard Johnsons do so cheerfully (the Ramadas indicate on each listing in their directory whether or not pets are welcome). Best Western usually frowns on pets (not all of them but enough to make it necessary to find out which do). Some of the smaller chains welcome pets. The majority of privately owned motels do not.

Have everything prepared the night before the show to expedite your departure. Be sure that the dog's identification and your judging program and other show information are in your purse or briefcase. If you are taking sandwiches, have them ready. Anything that goes into the car the night before will be one thing less to be concerned with in the morning. Decide upon what you will wear and have it out and ready. If there is any question in your mind about what to wear, try on the possibilities before the day of the show; don't risk feeling you may want to change when you see yourself dressed a few moments prior to departure time! In planning your outfit, wear something simple that will make an attractive background for your Golden, providing contrast to his color, calling attention to the *dog* rather than to yourself. Sports clothes always seem to look best at a dog show. What you wear on your feet is important, as many types of flooring are slippery, and wet grass, too, can present a hazard as you move the dog. Make it a rule to wear rubber soles and low or flat heels in the ring, so that you can move along smartly.

Your final step in pre-show preparation is to leave yourself plenty of time to reach the show that morning. Traffic can get extremely heavy as one nears the immediate vicinity of the show, finding a parking place can be difficult, and other delays may occur. You'll be in better humor if you can take it all in your stride without the pressure of watching every second because you figured the time too closely.

Am., Can. Ch. Russo's Pepperhill Poppy winning the breed at Old Dominion, 1980. Elliot More handling for Barbara and Jeffrey Pepper.

Ch. Mercer's Morning Glory at Staten Island 1980. Mercer Russo Ervin, owner.

Day of the Show

From the moment of your arrival at the dog show until after your Golden has been judged, keep foremost in your mind the fact that he is your purpose for being there. You will need to arrive in advance of the judging in order to give him a chance to exercise after the trip to the show and take care of personal matters. A dog arriving in the ring and immediately using it for an exercise pen hardly makes a favorable impression on the judge. You will also need time to put the final touches on your dog, making certain that he goes into the ring looking his very best.

When you reach ringside, ask the steward for your arm-card with your Golden's entry number on it and anchor it firmly into place on your arm with the elastic provided. Make sure that you are where you should be when your class is called. The fact that you have picked up your arm-card does not guarantee, as some seem to think, that the judge will wait for you more than a minute or two. Judges are expected to keep on schedule, which precludes delaying for the arrival of exhibitors who are tardy.

October's Bargello Diamond, owned by Barbara Tinker, Bargello Goldens.

On the left is Mercer Russo Ervin's bitch, Russo's Wildwood Flower and on the right, representing Springfield Farms, is Ch. Cummings' Gold-Rush Charlie, snapped informally at a dog show.

Even though you may be nervous, assume an air of cool, collected calm. Remember that this is a hobby to be enjoyed, so approach it in that state of mind. The dog will do better, too, as he will be quick to reflect your attitude.

If you make a mistake while presenting the dog, don't worry about it—next time you'll do better. Do not be intimidated by the more expert or experienced exhibitors. After all, they, too, were once newcomers.

Always show your Golden with an air of pride. An apologetic attitude on the part of the exhibitor does little to help the dog win, so try to appear self-confident as you gait and set up the dog.

The judging routine usually starts when the judge asks that the dogs be gaited in a circle around the ring. During this period the judge is watching each dog as it moves along, noting style, topline, reach and drive, head and tail carriage, and general balance. This is the time to keep your mind and your eye on your dog, moving him at his most becoming gait and keeping your place in line without coming too close to the dog ahead of you. Always keep your dog on the inside of the circle, between yourself and the judge, so that the judge's view of the dog is unobstructed.

Calmly pose the dog when requested to set up for examination. If you are at the head of the line and many dogs are in the class, do not stop halfway down the end of the ring and begin stacking the dog. Go forward enough so that sufficient space is left for the other dogs. Simple courtesy demands that we be considerate and give others a chance to follow the judge's instructions, too.

Space your Golden so that on all sides of the dog the judge will have room in which to make

Ch. Pepperhill's Peter Principle is first in line in this beautiful class of Goldens. Handled by Tom Tobin for Myra Moldawsky and Jeff Pepper.

Ch. Gold-Rush Lightnin', owned by R. Ann and Larry Johnson.

Ch. Gold-Rush Sweet Betsy, daughter of Ch. Cummings' Gold-Rush Charlie, owned by Craig Westergaard, Greensboro, North Carolina.

Am., Can. Ch. Pepperhill's Huggy Bear being "gone over" by the judge. Barbara Pepper handling.

Ch. Laurell's Heather of the Moor, U.D., owned by Ralph and Connie Ward and bred by Thomas C. Kling and Laura Ellis Kling. Sired by Ch. Laurell's Allspice, C.D., ex Ch. Duckdown's Veronica Laker, C.D.

his examination; this means that there must be sufficient room between each of the dogs for the judge to move around. Time is important when you are setting up your Golden, so practice in front of a full-length mirror at home, trying to accustom yourself to "getting it all together" correctly in the shortest possible time. When you set up your Golden, you want his forelegs well under the dog, feet directly below the elbows, toes pointing straight ahead, and hindquarters extended *correctly*, not overdone (stretched too far behind) or with the hind feet further forward than they should be. It is customary to remove the lead, dropping it beside you, when you set up a Golden. Hold the dog's head up with your hand at the back inner corner of the lips, your left hand extending the tail to its proper position. You want the dog to look "all of a piece," head carried proudly on a strong neck, correct topline, hindquarters nicely angulated, the front straight and true, and the dog standing firmly up on his feet.

Listen carefully as the judge instructs the manner in which the dog is to be gaited, whether it is straight down and straight back; down the ring, across, and back; or in a triangle. The latter has become the most popular pattern with the majority of judges. "In a triangle" means down the outer side of the ring to the first corner, across that end of the ring to the second corner, and then back to the judge from the second corner,

Ch. Laurell's Travlin' In Style, by Ch. Southern's Gold-Rush Travler ex Ch. Laurell's Kilimanjaro. Owned by Janet and Laurin Howard.

Ch. Laurell's Yours Truly, owned by Vicki Siegel and Laura Ellis Kling and bred by the Klings, is a daughter of Ch. Gold-Rush Lightnin' and Ch. Laurell's Kilimanjaro.

using the center of the ring in a diagonal line. Please learn to do this pattern without breaking at each corner to twirl the dog around you, a senseless maneuver we sometimes have noted. Judges like to see the dog move in an *uninterrupted* triangle, as they get a better idea of the dog's gait.

It is impossible to overemphasize that the gait at which you move your Golden is tremendously important, and considerable thought and study should be given to the matter. At home, have someone move the dog for you at different speeds so that you can tell which shows him off to best advantage. Your Golden should travel with powerful reach and drive, head up, and tail an extension of the firm, unbroken topline. Galloping or racing around the ring is out of character for a Golden and unbecoming to almost any dog.

Do not allow your Golden to sidetrack, flop, or weave as you gait him, and do not let him pull so that he appears to lean on the lead as you are gaiting him. He should move in a straight line, displaying strength and power. That is your goal as you work with him on a lead in preparation for his show career.

Ch. Pepperhill's Peter Principle coming at you as a Golden should. Owned by Myra Moldawsky and Jeff Pepper, Peter is at Ashwel Goldens.

Baiting your dog should be done in a manner which does not upset the other Goldens in the ring or cause problems for their handlers. A tasty morsel of well-cooked and dried-out liver is fine for keeping your own dog interested, but discarded on the ground or floor, it can throw off the behavior of someone else's dog who may attempt to get it. So please, if you drop liver on the ground, pick it up and take it with you when you have finished.

When the awards have been made, accept yours courteously, no matter how you may actually feel about it. To argue with a judge is unthinkable, and it will certainly not change the decision. Be gracious, congratulate the winners if your dog has been defeated, and try not to show your disappointment. By the same token, please be a gracious winner; this, surprisingly, sometimes seems to be even more difficult.

If you already show your Golden, if you plan on being an exhibitor in the future, or if you simply enjoy attending dog shows, there is a book, written by me, which you will find to be an invaluable source of detailed information about all aspects of show dog competition. This book is *Successful Dog Show Exhibiting* (T.F.H. Publications, Inc.) and is available wherever the one you are now reading was purchased.

Ch. Pepperhill Sam I Am at Rockland County in 1968, handled by Bob Forsyth for owners Jeffrey and Barbara Pepper, Pepperhill Farms.

John R. Mier, staff writer for the *St. Joseph Gazette*, has sent us this photo snapped by him showing the excellent form in which Ch. Thistledue's Shining Star is posed for the judge's examination by owner-handler Carter Foss. The Best in Show judge is approaching from the rear to examine the dog. See the photos on the facing page for the result.

Ch. Mercer's Morning Glory "baiting" in the show ring. Morning Glory is a daughter of Ch. Gold-Rush's Great Teddy Bear ex Ch. Russo's Cummings' Elsa. Breeder-owner, Mercer Russo Ervin.

Right: The thrill of victory! Note the mutual happiness of Carter Foss and Ch. Thistledue's Shining Star as they congratulate each other on Star's just being awarded Best in Show at St. Joseph Kennel Club. Photo catching the occasion by John R. Mier, a staff writer who had been assigned to cover the show for the *St. Joseph Gazette*.

Below: Carter Foss proudly presents Ch. Thistledue's Shining Star to the camera moments after being adjudged Best in Show at St. Joseph, Missouri. Photo courtesy of John R. Mier, staff writer for the *St. Joseph Gazette*.

Laurell's Riva Ridge, by Ch. Sutter Creek Goldrush Flyboy ex Ch. Laurell Yats of Luck, taking Winners at Dayton Kennel Club, 1982. Bred and owned by Thomas C. Kling and Laura Ellis Kling, Laurell Goldens.

Ch. Pepperhill's Bonni Valentine, C.D., taking Winners Bitch at Potomac Valley Golden Retriever Club, 1982. Handled by Barbara Pepper. Co-owned by Diane Dorry and Barbara and Jeffrey Pepper.

Ch. Laurell's Travlin' My Way, C.D., by Ch. Southern Gold-Rush Travler ex Ch. Laurell's Kilimanjaro. Bred and owned by Thomas C. Kling and Laura Ellis Kling.

Am., Can. Ch. Peachy's Technical Knockout, Best of Breed at Chenango Valley in 1982, is one of the handsome Goldens owned by Ginny Boyle, Charms Goldens, Joppa, Maryland.

Ch. Laurell's Yasmine of Jenesi, by Ch. Gold-Rush Lightnin', finishing title at Muncie Kennel Club in 1981 by taking Best of Opposite Sex. Bred by Thomas C. Kling and Laura Ellis Kling and owned by Judy Glasgow, Athens, Ohio.

Above: Ch. Sutter Creek Laurell Ruffian, by Ch. Sutter Creek Goldrush Playboy ex Ch. Laurell Yats of Luck, taking Winners Dog at Windham County Kennel Club, 1982. Bred by Thomas C. Kling and Laura Ellis Kling and owned by Susan Breakell. **Below:** Am., Can. Ch. Russo's Pepperhill Poppy taking Best of Breed at Mohawk Valley Kennel Club in 1980. Elliot More handling for Barbara and Jeffrey Pepper.

Above: Ch. Laurell's Secretariat, by Ch. Sutter Creek Goldrush Flyboy ex Ch. Laurell Yats of Luck. Bred and owned by Thomas C. Kling and Laura Ellis Kling. Bob Stebbins, handling. **Below:** Ch. Laurell's Jubilant Katie, C.D.X., also bred and owned by Thomas C. Kling and Laura Ellis Kling, Laurell Goldens.

Right: Ch. Laurell Yats of Luck, by Ch. Gold-Rush Lightnin' ex Ch. Laurell's Kilimanjaro. Owned by Thomas C. Kling and Laura Ellis Kling, Laurell Goldens. Janet Churchill, judge.

Below: Ch. Laurell's Honor's Grubstake, C.D., one of the splendid Goldens representing Laurell Kennels, Thomas C. Kling and Laura Ellis Kling.

Above: Ch. Georgia's Gran Prix, C.D., a son of Ch. Alstone Sutter Creek Charade, owned by Georgia Boyce.

Left: Ch. Pepperhill's Sam-I-Am, handled by Bob Forsyth for Barbara and Jeffrey Pepper.

Facing page: Can., Bda. Ch. Nanno Chrys-haefen Son of Skye, C.D., in 1976 at Elgin County. By Can., Bda. Ch. Skylon Lancelot ex Ch. Candace of Nanno, C.D. Owners, Jennifer and Ian McAuley of Canada.

ELGIN COUNTY
KENNEL CLUB 1976

GROUP 2nd

HAMON PHOTO

Ch. Laurell's Travlin' Alone, by Ch. Southern's Gold-Rush Travler ex Ch. Laurell's Kilimanjaro. Bred and owned by Thomas C. Kling and Laura Ellis Kling.

Ch. Sandy Hill's Wochica's Jenny, a multiple Specialty Best of Opposite Sex-winner, owned, handled, and loved by Mary E. Tompkins. Photo courtesy of Janet Bunce.

Ch. Pepperhill Allison Charlen, co-owned by Charles Ingher and Pepperhill Farms, taking Best of Winners at Mohawk Valley in 1980. Jeffrey Pepper handling.

Ch. Mercer's Morning Glory takes Best of Opposite Sex at Springfield in 1980. Mercer Russo Ervin, owner.

Ch. Wochica's Symphony, by Ch. Gold-Rush's Great Teddy Bear ex Ch. Wochica's Sandpiper, W.C., with Janet L. Bunce, Wochica Goldens.

Ch. Willow Lane's Sunswept Luke is owned by Mr. and Mrs. Charles Bradley, Wilton, Connecticut.

Ch. Copper Kettle's Headliner, known as "Clyde," is one of the many splendid Goldens owned by Donald Sturz. Bob Stebbins is handling here.

Sutter Creek's Ram Charger, litter-brother to Can. Ch. Sutter Creek's Crispy Critter, bred, owned, and handled by Susan Breakell, Sutter Creek Kennels.

Valhalla's Autumn Mist at the Long Island Golden Retriever Club Specialty in April 1974. Owner-handled by Kathy Liebler.

Russo's Wildwood Flower, by Ch. Misty Morn's Sunset, C.D., ex Ch. Russo's Cummings' Elsa, gained her championship with four majors within a month. Breeder-owner, Mercer Russo Ervin.

Ch. Westmont's Goldrush Dynamite, owned by Howard and Carol Falberg, Westport, Connecticut. Bob Stebbins, handling.

Ch. Laurell's Travlin' Too Far, by Ch. Southern's Gold-Rush Travler ex Ch. Laurell's Kilimanjaro, was bred by Thomas C. Kling and Laura Kling. Owned by John Freed, III.

Am., Can. Ch. Valhalla's Amber Waves at Mid-Hudson in 1975. Kathy and Larry Liebler, owners, Valhalla Farms.

Am., Can. Ch. Wylwind Tobey, Am., Can. C.D., by Am., Can. Ch. Meadowpond Dustin Sugarbear ex Topbrass Ruffian's Heide, belongs to Bruce and Ruth Wylie, Wylwind Goldens.

Ch. Copper Kettle's Society Page, W.C., handled by Marilyn Sturz to her title. Golden Glo Kennels, Marilyn and Don Sturz.

Ch. Sir Duncan of Woodbury, starting his show career at six years of age, is gaining some of the points toward his title to which he was handled by Bob Stebbins.

Am., Can. Ch. Cummings' Golden Princess, Best of Opposite Sex at a Golden Specialty in 1969, dam of Am., Can. Ch. Cummings' King Midas, Ch. Cummings' Copper Penny, Am., Can., Bda. Ch. Cummings' Gold-Rush Charlie, Ch. Cummings' Golden Sunshine, Ch. Cummings' Dame Pepperhill, Ch. Russo's Cummings' Elsa, and Ch. Sunset's Happy Duke II, just to name a few. One of the breed's great dams. Owned by Mrs. Mary W. Cummings.

Goldens from D.J.'s Kennel, owned by Dave, Jean, and J.D. Wacker, are equally at home in the field, conformation ring, obedience, or junior showmanship competition. This is D.J.'s Montana Kid's X-Rated, C.D., who represents five generations of D.J.'s breeding program.

Above: D.J.'s Stormy's Thunderbolt, C.D.X., Can. C.D., sitting proudly with his dumbbell in his mouth. "Thunder" just earned a *Dog World* Award, June 1982, for his C.D.X. title. Trained, owned, and handled by Nancy L. Sauer, Grafton, Wisconsin.

Facing page: Ch. Honor's Kickback, U.D.T., W.C.X., is the *first* champion U.D.T. and W.C.X. in the breed. Kitty Cathey, owner, Pekay's Goldens.

How it should be done! The mighty "Streaker" (Am., Can. Ch. and O.T. Ch. Sunstreak of Culynwood, T.D., W.C.X., Can. C.D.) performing obedience exercises in the manner which brought him fame. The David Blufords, owners. **Left:** "Streaker" heeling. **Center left:** "Streaker" doing a retrieve in the obedience ring. **Center right:** "Streaker" retrieving a dumbbell over the high jump. **Below left:** "Streaker" doing the broad jump, Open Class. **Below right:** "Streaker" at the finish of his day's obedience work.

Right: Am., Can. Ch. Sutter Creek Tessahoc Tigger, Am. and Can. C.D., by Ch. Alstone Sutter Creek Charade ex Am., Can. Ch. Fox Rock Sutter Creek Ulanda. Breeder, Susan Breakell. Owner, Pamela Tillotson. **Below:** Am., Can. Ch. Golden Pine's Courvoisier, Am. and Can. C.D.X., W.C., and Am. W.C.X. Owner, Nancy Kelly Belsaas. "Cognac" is pictured here, at ten years old, the day he won Best of Breed at Del Monte Kennel Club, May 1982.

Am., Can. Ch. High Farms Jantze of Curacao, C.D.X., T.D., W.C., Can. C.D., T.D.X. Barbara Tinker, owner, Bargello Goldens.

Right: Beskabekuk of Maine, W.C., C.D., outside Aintree Kennels, May 1979. Jennifer Kesner, owner. **Below:** Ch. Amberac's Mr. Beau Jangles, C.D., W.C., by Ch. Duckdown's Unpredictable, C.D., W.C., O.S., ex Amberac's Reeva Rustelle, was bred by Ellen Manke, Amberac Golden Retrievers, and is owned by Dennis Huber.

Facing page: Am., Can. Ch. October's Cal-Vo Spirit in September 1981, eight weeks after whelping her first litter, pictured following an afternoon of hunting. Ted and Beth Greenfield, owners, Westbrook Golden Retrievers. **Right:** Ch. Beckwith's Viking for Dasu, C.D., doing a balancing act! Photo courtesy of Mrs. R.E. Beckwith. **Below:** Am., Can. Ch. Golden Pine's Remy Martin, Am. and Can. C.D. Owners, Nancy Kelly Belsaas and Janis Teichman.

Mercer's Flowering Quince at work in the field. Homebred by Mercer Russo Ervin.

J.D. Wacker and Can. Ch. Amberac's D.J. Dixie Darlin in rural Wisconsin, during a successful pheasant hunting afternoon, autumn 1981. J.D., Jean, and Dave Wacker, owners.

Left: Am., Can. Ch. Chebaco's Brandywine, at three years of age, heading for the water. Mr. and Mrs. Jeffrey Gowing own him. **Below:** Duckpond's Graham Cracker working a water retrieve. Bruce Mittelstaedt, owner.

Right: A lovely photo of one of the Charms Goldens in the water. Ginny Boyle, owner. **Below:** Ch. Jake's Hanalei Valley Jam doing his favorite thing. Owned by Joan Luria.

Left: Amico of Maine, C.D., W.C.X., in November 1982 with a pheasant that he *caught* all by himself, with never a shot having been fired. Jennifer Kesner of Massachusetts, owner. **Below:** Amberac's Sungria De Ora, C.D., is the mother of many obedience title holders, grandam of champions. One of the best hunting dogs the Wacker family has ever owned and hunted. Pictured with Jean Wacker during a late afternoon pheasant hunt in rural Wisconsin.

Right: Proudly carrying her bird, the noted Ch. Topbrass Ad-Lib's Bangor, C.D., is a qualified open all-age bitch, one of only three in the U.S. now a bench show champion. Additionally she is a Golden Retriever Club of America Outstanding Dam. Mrs. Joseph Mertens, owner, Topbrass Kennels. **Below:** "Waiting for the Ducks" on Tea Pond, Eustis, Maine. Left to right, Amico of Maine, W.C.X., C.D., Beskabekuk of Maine, W.C., C.D., and Bittersweet Maine Seboomook, three magnificent Goldens belonging to Jennifer Kesner.

The very talented and versatile Am., Can. Ch. Ambertrail's Bargello Stitch, U.D.T., W.C.X., Can. U.D.T.X., W.C. Barbara Tinker, owner.

CHAPTER THIRTEEN

Obedience and Working Goldens

A Bargello puppy retrieving at six weeks of age. Barbara Tinker, owner.

Both beauty and brains are combined in a Golden Retriever, and the result is a multi-talented, versatile dog. Aside from possessing championship qualities, proven in the show ring, Goldens also exhibit intelligence, stamina, and a fine temperament—qualities which make this breed excel in obedience and several specialized fields of work.

Obedience

For its own protection and safety, every dog should be taught, at the very least, to recognize and respond promptly to the commands "Come," "No," "Down," "Sit," and "Stay." Doing so at some time might save the dog's life and in less extreme circumstances will certainly make him a better-behaved, more pleasant member of society. If you are patient and enjoy working with your dog, study some of the good books available on the subject of obedience and then teach your Golden these basic manners. If you need the stimulus of working with a group, find out where obedience training classes are held (your dog's veterinarian, your dog's breeder, or a dog-owning friend can tell you) and you and your Golden can join up. Alternatively, you could let someone else do the training by sending the dog to class, but this is not very rewarding, because you lose the opportunity of working with your dog and developing a rapport between the two of you.

If you are going to do it yourself, there are some basic rules which you should follow. You must remain calm and confident in attitude. Never lose your patience or temper and frighten or punish your dog unjustly. Never resort to cruelty. Be quick and lavish with praise each time a command is correctly followed. Make it fun for your dog, and he will be eager to please you by responding correctly. Repetition is the keynote, but it should not be continued without recess to the point of tedium. Limit the training sessions to ten- or fifteen-minute periods at a time.

Formal obedience training can be followed, and very frequently is, by entering the dog in obedience trial competition to work toward an obedience degree, or several of them, depending on the dog's aptitude and your own enjoyment. Obedience trials are held in conjunction with the majority of all-breed conformation dog shows, as Specialty events, and in conjunction with Golden Specialties. If you are working alone with your dog, a list of trial dates might be obtained from your dog's veterinarian, your dog's breeder, or a dog-owning friend; or write to the American Kennel Club. The A.K.C. *Gazette*

Left, Friar Tuck of Eagan Forest, C.D., born in 1971, with Big Red Paddy Waggin, U.D., born in 1976. They positioned themselves this way as their owner, Barbara Roy, of Hazelwood, Missouri, called "Stay" and grabbed a camera.

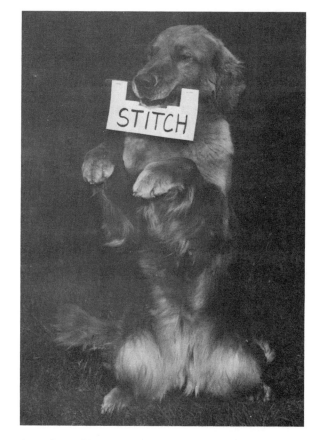

Am., Can. Ch. Ambertrail's Bargello Stitch, U.D.T., W.C.X., Can. U.D.T.X., W.C., in an informal moment. Barbara Tinker, owner, Bargello Goldens.

Beskabekuk of Maine, W.C., C.D., doing the "Halt" in obedience competition. Handled by owner Jennifer Kesner.

carries a monthly listing of all member or licensed dog shows and obedience trials to be held during the coming months in the United States. If you have been working with a training class, you will find information readily available regarding dates and locations of trials.

The basic goals for which one works in the formal American Kennel Club obedience trials are the following titles: Companion Dog (C.D.), Companion Dog Excellent (C.D.X.), and Utility Dog (U.D.). These degrees are earned by gaining three "legs," or qualifying scores, at each level of competition. The degrees must be earned in order, with one completed prior to starting work on the next. For example, a dog must have attained C.D. before starting work on C.D.X.; then C.D.X. must be completed before work on U.D. is started. The ultimate title attainable in obedience is Obedience Trial Champion (O.T.Ch.).

When you see the letters "C.D." following a dog's name, you will know that the dog has satisfactorily completed the following exercises: heel on leash, stand for examination, heel free, recall, long sit, and long stay. "C.D.X." indicates tests have been passed in all of the above plus heel free, drop on recall, retrieve over high jump, broad jump, long sit, and long stay. "U.D." indicates that the dog has additionally passed tests in scent discrimination (leather article), scent discrimination (metal article), signal exercises, directed retrieve, directed jumping, and group stand for examination.

Ch. Sundance's Melody, C.D.X., showing good form in obedience competition. Handled by Nancy Leakey, then twelve years old, to the C.D.X. title. Melody belongs to Nancy and Pat Leakey, Briarmoor Goldens.

Ch. Kinike Big Bad Dad of Topbrass, C.D.X., W.C., owned by J. and J. Mertens, Topbrass Kennels.

Am., Can. Ch. Ambertrail's Bargello Stitch, U.D.T., W.C.X., Can. U.D.T.X., W.C. Barbara Tinker, owner.

"Streaker" clears the Bar Jump, Utility Class, in his own incomparable style.

"Streaker" shows good form as he clears the jump with his dumb-bell in mouth.

Here comes "Streaker," that fantastic conformation and obedience star who achieved such inspiring records during his all-too-short lifetime. The late Am., Can. Ch. and O.T. Ch. Sunstreak of Culynwood, T.D., W.C.X., Can. C.D., owned by Suzi and Dave Bluford, Dasu Kennels.

O.T. Ch. Beckwith's Eta of Spindrift, U.D.T., W.C.X., in September 1975. Owned by Pat Klausman, Pekay Goldens.

The letters "O.T.Ch." are the abbreviation for the only obedience title which precedes rather than follows a dog's name. To gain an obedience trial championship, a dog who already holds a Utility Dog degree must win a total of one hundred points and must win three firsts, under three different judges, in Utility and Open B Classes. Fulfilling these requirements is certainly no small achievement but rather one in which to take tremendous pride.

There is also a Tracking Dog title (T.D.) which can be earned at tracking trials, and a dog who has this title can then take a Tracking Dog Excellent test which, if passed successfully, permits the dog to be known as a Tracking Dog Excellent (T.D.X.). In order to pass the Tracking Dog tests, the dog must follow the trail of a stranger along a path on which the trail was laid between thirty minutes and two hours previously. Along this trail there must be more than two right-angle turns, at least two of which are well out in the open where no fences or other boundaries exist for the guidance of the dog or the handler. The dog wears a harness and is connected to the handler by a lead twenty to forty feet in length. Inconspicuously dropped at the end of a track is an article to be retrieved, usually a glove or a wallet, which the dog is expected to locate and the handler to pick up. "T.D.X." is gained through completion of a more difficult version of the Tracking Dog test, with longer tracks being used and more turns through which the dog must work satisfactorily.

The owner of a dog holding the U.D. title and the T.D. title may then use the letters "U.D.T." following the dog's name. If the dog has gained his U.D. title and his T.D.X. title, then the letters "U.D.T.X." may follow his name, indicating that he is a Utility Dog and Tracker Excellent.

"The end of the track." Am., Can. Ch. Ambertrail's Bargello Stitch, U.D.T., W.C.X., Can. U.D.T.X., W.C. Barbara Tinker, owner.

It is interesting to note that since the American Kennel Club made the award of Highest Scoring Dog in the regular classes at obedience trials an official although optional title, Golden Retrievers have dominated this phase of all-breed competition to an extent beyond that of any other breed's dominance of any specific phase of activity in our world of purebred dogs. Since the American Kennel Club first instituted this award, the Ken-L-Products Division of the Quaker Oats Company has annually offered a trophy honoring the dog of any breed earning the greatest number of obedience trial championship points. As of July 1982, it has *never* been won by any breed of dog other than a Golden Retriever. During this same period, although the breed has registered somewhere around only 4-5% of all-breed total registrations annually, Goldens have annually gathered 25-30% of the Highest Scoring awards, published in *Pure-Bred Dogs American Kennel Gazette.*

Valhalla's After Dinner Licker, C.D.X., W.C.X., proudly holds his dumb-bell after taking Highest Scoring in Obedience at Monticello in September 1981. Kathy Liebler, owner, Valhalla Farms.

Ch. Pepperhill's Travelin' Bear, Am. and Can. C.D., winning another obedience first at Mispillion Kennel Club for Pepperhill Farms.

The first dog of any breed to gain the obedience trial championship when it was created by the American Kennel Club in 1977 was a Golden bitch, Obedience Trial Champion Moreland's Golden Tonka. The first bench show champion to gain the obedience trial champion title was the Golden bitch, Champion and Obedience Trial Champion Russo's Gold-Rush Sensation, U.D.

As of July 1982, the highest average score won in the Annual Gaines Super Dog Contest was won by Obedience Trial Champion Meadowpond Femme de Fortune.

The first and only Golden Retriever to attain *every show and every obedience title* offered by both the American Kennel Club and the Canadian Kennel Club was American and Canadian Champion and Obedience Trial Champion Bardfield Boomer, W.C., American U.D.T., Canadian U.D.T.X.

O.T. Champion Topbrass Ric O Shay Barty, owned by Sharon Long, is the winner of at least forty High in Trial awards. Here he is being honored with a Gaines Award for these achievements.

A triple retrieve! Beskabekuk of Maine, W.C., C.D.X., Amico of Maine, W.C.X., C.D., and Bittersweet Maine Seboomook. Owned by Jennifer Kesner of Massachusetts.

Big Red Paddy Waggin, U.D., shown holding his own High in Trial ribbon won from Novice B in May 1978 at Evansville, Indiana. Barbara Roy owns this distinguished obedience winner, and they live in Hazelwood, Missouri.

The 1981 Ken-L-Ration Quaker Oats Award for earning the greatest number of obedience trial championship points at American Kennel Club obedience trials during 1981 was won by Champion and Obedience Trial Champion Meadowpond Dust Commander, with a record 1,159 points. This was the third year in which he has earned this honor.

Mention must also be made of the great "Streaker," American and Canadian Champion and Obedience Trial Champion Sunstreak of Culynwood, T.D., W.C.X., Canadian C.D., whose untimely death during the spring of 1981 ended his spectacular career far too early.

Details about these and other great obedience performers may be found in the kennel stories presented in this book. We proudly salute all of these Goldens!

Amico of Maine, W.C.X., C.D., was born October 14th 1976 and is owned by Jennifer Kesner.

On the job at an early age, this is a puppy from Topbrass Kennels owned by Mrs. Joseph Mertens.

Sutter Creek Ruff 'n' Ready, at four months of age, with a quail wing. Breeder, Susan Breakell. Owners, Donna and Bruce Proudfoot.

Ch. Topbrass Ad-Lib Bangor, C.D., sitting in the blind. Owned by Mrs. Joseph Mertens.

Gun Dogs

Developing the natural instinct and talent that a Golden Retriever possesses for retrieving is not at all difficult. The instinct and inclination are there, merely waiting to be developed and guided by you to the proper channels. The big question is whether or not you are equipped to train the dog, as it takes knowledge, patience, and kindness to bring this about successfully.

Working with your own dog is far more satisfactory than turning him over to a trainer. The rapport and closeness that develop as the two of you work together is one of the great pleasures of dog ownership; and if you miss out on it, you will be losing something of great value. Before deciding that you feel unqualified to achieve success, study up on the subject (there are dozens of excellent books available which will help you train and hunt with your dog) and see if you are able to accomplish the job on your own.

We have already touched upon the importance of early obedience training for your puppy. The obedience commands, with the addition of "Fetch," are the first steps in field work which must be learned. Keep the commands short and brisk, always using the same word for the same act, so that the dog will immediately associate what you want with what he is hearing. This part of the training can, and should, be started as soon as the puppy is a few months old, the younger the better. The lessons should be short, pleasant, and lacking in tedium; and they can take place in the house as well as outdoors.

Coming through the water, bird in mouth, is Ch. Nordlys Australis. Owned by Karl and Lei Taft of Hawaii.

Just out of the water, two of the excellent Goldens at Valhalla Farms owned by Kathy Liebler.

You will perhaps gradually wish to add whistle or hand signals to the verbal commands. If you decide to use hand signals, do not swing or wave your arm about; this will be confusing to the dog. Hold your arm out straight, moving your hand to indicate "right" or "left," and hold your arm above your head to indicate "back." With repetition and practice, the commands can be learned by the dog far faster than you might anticipate.

Some people prefer to use a whistle or a combination of hand and whistle for signaling. One sharp blast generally means the dog should sit wherever he may be, or one blast can be used to call the dog's attention to the hand signal you are about to give. Three blasts usually mean that the dog is to return to you or come part way back to you.

D.J.'s Montana's Kid's X-Rated, C.D., owned by D.J.'s Golden Kennels, has just completed an excellent retrieve.

For training equipment, you will need a dummy that will hold up on land or in water. These come in assorted sizes and are made of canvas stuffed with shredded rubber. You will also need a lead with a choke collar, to prevent the dog from roaming too far away during the learning stage. The introduction to feathers is of primary importance and is usually accomplished by way of a chicken or turkey wing from which the feathers have not been removed or by a dummy with feathers tied securely to it. Any inclination on the part of the dog to go off with the feathered object or dummy after retrieving must be discouraged. It must be brought promptly and directly back to you. Never forget that a Golden's retrieve is to be made to your hand.

From the very beginning, see that your Golden puppy becomes accustomed to sudden sharp noises. Lots of pan-clattering at meal times and hand clapping are two good ways to help the dog get used to loud noises. The dog's introduction to the gun should start with the gun being fired a considerable distance away from him;

"Is it hunting season yet?" seems to be what this lovely Golden is asking as he quietly watches the ducks on the Ipswich River. Jennifer Kesner, owner.

then the gun should gradually be fired closer and closer until the sudden loud noise becomes routine. During this step great care should be taken not to frighten the dog, as by so doing you may make him forever gun-shy. Praise him, pet him, and be generally cheerful each time the gun is fired, until he grows to associate the sound with something he enjoys.

Introduction to the water also should be handled with care. A child's wading pool of shallow water might be a good starting place for him to get the feel of being in water. Be cautious the first time the puppy enters deep water, as you do not want him to become frightened. It is good to have along his dam or another experienced older

"Cookie" heading into the pool. One of the Lounsburys' Jolly Goldens.

Enjoying the pool, Ch. Peachy's Happy Lady of Charms, C.D. Owned by Ginny Boyle.

How to pass a hot afternoon, snapped at Valhalla Farms, Kathy Liebler. Notice the puppy getting into the act.

Relaxing in his pool is Valhalla's Silvery Sunlight, bred by Kathy Liebler and owned by Judye Anderson.

dog who enjoys being in the water to set an example for the pup, but be very careful that the baby Golden does not get into difficulty before he learns how to proceed.

If you are starting out with your first Golden, try to get a more experienced friend to come out with you for some of the earlier training sessions. This can be helpful to you as a "confidence booster" and to both you and your Golden by getting things off on the right foot. Good luck and happy hunting!

Working Certificate

The purpose of the Golden Retriever Club of America in establishing and making available a Working Certificate to all owners of Goldens is to encourage the use of and to maintain the natural hunting and retrieving abilities in these dogs. It is realized that the majority of Goldens gaining these certificates will not be so thoroughly trained as those competing in field trials; therefore, simple hand and water tests have been devised, using ducks, game birds, or pigeons. These tests are designed to demonstrate accurate marking and memory of falls, attention, intelligence, good nose, style, perseverence, desire, and trainability.

Working Certificate tests may be held at any American Kennel Club licensed retriever field trial or at any event held in the name of the Golden Retriever Club of America for any number of Golden Retrievers. Permission must be granted by the G.R.C.A., and the test is conducted under their requirements. All other retriever clubs wishing to hold a Working Certificate test must submit a written request to the parent club (national) sixty days prior to the first day of the trial, detailing test location, date, judges, and an estimate of the number of dogs to be tested, all of which must be at least six months old and individually registered with the American Kennel Club.

These tests for the Working Certificate include the retrieving of two birds on land in moderate cover (the birds should fall approximately forty to fifty yeards from the line and at least ninety degrees apart) and the retrieving of two live ducks in swimming water, as back-to-back singles, in light cover (the ducks should be approximately twenty-five to thirty yards from the line).

If a fee is to be charged for entering the Working Certificate test, the cost must be indicated in advance. The types of birds to be used are also indicated in advance. Each gun station uses a shotgun, and there is a gunner and a thrower at each station.

Working Certificate tests are conducted and judged under the Derby rules for non-slip retriever trials described by the A.K.C., with the following exceptions: artificial decoys are not used; dogs may be brought to the line on a leash and held, but they are not released until their number has been called; and although hand delivery of birds is not required, delivery must

Above: "Killer's" water entry (yes, he's in there). Ch. Beaumaris Pekay's Kilowatt owned by Pekay's Goldens. **Below:** "Killer" starting out from shore.

Ch. Beaumaris Pekay's Kilowatt, left, and Ch. Beaumaris Pekay's Natural Hi, C.D., showing how they love the water! Both owned by Pekay's Goldens.

be made to the area of the line which has been clearly marked prior to the beginning of the test.

A Working Certificate is issued to the owners of all dogs who have satisfactorily completed these tests.

For people who do not wish to compete in American Kennel Club field trials but who enjoy training their dogs beyond the level of a Working Certificate, the Golden Retriever Club of America has created a higher goal, a Working Certificate Excellent (W.C.X.), for which land and water marking tests have been devised similar to those of the American Kennel Club.

The land part of the Working Certificate Excellent test consists of three retrieves, one bird each time (two of them dead, one a flier) in moderate cover. Two of the falls must be between sixty and one hundred yards from the line, at least sixty degrees apart, and at a forty-five-degree angle back from the guns. The water part of the test consists of the retrieving of two shackled ducks from the water. Swimming water is preferable in both cases, but it is demanded for only one. The falls must be between forty-five and sixty yards from the line, at least sixty degrees apart, and at a forty-five-degree angle back from the guns. One bird, known as the memory bird, should be in natural moderate cover not visible from the line; the other should be in open water and should be fully visible from the line.

For these advanced tests the dog is brought to the line off leash and not wearing a collar, and the dog is not touched by the handler at any time during the test. The dog must remain steady on the line until the judge gives the handler his number, at which time the handler will send the dog. The dog should leave the line off leash and under control. For these tests, the dog must deliver each bird to hand, relinquishing it easily to the handler.

Upon satisfactory completion of these tests, a Working Certificate Excellent will be awarded by the Golden Retriever Club of America, and the owner of a dog who is so awarded may use "W.C.X." following the dog's name. This award for working ability made by the Golden Retriever Club of America should not be confused with the other titles one sees indicated, which are awarded by the American Kennel Club.

Mercer's Woodruff, by Ch. Mercer's Sweet William ex Ch. Russo's Cummings' Elsa at the water's edge. Mercer Russo Ervin, owner. Photograph by John Nichole of New Fairfield, Connecticut.

Mercer's Flowering Quince and Mercer's Woodruff beautifully photographed by John Nichole of Connecticut. Mercer Russo Ervin owns this handsome pair.

F.C., A.F.C. Topbrass Mandy belongs to Mrs. Joseph Mertens, Topbrass Goldens.

Field Trial Dogs

Golden Retrievers are excellent field dogs and are extremely popular with sportsmen, both for hunting and for formal field trial competition. The work of a Golden is what his name implies —to retrieve, on land or from the water.

The first field trial held in the United States under American Kennel Club rules was sponsored by the Labrador Retriever Club of America, at Port Chester, New York, December 1931. The sport has grown at a steady rate and, as of 1979, more than 150 trials are annually licensed by the A.K.C.

Only pure-bred retrievers, six months of age or over, are eligible for entry in an American Kennel Club member or licensed field trial. The regular official stakes at a retriever trial are Derby, Qualifying, Open-All Age, and Amateur All-Age.

A Derby Stake is for dogs who have not yet reached their second birthday on the first day of the trial at which they are to be run.

Mother and daughter snapped in the field. Valhalla Goldens, Kathy Liebler.

One of the Topbrass Goldens headed for the water. Mrs. Joseph Mertens, owner, Topbrass Kennels.

Am., Can. Ch. Ambertrail's Bargello Stitch, U.D.T., W.C.X., Can. U.D.T.X., W.C. This splendid Golden belongs to Barbara Tinker, Bargello Goldens.

A Qualifying Stake is for dogs who have not previously won a first, second, third, or fourth placement, or a Judges Award of Merit, in an Open All-Age or Limited All-Age Stake; a first, second, third, or fourth place in an Amateur All-Age Stake; or two first places in Qualifying Stakes at licensed or member club trials. In determining a dog's eligibility for the Qualifying Stake, no award received on or after the official closing date for entries is counted.

An Open All-Age Stake is exactly what it says —open to all dogs of all ages.

A Limited All-Age Stake is for dogs who have previously placed or been awarded a Judges Award of Merit in an Open All-Age Stake, who have placed first or second in a Qualifying Stake, or who have placed or been awarded a Judges Award of Merit in an Amateur All-Age Stake carrying championship points.

An Amateur All-Age Stake is for all dogs handled by persons who are amateurs, and whether or not a person is an amateur is determined by the field trial committee of the sponsoring club.

Each field trial has only one stake, either Open All-Age or Limited All-Age, and a club is allowed to hold no more than two such stakes annually.

National Championship Stakes and National Amateur Championship Stakes are held only once a year by the National Retriever Club and the National Amateur Retriever Club, respectively. The winners of these stakes, if registered with the A.K.C., become field or amateur field champions, respectively, and are entitled to their appropriate title (either "National Retriever Club Champion of 19--" or "National Amateur Retriever Club Champion of 19--").

To become a field champion, a retriever must win a National Championship Stake or win a total of ten points at Open All-Age or Limited All-Age Stakes. To become an amateur field champion, a retriever must win a National Amateur Championship Stake, win a total of ten points in Open All-Age or Limited All-Age Stakes, or win a total of fifteen points in Open All-Age, Limited All-Age, or Amateur All-Age Stakes.

Retriever trials may include A.K.C.-approved non-regular stakes, but such stakes do not carry championship points.

Non-slip retriever trials are held for the purpose of determining the relative merits of retrievers in the field. These trials simulate, as closely as possible, conditions that may be met on an ordinary day's shoot with the master.

D.J.'s Oak Hill Brandy's water entry on Lake Namekagon, Wisconsin. Owned by Hans and Dianne Mueller.

Amico of Maine, W.C.X., C.D., doing what he was bred to do. Jennifer Kesner, owner.

Bargello's Best Seller "marking" the bird at a field trial. Owners, B. Sellers and B. Tinker.

Pepperhill's My-T-Tuff Bear, C.D., returning from the water. Pepperhill Farms, Barbara and Jeffrey Pepper, owners.

It is a non-slip retriever's function to seek and retrieve, under all conditions, fallen game upon command; he is not expected to find or flush game. He should sit quietly on line in the blind, mark the fall, and, on command, retrieve quickly and briskly with little disturbance. The bird should be delivered tenderly to hand, and then the dog should patiently await further orders. Accurate marking is of primary importance.

If you are planning a field trial career for your Golden, you should write to the American Kennel Club and ask for a copy of their free booklet, *Registration and Field Trial Rules and Standard Procedures*. This booklet contains all of the detailed information you will need to know about field trials.

Retriever trials got underway in the United States in 1935, and it was this activity, first started in the Midwest, that brought the Golden into public demand—sportsmen began to realize the breed's many assets.

Nero of Roedare was the trailblazer for Goldens in the trials. He was the Top Derby Dog of 1937, and he was the first Golden to place in an Open All-Age Stake and in an obedience trial, the latter in 1939. Unfortunately, Nero met with an untimely death before he was able to complete his dual championship (he had fourteen points toward his show title and thir-

teen toward his field championship). He was owned by Richard Ryan.

It was Paul Bakewell, III, and his dog Rip who really put Goldens on the field trial map. Trained and handled by his amateur owner, this magnificent dog became the first Golden to achieve field dog championship in the United States. He completed his championship in 1939 and won the *Field and Stream* Challenge Cup for Retrievers that year and again in 1940. He acquired sixty-three championship points during his two-and-a-half year career. Field Trial Champion Rip, by Speedwell Reuben ex Champion Speedweli Tango, was born on November 25th 1935, and was bred by Whitebridge Kennels. He died on August 24th 1941.

The winner of the first National Championship Retriever Trial, in 1941, was another very distinguished Golden, National and Field Trial Champion King Midas of Woodend. King Midas, by Rockhaven Tuck ex Glittering Cloud, was bred by Winnebago Kennels and owned by E.N. Dodge. His grandsire, Tuck's sire, was Colonel Magoffin's American and Canadian Champion Speedwell Pluto, the first bench champion, the first Best in Show winner, and the first Sporting Group winner for the breed in the United States.

The second Golden to win the National Retriever Field Trial was a dog named Shelter Cove Beauty, owned by Dr. L.M. Evans. This dog won the day in 1944.

Left to right: F.C., A.F.C. Topbrass Mandy, Amateur first; Topbrass Gatsby, Qualifying first; and Topbrass Cotton, Derby first, at a licensed trial in Wisconsin, May 1980. Ben and Jeff Fenley own Gatsby and Cotton. All are from the Topbrass Kennels owned by Mrs. Joseph Mertens.

All of the intelligence that so well equips her for her job as guardian of the Statue of Liberty in New York Harbor is clearly evident as one studies the expressive face of Talli, the lovely Golden donated by Kathy Uhrman for this purpose.

Explosives Detection Dog—
A Dog Named Talli
by Kathy Uhrman

"Talli," formally known as Bridlewold's Alchemist, is a Golden Retriever who exemplifies all the adjectives usually used to describe a Golden Retriever: beautiful, friendly, talented, playful, and so on. The only people who would be unable to love her would be terrorists and madmen. She is a Golden Retriever with a big job—to protect the Statue of Liberty, *Liberty Enlightening the World*, from terrorists and bombers.

The Statue of Liberty is a national monument, and it is the popular target for terrorists and anyone else wanting to attract attention to themselves or their cause. The most recent bombing of "Miss Liberty" took place on June 3rd 1980, at 7:30 in the evening. All of the tourists had left; but had it not been for bad timing on the part of the bombers, many people could have been injured or killed.

In August 1981, after a rash of bomb threats, Alan and Marilyn Baruch of Las Sana/Argus, Ltd., the largest manufacturer of protection training equipment used by the military, city and state municipalities, commercial trainers, and Schutzhund competitors, decided to obtain a dog for explosives detection at the Statue of Liberty. They contacted Gerry Lapham, of Sentinel K-9 in Fayetteville, North Carolina, who trains police dogs, attack dogs, narcotic detection dogs, and explosives detection dogs. They suggested to Gerry that a dog be obtained, trained, and donated to the National Park Service to protect the statue. Gerry was in agreement with the Baruchs regarding the soundness of the idea and told them that a retriever was the type of dog needed. After many other telephone calls, Gerry called me and told me what he was looking for. I told him I had the type of dog he was describing, but I would have to think about parting with her and I would also have to talk to her co-owner, Ann Johnson of Gold-Rush Goldens. After much discussion with Ann, and more serious thinking on my part, I decided to donate "Talli," my three-and-a-half-year-old Golden.

Talli with her handlers Bill De Hart and Frank Mills at the Statue of Liberty. New York City's skyline is in the background.

"Talli" is a daughter of American, Canadian, and Bermudian Champion Cummings' Gold-Rush Charlie. She had been through a disastrous whelping problem in April, which necessitated her being spayed. I had kept telling myself all summer that I would start her in obedience "tomorrow," but "tomorrow" never seemed to come.

Above: Kelly's Honey of Bridlewold, C.D., grandmother of Talli. **Below:** Talli, the daughter of Am., Can., Bda. Ch. Cummings' Gold-Rush Charlie, was donated by Kathy Uhrman to be trained to protect the Lady of the Harbor, the Statue of Liberty, from terrorists and bombers.

Above: Talli and her friend Frank Mills exchange greetings on the Statue of Liberty grounds where both are employed. **Below:** Checking out her territory, Talli goes the rounds to ascertain that "all is well" on a snowy morning surrounding the Statue of Liberty. Photos courtesy of Kathy Uhrman, Bridlewold Goldens.

In August, "Talli" left me to go to Gerry Lapham, who planned to evaluate her and begin her training. After two weeks, Gerry called and told me that "Talli" was good—very good! An explosives detection dog, unlike a narcotics detection dog, has to be right 100% of the time. One dog in a hundred makes a bomb dog, and "Talli" was that *one*!

"Talli" was in training for ten weeks, at the end of which time she was ready for the two park rangers who would be her handlers. The two rangers, Bill DeHart and Frank Mills, went to North Carolina for a week of intensive training with "Talli" and Gerry. "Talli" and her handlers then left for New York; and on November 12th 1981, Talli became the guardian of one of America's proudest symbols.

Talli, on the job, thoughtfully inspects all visitors to "Miss Liberty."

"Talli" is the first explosives detection dog to be owned by the National Park Service to work at a national monument. She, however, does not think this is work. In order to demonstrate her talents, Gerry hid two bombs in the generator room in the compound. One bomb was in a tool bin and the other was in a closed metal locker. Despite the noise and the predominant odor of fuel oil, it took "Talli" only about thirty seconds to find both bombs, which she indicated by a passive response at each location. She then was rewarded with her favorite toy, a small sack filled with gunpowder to chase and fetch.

"Talli" will live on Liberty Island with the rangers and go to work with them each day. She also greets the tourists, a pastime she enjoys almost as much as finding bombs. Bill and Frank hope, however, that "Talli" does not suddenly sit down when greeting tourists, because that is her way of saying "Bomb!"

We wonder how many visitors will return home from meeting "Talli" at the Statue of Liberty thoroughly won over to the charms of a Golden Retriever, adding one to their own family as a result.

"Time to go home now," Frank Mills tells his friend as the shift changes at the Statue of Liberty.

This adorable Golden puppy, by Teakwood Farms Russo's Troy ex Ch. Mercer's Morning Glory, was bred by Mercer Russo Ervin, Mercer's Goldens.

CHAPTER FOURTEEN

Breeding Golden Retrievers

Valentine Torch of Topbrass stands behind the Topbrass Goldens of today. Mrs. Joseph Mertens, owner.

Breeding good dogs requires a lot of hard work. It is not easy to produce dogs who conform as closely as possible to the standard, and it takes years to develop a strain of good and successful dogs. A lot of time and effort must go into choosing the stud dog and brood bitch, and then more time must be spent with the litter once it arrives.

The Stud Dog

Choosing the best stud dog to complement your bitch is not an easy task. The principal factors to be considered are the stud's quality and conformation and his pedigree. The pedigree lists the various bloodlines involved with the ancestry of the dog. If you are a novice in the breed, I would suggest that you seek advice from some of the more experienced breeders who are old-timers in the fancy and thus would be able to discuss with you some of the various dogs behind the one to which you are planning to breed your bitch. Many times such people accurately recall in minute detail the dogs you need to know about, perhaps even having access to photos of them. And do be sure to carefully study the photos in this book, as they show representatives of important Golden bloodlines.

It is extremely important that the stud's pedigree be harmonious with that of your bitch. Do not just rush out and breed to a current win-

ner, with no regard for whether or not he can reproduce his quality. Take time to check out the progeny being sired by the dog, or dogs, under your consideration. A dog that has sired nothing of quality for others probably will do no better for you, unless, of course, it is a young stud just starting out; such a stud may not have had the opportunity to produce much of anything, good or bad, thus far. Do you want to waste your bitch's time on an unknown quantity? Wouldn't you prefer to use a dog with a good producing record? You may get a little-known or unproven dog for a less expensive stud fee, but is that really sensible?

Breeding dogs is not a moneymaking proposition. By the time you pay a stud fee, take care of the bitch during gestation, whelp the litter, and raise and care for the puppies (including shots, and food, among other things) until they reach selling age, you will be fortunate if you break even on the cost of the litter. Therefore, it is foolish to skimp on the stud fee. Let nothing influence your selection except that the dog be best suited to your bitch in background and conformation, with the best producing record, regardless of the cost. It is just as expensive to raise mediocre puppies as good ones, and you will certainly fare better financially if you have show-prospect puppies to sell than if you come up with nothing but pets, which you will probably wind up selling for far less than you had intended or you'll end up giving away to get them good homes. Remember, the only excuse for breeding and bringing puppies into the world is an honest effort to improve the breed. So in choosing the stud you use, remember that the best, most suitable one you can find with an impressive producing record will almost certainly be by far the greatest bargain in the long run.

You will have to decide on one of three courses to follow in planning the breeding of your bitch: inbreeding, line-breeding, or outcrossing. Inbreeding is normally considered to be father to daughter, mother to son, or sister to brother. Line-breeding is combining two dogs belonging originally to the same strain or family of Goldens, descended from the same ancestors, such as half-brother to half-sister, niece to uncle, granddaughter to grandsire, and so on. Outcross breeding is using a dog and a bitch of completely different bloodlines with no mutual ancestors, or only a few, and these far back, if at all.

Each of these methods has advantages and disadvantages; each has supporters and detractors. I would say that line-breeding is probably the safest, the most generally approved, and the most frequently used with the desired results. Thus, I would say, it is perfect for the novice breeder because it is the easiest to figure out, especially until one has acquired considerable experience with the breed and the various bloodlines of which it consists.

Inbreeding should be left for the experienced, very sophisticated breeder who knows the line extremely well and thus is in a position to evaluate the probable results. Outcrossing is normally done when you are trying to bring in a specific feature or trait, such as a shorter back, better head type, more correct bone or action, or better personality or temperament.

Everyone sincerely interested in breeding dogs wants to develop a line of their own, but this is not accomplished overnight. It takes at least several generations before you can claim to have done so, and during this time the close study of bloodlines and the observation of individual dogs are essential. Getting to know and truthfully evaluate the dogs with which you are working will go a long way in helping you preserve the best in what you have while at the same time remove weaknesses.

As a novice breeder, your wisest bet is to start by acquiring one or two bitches of the finest

Ch. Misty Morn's Sunset, top sire in Golden history with get still finishing. This is the sire of Ch. Wochica's Okeechobee Jake and the grandsire of Ch. Camelot's Noble Fella, C.D.X. Photo courtesy of Bob Stebbins, Jake's friend and handler.

quality and background you can buy. In the beginning, it is really foolish to own your own stud dog; you will make out better and have a wider range of dogs with which to work if you pay a stud fee to one of the outstanding producing Goldens available to service your bitch. In order to be attractive to breeders a stud dog must be well known, must have sired at least one champion (and usually one that has attracted considerable attention in Specials competition), and must have winning progeny in the ring; this represents a large expenditure of time and money before the dog begins to bring in returns on your investment. So start out by paying a stud fee a few times to use such a dog, or dogs, retaining the best bitch out of each of your first few litters and breeding those once or twice before you seriously think of owning your own stud dog. By that time, you will have gained the experience to recognize exactly what sort of dog you need for this purpose.

A future stud dog should be selected with the utmost care and consideration. He must be of very high standard as he may be responsible for siring many puppies each year, and he should not be used unless he clearly has something to contribute to the breed and carries no hereditary disease. Ideally, he should come from a line of excellent dogs on both sides of his pedigree, the latter containing not only *good* dogs but also ones which are *proven successful producers of quality*.

Ch. Pathfinder of Lazy Pines, C.D., W.C., relaxing for a bit. This lovely dog was the foundation sire and personal pet of Janet Bunce, Wochica Goldens.

The dog himself should be of sufficient quality to hold his own in competition in his breed. He should be robust and virile, a keen stud dog who has proved that he is able to transmit his best qualities to his progeny. Do not use an unsound dog or a dog with a major or outstanding fault. Not all champions seem able to pass along their individual splendid quality and, by the same token, occasionally one finds a dog who never finished but who does sire puppies better than himself *provided that his pedigree is star-studded with top producing dogs and bitches.* Remember, too, that the stud dog cannot do it alone; the bitch must have what it takes too, although I must admit that some stud dogs, the truly dominant ones, can consistently produce type and quality regardless of the bitch or her background. Great studs like this, however, are few and far between.

Ch. Wochica's Okeechobee Jake in the Stud Dog Class at the Garden State Specialty in 1978. Handled by Bob Stebbins for owner Susan Taylor of New York. The progeny pictured are Ch. Starfarms Coleen and Camelot's Free Spirit.

Ch. Sun Dance's Moonlight Gambler, C.D., W.C., owned by Howard and Marcia Henderson of Duckdown Kennels, was the sire of those famed producers, Ch. Duckdown's Veronica Laker and Ch. Duckdown's Unpredictable, C.D., W.C.

If you are the proud owner of a promising young stud dog, one that you have either bred from one of your own bitches or that you have purchased after much serious thought and deliberation, do not permit him to be used for the first time until he is about a year old. The initial breeding should be to a proven matron, experienced in what is expected of her and thus not likely to give the stud a bad time. His first encounter should be pleasant and easy, as he could be put off breeding forever by a maiden bitch that fights and resents his advances. His first breeding should help him develop confidence and assurance. It should be done in quiet surroundings, with only you and one other person (to hold the bitch) present. Do not make a circus of it, as the first time will determine your stud's attitude and feeling about future breeding.

Your young stud dog must allow you to help with the breeding, as later there will be bitches who will not be cooperative and he will need to develop the habit of accepting assistance. If, right from the beginning, you are there helping and praising him, he will expect and accept this as a matter of course whenever it may be necessary.

Before you introduce the dogs, be sure to have some K-Y Jelly at hand (this is the only lubricant that should be used) and either a stocking or a length of gauze with which to muzzle the bitch should it seem necessary, as you do not want either yourself or your stud dog bitten. Once they are "tied," you will be able to remove the muzzle, but, for the preliminaries, it is best to play it safe by muzzling her.

The stud fee is paid at the time of the breeding. Normally a return service is offered should the bitch fail to produce. Usually one live puppy is considered to be a litter. In order to avoid any misunderstanding regarding the terms of the breeding, it is wise to have a breeding certificate which both the owner of the stud and the owner of the bitch should sign. This should spell out quite specifically all the conditions of the breeding, along with listing the dates of the matings (usually the bitch is bred twice with one day in between, especially if she is a maiden bitch). The owner of the stud should also at this time provide the owner of the bitch with a copy of the stud dog's pedigree, if this has not previously been done.

Sometimes a pick of the litter puppy is taken instead of a stud fee, and this should be noted on the breeding certificate along with such terms as at what age the owner of the stud dog is to select the puppy and whether it is to be a dog puppy, a bitch puppy, or just the "pick" puppy. All of this should be clearly stated to avoid any misunderstandings later on.

Ch. Sutter Creek's Libra Bearhug, C.D., bred by Cheryl Blair and purchased by Susan Breakell when he was ten months old, was shown as a Special and now has several progeny in the show ring.

In almost every case, the bitch must come to the stud dog for breeding. Once the owner of the bitch decides to what stud dog she will preferably be bred, it is important that the owner of the stud be contacted immediately to discuss the stud fee, terms, approximate time the bitch is due in season, and whether she will be shipped in or brought to the stud owner. Then, as soon as the bitch shows signs of coming into season, another phone call to the stud owner must follow to finalize the arrangements. I have experienced times when the bitch's owner has waited until a day or two before the bitch should be bred to contact me, only to meet with disappointment owing to the dog's absence from home.

It is essential that the stud owner have proper facilities for housing the bitch while she is there. Nothing can be more disheartening than to have a bitch misbred or, still worse, to have her get away and become lost. Unless you can provide safe and proper care for visiting bitches, do not offer your dog at public stud.

Above: Ch. Vagabond's Cougar Bill, C.D., the sire of Ch. Laurell's Kilimanjaro, at the North Kentucky Kennel Club, July 25th 1971. Photo courtesy of Laura Kling, Laurell Kennels. **Below:** Ch. Malagold High Voltage, the first homebred Best in Show-winner from Connie Gerstner's Malagold Kennels. Sired by Ch. Malagold Beckwith O.K. Ivan, C.D., ex Malagold Beckwith Bootes, this dog was in the Top Ten Goldens of 1978, going on to produce several champions for Pat Haines and Oncore Kennels.

Owning a stud dog is no easy road to riches, as some who have not experienced it seem to think; making the dog sufficiently well known is expensive and time-consuming. Be selective in the bitches you permit this dog to service. It takes two to make the puppies; and while some stud dogs do seem almost to achieve miracles, it is a general rule that an inferior bitch from a mediocre background will probably never produce well no matter how dominant and splendid may be the stud to whom she is bred. Remember that these puppies will be advertised and perhaps shown as sired by your dog. You do not want them to be an embarrassment to yourself or to him, so do not accept just any bitch who comes along in order to get the stud fee. It may prove far too expensive in the long run.

A stud fee is generally based on the going price of one show-type puppy and on the sire's record as a producer of winners. Obviously, a stud throwing champions in every litter is worth a greater price than a dog that sires mediocre puppies. Thus a young stud, just starting his career as a sire, is less expensive before proven than a dog with, say, forty or fifty champions already on the record. And a dog that has been used more than a few times but has no winning progeny should, it goes without saying, be avoided no matter how small the fee; he will almost certainly be a waste of your bitch's time.

Ch. Mercer's Sweet William, the first homebred male belonging to Mrs. Mercer Russo Ervin, in November 1978.

Am., Can. Ch. Sutter Creek Goldrush Flyboy at five-and-a-half years of age. Owner-handler Susan Breakell, Sutter Creek Kennel. Breeder, D. Jean Baird. Flyboy has sired nine champions and is an Outstanding Sire in the Hall of Fame.

I do not feel that we need to go into the actual breeding procedure here, as the experienced fancier already knows how it should be handled and the novice should not attempt it for the first time by reading instructions in a book. Plan to have a breeder or handler friend help you until you have become accustomed to handling such matters or, if this is not practical for you, it is very likely your veterinarian can arrange to do it for you or get someone from his staff to preside.

If a complete "tie" is made, that breeding should be all that is actually necessary. However, with a maiden bitch, a bitch who has "missed" (failed to conceive) in the past, or one who has come a long distance, most people like to give a second breeding, allowing one day to elapse in between the two. This second service gives additional insurance that a litter will result; and if the bitch is one with a past record for misses, sometimes even a third mating takes place in an effort to take every precaution.

Once the "tie" has been completed, be sure that the penis goes back completely into its sheath. The dog should be offered a drink of water and a short walk, and then he should be put in his crate or kennel somewhere alone to settle down. Do not permit him to mingle with the other males for a while, as he will carry the odor of the bitch about him and this could result in a fight.

The bitch should not be allowed to urinate for at least an hour. In fact, many people feel that she should be "upended" (held with her rear end above her front) for several minutes following the "tie" in order to permit the sperm to travel deeper. She should then be offered water, crated, and kept quiet.

There are no set rules governing the conditions of a stud service. They are whatever the owner of the stud dog chooses to make them. The stud fee is paid for the act, not for the litter; and if a bitch fails to conceive, this does not automatically call for a return service unless the owner of the stud sees it that way. A return ser-

Sutter Creek Laurell Ruffian, owned by Susan J. Breakell, is contributing to the breeding program at Sutter Creek Goldens. Ruffian is shown here taking points at Windham in 1982.

A lovely head study of Am., Can. Ch. High Farms Jantze of Curacao, C.D.X., T.D., W.C., Can. C.D., T.D.X., first stud dog owned by Barbara Tinker, Bargello Goldens.

vice is a courtesy, not something that can be regarded as a right, particularly as in many cases the failure has been on the part of the bitch, not the stud dog. Owners of a stud in whom they take pride and whom they are anxious to have make records as the sire of numerous champions, however, are usually most generous in this respect; and I do not know of any instances where this courtesy has been refused when no puppies resulted from the breeding. Some stud owners insist on the return service being given to the same bitch only, while others will accept a different bitch in her place if the owner wishes, particularly if the original one has a previous record for missing.

When a bitch has been given one return breeding and misses again, the stud owner's responsibility has ended. If the stud dog is one who consistently sires puppies, then obviously the bitch is at fault; and she will quite likely never conceive, no matter how often or to how many different studs she is bred. It is unreasonable for the owner of a bitch to expect a stud's owner to give more than one return service.

Ch. Ashwell's Gold-Rush Logan, now settled down to motherhood following a fine show career. Owned by Ashwell Goldens, Myra Moldawsky.

The Brood Bitch

One of the most important purchases you will make in dogs is the selection of your foundation brood bitch, or bitches, on whom you plan to base your breeding program. You want marvelous bloodlines representing top producing strains; you want sound bitches of basic quality, free of any hereditary problems.

Your Golden bitch should not be bred until her second period in season; but if she starts her season at an extra early age, say, barely over six months of age and then for the second time just past one year of age, you would be wise to wait until her third heat. The waiting period can be profitably spent carefully watching for the ideal stud to complement her own qualities and be compatible with her background. Keeping this in mind, attend dog shows and watch the males who are winning and, even more important, siring the winners. Subscribe to any dog magazines which include Goldens and study the pictures

Ch. Laurell's Kilimanjaro winning the Brood Bitch Class at Fort Detroit Golden Retriever Club in November 1981, judged by Janet Churchill. The progeny pictured are Ch. Laurell's York, center, and Ch. Laurell's Travlin' Too Far on the right. Fine representatives of the Klings' famed Laurell breeding program.

The foundation of Golden Charms Kennels, Apollo's Golden Charmer, Am. and Can. C.D.X., the dam of one champion and other pointed progeny plus fourteen obedience trial dogs. Owned by Virginia Boyle.

Above: Foundation bitch for Laurell Kennels, Ch. Rusticana's Princess Teena, C.D. After being mistreated elsewhere, Teena was given a good home by Laura Ellis (now Laura Ellis Kling). Below: This impressive Golden lady is Morningsage Malagold Honey, by Ch. Malagold Beckwith's Om K Ivan, C.D., ex Ch. Dangret Emerald of Yeo. She is the foundation bitch at Joanne A. Lastoka's Morningsage Kennels.

and stories accompanying them to familiarize yourself with dogs in other areas of which you may have not been aware. Be sure to keep in mind that the stud should be strong in the bitch's weak points; carefully note his progeny to see if he passes along the features you want and admire. Make special note of any offspring from bitches with backgrounds similar to your bitch's; then you can get an idea of how well the background fits with his. When you see a stud dog that interests you, discuss your bitch with the owner and request a copy of his dog's pedigree for your study and perusal.

When you have made a tentative choice, contact the stud's owner to make the preliminary arrangements regarding the stud fee (whether it will be in cash or a puppy), approximate time the bitch should be ready, and so on. Find out, too, the requirements (such as health certificates and tests) the stud owner has regarding bitches accepted for breeding. If you will be shipping the bitch, find out which airport and airline should be used.

The airlines will probably have special requirements, too, regarding conditions under which they will or will not take dogs. These requirements, which change from time to time, include such things as crate size and type they will accept. Most airlines have their own crates

Ch. Mercer's Morning Glory is on the way to becoming an Outstanding Dam. Owned by Mercer Russo Ervin.

Ch. Sunstream Gypsy of Topbrass, an excellent winning and producing bitch from the Topbrass Goldens owned by Mrs. Joseph Mertens.

Ch. Russo's Cummings' Elsa, litter-sister to Ch. Cummings' Gold-Rush Charlie, is a great producer owned by Mercer Russo Ervin.

available for sale which may be purchased at a nominal cost, if you do not already have one that they consider suitable. These are made of fiberglass and are the safest type in which to ship a dog. Most airlines also require that the dog be at the airport two hours before the flight is scheduled to depart and that the dog is accompanied by a health certificate from your veterinarian, including information about rabies inoculation. If the airline does not wish to accept the bitch because of extreme temperature changes in the weather but will do so if you sign a waiver stating that she is accustomed to them and should have no problem, think it over carefully before doing so, as you are thus relieving them of any responsibility should the bitch not reach her destination alive or in good condition. And always insure the bitch when you can.

Normally the airline must be notified several days in advance for the bitch's reservation, as only a limited number of dogs can be accommodated on each flight. Plan on shipping the bitch on her eighth or ninth day, but if at all possible arrange it so that she avoids travelling on the weekend when schedules are not always the same and freight offices are likely to be closed.

It is important that whenever possible you ship your bitch on a flight that goes directly to the airport which is her destination. It is not at all unusual, when stopovers are made along the way, for a dog to be removed from the plane with other cargo and either incorrectly loaded for the next leg of the flight or left behind. Take every precaution that you can against human error!

It is simpler if you can plan to bring the bitch to the stud dog. Some people feel that the trauma of the plane trip may cause the bitch not to conceive; others just plain prefer not sending them that way. If you have a choice, you might do better to take the bitch in your own car where she will feel more relaxed and at ease. If you are doing it this way, be sure to allow sufficient time for the drive to get her to her destination at the correct time for the breeding. This usually is any time from the eighth to the fourteenth day, depending on the individual bitch and her cycle. Remember that if you want the bitch bred twice, you must allow a day in between the two services. Do not expect the stud's owner to put you up during your stay. Find a good, nearby motel that accepts dogs, and make a reservation for yourself there.

Above: This is Ch. Lady Sonata, foundation bitch at Tangleburr Goldens, winning a two-point major at Skyline Kennel Club, 1977. Bob Stebbins, handling. **Below:** Ch. Cummings' Dame Pepperhill winning the Brood Bitch Class under Arlene Thompson at the Garden State Specialty in 1977. The progeny pictured are Am., Can. Ch. Pepperhill's Basically Bear and Pepperhill's Sugar Bear. Pepperhill Farms, owners.

Professional handler Elliot More in an informal moment with one of his particularly successful favorites, the great bitch Am., Can. Ch. Russo's Pepperhill Poppy, owned by Jeffrey and Barbara Pepper's Pepperhill Farms. Poppy is an Outstanding Dam with at least eight champion get.

Just prior to your bitch's season, you should make a visit to your veterinarian with her. Have her checked for worms, make sure that she is up-to-date on all her shots, and attend to any other tests the stud owner may have requested. The bitch may act and be perfectly normal up until her third or fourth week of pregnancy, but it is better for her to have a clean bill of health before the breeding than to bother her after it. If she is overweight, right now is when you should start getting the fat off her; she should be in good hard condition, neither fat nor thin, when bred.

The day you've been waiting for finally arrives, and you notice the swelling of her vulva, followed within a day or two by the appearance of a colored discharge. Immediately call the stud's owner to finalize arrangements, advising whether you will ship her or bring her, the exact day she will arrive, and so on. Then, if she is going by plane, as soon as you know the details, advise the stud owner of the flight number, the time of arrival, and any other pertinent information. If you are shipping the bitch, the check for the stud fee should be mailed now. If the owner of the stud dog charges for his trips to the airport, for picking the bitch up and then returning her, reimbursement for this should either be included with the stud fee or sent as soon as you know the amount of the charge.

If you are going to ship your bitch, do not feed her on the day of the flight; the stud's owner will do so when she arrives. Be sure that she has had access to a drink of water just before you leave her and that she has been exercised prior to being put in her crate. Place several layers of newspapers, topped with some shredded papers, on the bottom of the crate for a good bed. The papers can be discarded and replaced when she reaches her destination prior to the trip home. Rugs and towels are not suitable for bedding material as they may become soiled, necessitating laundering when she reaches her destination. A small towel may be included to make her feel more at home if you wish. Remember to have her at the airport two hours ahead of flight time.

If you are driving, be sure to arrive at a reasonable time of day. If you are coming from a distance and get in late, have a good night's sleep before contacting the stud's owner first thing in the morning. If possible, leave the children and relatives at home; they will not only be in the way, but also most stud owners definitely object to too many people around during the actual breeding.

Best of Breed, Wallkill K.C. in 1972, Ch. Cummings' Puf O'Golden Springs, second generation champion from Am., Can. Ch. Cummings' Golden Princess. Mrs. Mary W. Cummings, owner.

Ch. Wochica's Gold-Rush Bonanza, grandmother of two Best in Show winners, at Westbury in 1973. Photo courtesy of Janet Bunce.

Once the breeding has been completed, if you wish to sit and visit for a while, that is fine; but do not leave the bitch at loose ends. Take her to her crate in the car where she can be quiet (you should first, of course, ascertain that the temperature is comfortable for her there and that she has proper ventilation). Remember that she should not urinate for at least an hour following the breeding.

If you have not already done so, pay the stud fee now, and be sure that you receive your breeding certificate and a copy of the dog's pedigree if you do not have one.

Now you are all set to await, with happy anticipation, the arrival of the puppies.

Am., Can. Ch. Cummings' Golden Princess winning the Brood Bitch Class at a Specialty in 1969. Left to right: Princess, Cummings' Golden Doubloon, and Thunder Cloud of Stillwater. Mrs. Mary W. Cummings.

Pedigrees

To anyone interested in the breeding of dogs, pedigrees are the basic component with which this is best accomplished. It is not sufficient to just breed two nice-looking dogs to one another and then sit back and await outstanding results. Chances are they will be disappointing, as there is no equal to a scientific approach to the breeding of dogs if quality results are the ultimate goal.

We have selected for you pedigrees of Golden Retreiver dogs and bitches who either are great producers or have come from consistently outstanding producing lines. Some of these dogs are so dominant that they have seemed to "click" with almost every strain or bloodline. Others, for best results, need to be carefully line-bred. The study of pedigrees and breeding is both a challenge and an exciting occupation.

Even if you have no plans to involve yourself in breeding and just anticipate owning and loving a dog or two, it is fun to trace back the pedigree of your dog, or dogs, to earlier generations and thus learn the sort of ancestors behind your own. Throughout this book you will find a great many pictures of dogs and bitches whose names appear in these pedigrees, enabling you not only to trace the names in the background of your Golden Retriever but also to see what the forebears look like.

Ch. Golden Pine's Easy Ace with Lloyd M. Case at the Longshore-Southport Kennel Club Dog Show, June 1961. Easy Ace is a grandsire of Cummings' Golden Princess, whose pedigree is shown at the top of the facing page and who went on to produce many champions.

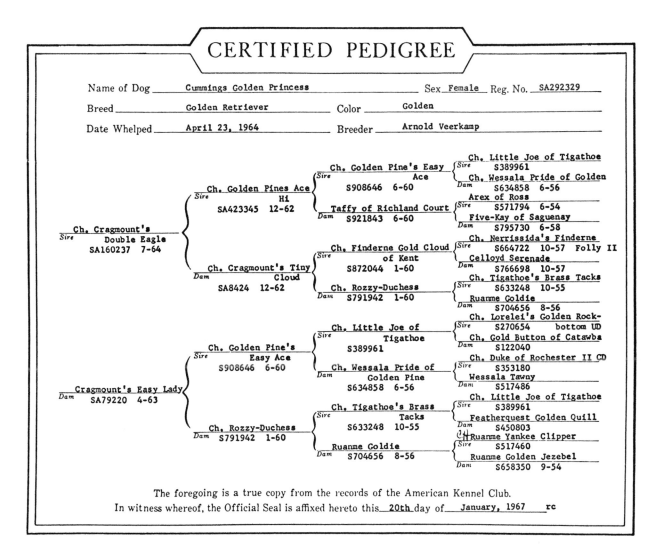

CERTIFIED PEDIGREE

Name of Dog ___Cummings Golden Princess___   Sex ___Female___   Reg. No. ___SA292329___

Breed ___Golden Retriever___   Color ___Golden___

Date Whelped ___April 23, 1964___   Breeder ___Arnold Veerkamp___

				Ch. Little Joe of Tigathoe
			Ch. Golden Pine's Easy	*Sire* S389961
		Ch. Golden Pines Ace	Ace	Ch. Wessala Pride of Golden
		Sire Hi	S908646 6-60	*Dam* S634858 6-56
		SA423345 12-62		Arex of Ross
			Taffy of Richland Court	*Sire* S571794 6-54
	Ch. Cragmount's	*Dam*	S921843 6-60	Five-Kay of Saguenay
	Sire Double Eagle			*Dam* S795730 6-58
	SA160237 7-64			Ch. Nerrissida's Finderne
			Ch. Finderne Gold Cloud	*Sire* S664722 10-57 Folly II
		Ch. Cragmount's Tiny	of Kent	Celloyd Serenade
		Dam Cloud	S872044 1-60	*Dam* S766698 10-57
		SA8424 12-62		Ch. Tigathoe's Brass Tacks
			Ch. Rozzy-Duchess	*Sire* S633248 10-55
			Dam S791942 1-60	Ruanme Goldie
				Dam S704656 8-56
				Ch. Lorelei's Golden Rock-
			Ch. Little Joe of	*Sire* S270654 bottom UD
		Ch. Golden Pine's	*Sire* Tigathoe	Ch. Gold Button of Catawba
		Sire Easy Ace	S389961	*Dam* S122040
		S908646 6-60		Ch. Duke of Rochester II CD
			Ch. Wessala Pride of	*Sire* S353180
			Dam Golden Pine	Wessala Tawny
	Cragmount's Easy Lady		S634858 6-56	*Dam* S517486
	Dam SA79220 4-63			Ch. Little Joe of Tigathoe
			Ch. Tigathoe's Brass	*Sire* S389961
		Ch. Rozzy-Duchess	*Sire* Tacks	Featherquest Golden Quill
		Dam S791942 1-60	S633248 10-55	*Dam* S450803
				Ch. Ruanme Yankee Clipper
			Ruanme Goldie	*Sire* S517460
			Dam S704656 8-56	Ruanme Golden Jezebel
				Dam S658350 9-54

The foregoing is a true copy from the records of the American Kennel Club.
In witness whereof, the Official Seal is affixed hereto this __20th__ day of __January, 1967__   rc

Ch. Cummings' Goldilocks, second generation champion from Am., Can. Ch. Cummings' Golden Princess and Ch. Cragmount's Hi-Lo. By Am., Can. Ch. Cummings' King Midas ex Chamois Beige. Mrs. Mary W. Cummings.

Ch. Cummings' Alexander the Great, a fourth generation champion from Am., Can. Ch. Cummings' Golden Princess, taking winners at Elm City in 1981 for owner Mrs. Mary W. Cummings.

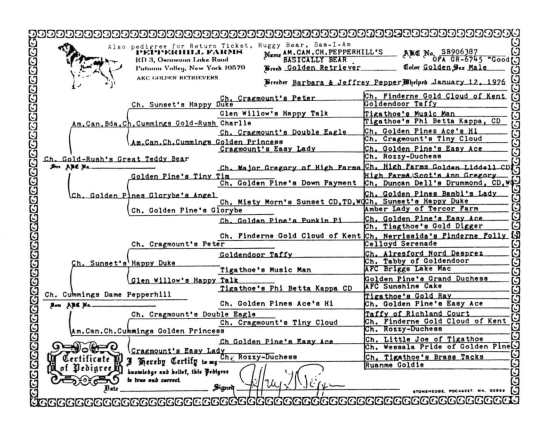

Also pedigree for Return Ticket, Huggy Bear, Sam-I-Am

PEPPERHILL FARMS
RD 3, Oscawana Lake Road
Putnam Valley, New York 10579
AKC GOLDEN RETRIEVERS

Name AM.CAN.CH.PEPPERHILL'S BASICALLY BEAR
AKC No. SB906387
OFA GR-6745 "Good"
Breed Golden Retriever
Color Golden Sex Male
Breeder Barbara & Jeffrey Pepper Whelped January 12, 1976

Ch. Gold-Rush's Great Teddy Bear

- Am.Can.Bda.Ch.Cummings Gold-Rush Charlie
  - Ch. Sunset's Happy Duke
    - Ch. Cragmount's Peter
      - Ch. Finderne Gold Cloud of Kent
      - Goldendoor Taffy
    - Glen Willow's Happy Talk
      - Tigathoe's Music Man
      - Tigathoe's Phi Betta Kappa, CD
  - Am.Can.Ch.Cummings Golden Princess
    - Ch. Cragmount's Double Eagle
      - Ch. Golden Pines Ace's Hi
      - Ch. Cragmount's Tiny Cloud
    - Cragmount's Easy Lady
      - Ch. Golden Pine's Easy Ace
      - Ch. Rozzy-Duchess

- Ch. Golden Pines Glorybe's Angel
  - Golden Pine's Tiny Tim
    - Ch. Major Gregory of High Farms
      - Ch. High Farms Golden Liddell CD
      - High Farms Scot's Ann Gregory
    - Ch. Golden Pine's Down Payment
      - Ch. Duncan Dell's Drummond, CD, WC
      - Ch. Golden Pines Bambi's Lady
  - Ch. Golden Pine's Glorybe
    - Ch. Misty Morn's Sunset CD,TD,WC
      - Ch. Sunset's Happy Duke
      - Amber Lady of Tercor Farm
    - Ch. Golden Pine's Punkin Pi
      - Ch. Golden Pine's Easy Ace
      - Ch. Tiagthoe's Gold Digger

Ch. Cummings Dame Pepperhill

- Ch. Sunset's Happy Duke
  - Ch. Cragmount's Peter
    - Ch. Finderne Gold Cloud of Kent
      - Ch. Nerrissida's Finderne Folly
      - Celloyd Serenade
    - Goldendoor Taffy
      - Ch. Alresford Nord Desprez
      - Ch. Tabby of Goldendoor
  - Glen Willow's Happy Talk
    - Tigathoe's Music Man
      - AFC Briggs Lake Mac
      - Golden Pine's Grand Duchess
    - Tigathoe's Phi Betta Kappa CD
      - AFC Sunshine Cake
      - Tigathoe's Gold Ray
- Am.Can.Ch.Cummings Golden Princess
  - Ch. Cragmount's Double Eagle
    - Ch. Golden Pines Ace's Hi
      - Ch. Golden Pine's Easy Ace
      - Taffy of Richland Court
    - Ch. Cragmount's Tiny Cloud
      - Ch. Finderne Gold Cloud of Kent
      - Ch. Rozzy-Duchess
  - Cragmount's Easy Lady
    - Ch Golden Pine's Easy Ace
      - Ch. Little Joe of Tigathoe
      - Ch. Wessala Pride of Golden Pine
    - Ch. Rozzy-Duchess
      - Ch. Tigathoe's Brass Tacks
      - Ruanme Goldie

Certificate of Pedigree

I Hereby Certify to my knowledge and belief, this Pedigree is true and correct.

Date _____ Signed _____

STONEHEDGE, POCASSET, MA. 02559

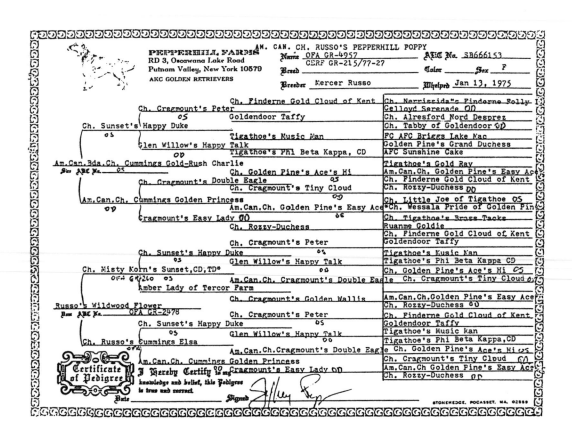

AM. CAN. CH. RUSSO'S PEPPERHILL POPPY

PEPPERHILL FARMS
RD 3, Oscawana Lake Road
Putnam Valley, New York 10579
AKC GOLDEN RETRIEVERS

Name OFA GR-4957
CERF GR-215/77-27
AKC No. SB666153
Breed
Color Sex F
Breeder Mercer Russo Whelped Jan 13, 1975

- Am.Can.Bda.Ch. Cummings Gold-Rush Charlie
  - Ch. Sunset's Happy Duke
    - Ch. Cragmount's Peter
      - Ch. Finderne Gold Cloud of Kent
        - Ch. Nerrissida"s Finderne Folly
        - Celloyd Serenade OD
      - Goldendoor Taffy
        - Ch. Alresford Nord Desprez
        - Ch. Tabby of Goldendoor OD
    - Glen Willow's Happy Talk
      - Tigathoe's Music Man
        - FC AFC Briggs Lake Mac
        - Golden Pine's Grand Duchess
      - Tigathoe's Phi Beta Kappa, CD
        - AFC Sunshine Cake
        - Tigathoe's Gold Ray
  - Am.Can.Ch. Cummings Golden Princess
    - Ch. Cragmount's Double Eagle
      - Ch. Golden Pine's Ace's Hi
        - Am.Can.Ch. Golden Pine's Easy Ace
        - Ch. Finderne Gold Cloud of Kent
      - Ch. Cragmount's Tiny Cloud
        - Ch. Rozzy-Duchess OD
    - Cragmount's Easy Lady OD
      - Am.Can.Ch. Golden Pine's Easy Ace
        - Ch. Little Joe of Tigathoe OS
        - Ch. Wessala Pride of Golden Pine
      - Ch. Rozzy-Duchess
        - Ch. Tigathoe's Brass Tacks
        - Ruanme Goldie

- Russo's Wildwood Flower OFA GR-2478
  - Ch. Misty Morn's Sunset,CD,TD OFA GR-260
    - Ch. Sunset's Happy Duke
      - Ch. Cragmount's Peter
        - Ch. Finderne Gold Cloud of Kent
        - Goldendoor Taffy
      - Glen Willow's Happy Talk
        - Tigathoe's Music Man
        - Tigathoe's Phi Beta Kappa CD
    - Amber Lady of Tercor Farm
      - Ch. Cragmount's Double Eagle
        - Ch. Golden Pine's Ace's Hi OS
        - Ch. Cragmount's Tiny Cloud
      - Ch. Cragmount's Golden Wallis
        - Am.Can.Ch.Golden Pine's Easy Ace
        - Ch. Rozzy-Duchess OD
  - Ch. Russo's Cummings Elsa
    - Ch. Sunset's Happy Duke
      - Ch. Cragmount's Peter
        - Ch. Finderne Gold Cloud of Kent
        - Goldendoor Taffy
      - Glen Willow's Happy Talk
        - Tigathoe's Music Man
        - Tigathoe's Phi Beta Kappa,CD
    - Am.Can.Ch. Cummings Golden Princess
      - Am.Can.Ch.Cragmount's Double Eagle
        - Ch. Golden Pine's Ace's Hi OS
        - Ch. Cragmount's Tiny Cloud OD
      - Cragmount's Easy Lady OD
        - Am.Can.Ch Golden Pine's Ace's Hi
        - Ch. Rozzy-Duchess OD

Certificate of Pedigree

I Hereby Certify to my knowledge and belief, this Pedigree is true and correct.

Date _____ Signed _____

STONEHEDGE, POCASSET, MA. 02559

390

Top Certificate

AM.CAN.CH. GOLDRUSH'S Sire CONTENDER U.D. (OS)

Reg No SB483011
OFA No GR 3643
EYES CLEAR
BIS WINNER

CH. WINDSOR'S MARK OF GOLD
OFA GR 109 03
EYES CLEAR
HALL OF FAME
BIS WINNER

ROCKGOLD'S Dam FANFARE OF BRASS
Reg No SB755946
OFA No GR6511
EYES CLEAR
8PTS 1 MAJOR
SPECIALTY RWB

Breed GOLDEN RETRIEVER
Whelped 11-18-78   Color GOLDEN
Height ___ Weight ___ Sex ___
BREEDER SUSAN McDONALD
OWNER J. HEINL

CH. MISTY MORN'S SUNSET C.D. T.D. W.C. (OS) OFA GR 260 HALL OF FAME	CH. SUNSET'S HAPPY DUKE (OS)	CH. CRAGMOUNT'S PETER (OS) HALL OF FAME	CH. FINDERNE GOLD CLOUD OF KENT (OS) HALL OF FAME
			GOLDENDOOR TAFFY
		GLEN WILLOW'S HAPPY TALK	CH. TIGATHOE'S MUSIC MAN
			TIGATHOE'S PHI BETA KAPPA
	AMBER LADY OF TERCOR FARM	AM.CAN.CH. CRAGMOUNT'S DOUBLE EAGLE	CH. GOLDEN PINE'S ACE HI
			CH. CRAGMOUNT'S TINY CLOUD
		CH. CRAGMOUNT'S GOLDEN WALLIS	AM.CAN.CH. GOLDEN PINE EASY ACE WC. (OS) HALL OF FAME
			CH. ROZZY DUCHESS
CH. GOLDRUSH'S BIRCH OF BEARWOOD AM.CAN CD. WC. (OD) OFA GR 1868	CH. SUN DANCE'S ESQUIRE'S PLAYBOY CDX	CH. SUN DANCE'S ESQUIRE CD (OS) HALL OF FAME	CH. SUN DANCE'S YANKEE DOLLAR CD
			CH. SUN DANCE'S GULIE
		CH. HARLENHEIM'S RUST HAVEN	CH. SUN DANCE'S VEGAS DEALER CD
			SUN DANCE'S DAWN OF HARLEN
	BEARWOOD'S HONEY BEAR CD	CH. SUN DANCE'S ESQUIRE CD. (OS) HALL OF FAME	CH. SUN DANCE'S YANKEE DOLLAR CD "Adim"
			CH. SUN DANCE'S GULIE
		CH. DUCKDOWN TUFFY OF BUCKSKIN CD.	CH. MAPLE LEAF'S TRACE-O- COPPER
			SUNDANCE'S GOLD INGOT
CH. ROCKGOLD CHUG'S RIC-O-SHAY (OS) OFA GR 159 EYES CLEAR GROUP PLACEMENTS	ROCKGOLD'S CHUG-O- LUG	AM.CAN. CH. STAR SPRAY MARIA'S RAYO DEL SOL	CH. FEATHERQUEST JAY'S BLOND TOM
			CH. STAR SPRAY ENID'S MARIA
		CH. ROCKGOLD'S FROLICKING GYPSY WC. OFA GR 32	CH. FLAMING ROCK (X-RAYED NORMAL)
			SCARSDALE'S LCON MARJORIE
	TENAURUM'S HOLKA OFA GR 301 7PTS. 1 MAJOR	CH. SCARSDALE'S BUCKSHOT X-RAYED NORMAL	TIMOTHY OF SCOTWELL
			SHERRY OF SCOTWELL
		JUDIANA'S GOLDEN GINGER	CH. GOLDEN KNOLLS TONKA
			JUDIANA'S HONEY DREAMER
CH. ROCKGOLD'S LYSISTRATA X-RAYED NORMAL EYES CLEAR	CH. HUNT'S COPPERFIELD DAEMON WC. (OS) OFA GR 885	AM.CAN.CH. KYRIE DAEMON CDX, WC. CAN.CD (OS) OFA GR. 148	DES LACS DELAWARE
			CH. GAYHAVEN HARMONY
		CH. HUNT'S ANNABELLE OF VEGAS CDX, WC. OFA GR 394	CH. SUN DANCE'S VEGAS DEALER CDX. WC.
			HUNT'S GOLDEN TANGERINE
	CH. RYDEN'S CHARISMA	CH. ROCKGOLD CHUG'S RIC-O-SHAY OFA GR 159	ROCKGOLD'S CHUG-O-LUG CD
			TENAURUM'S HOLKA
		HONEYSUCKLE OF YEO (ENG. IMPORT) OFA GR 211	ENG. IRISH CH. MANDINGO BUIDHE COLUM
			BRANDY O'COLY

I certify that this pedigree is true and correct to the best of my knowledge and belief.

Name Susan Heinl

Bottom Certificate

BUGABOO REG.
JOHN AND EDIE SHIELDS
R.R. #8 CALGARY, ALBERTA
T3J 2T9

9815 E. Parker Rd.
Parker, Co. 80134
841-2004

REGISTERED NAME: BUGABOO'S BARBIE-DOLL *
INDIVIDUAL REGISTRATION NO. SO 336486
REGISTERED LITTER NO. SM011635   CALL NAME "BARBIE"   BREED GOLDEN RETRIEVER
SEX Female   BORN OCT 18, 1981   COLOR AND MARKINGS LIGHT GOLDEN
BREEDER ___ ADDRESS ___
CITY ___ TATOO NO. ___

*EYES NORMAL 3/82
VWD NORMAL

CH. GOLDWING TRUE BEAR
SIRE
OFA #GR-10116 (GOOD)
EYES CLEAR 3/19/80

AM. & CAN. CH. BUGABOO'S APACHE DOLL
DAM
GR-11833-T
OFA - EYES CLEAR 9/81
VWD NORMAL

This pedigree is certified to be correct to the best of my knowledge and belief.

Signed ___   Date July 30 19 81

PARENTS	GRANDPARENTS	GREAT GRANDPARENTS	GREAT GREAT GRANDPARENTS
CH. GOLDWING TRUE BEAR	AM. & CAN. CH. GOLD-RUSH'S GREAT TEDDY BEAR SIRE OFA - CERF	AM. BMDA. & CAN. CH. CUMMINGS' GOLD-RUSH CHARLIE SIRE RADIOLOGIST - CERF	CH. SUNSET'S HAPPY DUKE
			AM. & CAN. CH. CUMMINGS' GOLDEN PRINCESS
		CH. GOLDEN PINES GLORYBE'S ANGEL DAM OFA - CERF	GOLDEN PINE'S TINY TIM OFA - EYES CLEAR
			CH. GOLDEN PINE GLORYBE HIPS & EYES NORMAL
	CH. GOLDWING RHYTHM-N-BLUE DAM HIPS NORMAL - CERF	AM BMDA & CAN. CH. CUMMINGS' GOLD-RUSH CHARLIE SIRE RADIOLOGIST - CERF	CH SUNSET'S HAPPY DUKE
			AM. & CAN. CH. CUMMINGS' GOLDEN PRINCESS
		CH. GOLDEN PINE JUST-A-MINUTE DAM HIPS NORMAL - CERF	GOLDEN PINE'S TINY TIM
			CH. GOLDEN PINE GLORYBE
AM. & CAN. CH. BUGABOO'S APACHE DOLL	AM. & CAN. CH. KRISHNA'S KLASSIC KACHINA SIRE OFA #GR-6493 CERF #GR-434/78-36	CH. AUTUMN LODGES MR. ZAP SIRE OFA #GR-2600	CH. MISTY MORN'S SUNSET OFA #GR-260 CO TD
			AUTUMN LODGE'S LI'L INDIAN
		CH. LARK MILL GENEVIVE CD DAM	AM CAN & MEX CH CALVO'S HAPPY AMBASSADOR OFA #GR-1102
			CH MISS LIBERTY O'LARK HILL OFA
	AM. & CAN. CH. COUNTRY SUN'S MS. CRICKET DAM OFA #GR-7173-T CERF #GR-1236/78-30 VWD NORMAL	AM. BMDA. & CAN. CH. CUMMINGS' GOLD-RUSH CHARLIE SIRE RADIOLOGIST - CERF	CH. SUNSET'S HAPPY DUKE
			CH. CUMMINGS' GOLDEN PRINCESS
		CH. BOCKOUT'S COUNTRY SUNSHINE DAM OFA #GR-3575-T CO	CH. GOLDENWIRE'S GAY CADET
			HONEY GIRL'S STORMY SUNSET CO

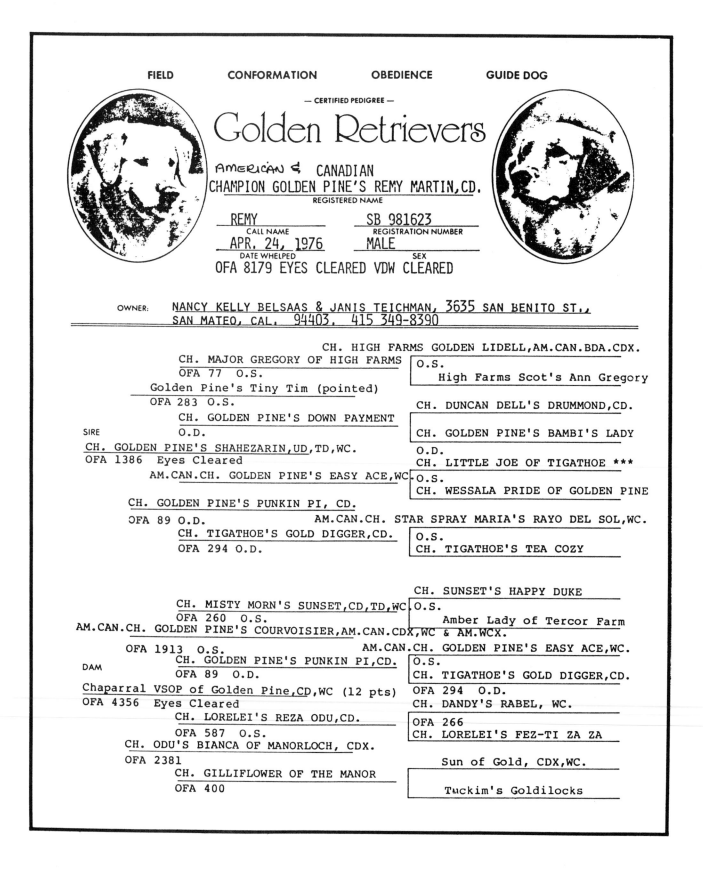

FIELD   CONFORMATION   OBEDIENCE   GUIDE DOG

— CERTIFIED PEDIGREE —

Golden Retrievers

AMERICAN & CANADIAN
CHAMPION GOLDEN PINE'S REMY MARTIN, CD.
REGISTERED NAME

REMY   SB 981623
CALL NAME   REGISTRATION NUMBER
APR. 24, 1976   MALE
DATE WHELPED   SEX
OFA 8179 EYES CLEARED VDW CLEARED

OWNER: NANCY KELLY BELSAAS & JANIS TEICHMAN, 3635 SAN BENITO ST.,
SAN MATEO, CAL. 94403. 415 349-8390

			CH. HIGH FARMS GOLDEN LIDELL,AM.CAN.BDA.CDX.
	CH. MAJOR GREGORY OF HIGH FARMS	O.S.	
	OFA 77 O.S.		High Farms Scot's Ann Gregory
	Golden Pine's Tiny Tim (pointed)		
	OFA 283 O.S.	CH. DUNCAN DELL'S DRUMMOND,CD.	
	CH. GOLDEN PINE'S DOWN PAYMENT		
SIRE	O.D.	CH. GOLDEN PINE'S BAMBI'S LADY	
CH. GOLDEN PINE'S SHAHEZARIN,UD,TD,WC.	O.D.		
OFA 1386 Eyes Cleared	CH. LITTLE JOE OF TIGATHOE ***		
	AM.CAN.CH. GOLDEN PINE'S EASY ACE,WC	O.S.	
	CH. GOLDEN PINE'S PUNKIN PI, CD.	CH. WESSALA PRIDE OF GOLDEN PINE	
	OFA 89 O.D.	AM.CAN.CH. STAR SPRAY MARIA'S RAYO DEL SOL,WC.	
	CH. TIGATHOE'S GOLD DIGGER,CD.	O.S.	
	OFA 294 O.D.	CH. TIGATHOE'S TEA COZY	

			CH. SUNSET'S HAPPY DUKE
	CH. MISTY MORN'S SUNSET,CD,TD,WC	O.S.	
	OFA 260 O.S.		Amber Lady of Tercor Farm
AM.CAN.CH. GOLDEN PINE'S COURVOISIER,AM.CAN.CDX,WC & AM.WCX.			
OFA 1913 O.S.	CH. GOLDEN PINE'S PUNKIN PI,CD.	AM.CAN.CH. GOLDEN PINE'S EASY ACE,WC.	
DAM	OFA 89 O.D.	O.S.	
		CH. TIGATHOE'S GOLD DIGGER,CD.	
Chaparral VSOP of Golden Pine,CD,WC (12 pts)	OFA 294 O.D.		
OFA 4356 Eyes Cleared	CH. DANDY'S RABEL, WC.		
	CH. LORELEI'S REZA ODU,CD.	OFA 266	
	OFA 587 O.S.	CH. LORELEI'S FEZ-TI ZA ZA	
CH. ODU'S BIANCA OF MANORLOCH, CDX.			
OFA 2381	Sun of Gold, CDX,WC.		
	CH. GILLIFLOWER OF THE MANOR		
	OFA 400	Tuckim's Goldilocks	

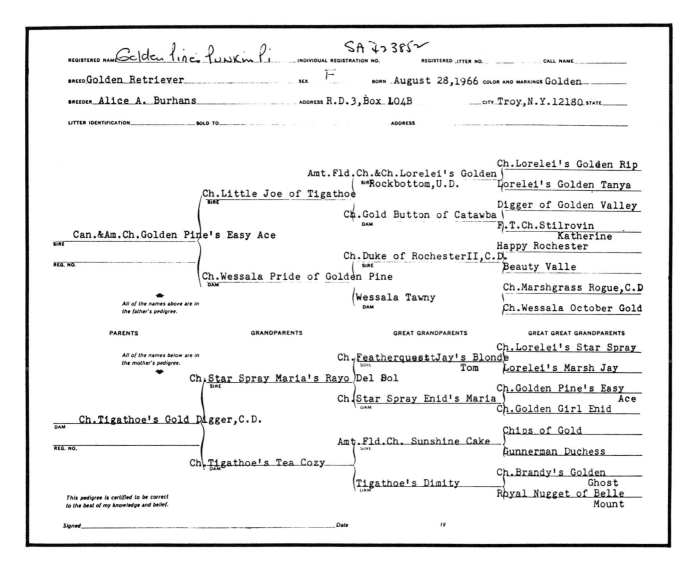

REGISTERED NAME Golden Pine Punkin Pi   SA 72385   INDIVIDUAL REGISTRATION NO.   REGISTERED LITTER NO.   CALL NAME

BREED Golden Retriever   SEX F   BORN August 28,1966   COLOR AND MARKINGS Golden

BREEDER Alice A. Burhans   ADDRESS R.D.3, Box 104B   CITY Troy, N.Y. 12180 STATE

LITTER IDENTIFICATION   SOLD TO   ADDRESS

Ch.Little Joe of Tigathoe
SIRE

Amt.Fld.Ch.&Ch.Lorelei's Golden
SIRE Rockbottom,U.D.

Ch.Lorelei's Golden Rip

Lorelei's Golden Tanya

Ch.Gold Button of Catawba
DAM

Digger of Golden Valley

F.T.Ch.Stilrovin Katherine

Can.&Am.Ch.Golden Pine's Easy Ace
SIRE

REG. NO.

Ch.Wessala Pride of Golden Pine
DAM

Ch.Duke of RochesterII,C.D.
SIRE

Happy Rochester

Beauty Valle

Wessala Tawny
DAM

Ch.Marshgrass Rogue,C.D

Ch.Wessala October Gold

All of the names above are in the father's pedigree.

PARENTS   GRANDPARENTS   GREAT GRANDPARENTS   GREAT GREAT GRANDPARENTS

All of the names below are in the mother's pedigree.

Ch.Star Spray Maria's Rayo Del Bol
SIRE

Ch.Featherquest Jay's Blonde Tom
SIRE

Ch.Lorelei's Star Spray

Lorelei's Marsh Jay

Ch.Star Spray Enid's Maria
DAM

Ch.Golden Pine's Easy Ace

Ch.Golden Girl Enid

Ch.Tigathoe's Gold Digger,C.D.
DAM

REG. NO.

Ch.Tigathoe's Tea Cozy
DAM

Amt.Fld.Ch. Sunshine Cake
SIRE

Chips of Gold

Gunnerman Duchess

Tigathoe's Dimity
DAM

Ch.Brandy's Golden Ghost

Royal Nugget of Belle Mount

This pedigree is certified to be correct to the best of my knowledge and belief.

Signed   Date   19

PEDIGREE OF Ch. Golden Pine Glorybe's Angel

Sire Golden Pine's Tiny Tim
Reg. No.
Reg. No.

Ch. Major Gregory of High Farms

Ch. High Farms Golden Liddell Am. & Can. C.D.X.

Eng. Ch. Crusader of Carthew

Eng. Ch. Camrose Fantango
Caona of Carthew

Ch. Lucky Penny of High Farms

Ch. Ritz of High Farms
Meadow Creek Ko-Ko

High Farms Scot's Ann Gregory

Ch. Golden Scot of High Farms

Ch. Ritz of High Farms
Meadow Creek Ko-Ko

Zeta's Bright Star

Ch. Golden Band of High Farms
Dipper's Zeta of High Farms

Ch. Golden Pine's Down Payment

Ch. Duncan Dell's Drummond C.D.

Ch. Hilane Sirroco

Ch. Sprucewood Ching
Kellys Kier of Kieps

Ch. Hillcrest Marigold

Ch. Sprucewood Chore Boy
Sunbonnet Sue of Hillcrest C.D.

Ch. Golden Pine's Bambi's Lady

Ch. Little Joe of Tigathoe

Amt. Fld. Ch. & Ch. Lorelei's Golden Rockbottom UD
Ch. Gold Button of Catawba

Ch. Wessala Pride of Golden Pine

Ch. Duke of Rochester C. D.
Wessala Tawny

Dam Golden Pine Glorybe
Reg. No.
Reg. No.

Ch. Misty Morn's Sunset

Ch. Sunset's Happy Duke

Ch. Cragmount's Peter

Ch. Finderne Gold Cloud of Kent
Goldendoor Taffy

Glen Willow's Happy Talk

Ch. Tigathoe's Music Man
Tigathoe's Phi Beta Kappa CD

Amber Lady of Tercor Farm

Ch. Cragmount's Double Eagle

Ch. Golden Pine's Ace's Hi
Ch. Cragmount's Tiny Cloud

Ch. Cragmount's Golden Wallis

Ch. Golden Pine's Easy Ace
Ch. Rozzy-Duchess

Golden Pine's Punkin Pi

Am. & Can. Ch. Golden Pine's Easy Ace

Ch. Little Joe of Tigathoe

Amt. Fld. Ch. & Ch. Lorelei's Golden Rockbottom UD
Ch. Gold Button of Catawba

Ch. Wessala Pride of Golden Pine

Ch. Duke of Rochester II C. D.
Wessala Tawny

Ch. Tigathoe's Gold Digger C.D.

Ch. Star Spray Maria's Rayo Del Sol

Ch. Featherquest Jay's Blonde Tom
Ch. Star Spray Enid's Maria

Ch. Tigathoe's Tea Cozy

Amt. Fld. Ch. Sunshine Cake
Tigathoe's Dimity

Breed
Whelped   Color
Height   Weight   Sex F
BREEDER Mary-Luise Semans
OWNER Ann R. Johnson, Gold-Rush Kennels

I certify that this pedigree is true and correct to the best of my knowledge and belief.

(Signed)

393

Am-Can Ch Sugarbear's Wylwind Tobey Am-Can CD
OFA GR-12158
Eyes vet. opthamologist clear

- **Am/Can Ch Meadowpond Dustin Sugarbear**
  OFA #GR-7255, CERF #GR-734/79-31
  Group Placements
  - **Ch Jungold Legend of Golden Pine**
    OFA #GR-1982, Brother to 3 Ch
    - **Golden Pine's Tiny Tim**
      OFA #GR-283, Ch pts., 1 mjr
      GRCA Outstanding Sire (9)
      - Ch Major Gregory of High Farms
        OFA, GRCA Outstanding Sire (23)
      - Ch Golden Pine's Down Payment
        GRCA Outstanding Dam
    - **Ch Golden Pine's Glorybe**
      GRCA Outstanding Dam (6)
      - Ch Misty Morn Sunset CD TD*
        OFA, CERF, GRCA Show Hall of Fame
        GRCA Outstanding Sire (95)
      - Ch Golden Pine's Punkin Pie CD
        OFA, GRCA Outstanding Dam
  - **Am/Can Ch Cimaron's Dazzle Dust**
    CDX, TD, WC CERF #GR-264/76-31
    Sister to 2 Ch
    - **Am/Can Ch Laurell's Especial Jason UDT*, Can UDT, OFA, CERF**
      GRCA Show Hall of Fame
      GRCA OS
      - Ch Major Gregory of High Farms
        (See above)
      - Ch Laurell's Amiable Caboose
        OFA, CERF, GRCA Outstanding Dam
    - **Ch Duckdown's Voodoo Charm UD**
      OFA #GR-734
      GRCA Outstanding Dam
      - Ch Sun Dance's Moonlight Gambler
        CDX, GRCA Outstanding Sire (12)
      - Ch Sprucewood's Harvest Sugar CD
        GRCA Outstanding Dam (19)

- **Topbrass Ruffian's Maida**
  OFA #GR-6194, CERF #GR-264/77-44
  - **Ch Malagold Beckwith Om K Ivan CD**
    OFA #GR-542, CERF #GR-108/75-85
    GRCA Outstanding Sire
    Brother to 6 Ch
    - **Am/Can/Mex Ch Beckwith's Copper Ingot**
      OFA #GR-63
      GRCA Outstanding Sire (24 Ch)
      - Am/Can/Mex/Ber/Col
        Ch Beckwith's Copper Coin
        GRCA Hall of Fame, 16 BIS
      - Beckwith's Gayhaven Fancy
        OFA #GR-4
    - **Am/Can Ch Beckwith's Frolic of Yeo CDX, OFA #GR-235**
      GRCA Outstanding Dam
      - Ch Orlando of Yeo
        (English Import)
      - Jessica of Yeo
        GRCA Outstanding Dam
  - **Topbrass Fiery Saffron CDX**
    OFA #GR-1111 (Exc.), CERF #GR316/76-17
    - **Polka of Handjem**
      OFA #GR-092
      GRCA OS of 3 Fld. Ch. and 2 Bench Champions
      - FC & AFC Brandy Snifter
      - Ch Torch of Handjem***
    - **Valentine Torch of Topbrass**
      OFA #GR-675, CERF #GR-207/76-84
      Dam of 9 Ch. & 7 HIT Dogs
      - Ch Rockgold Chug's Ric O Shay
        OFA #GR-159, GRCA OS
      - Ch Goldenloe's Bronze Lustre
        OFA #GR-268

- **Am-Can Ch. Duckdown's Unpredictable CD WC OFA CERF O.S. SDHF** Group & Specialty Winner Top 10 Goldens
  - **Ch. Sundance's Moonlight Gambler CDX WC O.S.** X-rayed Group & Specialty winner
    - **Ch. Sundances Sir Ivan CDX**
      - Am-Can Ch. Sprucewoods Chocki 12 BIS 45 Group win
      - Sundances Gold Lightening UD
    - **Sundances Gold Ingot CD**
      - Ch. Indian Knolls RocCloud UD O.S.
      - Ch. Sprucewood's Glamour Girl CDX O.D.
  - **Ch. Sprucewoods Harvest Sugar CD** X-rayed
    GRCA Outstanding Dam
    - **Ch. Furore Harvest Gold** Best-In-Show winner
      - Ch. Sprucewoods Ching
      - Des Lac's Golden Heart O.D.
    - **Am-Can Ch. Sprucewood Chiniki** Specialty Winner
      - Am-Can Ch. Golden Knolls King Alphonzo O.S. 21 BIS
      - Am-Can Ch. Chee Chee of Sprucewood O.D. (16) 5 BIS

- **Am-Can Ch Amberac's Beausoliel CD**
  OFA GR-9471
  Eyes vet. opthamologist clear
  - **Laurell's Etego Catawba CD**
    6 points (1 major) OFA
    Littermate to: 3 champions including Am-Can Ch. Laurell's Especial Jason Am-Can UDT SDHF Top 10 Goldens OFA CERF
    - **Ch. Major Gregory of High Farms OFA O.S.** Group Wins Top Ten Goldens
      - Ch. High Farms Golden Liddell Am-Can-Ber CDX
      - High Farms Scots Ann Gregory
    - **Ch. Laurell's Amiable Caboose OFA O.D.**
      - Ch. High Farms Sutters Gold OFA 5 Group 1st
      - Ch. Rusticanas Princess Teena OFA Am-Can CD
  - **Amberac's Reeva Rustelle**
    OFA CERF GRCA Outstanding Dam of 5 Champions
    - **Zeurcher's Tawneika Lass** pointed X-rayed
      - **Wildwing Topbrass OFA**
        - Ch. Wildwing Stormy** OFA O.S.
        - Tigerdales Brazen Angel
      - **Zuercher's Replica of Taffy** X-rayed
        - Ch. Hilltops Tawny Lad Westminster win
        - Zeurcher's Golden Rod CDX

Co-owner: Mary Wuestenberg
Asterling Goldens

Pedigree Certificate

Name: Ch. Sunset's Happy Duke   A.K.C.# SG-341289
Breed: Golden Retriever   Sex: M   Breeder: Charles A. Cronheim
Color: Golden   Whelped: 1-8-1964

		SIRE Ch. Loreleis Marshgrass Rebel	SIRE Ch. Loreleis Golden Rip
	SIRE Ch. Nerrissida's Finderne Folly II		DAM Ch. Golden Tassie III
		DAM Loreleis Lucky Penny	SIRE Ch. Loreleis Golden Rockbottes
SIRE Ch. Finderne gold cloud of kent S-872644			DAM FeatherGuest Pamela
		SIRE Ch. Copper's Czar Again	SIRE Ch. Prince Copper of Malibu
	DAM Celloyd Serenade S-766698		DAM Ch. Czar Bracken of Coastwi:
		DAM Celloyd Bess of Nashoba	SIRE Ch. Marshgrass Rogue
SIRE Ch. Cragmount's Peter SA-31166			DAM Tonkah of Penny
		SIRE E.Ch. Alexander of Elsiville	SIRE Torrydale Tinker
	SIRE Ch. Alresford Nord Desprez S-703618		DAM Zens of Elsiville
		DAM E.Ch. Alresford Mail	SIRE Alresford Last langt
DAM Goldendoor Taffy S-727634			DAM Windwood Honey Al
		SIRE Ch. Loreleis Marshgrass Rebel	SIRE Ch. Loreleis Golden Rip
	DAM Tabby of Goldendoor S-553460		DAM Ch. Loreleis Tassie III
		DAM Sherrymont Sarah	SIRE Stubbings Golden Simon
			DAM Stubbings Golden Olive
		SIRE Granite City Red	SIRE Kin Kem
	SIRE Briggs Lake Mac Ad.Ch. Amt.Fld Ch. S-752673		DAM Tondahal June
		DAM Briggs Lake Ginger	SIRE Golden Boy Hanaver
Tigathoe's SIRE Music Man			DAM Lady of the Valley
		SIRE Ch.Ritz of High Farms S-604651	SIRE Featherfetch Tucker Ch.
	DAM Golden Pines Grand Duchess		DAM Ch.Golden Gal of High Farm:
		DAM Golden Pine Belle Tigathoe	SIRE Ch. Little Toe of Tigathoe
DAM Glen Willow's Happy Talk SA-86357			DAM Ch. Wessala Pride of Gold
		SIRE Chips of Gold S-458914	SIRE Rival of Wolf River
	SIRE Amt Fld Cn. Sunshine Cake S-659147		DAM Beaver Tail Bean
		DAM Gummerman Duchess II	SIRE Kingdale Buck Fld.Ch.
S-998744 DAM Tigathoe's Phi Beta Kappa ed			DAM Flaming Copper
		SIRE Ch. Rockhaven Raynard of Fo-Ga-Ta S-44764 Fld.Ch. Amt.Ch. Can.Dual	SIRE Rockhaven Rastus
	DAM Tigathoe's Gold Ray		DAM Judge of Dewstraw (Importe:
		DAM Tigathoe's Fireball	SIRE Loreleis Sanchar Danny C.D.
			DAM Gold Button of Catawba

THIS PEDIGREE IS CERTIFIED TO BE CORRECT TO THE BEST OF MY KNOWLEDGE AND BELIEF.
Signed _____ Date _____

MAGGIE STRAUB, P. O. BOX 98, NEWTOWN, CONN.

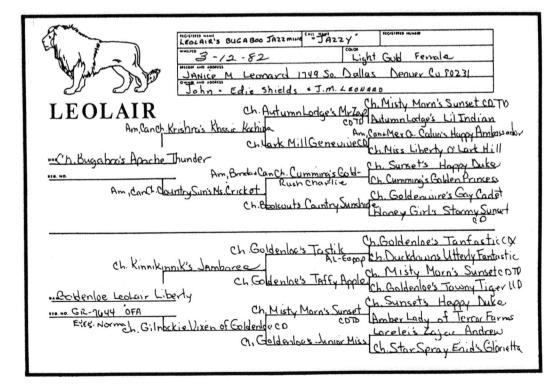

LEOLAIR

REGISTERED NAME	LEOLAIR's BUGABOO JAZZMINE	CALL NAME "JAZZY"	REGISTERED NUMBER
WHELPED 3-12-82		COLOR Light Gold Female	

BREEDER AND ADDRESS: Janice M Leonard 1749 So. Dallas Denver Co 80231
OWNER AND ADDRESS: John · Edie Shields & J.M. Leonard

Ch. Bugaboo's Apache Thunder
REG. NO.

- Am,Canch Krishna's Khssic Kachina
  - Ch. Autumn Lodge's Mr Zap CDTD
    - Ch. Misty Morn's Sunset CD TD
    - Autumn Lodge's Li'l Indian
  - Ch. Lark Mill Genevieve CD
    - Am,Can&Mex Ch. Calvin's Happy Ambassador
    - Ch. Miss Liberty O'Lark Hill
- Am,Canch Country Sun's Ms.Cricket
  - Am,Brmd&CanCh. Cummings Gold- Rush Charlie
    - Ch. Sunset's Happy Duke
    - Ch. Cumming's Golden Princess
  - Ch. Brookouts Country Sunshine
    - Ch. Goldenwire's Gay Cadet
    - Honey Girl's Stormy Sunset CD

..Goldenloe Leolair Liberty
REG. NO. GR-7644 OFA
EYES: Norm

- Ch. Kinnikinnik's Jamboree
  - Ch. Goldenloe's Tastik
    - Ch. Goldenloe's Tanfastic CDX
    - Ch. Duckdowns Utterly Fantastic
  - Ch. Goldenloe's Taffy Apple AL-Eopop
    - Ch. Misty Morn's Sunset CD TD
    - Ch. Goldenloe's Tawny Tiger UD
- Ch. Gilnockie Vixen of Goldenloe CD
  - Ch. Misty Morn's Sunset CD TD
    - Ch. Sunset's Happy Duke
    - Amber Lady of Terrar Farms
  - Ch. Goldenloe's Junior Miss
    - Loreleis Zajac Andrew
    - Ch. Star Spray Enid's Glorietta

Certified Pedigree

SC471754
INDIVIDUAL REG NO

SC471754
LITTER REG NO

Rabbit
CALL NAME

AKC
REGISTERED WITH

CH DASUS CHAMPAGNE EDITION CDX CAN CD
REGISTERED NAME OF DOG

BREED ___

DATE WHELPED 6-9-78

SEX Female

BREEDER Dave + Suzi Bluford   ADDRESS ___

OWNER "   "   "   ADDRESS ___

GENERAL DESCRIPTION ___

SIRE

CH FOOTPRINT OF YEO CD

- INT CH MANDINGO BUIDHE COLUM
  - ALRESFORD NICE FELLA
    - ALRESFORD CARLETON KIM
    - ALRESFORD CHIQUITA
  - BUIDHE DEARG
    - CH & FTCH DAVID OF WESTLEY
    - CH STUBBLESDOWN VANDA
- JESSICA OF YEO
  - RINGMASTER OF YEO
    - CH ALRESFORD ADVERTISER
    - CH PANDOWN POPPET OF YEO
  - JUDITH OF YEO
    - TREGASSA BRUSH OF YEO
    - DARTMOOR GOLDEN GLORIOUS

CH SABAHKAS ALEXANDER OF CAL-VO CD - GRCA Outstanding Sire

REG. NO. SA823141

- CH MALAGOLD BECKWITH BIG BUFF
  - INT CH BECKWITHS COPPER COIN
    - BECKWITHS GOLDEN BLAZE CD
    - VENOS VIXEN CD
  - BECKWITHS CHRYS-HAEFEN BELINDA
    - CH MEL-BACHS CURLEY CDX
    - BECKWITHS FLAVIA CD
- CH BECKWITHS MALAGOLD STARFARM
  - CH GOLDEN BAND OF HIGH FARMS
    - CH RITZ OF HIGH FARMS
    - MEADOW CREEK KO-KO
  - BECKWITHS CHICKASAW JINGLE
    - CH CHICKASAW MISCHIEF MAKER
      - CH GOLDEN PINES HIGH FARMS FEZ
      - HIGH FARMS CHICKASAWS GALE

DAM

CH WENDY VIII UD ✴ WCX — GRCA Outstanding Dam

REG. NO. ___

- LEO OF LOS ALTOS
  - ROYAL GOLDEN OF PARK LANE
    - FOREVER SANDY
      - SANDYMAN OF BRIGHT RIDGE
      - FOREVER AMBER RAH
    - LADY MILLICENT
      - ALRESFORD BOUVERIE CD
      - GRAND DUCHESS MILISSA
  - GOLDEN MARIDEAN OF LOS ALTOS
    - CH JASON OF GOLDEN ANNO NUEVO UD
      - CH JEWELITES MR SWAGGER CD
      - SAMIRA OF GOLDEN ANNO NUEVA
    - PRINCESS PAT OF LOS ALTOS
      - CH OAKWIN JUNIOR
      - QUEEN ANN 11
- AMANDA OF LYNN D'OR
  - TRADEWIND CLIPPER OF GOLD
    - GOLDEN ROCKET OF WAKEFIELD
      - CH AGNEWS JABBER
      - SWAGS GOLDEN FLARE
    - GOLDEN MISSILE OF WAKEFIELD
      - MR SWAGGERS GOLD CHIP
      - HESPERIAN TINA
  - BECKWITHS PROMISE OF DALKA CDX✴
    - COL AMER CAN BER MEX CH BECKWITHS COPPER COIN
      - BECKWITHS GOLDEN BLAZE CD
      - VENOS VIXEN CD
    - BECKWITHS CHRYS-HAEFEN BELINDA
      - CH MEL-BACHS CURLEY CDX
      - BECKWITHS FLAVIA CD

I HEREBY CERTIFY THAT THIS PEDIGREE IS TRUE AND CORRECT
TO THE BEST OF MY KNOWLEDGE AND BELIEF

SIGNED ___

DATE ___ 19__

CERTIFIED PEDIGREE

CH. BIRNAM WOOD'S RITA D RIOT ACT   OFA GR-8292 "Good"
REGISTERED NAME OF DOG

BREED **Golden Retriever**   DATE WHELPED **4-1-77**   SEX **Bitch**

BREEDER **Sylvia Donahey**   ADDRESS

OWNER **Linda & Doug Walker**   ADDRESS **7882 Springport Rd., Parma, Mi. 49269**

GENERAL DESCRIPTION

SIRE

OTCH. Windy's the Forecast
OFA, OCHOF
OS

- AM-CAN CH. Bardfield Boomer AM-CAN UDT*
  OCHOF, OS, OFA
  - AM-CAN CH. Duckdown's Unpredictable CD*
    OFA, OS, SCHOF
    - *CH. Sun Dance's Moonlight Gambler CDX* OS, SCHOF
    - *CH. Sprucewood's Harvest Sugar CD* OD
  - Sandia's Flaxen Babe CD
    OD
    - Wessala Flaxen
    - Sandia
- Sunstream's Little Echo
  OFA GR-1514
  - Conquest of Anbria
    OFA GR-067
    - ENG-IR. Dual CH. David of Westley
    - ENG.CH. Jane of Anbria
  - Sunstream's Golden Taffy
    - CH. Prince Royal of Los Altos CD
    - AM-CAN CH. Sunstream's Gold Dust CD

CH. DECOY'S BUCKINGHAM GROVER CDX, AM-CAN WC
REG. NO. OFA "Good"

- CH. Honor's Grandeur CDX*
  OFA, OS, SCHOF
  - AM-CAN-MEX CH. Beckwith's Copper Ingot
    OS OFA
    - AM-CAN-MEX-COL-BDA CH. Beckwith's Copper Coin
    - Beckwith's Gayhaven Fancy
  - Ch. Honor's Charade
    OFA
    - CH. Milaur's Baal Benefactor
    - CH. Honor's Coed*
- Laurell's Honor's Gibson Girl CDX
  OFA "GOOD"
  OD-4
  - CH. Duckdown's Veronica Laker CD
    OFA, OD
    - *CH. Sun Dance's Moonlight Gambler CDX* OS, SCHOF
      - *CH. Sun Dance's Sir Ivan CDX OS
      - *Sun Dance's Gold Ingot CD OD
    - *CH. Sprucewood's Harvest Sugar CD OD-19
      - *CH. Furore Harvest Gold
      - *AM-CAN CH. Sprucewood's Chinki

DAM

CH. Duckdown's Spannew CD
SCHOF, OS

- CH. Sun Dance's Bronze CD
  OS
  - CH. Indian Knoll's Roc-Cloud
    UD OCHOF, OS-23
    - CH. Rocky of Holland Farm
    - Indian Knoll's Misty
  - Sidram Kapering Korky CD
    - Sidram Shortstop
    - Sidram Sawanee
- CH. Sprucewood's Harvest Sugar CD
  OD-19
  - *CH. Furore Harvest Gold
    SCHOF
    - *CH. Sprucewood's Ching
    - Des Lac's Golden Heart
  - *AM-CAN CH. Sprucewood's Chinki
    - AM-CAN CH. Golden Knoll's King Alphonzo SCHOF, OS
    - *AM-CAN CH. Chee-Chee of Sprucewood SCHOF, OD

Spannen's Winged Victory
OFA, OD
REG. NO. ....

- CH. Sun Dance's Vegas Dealer CDX*
  - CH. Sun Dance's Bronze CD
    - CH. Indian Knoll's Roc-Cloud UD
    - Sidram Kapering Korky CD
  - *CH. Sprucewood's Glamour Girl
    CDX OD
    - *AM-CAN CH. Sprucewood's Chocki
    - Des Lac's Golden Heart
- CH. Dealer's Donation to Duckdown CD
  OD
  - CH. Sun Dance's Sprig of Holly CDX**
    - *Sun Dance's Shadrack CD
      - *AM-CAN CH. Sprucewood's Chocki
      - Sun Dance's Gold Lightening UD
    - CH. Sun Dance's Athena CD
      OD
      - CH. Sun Dance's Bronze CD
      - Heatherington Jeane CD

I HEREBY CERTIFY THAT THIS PEDIGREE IS TRUE AND CORRECT
TO THE BEST OF MY KNOWLEDGE AND BELIEF

SIGNED *Linda J. Walker*

DATE *August 6* 19 80

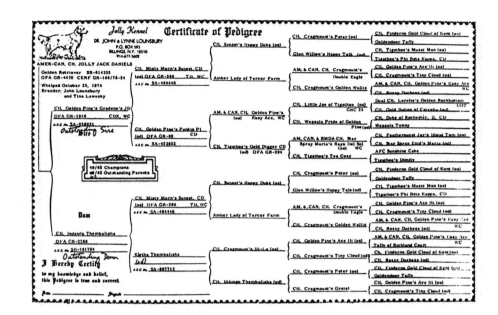

Jolly Kennel — Certificate of Pedigree

DR. JOHN & LYNNE LOUNSBURY
P.O. BOX 593
BILLINGS, N.Y. 12510
914-677-5602

AMER-CAN. CH. JOLLY JACK DANIELS
Golden Retriever SB-614352
OFA GR-4470 CERF GR-196/76-24
Whelped October 25, 1974
Breeder: John Lounsbury and Tina Lewesky

	CH. Sunset's Happy Duke (os)	CH. Cragmount's Peter (os)	CH. Finderne Gold Cloud of Kent (os)
			Goldendoor Taffy
CH. Misty Morn's Sunset, CD		Glen Willow's Happy Talk (od)	CH. Tigathoe's Music Man (os)
(os) OFA GR-280 TD, WC			Tigathoe's Phi Beta Kappa, CD
A.E.C. no. SA-464440	Amber Lady of Tercor Farm	AM. & CAN. CH. Cragmount's Double Eagle	CH. Golden Pine's Ace Hi (os)
CH. Golden Pine's Gradene's JD			CH. Cragmount's Tiny Cloud (od)
OFA GR-1816 CDX, WC		CH. Cragmount's Golden Wallis	AM. & CAN. CH. Golden Pine's Easy Ace WC
A.E.C. no. SA-358931			CH. Rozzy Duchess (od)
Outstanding Sire	AM. & CAN. CH. Golden Pine's Easy Ace, WC	CH. Little Joe of Tigathoe (os) GMC 25	Dual CH. Lorelei's Golden Rockbottom UDT
			CH. Gold Button of Catawba (od)
CH. Golden Pine's Punkin Pi		CH. Wessala Pride of Golden Pine (od)	CH. Duke of Rochester, II, CD
(od) OFA GR-69 CD			Wessala Tawny
A.E.C. no. SA-422052	CH. Tigathoe's Gold Digger CD	AM. CAN. & BMDA CH. Star Spray Maria's Rayo Del Sol (os) WC	CH. Featherquest Jay's Blund Tom (os)
	(od) OFA GR-294		CH. Star Spray Enid's Maria (od)
49/62 Champions		CH. Tigathoe's Tea Cozy	AFC Sunshine Cake
49/62 Outstanding Parents			Tigathoe's Dimity
	CH. Misty Morn's Sunset, CD	CH. Sunset's Happy Duke (os)	CH. Cragmount's Peter (os)
	(os) OFA GR-280 TD, WC		CH. Finderne Gold Cloud of Kent (os)
Dam	A.E.C. no. SA-464440		Goldendoor Taffy
		Glen Willow's Happy Talk (od)	CH. Tigathoe's Music Man (os)
			Tigathoe's Phi Beta Kappa, CD
CH. Indiana Thembalisha	Amber Lady of Tercor Farm	AM. & CAN. CH. Cragmount's Double Eagle	CH. Golden Pine's Ace Hi (os)
OFA GR-2288			CH. Cragmount's Tiny Cloud (od)
A.E.C. no. SH-181704		CH. Cragmount's Golden Wallis	AM. & CAN. CH. Golden Pine's Easy Ace WC
Outstanding Dam			CH. Rozzy Duchess (od) WC
	Kletha Thembalisha (ad)	CH. Cragmount's Hi-Lo (os)	AM. & CAN. CH. Golden Pine's Easy Ace
	A.E.C. no. SA-807713		Taffy of Richland Court
I Hereby Certify			Ch. Finderne Gold Cloud of Kent (os)
to my knowledge and belief,		CH. Cragmount's Tiny Cloud (od)	CH. Rozzy Duchess (od)
this Pedigree is true and correct.	CH. Bhinga Thembalisha (od)	CH. Cragmount's Peter (os)	CH. Finderne Gold Cloud of Kent (os)
			Goldendoor Taffy
Date _____ Signed _____		CH. Cragmount's Gretel	CH. Golden Pine's Ace Hi (os)
			CH. Cragmount's Tiny Cloud (od)

Jolly Kennel — Certificate of Pedigree

DR. JOHN & LYNNE LOUNSBURY
P.O. BOX 593
BILLINGS, N.Y. 12510
914-677-5602

Name CH. SIR DUNCAN OF WOODBURY **AKC No.** SB-023769
OFA GR-4962 CERF GR-684/78-79
Breed Golden Retriever **Color** Lt. Gold **Sex** Male
Breeder Mrs. Robert Krause **Whelped** June 12, 1971

	CH. CRAGMOUNT'S PETER (OS)	CH FINDERNE GOLD CLOUD OF KENT (OS)	CH. NERRISSIDA'S FINDERNE FOLLY II
			Cellovd Serenade (OD) (OS)
CH. SUNSET'S HAPPY DUKE		Goldendoor Taffy	CH. ALRESFORD NORD DESPREZ
Outstanding Sire			CH. TABBY OF GOLDENDOOR (OD)
	CH TIGATHOE'S MUSIC MAN	FC-AFC BRIGGS LAKE MAC	
CH. MISTY MORN'S SUNSET, CD *	Glen Willow's Happy Talk (OD)		Golden Pines Grand Duchess
Sire AKC No. SA-464440		Tigathoe's Phi Beta Kappa, CD	AFC SUNSHINE CAKE
Outstanding Sire			Tigathoe's Gold Ray
	CH CRAGMOUNT'S DOUBLE EAGLE	CH GOLDEN PINE'S ACE HI	CH GOLDEN PINE'S EASY ACE * (OS)
			Taffy of Richland Court
Amber Lady of Tercor Farm		CH CRAGMOUNT'S TINY CLOUD (OD)	CH FINDERNE GOLD CLOUD OF KENT
			CH ROZZY DUCHESS (OD) (OS)
	CH CRAGMOUNT'S GOLDEN WALLIS	CH GOLDEN PINE'S EASY ACE * (OS)	CH LITTLE JOE OF TIGATHOE*** (OS)
			CH WESSALA PRIDE OF GOLDEN PINE
		CH. ROZZY DUCHESS (OD)	CH TIGATHOE'S BRASS TACKS (OD)
			Ruame Goldie
	AFC GOLDEN STAR OF OAK RIDGE	Aureal Wood's Autumn Fury	RR Rival II ***
			Sudden Sandy *** (OD)
CH AUREAL WOOD'S OKEMO *		Aureal Wood's Widgeon	CH GOLDEN SUNSET OF NERRISSIDA
			Aureal Wood's Tanya
	CH AUREAL WOOD'S CHICKADEE	CH GOLDEN SUNSET OF NERRISSIDA	CH LORELEI'S MARSHGRASS REBEL
			Lorelei's Lucky Penny
Autumn Lodge's Li'l Indian		Aureal Wood's Tanya	Lorelei's Aureal Basil
Dam AKC No. SA-505184			Gina Tanyamarsh
13 Points, 1 Major	CH. RITZ OF HIGH FARMS (OS)	Featherfetch Tucker (OD)	
	CH GOLDEN PINE'S HIGH FARM FEZ (OS)	CH GOLDEN PINE'S BAMBI LADY (OD)	CH GOLDEN GAL OF HIGH FARMS, CDX
CH LORELEI FEZ-TI ZU-ZU			CH LITTLE JOE OF TIGATHOE*** (OS)
			CH WESSALA PRIDE OF GOLDEN PINE (OD)
	CH PRINCE OBERON OF NERRISSIDA		CH LORELEI'S MARSHGRASS REBEL
	CH LORELEI'S HAPPY TI-JI-GEE (OD)		Lorelei's Lucky Penny
		CH LORELEI'S STAR LUCK	CH LORELEI'S MARSH PIPER
			Lorelei's Lucky Star

Certificate of Pedigree

I Hereby Certify to my knowledge and belief, this Pedigree is true and correct.

Date July 26, 1977 Signed John B Lounsbury

STONEHEDGE, POCASSET, MA. 02559

Morningsage Goldens

PEDIGREE OF

CH ROCKGOLD CHUG'S RIC O' SHAY
Reg. No. SA387937
Reg. No. OFA GR-159
GRCA C.S.
Eyes Normal

Sire: CH MORNINGSAGE MARIA'S CAIN
Reg. No. SB660950
Reg. No. OFA GR-4712
Eyes Normal 3/80
owner handled Group First
& multiple Group placings

Dam: CH STARFARM'S CAROLINA GINGER, CD
Reg. No. OFA GR-1551
Reg. No. GRCA O.D.
Eyes Normal

AM/CAN CH STAR SPRAY MARIA'S RAYO DEL SOL** XRAYED NORMAL Group Winner	CH FEATHERQUEST JAY'S BLONDE TOM ORCA O.S.	CH LORELEI'S STAR SPRAY
		LORELEI'S MARSH JAY
	CH STAR SPRAY'S ENID'S MARIA	AM/CAN CH GOLDEN PINE'S EASY ACE* O.S.
		CH GOLDEN GIRL ENID
ROCKGOLD'S CHUG O'LUG OFA GR-45	CH FLAMING ROCK Xrayed Normal at 5 yrs.	STEITZ'S GOLDEN NUGGET
		STEITZ'S GOLDEN FLAME
CH ROCKGOLD'S FROLICKING GYPSY* OFA GR-32	SCARSDALE'S L CON MAR* Xrayed Normal at 4 yrs.	CH INDIAN KNOLL'S COLONEL, UD***
		SHAWANNA OF SCARSDALE
CH SCARSDALE'S BUCKSHOT Xrayed Normal 5 yrs.	TIMOTHY OF SCOTWELL	FIELD MARSHALL II
		FLOSSIE OF OLDMORE
TENAURUM'S HOLKA OFA GR-301 7 Pts. (1 major) USA	SHERRY OF SCOTWELL	STEITZ'S GOLDEN NUGGET
		STEITZ'S GOLDEN FLAME
JUDIANNA'S GOLDEN GINGER Xrayed Normal	CH GOLDEN KNOLL'S TONKA, CD	CH TONKAHOF KELLY
		CH R R ECHO V
	JUDIANNA'S HONEY DREAMER, CD	CH BETTENYE'S ALMINO HIGH
		DUCHESS OF HEBRON
CH MISTY MORN'S SUNSET, CDTWC OFA GR-260 GRCA O.S.	CH SUNSET'S HAPPY DUKE	CH CRAGMOUNT'S PETER	CH FINDERNE GOLD CLOUD OF KENT O.S.
			GOLDENDOOR TAFFY
		GLEN WILLOW'S HAPPY TALK GRCA O.D.	CH TIGATHOE'S MUSIC MAN
			CH TIGATHOE'S PHI BETA KAPPA
	AMBER LADY OF TERCOR FARMS	AM/CAN CH CRAGMOUNT'S DOUBLE EAGLE	CH GOLDEN PINE'S ACE'S HI
			CH CRAGMOUNT'S TINY CLOUD O.D.
		CH CRAGMOUNT'S GOLDEN WALLIS	AM/CAN CH GOLDEN PINE'S EASY ACE* O.S.
			CH ROZZY DUCHESS ORCA O.D.
CH CRAGMOUNT'S AUSTER, CD OFA GR-317 ORCA O.D.	CH CRAGMOUNT'S HI-LO GRCA O.S.	CH GOLDEN PINE'S ACE'S HI	AM/CAN CH GOLDEN PINE'S EASY ACE* O.S.
			TAFFY OF RICHLAND COURT
		CH CRAGMOUNT'S TINY CLOUD GRCA O.D.	CH FINDERNE GOLD CLOUD OF KENT O.S.
			CH ROZZY DUCHESS GRCA O.D.
	GOLDEN PINE'S TWINK	CH HIGH FARM'S BRASSY GOLD BRAID	CH HIGH FARM'S GOLDEN LIDDELL
			HIGH FARM'S DAYDREAM
		CH GOLDEN PINE'S DOWN PAYMENT	CH DUNCAN DELL'S DRUMMOND, CD**
			CH GOLDEN PINE'S BAMBI LADY

Breed: Golden Retriever
Whelped: December 2, 1974 Color: Golden
Height: 21½" Weight: 80 lbs. Sex: Male
BREEDER: Arthur D. & Shirley Cahoon, Chesapeake, VA
OWNER: Joanne A. Lastoka, 537 Morningside Dr., Worthington, MN 56187

I certify that this pedigree is true and correct to the best of my knowledge and belief.
(Signed) Joanne A. Lastoka

Morningsage Goldens

PEDIGREE OF

H HONOR'S LET 'EM HAVE IT, CD WC
Reg. No. SB 143862
Reg. No. OFA GR-2967
CERF GR-634/77-59
Eyes Normal

Sire: AM/CAN CH MORNINGSAGE LAST TANGO
Reg. No. SB 86101
Reg. No. OFA GR-6517
Eyes Normal 3/80
Multiple Group wins
breeder/owner handled in
U.S. & Can.
Best of Breed Manitoba
Golden Retr. Spec. 5/81

Dam: MORNINGSAGE MALAGOLD HONEY
Reg. No. SB 261008
Reg. No. OFA GR-2970
CERF GR-544/78-67
Multiple Specialty Brood
Bitch class wins. GRCA O.D.
Pts. U.S. & Can.
Breed: GOLDEN RETRIEVER

DUAL CH/AFC RONAKER'S NOVATO CAIN CD OFA GR-437 ORCA C.S. Eyes Normal	CH GOLDEN DUKE OF TREY-C* GRCA O.S. Vet. Normal	LAKEWOOD'S RED GOLD	WINYON'S JEREMIAH
			ROUNDWOOD GOLDEN MIST
		THE DUCHESS OF OGDEN	OAKCREEK'S SILVER SKEET
			OAKCREEK'S GOLDEN MERLE
	CH J'S KATE OFA Normal GRCA O.D.	FC/AFC NICKOLAS OF LOGAN'S END U of CA Normal	SIR CHARLES OF MT WHITNEY***
			tiny ALICE
		CH J'S TEEKO OF TIGATHOE***	CH LITTLE JOE OF TIGATHOE***
			PRINCESS KILROY
CH HONOR'S CHANCES ARE, CD U of MN Normal GRCA O.D. Eyes Normal	BRIGG'S LAKE WOODY**	FC/AFC BRIGG'S LAKE MAC U of Boston Normal	GRANITE CITY RED
			BRIGG'S LAKE GINGER
		POLLY	GRANITE CITY STRETCH
			DAISY OF STONEY CREEK
	NORTON'S GOLDEN QUEEN	SAUSEN'S GOLDEN PRINCE	PIRATE OF SUN-N-AIRE**
			GOLDEN KAY OF SAXONETTE
		SAUSEN'S GOLDEN SASSAFRAS	GOLD STRIKE BARON
			GOLD STRIKE TAWNY
AM/MEX CH BECKWITH'S COPPER RICOT OFA Normal GRCA C.S.	AM/UK/MEX/BDA/COL CH BECKWITH'S COPPER COIN GRCA O.S. U of MN Normal	BECKWITH'S GOLDEN BLAZE, CD Xrayn	WYNOS VIXEN, CD
			GAYHAVEN DAMSEL CH KYRIS GR-031
		BECKWITH'S GAYHAVEN FANCY OFA GR-4	CH GALUSTO OF YEO
			ENI/AM CH FIGARO OF YEO*
CH MALAGOLD BECKWITH'S OM K IVAN OFA GR-542 GRCA O.S. CERF GR-108/85-54	AM/CAN CH BECKWITH'S FROLIC OF YEO CDX GRCA O.D. OFA Normal	CH GALUSTO OF YEO	MANA OF YEO
			RINGMASTER OF YEO Stud Dog Cup '6l
		JESSICA OF YEO	JUDITH OF YEO
			ALRESFORD CARLTON KIM
	MANDINGO BEAU GESTE OF YEO	ALRESFORD NICE FELLA	ALRESFORD CHIQUITA
			RINGMASTER OF YEO
		LUCKY CHARM OF YEO	JINGLE JILL
CH DANGILT EMERALD OF YEO OFA GR-1071 English Imp. CERF GR-140/76-75		IR/ENG CH MANDINGO BUIDHE COLUM	ALRESFORD NICE FELLA
			BUIDHE DEARG
	SAPPHIRE OF YEO	JESSICA OF YEO	RINGMASTER OF YEO
			JUDITH OF YEO

Whelped: June 7, 1975 Color: Golden
Height: 24" Weight: 80 lbs. Sex: Male
BREEDER: Joanne A. Lastoka, Morningsage Goldens, Worthington, MN 56187
OWNER: J.A. Lastoka, 537 Morningside Dr., Worthington, MN 56187

I certify that this pedigree is true and correct to the best of my knowledge and belief.
(Signed) Joanne A. Lastoka

Pedigree

CH. SUTTER CREEK

Susan Breakell & Pam Tillotson	TESSAHOC WILOBY	
Breeder (owner of Dam)	Name of Dog	Litter Registration Number
	M SEPTEMBER, 1979	
Address of Breeder	Sex Date Whelped	Individual Registration Number
"WILLIE"	Rich Gold	
"Call" Name of Dog	Color, Markings or Other Identification	Registered With

PARENTS	GRAND PARENTS	GREAT GRAND PARENTS	GR. GR. GRAND PARENTS	GR. GR. GR. GRAND PARENTS

CH SUTTER CREEK GOLDRUSH FLYBOY — SIRE, Reg. No. _____

- CH GOLD-RUSH'S GREAT TEDDY BEAR (Grand Sire)
  - CH CUMMINGS GOLD-RUSH CHARLIE
    - CH SUNSET'S HAPPY DUKE
      - C CRAGMOUNT'S PETER
      - Glen Willow"s Happy Talk
    - CH CUMMINGS GOLDEN PRINCESS
      - C CRAGMOUNT'S DOUBLE EAGLE
      - Cragmount's Easy Lady
  - CH GOLDEN PINE'S GLORYBE'S ANGEL
    - Golden Pine's Tiny Tim
      - C MAJOR GREGORY OF HIGH FARMS
      - C GOLDEN PINE'S DOWN PAYMENT
    - CH GOLDEN PINES GLORYBE
      - C MISTY MORN'S SUNSET CD TD
      - C GOLDEN PINE'S PUNKIN PI CD
- CH GOLDRUSH'S BIRCH OF BEARWOOD, CD (Grand Dam)
  - CH SUN DANCE'S ESQUIRE'S PLAYBOY CDX
    - CH SUN DANCE'S ESQUIRE CD
      - C SUN DANCE'S YANKEE DOLLAR CD
      - C SUN DANCE'S GULIE
    - CH HARLENHEIM'S RUST HAVEN
      - C SUN DANCE'S VEGAS DEALER CDX
      - Sun Dance"s Dawn of Harlenheim
  - Bearwood's Honey Bear CD
    - CH SUN DANCE'S ESQUIRE CD
      - C SUN DANCE'S YANKEE DOLLAR CD
      - C SUN DANCE'S GULIE
    - CH DUCKDOWN TUFFY OF BUCKSKIN CD
      - C MAPLE LEAF'S TRACE-O-COPPER
      - Sun Dance's Gold Ingot CD

CAN. CH GOLDENQUEST SUTTER CREEK LYRIC CD — DAM, Reg. No. _____

- CH MISTY MORN"S SUNSET CD TD* (Grand Sire)
  - CH SUNSET'S HAPPY DUKE
    - CH CRAGMOUNT'S PETER
      - C FINDERNE GOLD CLOUD OF KENT
      - Goldendoor Taffy
    - Glen Willow"s Happy Talk
      - C TIGATHOE'S MUSIC MAN
      - Tigathoe's phi beta kappa CD
  - Amber lady of Tercor Farm
    - CH CRAGMOUNT'S DOUBLE EAGLE
      - C GOLDEN PINE'S ACE'S HI
      - C CRAGMOUNT'S TINY CLOUD
    - CH CRAGMOUNT'S GOLDEN WALL
      - C GOLDEN PINE"S EASY ACE
      - C ROZZY DUCHESS
- CAN. CH DEEGOLJAY'S AMOROUS ASPASIA CD (Grand Dam)
  - CH BECKWITH'S MALAGOLD FLASH UDT
    - CH BECKWITH'S COPPER INGOT
      - C BECKWITH'S COPPER COIN
      - Beckwith's Gayhaven Fancy
    - CH BECKWITH'S FROLIC OF YEO CDX
      - C ORLANDO OF YEO
      - Jessica of Yeo
  - Beckwith"s Allegro of Sand
    - CH BECKWITH'S MALAGOLD OJIBWAY
      - C BECKWITH'S COPPER INGOT
      - BECKWITH'S FROLIC OF YEO CD
    - CH BECKWITH'S NORTHGAME BELLE CDX
      - CH BECKWITH'S EMBLEM OF GOLD
      - C BECKWITH FLARE OF NORTHGAME (CAN)

I HEREBY CERTIFY THAT, this Pedigree is true and correct to the best of my knowledge and belief.

This dog to the best of my knowledge is in good health.

Signature of Seller _____

Signed _____

Name of Purchaser _____

Date of Purchase _____

Pedigree forms by Elizabeth Harvey Treharne, Guilford, N.Y. 13780

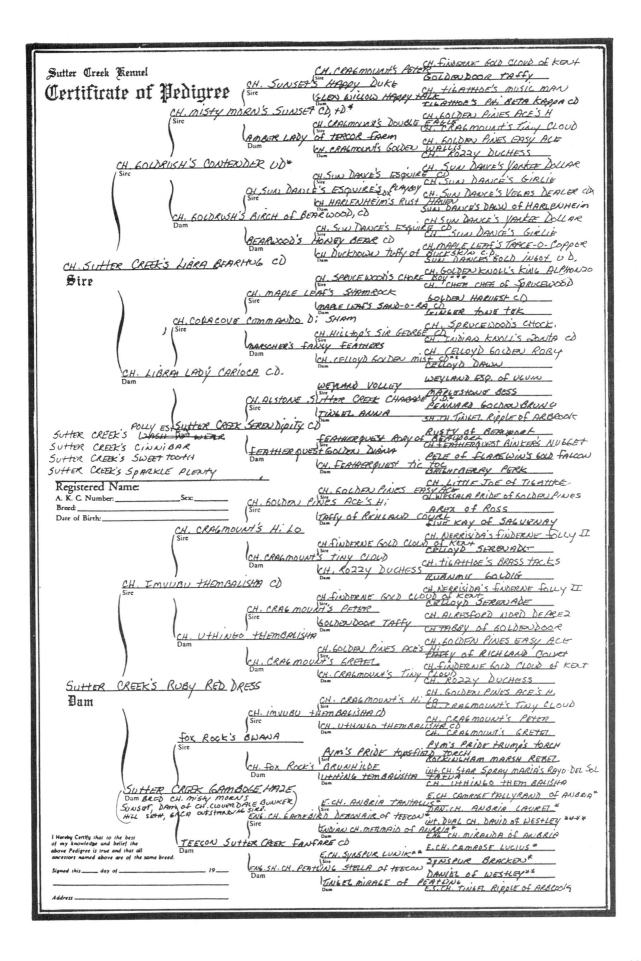

Sutter Creek Kennel

Certificate of Pedigree

Registered Name:

A. K. C. Number: _____ Sex: _____
Breed: _____
Date of Birth: _____

I Hereby Certify that to the best
of my knowledge and belief the
above Pedigree is true and that all
ancestors named above are of the same breed.

Signed this _____ day of _____ 19 ___

_____

Address _____

Sire

CH. SUTTER CREEK'S LIBRA BEARHUG CD

CH. GOLDRUSH'S CONTENDER UD*
CH. MISTY MORN'S SUNSET CD, TD*
CH. SUNSET'S HAPPY DUKE
CH. CRAGMOUNT'S PETER
CH. FINDERNE GOLD CLOUD OF KENT
GOLDENDOOR TAFFY
GLEN WILLOW HAPPY TALK
CH. TIGATHOE'S MUSIC MAN
TIGATHOE'S PHI BETA KAPPA CD
AMBER LADY OF TERCOR FARM
CH. CRAGMOUNT'S DOUBLE EAGLE
CH. GOLDEN PINES ACE'S H
CH. CRAGMOUNT'S TINY CLOUD
CH. CRAGMOUNT'S GOLDEN WALLIS
CH. GOLDEN PINES EASY ACE
CH. ROZZY DUCHESS

CH. GOLDRUSH'S BIRCH OF BEARWOOD, CD
CH. SUN DANCE'S ESQUIRE'S PLAYBOY
CH. SUN DANCE'S ESQUIRE CD
CH. SUN DANCE'S YANKEE DOLLAR
CH. SUN DANCE'S GIRLIE
CH. HARLENHEIM'S RUST HAVEN
CH. SUN DANCE'S VEGAS DEALER CD
SUN DANCE'S DAWN OF HARLENHEIM
BEARWOOD'S HONEY BEAR CD
CH. SUN DANCE'S ESQUIRE CD
CH. SUN DANCE'S YANKEE DOLLAR
CH. SUN DANCE'S GIRLIE
CH. DUCKDOWN TUFFY OF BUCKSKIN C.D
CH. MAPLE LEAF'S TRACE-O-COPPER
SUN DANCE'S GOLD INGOT UD

CH. LIBRA LADY CARIOCA C.D.
CH. COLACOVE COMMANDO D'SHAM
CH. MAPLE LEAF'S SHAMROCK
CH. SPRUCEWOOD'S CHORE BOY***
CH. GOLDEN KNOLL'S KING ALPHONZO
CH. CHEE CHEE OF SPRUCEWOOD
MAPLE LEAF'S SAND-O-RA CD
GOLDEN HARVEST CD
GINGER TONE TEK
MARSCHER'S FANCY FEATHERS
CH. HILLTOP'S SIR GEORGE CD
CH. SPRUCEWOOD'S CHOCK
CH. INDIAN KNOLL'S ZONTA CD
CH. CELLOYD GOLDEN MIST CD*
CH. CELLOYD GOLDEN RORY
CELLOYD DAWN

SUTTER CREEK'S CINNIBAR
SUTTER CREEK'S SWEET TOOTH
SUTTER CREEK'S SPARKLE PLENTY
POLLY ES SUTTER CREEK SERENDIPITY CD
SUTTER CREEK'S WASH
CH. ALSTONE SUTTER CREEK CHAMADE U.D.
WEYLAND VOLLEY
WEYLAND ESQ. OF ULUM
MAPLESTONE BESS
TINKEL ANNA
PENNARD GOLDEN BRUNO
SH. TH. TINKEL RIPPLE OF ARBROOK
FEATHERQUEST GOLDEN DIANA
FEATHERQUEST RORY OF BEAUPORT
RUSTY OF BEAUPORT
CH. FEATHERQUEST BINKER'S NUGGET
CH. FEATHERQUEST TIC TOC
PETE OF FLAREWIN'S GOLD FALCON
BRIGHTBERRY PERK

Dam

SUTTER CREEK'S RUBY RED DRESS

CH. IMVUBU THEMBALISHA CD
CH. CRAGMOUNT'S HI-LO
CH. GOLDEN PINES ACE'S HI
CH. GOLDEN PINES EASY ACE
CH. LITTLE JOE OF TIGATHOE
CH. WESSALA PRIDE OF GOLDEN PINES
TAFFY OF RICHLAND COURT
AREX OF ROSS
LIVE KAY OF SAGUENAY
CH. CRAGMOUNT'S TINY CLOUD
CH. FINDERNE GOLD CLOUD OF KENT
CH. NERRISIDA'S FINDERNE FOLLY II
CELLOYD SERENADE
CH. ROZZY DUCHESS
CH. TIGATHOE'S BRASS TACKS
RUANME GOLDIE

CH. UTHINGO THEMBALISHA
CH. CRAGMOUNT'S PETER
CH. FINDERNE GOLD CLOUD OF KENT
CELLOYD SERENADE
GOLDENDOOR TAFFY
CH. ALRESFORD NORD DE AREZ
CH. TABBY OF GOLDENDOOR
CH. CRAGMOUNT'S GRETEL
CH. GOLDEN PINES ACE'S HI
CH. GOLDEN PINES EASY ACE
TAFFY OF RICHLAND COURT
CH. CRAGMOUNT'S TINY CLOUD
CH. FINDERNE GOLD CLOUD OF KENT
CH. ROZZY DUCHESS

FOX ROCK'S BWANA
CH. IMVUBU THEMBALISHA CD
CH. CRAGMOUNT'S HI
CH. GOLDEN PINES ACE'S H.
CH. CRAGMOUNT'S TINY CLOUD
CH. UTHINGO THEMBALISHA CD
CH. CRAGMOUNT'S PETER
CH. CRAGMOUNT'S GRETEL
CH. FOX ROCK'S BRUNHILDE
AJM'S PRIDE TOPSFIELD TORCH
PYM'S PRIDE TRUMP'S TORCH
ROCKINGHAM MARSH REBEL
UTHINIG THEMBALISHA
INT. CH. STAR SPRAY MARIA'S RAYO-DEL-SOL TATUA
CH. UTHINGO THEMBALISHA

SUTTER CREEK GAMBOGE HAZE
(Dam BRED CH. MISTY MORN'S
SUNSET, DAM OF CH. CLOVERDALE BUNKER
HILL SETH, GACA OUTSTANDING SIRE)
TEECON SUTTER CREEK FANFARE CD
ENG. CH. GAMEBIRD DEBONAIR OF TEECON
E. CH. ANBRIA TANTALUS*
E. CH. CAMROSE TALLYRAND OF ANBRA*
DAN. CH. ANBRIA LAUREL*
INDIAN CH. MERMAID OF ANBRIA*
INT. DUAL CH. DAVID OF WESTLEY****
ENG. CH. MIRANDA OF ANBRIA*
ENG. SH. CH. PEATLING STELLA OF TEECON
E. CH. SUNSPUR LUNIK**
E. CH. CAMROSE LUCIUS*
SUNSPUR BRACKEN*
TINKEL MIRALE OF PEATLING
DANIEL OF WESTLEY**
E. S. TH. TINKEL RIPPLE OF ARBROOK

401

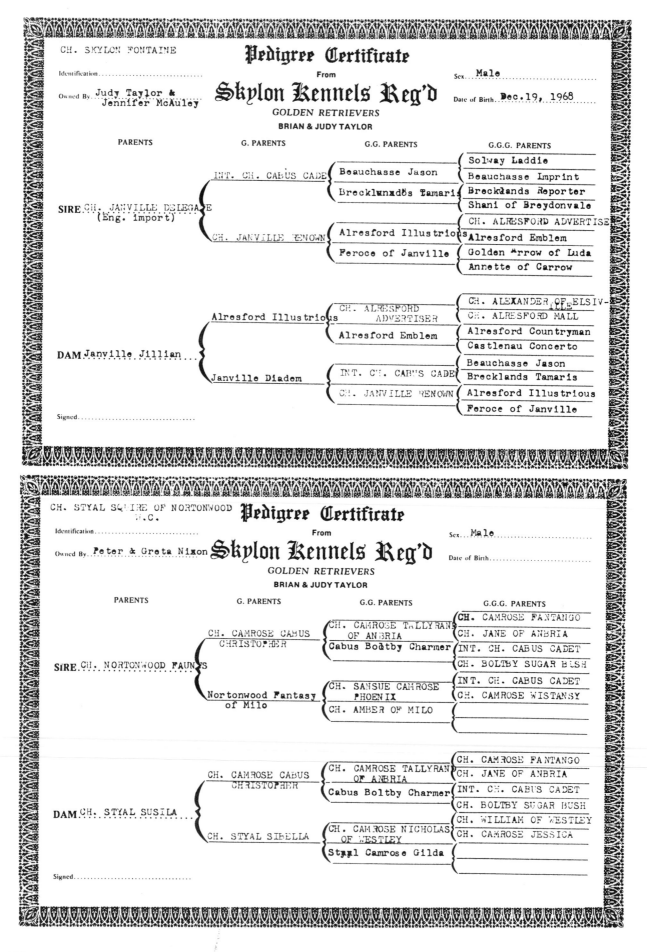

Pedigree Certificate

From

Skylon Kennels Reg'd
GOLDEN RETRIEVERS
BRIAN & JUDY TAYLOR

CH. SKYLON FONTAINE

Identification ....

Owned By Judy Taylor & Jennifer McAuley

Sex Male

Date of Birth Dec.19, 1968

PARENTS	G. PARENTS	G.G. PARENTS	G.G.G. PARENTS
SIRE CH. JANVILLE DELEGATE (Eng. import)	INT. CH. CABUS CADET	Beauchasse Jason	Solway Laddie
			Beauchasse Imprint
		Brecklands Tamaris	Brecklands Reporter
			Shani of Breydonvale
	CH. JANVILLE RENOWN	Alresford Illustrious	CH. ALRESFORD ADVERTISER
			Alresford Emblem
		Feroce of Janville	Golden Arrow of Luda
			Annette of Carrow
DAM Janville Jillian	Alresford Illustrious	CH. ALRESFORD ADVERTISER	CH. ALEXANDER OF ELSIVILLE
			CH. ALRESFORD MALL
		Alresford Emblem	Alresford Countryman
			Castlenau Concerto
	Janville Diadem	INT. CH. CABUS CADET	Beauchasse Jason
			Brecklands Tamaris
		CH. JANVILLE RENOWN	Alresford Illustrious
			Feroce of Janville

Signed ....

Pedigree Certificate

From

Skylon Kennels Reg'd
GOLDEN RETRIEVERS
BRIAN & JUDY TAYLOR

CH. STYAL SQUIRE OF NORTONWOOD W.C.

Identification ....

Owned By Peter & Greta Nixon

Sex Male

Date of Birth ....

PARENTS	G. PARENTS	G.G. PARENTS	G.G.G. PARENTS
SIRE CH. NORTONWOOD FAUNUS	CH. CAMROSE CABUS CHRISTOPHER	CH. CAMROSE TALLYRAND OF ANBRIA	CH. CAMROSE FANTANGO
			CH. JANE OF ANBRIA
		Cabus Boltby Charmer	INT. CH. CABUS CADET
			CH. BOLTBY SUGAR BUSH
	Nortonwood Fantasy of Milo	CH. SANSUE CAMROSE PHOENIX	INT. CH. CABUS CADET
			CH. CAMROSE WISTANSY
		CH. AMBER OF MILO	
DAM CH. STYAL SUSILA	CH. CAMROSE CABUS CHRISTOPHER	CH. CAMROSE TALLYRAND OF ANBRIA	CH. CAMROSE FANTANGO
			CH. JANE OF ANBRIA
		Cabus Boltby Charmer	INT. CH. CABUS CADET
			CH. BOLTBY SUGAR BUSH
	CH. STYAL SIBELLA	CH. CAMROSE NICHOLAS OF WESTLEY	CH. WILLIAM OF WESTLEY
			CH. CAMROSE JESSICA
		Styal Camrose Gilda	

Signed ....

402

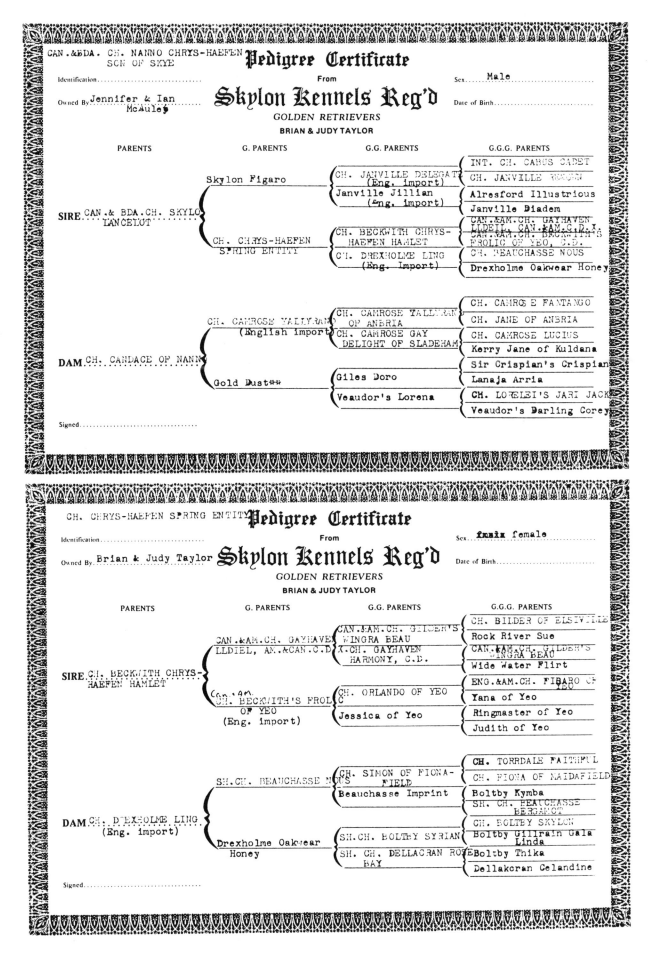

Pedigree Certificate

From

Skylon Kennels Reg'd

GOLDEN RETRIEVERS

BRIAN & JUDY TAYLOR

CAN.&BDA. CH. NANNO CHRYS-HAEFEN SON OF SKYE

Identification.....................

Owned By: Jennifer & Ian McAuley

Sex: Male

Date of Birth.....................

PARENTS	G. PARENTS	G.G. PARENTS	G.G.G. PARENTS
SIRE CAN.& BDA.CH. SKYLON LANCELOT	Skylon Figaro	CH. JANVILLE DELEGATE (Eng. import)	INT. CH. CABUS CADET
			CH. JANVILLE RECCO
		Janville Jillian (Eng. import)	Alresford Illustrious
			Janville Diadem
	CH. CHRYS-HAEFEN SPRING ENTITY	CH. BECKWITH CHRYS-HAEFEN HAMLET	CAN.&AM.CH. GAYHAVEN LLDEIL, CAN.&AM.C.D.X.
			CAN.&AM.CH. BECKWITH'S FROLIC OF YEO, C.D.
		CH. DREXHOLME LING (Eng. Import)	CH. BEAUCHASSE NOUS
			Drexholme Oakwear Honey
DAM CH. CANDACE OF NANNO	CH. CAMROSE VALLYRAND (English import)	CH. CAMROSE TALLYRAND OF ANBRIA	CH. CAMROSE FANTANGO
			CH. JANE OF ANBRIA
		CH. CAMROSE GAY DELIGHT OF SLADEHAM	CH. CAMROSE LUCIUS
			Kerry Jane of Kuldana
	Gold Dust**	Giles Doro	Sir Crispian's Crispian
			Lanaja Arria
		Veaudor's Lorena	CH. LORELEI'S JARI JACK
			Veaudor's Darling Corey

Signed.....................

Pedigree Certificate

From

Skylon Kennels Reg'd

GOLDEN RETRIEVERS

BRIAN & JUDY TAYLOR

CH. CHRYS-HAEFEN SPRING ENTITY

Identification.....................

Owned By: Brian & Judy Taylor

Sex: female

Date of Birth.....................

PARENTS	G. PARENTS	G.G. PARENTS	G.G.G. PARENTS
SIRE CH. BECKWITH CHRYS-HAEFEN HAMLET	CAN.&AM.CH. GAYHAVEN LLDIEL, AM.&CAN.C.D.	CAN.&AM.CH. GILDER'S WINGRA BEAU	CH. BILDER OF ELSIVILLE
			Rock River Sue
		X.CH. GAYHAVEN HARMONY, C.D.	CAN.&AM.CH. GILDER'S WINGRA BEAU
			Wide Water Flirt
	Can.&Am. CH. BECKWITH'S FROLIC OF YEO (Eng. import)	CH. ORLANDO OF YEO	ENG.&AM.CH. FIGARO OF YEO
			Yana of Yeo
		Jessica of Yeo	Ringmaster of Yeo
			Judith of Yeo
DAM CH. DREXHOLME LING (Eng. import)	SH.CH. BEAUCHASSE NOUS	CH. SIMON OF FIONA-FIELD	CH. TORRDALE FAITHFUL
			CH. FIONA OF MAIDAFIELD
		Beauchasse Imprint	Boltby Kymba
			SH. CH. BEAUCHASSE BERGAMOT
	Drexholme Oakwear Honey	SH.CH. BOLTBY SYRIAN	CH. BOLTBY SKYLON
			Boltby Gillrain Gala Linda
		SH. CH. DELLACRAN ROSE BAY	Boltby Thika
			Dellacran Celandine

Signed.....................

403

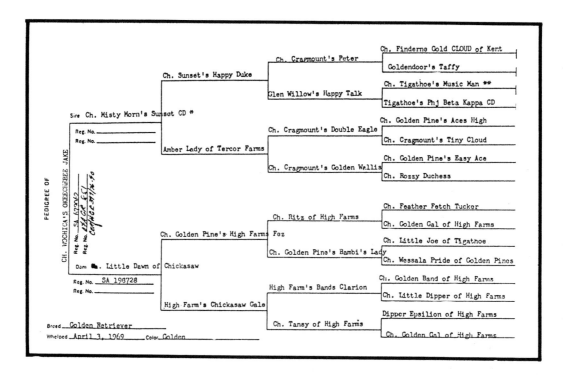

PEDIGREE OF

CH. VOCHICA'S OKEECHOBEE JAKE

Sire: Ch. Misty Morn's Sunset CD #
Reg. No. SA 639062
Reg. No. _____

Dam: Little Dawn of Chickasaw
Reg. No. SA 198728
Reg. No. _____

Breed Golden Retriever
Whelped April 3, 1969   Color Golden

Ch. Misty Morn's Sunset CD #
— Ch. Sunset's Happy Duke
  — Ch. Cragmount's Peter
    — Ch. Finderne Gold CLOUD of Kent
    — Goldendoor's Taffy
  — Glen Willow's Happy Talk
    — Ch. Tigathoe's Music Man **
    — Tigathoe's Phi Beta Kappa CD
— Amber Lady of Tercor Farms
  — Ch. Cragmount's Double Eagle
    — Ch. Golden Pine's Aces High
    — Ch. Cragmount's Tiny Cloud
  — Ch. Cragmount's Golden Wallis
    — Ch. Golden Pine's Easy Ace
    — Ch. Rozzy Duchess

Little Dawn of Chickasaw
— Ch. Golden Pine's High Farms Fez
  — Ch. Ritz of High Farms
    — Ch. Feather Fetch Tucker
    — Ch. Golden Gal of High Farms
  — Ch. Golden Pine's Bambi's Lady
    — Ch. Little Joe of Tigathoe
    — Ch. Wessala Pride of Golden Pines
— High Farm's Chickasaw Gale
  — High Farm's Bands Clarion
    — Ch. Golden Band of High Farms
    — Ch. Little Dipper of High Farms
  — Ch. Tansy of High Farms
    — Dipper Epsilon of High Farms
    — Ch. Golden Gal of High Farms

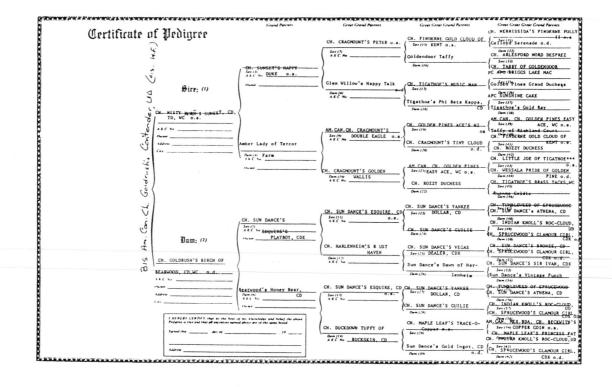

Certificate of Pedigree

BIS Am. Can. Ch. Goldrush's Contender, UD (Ess. M.F.)

	Grand Parents	Great Grand Parents	Great Great Grand Parents	Great Great Great Grand Parents

Sire: (1)
CH. MISTY MORN'S SUNSET, CD,
TD, WC o.s.

CH. SUNSET'S HAPPY DUKE o.s.
— CH. CRAGMOUNT'S PETER o.s.
  — CH. FINDERNE GOLD CLOUD OF KENT o.s.
    — CH. MERRISSIDA'S FINDERNE FOLLY
    — Celloyd Serenade o.d.
  — Goldendoor Taffy
    — CH. ARLESFORD NORD DESPREZ
    — CH. TABBY OF GOLDENDOOR
— Glen Willow's Happy Talk
  — CH. TIGATHOE'S MUSIC MAN
    — FC AND BRIGGS LAKE MAC
    — Golden Pines Grand Duchess
  — Tigathoe's Phi Beta Kappa, CD
    — AFC SUNSHINE CAKE
    — Tigathoe's Gold Ray

Amber Lady of Tercor Farm
— AM. CAN. CH. CRAGMOUNT'S DOUBLE EAGLE o.s.
  — CH. GOLDEN PINES ACE'S HI o.s.
    — AM. CAN. CH. GOLDEN PINES EASY ACE, WC o.s.
    — CH. FINDERNE GOLD CLOUD OF KENT o.s.
  — CH. CRAGMOUNT'S TINY CLOUD o.d.
    — Taffy of Richland County
    — CH. ROZZY DUCHESS
— CH. CRAGMOUNT'S GOLDEN WALLIS
  — AM. CAN. CH. GOLDEN PINES EASY ACE, WC o.s.
    — CH. LITTLE JOE OF TIGATHOE ***
    — CH. WESSALA PRIDE OF GOLDEN PINE o.d.
  — CH. ROZZY DUCHESS
    — CH. TIGATHOE'S BRASS TACKS, WC
    — Ruenne Goldie

Dam: (2)
CH. GOLDRUSH'S BIRCH OF BEARWOOD, CD, WC o.d.

CH. SUN DANCE'S ESQUIRE'S PLAYBOY, CDX
— CH. SUN DANCE'S ESQUIRE, CD o.s.
  — CH. SUN DANCE'S YANKEE DOLLAR, CD o.s.
    — CH. TUMBLEWEED OF SPRUCEWOOD
    — CH. SUN DANCE'S ATHENA, CD
  — CH. SUN DANCE'S GUILIE
    — CH. INDIAN KNOLL'S ROC-CLOUD, UD
    — CH. SPRUCEWOOD'S GLAMOUR GIRL, CDX o.d.
— CH. HARLENHEIM'S R UST HAVEN
  — CH. SUN DANCE'S VEGAS DEALER, CDX
    — CH. SPRUCEWOOD'S BRONZE, CD
    — CH. SPRUCEWOOD'S GLAMOUR GIRL, CDX o.d.
  — Sun Dance's Dawn of Harlenheim
    — CH. SUN DANCE'S SIR IVAN, CDX
    — Sun Dance's Vintage Punch

Bearwood's Honey Bear, CD
— CH. SUN DANCE'S ESQUIRE, CD o.s.
  — CH. SUN DANCE'S YANKEE DOLLAR, CD o.s.
    — CH. TUMBLEWEED OF SPRUCEWOOD
    — CH. SUN DANCE'S ATHENA, CD
  — CH. SUN DANCE'S GUILIE
    — CH. INDIAN KNOLL'S ROC-CLOUD, UD
    — CH. SPRUCEWOOD'S GLAMOUR GIRL, CDX o.d.
— CH. DUCKDOWN TUFFY OF BUCKSKIN, CD
  — CH. MAPLE LEAF'S TRACE-O-COPPER o.s.
    — AM. CAN. MEX. BDA. CH. BECKWITH'S COPPER COIN o.s.
    — CH. MAPLE LEAF'S PRINCESS PAT
  — Sun Dance's Gold Ingot, CD o.d.
    — CH. INDIAN KNOLL'S ROC-CLOUD, UD
    — CH. SPRUCEWOOD'S GLAMOUR GIRL, CDX o.d.

I HEREBY CERTIFY that to the best of my knowledge and belief the above Pedigree is true and that all ancestors named above are of the same breed.

Signed this _____ day of _____, 19__
Address _____

Pedigree
FOX ROCK KENNELS

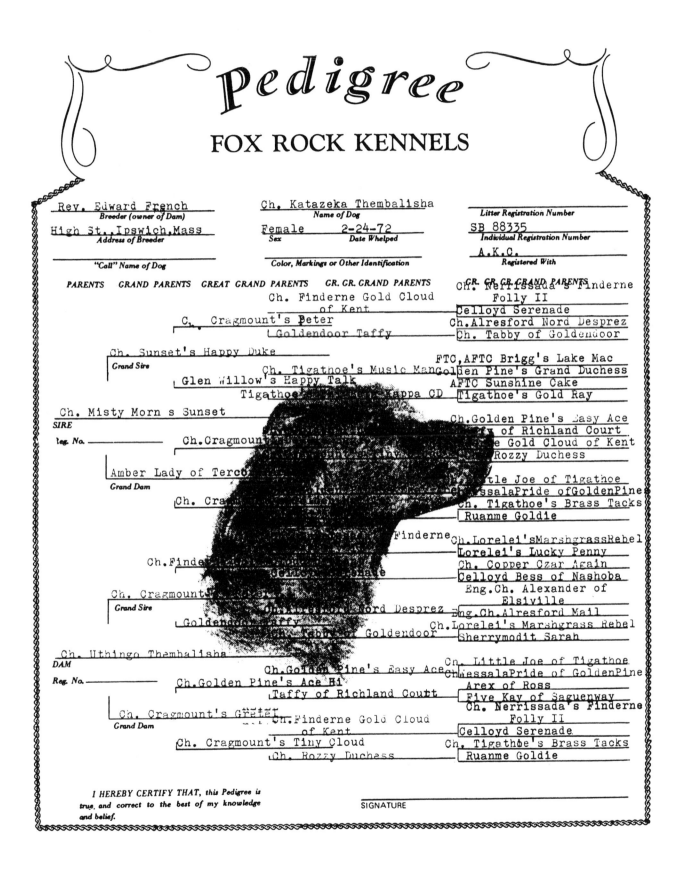

Rev. Edward French	Ch. Katazeka Thembalisha		Litter Registration Number
Breeder (owner of Dam)	*Name of Dog*		
High St.,Ipswich,Mass	Female 2-24-72		SB 88335
Address of Breeder	*Sex Date Whelped*		*Individual Registration Number*
			A.K.C.
"Call" Name of Dog	*Color, Markings or Other Identification*		*Registered With*

PARENTS   GRAND PARENTS   GREAT GRAND PARENTS   GR. GR. GRAND PARENTS   GR. GR. GR. GRAND PARENTS

Ch. Finderne Gold Cloud
of Kent
C. Cragmount's Peter
Goldendoor Taffy

Ch. Sunset's Happy Duke
Grand Sire
Ch. Tigathoe's Music Man
Glen Willow's Happy Talk
Tigathoe's Kappa CD

Ch. Misty Morn's Sunset
SIRE
Reg. No. _____
Ch.Cragmoun...

Amber Lady of Terco...
Grand Dam
Ch. Cra...

Ch.Finder...

Ch. Cragmount...
Grand Sire
Goldendoor...

Ch. Uthingo Thembalisha
DAM
Reg. No. _____
Ch.Golden Pine's Ace Hi
Taffy of Richland Court

Ch. Cragmount's Gretel
Grand Dam
Ch.Finderne Gold Cloud
of Kent
Ch. Cragmount's Tiny Cloud
Ch. Rozzy Duchess

Ch. Nerrissada's Finderne
Folly II
Celloyd Serenade
Ch.Alresford Nord Desprez
Ch. Tabby of Goldendoor

FTC,AFTC Brigg's Lake Mac
Golden Pine's Grand Duchess
AFTC Sunshine Cake
Tigathoe's Gold Ray

Ch.Golden Pine's Easy Ace
...fy of Richland Court
...ne Gold Cloud of Kent
...Rozzy Duchess

...ttle Joe of Tigathoe
...essalaPride ofGoldenPines
Ch. Tigathoe's Brass Tacks
Ruanme Goldie

Ch.Lorelei'sMarshgrassRebel
Lorelei's Lucky Penny
Ch. Copper Czar Again
Celloyd Bess of Nashoba
Eng.Ch. Alexander of
Elsiville
Eng.Ch.Alresford Mail
Ch.Lorelei's Marshgrass Rebel
Sherrymodit Sarah

Ch. Little Joe of Tigathoe
Ch.essalaPride of GoldenPine
Arex of Ross
Five Kay of Saguenway
Ch. Nerrissada's Finderne
Folly II
Celloyd Serenade
Ch. Tigathoe's Brass Tacks
Ruanme Goldie

I HEREBY CERTIFY THAT, this Pedigree is true, and correct to the best of my knowledge and belief.

SIGNATURE

405

Gestation, Whelping, and the Litter

When your bitch has been bred and is back at home, remain ever watchful that no other male gets to her until at least the twenty-second day of her season has passed. Prior to that time, it will still be possible for an undesired breeding to take place, which, at this point, would be catastrophic. Remember, she actually can have two separate litters by two different dogs, so *be alert and take care.*

In all other ways, the bitch should be treated quite normally. It is not necessary for her to have any additives to her diet until she is at least four to five weeks pregnant. It is also unnecessary for her to have additional food. It is better to underfeed the bitch this early in her pregnancy than to overfeed her. A fat bitch is not an easy whelper, so by "feeding her up" during the first few weeks, you may be creating problems for her.

Controlled exercise is good, and necessary, for your pregnant bitch. She should not be permitted to just lie around. At about seven weeks, the exercise should be slowed down to several sedate walks daily, not too long and preferably on the leash.

In the fourth or fifth week of pregnancy, calcium may be added to the diet; and at seven weeks, the one meal a day may be increased to two meals with some nutritional additives in each. Canned milk may be added to her meals at this time.

A week before she is due to whelp, your Golden bitch should be introduced to her whelping box, so that she will have accustomed herself to it and feel at home there by the time the puppies arrive. She should be encouraged to sleep there and be permitted to come and go as she pleases. The box should be roomy enough for her to lie down and stretch out in it; but it

Wellsley's Lady Ashley, C.D., with her puppies. Myra Moldawsky, owner, Ashwel Goldens.

These twelve-day-old puppies are by Ch. Amberac's Aristocrat, owned by Mary Wuestenberg, ex Can. Ch. Amberac's D.J.'s Dixie Darlin. Dave, Jean, and J.D. Wacker, owners.

should not be too large or the pups will have too much room in which to roam, and they may get chilled if they move too far away from the warmth of their mother. Be sure that there is a "pig rail" for the box, which will prevent the puppies from being crushed against the side of the box. The box should be lined with newspapers, which can easily be changed as they become soiled.

The room where the whelping box is placed, either in the home or in the kennel, should be free from drafts and should be kept at about seventy-five degrees Fahrenheit. It may be necessary during the cold months to install an infrared lamp in order to maintain sufficient warmth, in which case guard against the lamp being placed too low or too close to the puppies.

Keep a big pile of newspapers near the box. You'll find that you never have enough of these when there is a litter, so start accumulating them ahead of time. A pile of clean towels, a pair of scissors, and a bottle of alcohol should also be close at hand. Have all of these things ready at least a week before the bitch is due to whelp, as you never know exactly when she may start.

The day or night before she is due, the bitch will become restless; she'll be in and out of her box and in and out of the door. She may refuse food, and at this point her temperature will start to drop. She will start to dig and tear up the newspapers in her box, shiver, and generally look uncomfortable. You alone should be with her at this time (or one other person who is an experienced breeder, to give you confidence if this is one of your first litters). The bitch does not need an audience or any extra people around. This is not a sideshow, and several people hovering over the bitch may upset her to the point where she may hurt the puppies. Stay nearby, but do not fuss too much over her. Keep a calm attitude; this will give her confidence. Eventually she will settle down in her box and begin to pant; shortly thereafter she will start to have contractions and soon a puppy will begin to emerge, sliding out with one of the contractions. The mother immediately should open the sac and bite the cord and clean up the puppy. She will also eat the placenta, which you should permit. Once the puppy is cleaned, it should be placed next to the bitch, unless she is showing signs of having another one immediately. The puppy should start looking for a nipple on which to nurse, and you should make certain that it is able to latch on and start doing so at once.

Can. Ch. Amberac's D.J.'s Dixie Darlin with her one-week-old puppies by Ch. Amberac's Aristocrat. Jean, Dave, and J.D. Wacker, owners.

If a puppy is a breech birth (*i.e.*, born feet first), then you must watch carefully that it is delivered as quickly as possible and the sac removed very quickly, so that the puppy does not drown. Sometimes even a normally positioned birth will seem extremely slow in coming. Should either of these events occur, you might take a clean towel and, as the bitch contracts, pull the puppy out, doing so gently and with utmost care. If the bitch does not open the sac and cut the cord, you will have to do so. If the puppy shows little sign of life, make sure the mouth is free of liquid and then, using a Turkish towel or terry cloth, massage the puppy's chest, rubbing back and forth quite briskly. Continue this for about fifteen minutes. It may be necessary to try mouth-to-mouth breathing. Open the puppy's jaws and, using a finger, depress the tongue which may be stuck to the roof of the puppy's mouth. Then blow hard down the puppy's throat. Bubbles may pop out of its nose, but keep on blowing. Rub with the towel again across the chest, and try artificial respiration, pressing the sides of the chest together, slowly and rhythmically, in and out, in and out. Keep trying one method or the other for at least fifteen minutes (actual time—not how long it seems to you) before giving up. You may be rewarded with a live puppy who otherwise would not have made it.

If you are able to revive the puppy, it should not be put with the mother immediately, as it should be kept extra warm for a while. Put it in a cardboard box near a stove, on an electric heating pad, or, if it is the time of year when your heat is running, near a radiator until the rest of the litter has been born. Then it can be put in with the others.

The bitch may go for an hour or more between puppies, which is fine as long as she seems comfortable and is not straining or contracting. She should not be allowed to remain unassisted for more than an hour if she does continue to contract. This is when you should call your veterinarian, whom you should have alerted ahead of time of the possibility so that he will be somewhere within easy reach. He may want the bitch brought in so that he can examine her and perhaps give her a shot of Pituitrin. In some cases, the veterinarian may find that a Caesarean operation is necessary, because a puppy may be lodged in some manner that makes normal delivery impossible. This can occur due to the size of a puppy or may be due to the fact that the puppy is turned wrong. If any of the foregoing occurs, the puppies already born must be kept warm in their cardboard box, which should have been lined with shredded newspapers in advance and which should have a heating pad beneath it.

Once the Caesarean section has been completed, get the bitch and the puppies home. Do not attempt to put the pups in with the bitch until she is at least fairly conscious, as she might unknowingly hurt them. But do get them back as soon as possible so that they can start nursing.

Russo's Gold-Rush Periwinkle, ten days old—from the second litter by Ch. Cummings' Gold-Rush Charlie ex Ch. Russo's Wildwood Flower. Mercer Russo Ervin, owner.

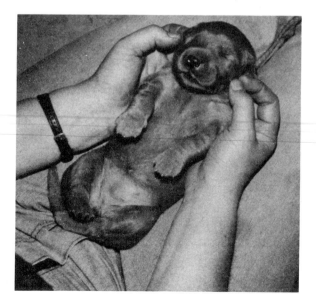

If the mother lacks milk at this point, the puppies will need to be fed by hand, kept very warm, and held against the mother's teats several times a day in order to stimulate and encourage the secretion of her milk, which will probably start shortly.

Assuming that there have been no problems, and the bitch has whelped normally, you should insist that she go outside to exercise, staying just long enough to make herself comfortable. She can be offered a bowl of milk and a biscuit, but then she should settle down with her family. Be sure to clean out the whelping box and change the newspapers so that she will have a fresh bed.

Unless some problem arises, there is little you need do about the puppies until they become three to four weeks old. Keep the box clean with fresh papers. When the puppies are a couple of days old, the papers should be removed and Turkish towels should be tacked down to the bottom of the box so that the puppies will have traction when they move. This is important.

If the bitch has difficulties with her milk supply, or if you should be so unfortunate as to lose the bitch, then you must be prepared to either hand-feed or tube-feed the puppies if they are to survive. We prefer the tube method as it is so much faster and easier. If the bitch is available, it is better that she continue to clean and care for the puppies in the normal manner, except for the food supplements you will provide. If she is unable to do this, then after every feeding, you must gently rub each puppy's abdomen with wet cotton to induce urination, and the rectum should be gently rubbed to open the bowels.

Newborn puppies must be fed every three or four hours around the clock. The puppies must be kept warm during that time. Have your veterinarian show you how to tube-feed. Once learned it is really quite simple, fast, and efficient.

After a normal whelping, the bitch will require additional food to enable her to produce sufficient milk. She should be fed twice daily now, and some canned milk should be available to her several times during the day.

When the puppies are two weeks old, you should clip their nails, as they are needle-sharp

Featherquest Golden Diana with her litter of fourteen puppies by Ch. Alstone Sutter Creek Charade, U.D.*. Susan Breakell, owner, Sutter Creek.

at this point and can hurt or damage the mother's teats and stomach as the pups hold on to nurse.

Between three and four weeks of age, the puppies should begin to be weaned. Scraped beef (prepared by scraping it off slices of raw beef with a spoon, so that none of the muscle or gristle is included) may be offered in very small quantities a couple of times daily for the first few days. If the puppy is reluctant to try it, put a little on your finger and rub it on the puppy's lips; this should get things going. By the third day, you can mix in ground puppy chow with warm water as directed on the package, offering it four times daily. By now the mother should be kept out of the box and away from the puppies for several hours at a time. After the puppies reach five weeks of age, she should be left in with them only overnight. By the time they are six weeks old, the puppies should be entirely weaned and the mother should only check on them with occasional visits.

Above: Goldens like cats, too—at least Am., Can. Ch. Russo's Pepperhill Poppy does, and so do the others at Pepperhill Farms. We love this photo of Poppy with her litter being visited by their cat friend. **Below:** Rusticana Ms. Traci with her babies. Linda Smith, owner.

Above: Three-week-old baby Goldens at Valhalla Farms. **Below:** The rest of the story! More from the same litter of Valhalla three-week-old babies. Kathy Liebler, owner.

A family portrait of Goldens at Valhalla Farms. Left to right: Charm (Dad), Kahlua (Mom), Kate (Grandam), and the baby Magic, at seven weeks of age. Kathy Liebler, owner.

Above: First steps, at three weeks old. These Golden puppies belong to Mary Lou Burke of Rhode Island. **Left:** Can. Ch. Bargello's Pomegranate, Am. and Can. C.D., W.C., with her puppies. Barbara Tinker, owner, Bargello Goldens.

Most veterinarians recommend a temporary DHL (distemper, hepatitis, leptospirosis) shot when the puppies are six weeks old. This remains effective for about two weeks. Then, at eight weeks, the series of permanent shots begins for the DHL protection. It is a good idea to discuss with your vet the advisability of having your puppies inoculated against the dreaded parvovirus at the same time. Each time the pups go to the vet for shots, you should bring stool samples so that they can be examined for worms. Worms go through various stages of development and may be present in a stool sample even though the sample does not test positive. So do not neglect to keep careful watch on this.

The puppies should be fed four times daily until they are three months old. Then you can cut back to three feedings daily. By the time the

Apollo's Golden Charmer, Am. and Can. C.D. with her three-month-old daughter, Charms Two Toots and Holler, both owned by Ginny Boyle, Charms Goldens, Joppa, Maryland.

puppies are six months old, two meals daily are sufficient. Some people feed their dogs twice daily throughout their lifetime, while others cut back to one meal daily when the puppy reaches one year of age.

The ideal time for Golden puppies to go to their new homes is when they are between eight and twelve weeks old, although some puppies successfully adjust to a new home when they are six weeks of age. Be certain that they go to their future owners accompanied by a description of the diet you've been feeding them and a schedule of the shots they have received and those they still need. These should be included with a registration application and a copy of the pedigree.

Above: Playtime for Gosling Golden youngsters. **Below:** Growing up is tiring work, so this Golden baby is catching forty winks. One of the Gosling Goldens.

Coming through the snow, Pepperhill's Sands of Charlen obviously enjoys the experience as a very young puppy. Barbara and Jeffrey Pepper, owners.

412

Left: Faera Rain Dance seven weeks following her litter's birth. Wanda Metz of Illinois, owner. **Above:** Fun in the snow! Goldens owned by Kathy Liebler of New York.

Wochica's Taste of Honey content on a fertilizer pile! By Ch. Misty Morn's Sunset ex Wochica's Apple Wine. Janet Bunce, owner, Wochica Goldens.

Guarding Dad's shoes. Golden puppy from D.J.'s Kennels owned by the Wackers.

Little Dawn of Chickasaw with the tiger cubs to which she was foster mother for Ringling Brothers Barnum and Bailey Circus. Janet Bunce, owner, Wochica Goldens.

Enjoying a swim. Valhalla Farms, Kathy Liebler.

Above: Three future champions at Sun Dance Kennels, Lisa Schultz, owner. **Below:** Two stages of puppy development. Sarah, left, is three-and-a-half months old and Tinker is eleven months old. From Pepperhill Goldens, Barbara and Jeffrey Pepper.

Game time being enjoyed by a couple of the Ashwel puppies. Myra Moldawsky, owner.

Topbrass Chivas Regal, a homebred from the Topbrass Kennels of Mrs. Joseph Mertens.

A lovely informal pose of Am., Can. Ch. Russo's Pepperhill Poppy, the third Golden bitch to be included in the Hall of Fame, based on show wins, and a great producer of champions.

Ch. Misty Morn's Sunset winning the Veterans Dog Class at the National in 1975. Sunset, famous and great as both a show dog and a producer, is owned by Peter and Rose Lewesky.

Henry

Facing page: Ch. Wendy, VIII, U.D., W.C.X., Golden Retriever Club of America Outstanding Dam, was sired by Leo of Los Altos ex Amanda of Lynn D'Or. Foundation bitch at Dasu Goldens, Wendy has produced Ch. Dasu's Champagne Edition, C.D.X., Dasu's Candy Cain, U.D., W.C.X., and Dasu's Solitaire For Zeravia, U.D. Owned by Dave and Suzi Bluford. **Right:** Am., Can. Ch. Beckwith's Apricot Brandy, U.D.T., Can. C.D.X., at ten years of age, left, with her dam, Am., Can. Ch. Beckwith's Malagold Cherub, U.D.T., Can. C.D.X., at eleven years of age. These are the only mother and daughter combined champions and U.D.T. dogs in Golden history. Breeder-owners, Mr. and Mrs. R.E. Beckwith. **Below:** This son and father brace won Best Brace in the Sporting Group at the Rapid City Kennel Club and the Central Wyoming Kennel Club shows during October of 1981. Left, Ch. Morningsage Little Big Shot, C.D., with his sire on the right, Ch. Sweetbay Morningsage Cajun, C.D. Owned by Joanne A. Lastoka and Sheri DeVries.

Four of the Southern Goldens belonging to Colleen and Clark Williams. Middle back is Best in Show-winning Am., Can. Ch. Goldrush's Contender, U.D. (Ch. Misty Morn's Sunset, C.D., T.D., W.C., ex Ch. Goldrush's Birch of Bearwood, C.D., W.C.). Far left, Am., Can. Ch. Southern's Gold-Rush Traveler, multiple Group-winner (Am., Can., Bda. Ch. Cummings' Gold-Rush Charlie ex Ch. Golden Pine's Glorybe's Angel). Far right, Ch. Southern's Goldrush Flair, C.D. (Ch. Gold-Rush's Great Teddy Bear ex Ch. Goldrush's Birch of Bearwood, C.D., W.C.). Middle front, a six-month-old pup out of Ch. Goldrush's Contender, U.D., line-bred on Ch. Misty Morn's Sunset, C.D., W.C., T.D. These four handsome Goldens are all closely related and all of the highest caliber. **Below:** The Charms gang! Left to right: Ch. Happy, C.D., two years old; Ely, C.D., six years old; Tootsie, Am. and Can. C.D.X., eight years old; Am., Can. Ch. Teak, four years old; Am., Can. Ch. Pugbear, three years old; and up front, Chet, C.D., six years old. All owned by Ginny Boyle, Charms Goldens, Joppa, Maryland.

A father and two sons: Amico of Maine, W.C.X., C.D., in the background, with his handsome offspring Beskabekuk of Maine, W.C., C.D., and Bittersweet Maine Seboomook. Jennifer Kesner, owner.

Left: This lovely puppy in the garden is by Ch. Westley Mervin ex Ch. Brador-Chryshaefen Bionic Gal and is typical of the type Golden raised at Matglo Kennels, M.D. Wilson, Canada. **Below:** Amico of Maine, W.C.X., C.D., in the foreground, with his young son who is now Beskabe-kuk of Maine, W.C., C.D. Both belong to Jennifer Kesner of Ipswich, Massachusetts.

This sensational puppy is Freedom's Celebration at nine months of age. This son of Ch. Gold Coast Here Comes The Sun, C.D., ex Ch. Laurell's Xpectations was born in June 1981. "Rally" has been gaining points at a rapid rate from the Puppy Classes, including both majors, and has been Best of Breed over Specialty winners and a Best in Show dog—certainly exciting successes for one so young. Owned by Judy Glasgow, Athens, Ohio; handled by his owner or by Jim Rathbun.

Left: October's Bargello's Diamond at nine weeks of age. Owners, Barbara Tinker and Sharon Smith. **Below:** A lovely Bargello puppy owned by Barbara Tinker.

Ch. Cummings' Chip of Gold at six months of age. Mrs. Mary W. Cummings, owner, Cummings' Goldens.

Left: Seven-week-old Golden Retriever puppies, bred and owned by Pam German, Goldust Kennels. **Below:** "Snow babies." Golden puppies at Valhalla Farms, owned by the Lieblers.

Right: Stopping to smell the flower, this puppy is a homebred belonging to Mercer Russo Ervin. **Below:** Kyle DeWitt with puppies raised by his family out of D.J.'s Montana Kid's X-Rated, C.D.

Above: At the lunch bar! Golden puppies owned by D.J.'s Golden Kennel, Dave, Jean, and J.D. Wacker.

Facing page, top: Baby "Coda" snatches a quick nap alongside the toy duck. Amberac Goldens, owner, Ellen Manke.
Facing page, bottom: "I *knew* that bowl was under there!" An adorable Ashwel Golden puppy belonging to Myra Moldawsky.

Left: Pepperhill's Beaujolais in January 1980 practicing to become a field dog. **Below:** Eight-week-old puppies by Ch. Gold-Rush's Great Teddy Bear ex Am., Can. Ch. Goldenquest's Lucky Charm. Mrs. Jay S. Cox, owner.

Pictured after a romp in the snow is this baby Golden from Topbrass Kennels, Mrs. Joseph Mertens, owner.

Goldens at play. These Australian-bred littermates, pictured here as puppies, are Semperidem Sunrunner and Semperidem Sunflower and they were imported to Hawaii by Karl and Lei Taft.

CHAPTER FIFTEEN

You and Your Golden

Portrait of a Golden from Valhalla Farms, owned by Kathy Liebler.

Over the years, Golden Retrievers have steadily grown in popularity, and today they rank in the top ten most popular dog breeds. There is good reason for this popularity, for Goldens are even-tempered and very trainable dogs. They are valued workers and are held in high esteem by people from many walks of life. Ownership of a Golden, of course, demands certain responsibilities, but these responsibilities are a joy to fulfill for such a versatile breed of dog.

Versatility of Goldens

Ask any Golden owner what he or she likes best about the breed, and on the majority of occasions the reply will be "its versatility." This dog really *does* fill the bill perfectly as an ideal all-around family companion, with numerous other attributes as well.

Not only is this a breed beautiful in physical appearance, but it also is one which possesses superior intelligence (just pause and review the outstanding achievements of Goldens in the world of obedience competition); stamina (the longest day in the field does not faze a Golden in the least); patience and good temper (this is what makes it so great as a companion for children); gentlemanly habits (this makes it an ideal house-hold member); liking for other dogs, cats, and various other household pets (you will note this fact in our illustrations depicting Goldens with "friends" which might be considered anything but by members of a less sociable breed); alertness as a watch dog (attack duty may be contrary to a Golden's personality, but being watchful and vigilant is part of a Golden's stock in trade); and many, many more good qualities.

Since a Golden requires little in the way of specialized pre-show preparation, this is a fun breed for an amateur exhibitor as well as for the more sophisticated competitor. Their gentleness and amiability make them great for young owners who wish to compete in Junior Showmanship. Their good nose makes them especially proficient workers in the field, and their expertise as retrievers has earned them many honors in the world of field trial competition. Brains and beauty merge in the Golden, and it is not unusual to find the same dog a successful competitor in the show ring, obedience, and field—a combination which has long since disappeared from numerous other breeds.

Goldens are one of the three most popular breeds for guiding the blind, sharing this distinction with German Shepherds and Labrador Retrievers. They are used extensively

Valhalla's Chip off the Ol' Block, at about one-and-a-half years of age. Owned by Kathleen M. Liebler.

Above: Valhalla's Goldenrod Cadet, by Camrose Edmundo ex Ch. Ropahi's Valhalla Jingle Too, at twenty-two months of age. Cadet is wearing his Guide Dog harness. Kathy Liebler. **Below:** This is "Shonie," a leader dog daughter of Ch. Kendra, from Amberac Goldens, Ellen Manke.

by Guide Dogs for the Blind, Leader Dogs, and other similar organizations. It is interesting to note that one Golden owned by the Guiding Eye organization, Rockhill's Guiding Eyes Jake, is being campaigned for an American Kennel Club championship and has at least twelve points toward this goal. Even though the blind owner may not be able to appreciate his dog's beauty, the admiration of friends and strangers who notice the dog is a source of pleasure to the owner. It is interesting, too, that this dog was sired by Susan Taylor's very famous Champion Wochica's Okeechobee Jake.

Goldens are also being used in therapy for the mentally ill and the elderly, and the results are good in both types of situation. Their gentleness and intelligence well equip them for helpfulness of this nature! Experiments to use Goldens as "ears" for the deaf are now being conducted and there is great hope that these dogs will be as successful as their "brothers" who act as "eyes" for the blind.

It is a Golden Retriever who guards the Statue of Liberty in New York Harbor, and she has received considerable admiration for the fine job she is doing.

Am., Can. Ch. Pepperhill's Lady Ruston with a friend. One of the many lovely Goldens from Pepperhill Farms.

The real heros of the Golden world, however, are all those who bring joy to their families by sharing their daily lives. What a delight it was recently, visiting Jeff and Barbara Pepper, to see several of their famous winners relaxing around the house, in company with the Peppers' assorted cats, several Whippets and a Springer. Ideal temperament such as this makes for very pleasant living and dog ownership at its best.

Children find that Goldens make great pillows, are fun to play a game of ball with, and are super companions on land or in the water, being equally at home in both places, and parents can be assured that the Goldens will safeguard "their" kids. They will also pull a cart if asked to do so.

Goldens are also good travellers and enjoy being in the car and accompanying you on short errands or long trips; and if you are fond of sailing, they'll be glad to accompany you on your boat.

Lochan Ora Sam, bred by Lochan Ora Goldens and owned by Tommy Blanchette. Our favorite "boy with his dog" photo!

Goldens make great pillows, too. Starkin's Royal King Tut, by Ch. Misty Morn's Sunset ex Bracken Hollow Sacaganga, with two-year-old Greg Havens. Wanda Metz, Starkin's Kennel, owns Tut.

Ch. Wochica's Okeechobee Jake with his favorite pal, Domi, in November 1977. Susan Taylor, owner.

A group of friends at Valhalla Farms owned by Kathy Liebler.

Goldens can be used to pull! Note the roller skates this youngster is wearing as his Golden waits for the signal to go. Jennifer Kesner, owner.

On guard, Amico of Maine, W.C.X., C.D., sits majestically atop the wall and waits. Jennifer Kesner, owner.

Two of Jennifer Kesner's Goldens enjoying a camping trip in Maine at Tea Pond.

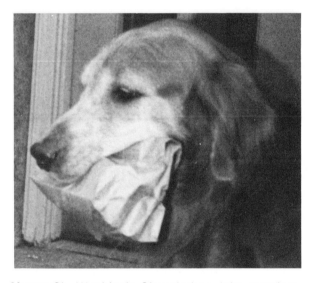

Above: Ch. Wochica's Okeechobee Jake carrying home the groceries, as was his custom, for his owner Susan Taylor. **Below:** Jake playing cards with Sue Taylor's brother.

Goldens make excellent sailors, too. This one is from Valhalla Farms.

Responsibilities of Golden Owners

Whether you are a one-dog owner, the owner of a show kennel, one involved in obedience or field trial dogs, or a breeder, there are definite responsibilites—to your dog or dogs, to your breed, and to the general public—involved which should never be overlooked or taken lightly.

It is inexcusable for anyone to breed dogs promiscuously, producing unneeded litters. The only time a responsible breeder plans a litter is when it is *needed* to carry on a bloodline or to provide dogs for which this breeder has very definite plans, including orders for at least half the number of puppies which will probably be born. Every healthy puppy deserves a good and loving home, assuring its future well-being. No puppy should be born to an uncertain future on someone's assumption that there will be no problem selling or otherwise finding a home for it, as very definitely this is not always easy. Overpopulation is the dog world's most heartbreaking tragedy. Those of us who love dogs should not add to it by carelessly producing more. If you have any reason to feel that the puppies may not be assured of homes, don't breed the bitch; wait for a more propitious time. Certainly no Golden breeder likes the thought of running around frantically trying to find someone who will take puppies off his hands, even if they must be given away. The latter usually is not a good idea anyway, as many people cannot resist saying "yes" to something which costs nothing, regardless of whether or not they really want it. As the Golden grows larger and demands more care, their enthusiasm wanes to the point that the dog soon is left to roam the streets where he is subject to all sorts of dangers, and the owner simply could not care less. If one pays for something, one seems to respect it more.

One litter at a time is all that any breeder should produce, making sure that all those puppies are well provided for prior to breeding for another litter. Breeders should do all in their power to ascertain that the home to which each of his puppies goes is a *good* home, one that offers proper care, a fenced in area, and a really enthusiastic owner. I have tremendous respect for those breeders who make it a point to carefully check out the credentials of prospective purchasers, and I firmly believe that all breeders should do likewise on this important point. I am certain that no breeder wants any Golden puppy to wind up in an animal shelter, in an experimental laboratory, or as a victim of a speeding car. While complete control of such situations may not be possible, it is at least our responsibility to make every effort to turn our puppies over to people who have the same outlook as our own where love of dogs and responsibility toward them are concerned and who realize that the ownership of a dog involves care, not neglect.

Fleetwood's Lady Taffeta, C.D., owned by Barbara and Jeffrey Pepper.

Am., Can. Ch. Jolly's December Charm at two years of age. Ginny Boyle, owner, Charms Goldens.

It is the breeder's responsibility to sell every puppy with the understanding that should the new owner find it necessary to place the dog elsewhere, you, the breeder, must be contacted immediately and given the opportunity to take back the dog or to help in finding it a new home. Many a dog starting out in what has seemed a good home has, under unforeseen circumstances, been passed along to others, only to wind up in exactly the sort of situation we most want to avoid. Keep in touch with what is happening to your dogs after they are sold.

The final obligation every dog owner shares, be there just one dog or many, is that of leaving detailed and up-to-date instructions in our wills about what is to become of our animals in the event of our death. Far too many of us are apt to procrastinate and leave this matter unattended to, feeling that everything will work out all right or that "someone will see to them." The latter is not too likely to happen, at least not to the benefit of the dogs, unless the owner makes absolutely certain that all will be well for them in the future.

Hogan Burke at two-and-a-half years of age. This good friend and family dog owned by Mary Lou Burke typifies the Golden personality and beauty.

If you have not already done so, please get together with your lawyer and set up a clause in your will specifying what is to be done with each and every dog you own and to whom each will be entrusted (after first ascertaining that this person is willing and able to assume the responsibility); also include details about the location of all registration papers, pedigrees, and kennel records, along with ways of identifying each dog. Just think of the possibilities of what might happen otherwise!

It is not wise to count on family members, unless they share your involvement with the dogs. In many cases our relatives are not the least bit "dog-oriented," perhaps they think we're a trifle crazy for being such enthusiasts, and they might absolutely panic at the thought of suddenly having even *one* dog thrust upon them. They might mean well, and they might try; but it is unfair to them and to the dogs to leave the one stuck with the other!

If you travel a great deal with your dogs, another wise idea is to post prominently in your vehicle and carry in your wallet the name, address, and telephone number of someone to be called to take charge of them in case of an accident. Of course, this should be done by pre-arrangement with the person named. We have such a friend, and she has a signed check of ours to be used in case of an emergency or accident when we are travelling with our dogs; this check will be used to cover her expenses to come and take over the care of our dogs should anything happen to make it impossible for us to do so.

The registration certificates of all our dogs are enclosed in an envelope with our wills, and the person who will be in charge knows each of them, and one from the other, so there will be no identification problem. These are all points to be considered, for which provision should be made.

We also owe an obligation to our older dogs who too often are disregarded. It disgusts me that so many supposedly great dog lovers think nothing of getting an older dog, even though well, happy, and enjoying life, out of the way to make room for younger show prospects or additional puppies. The people I consider to be genuine dog lovers are the ones who permit their dogs to live out their lives in comfort as loved, respected members of the household or kennel. How quickly some of us seem to forget the pleasures these dogs have brought us with exciting wins and the devotion they have shown to us and our families!

Ch. Peachy's Happy Lady of Charms, C.D., at two years of age. Ginny Boyle, owner.

The senior citizens, Amber and Kate (Am., Can. Ch. Valhalla's Amber Waves and his sister Ch. Valhalla's Amber Kate) enjoying life at home with Kathy Liebler at Valhalla Farms.

Am., Can. Ch. Ambertrail's Bargello Stitch, U.D.T., W.C.X., Can. U.D.T.X., W.C., "speaking." Barbara Tinker, owner, Bargello Goldens.

So much for our responsibility to our dogs, but we also owe a responsibility to our breed: to keep up its quality and to protect its image. Every Golden breeder should breed only from and for high-grade stock and should guard against the market being flooded with excess puppies. We should display good sportsmanship and concern for the dogs at all times, and we should involve ourselves whenever possible in activities beneficial to the breed.

To the general public we owe the consideration of good dog ownership. Our dogs should not be permitted to run at large and annoy others. Dogs should not be left barking endlessly, tied outside or closed in the house. We should pick up after our dogs, as required in most cities, when we exercise them where people must walk. We should, in other words, enjoy our dogs without allowing them to infringe on those who may be less enthusiastic.

Mercer Russo Ervin with two of her Goldens.

These three Goldens, sitting proudly at attention, are all dressed up for Christmas morning. Owned by Jennifer Kesner.

Travelling With Your Golden

When you travel with a dog, you must always remember that everyone does not necessarily share your love of dogs and that those who do not, strange creatures though they may seem, have their rights too. These rights, on which we should not encroach, include not being disturbed, annoyed, or made uncomfortable by the presence and behavior of other people's pets. Golden owners, since theirs is an intelligent and easily trained breed, should have the dog well schooled in proper canine behavior by the time maturity is reached. Your dog should not jump enthusiastically on strangers, no matter how playful or friendly the dog's intentions. We may love having them do this to us, but it is unlikely that someone else will share our enthusiasm, especially in the case of muddy paws on delicate or light-colored clothes which may be soiled or damaged. A sharp "Down" from you should be promptly obeyed, as should be "Sit," "Stay," and "Come."

Ch. Jolly Krishna Mr. Beau Jangles, C.D., by Ch. Sir Duncan of Woodbury ex Ch. Larkmill Genevieve, is all dressed up for the party. Sandra Haber of New York, owner.

Amico of Maine, W.C.X., C.D., graced the front of Jennifer Kesner's 1977 Christmas card.

If you expect to take your Golden on many trips, he should have, for your sake and for his, a crate of appropriate size for him to relax in comfortably. In cases of emergency or accident, a crated dog is far more likely to escape injury. Left in a parked car, a crated dog should have the car windows fully open in hot weather, thus being assured sufficient ventilation. For your own comfort, a dog in a crate does not hang from the car window, climb over you and your passengers, and shed hair on the upholstery. Dogs quickly become accustomed to their crates, especially when started with one, as they should be, from puppyhood. Both you and the dog will have a more enjoyable trip when you provide him with this safeguard.

If you do permit your dog to ride loose in the car, see to it that he does not hang from the windows, ears blowing in the breeze. He could become overly excited by something he sees and jump out; he could lose his balance and fall out should you stop short or swerve unexpectedly; he could suffer an eye injury induced by the strong wind generated by the moving car. All of these unnecessary risks can so easily be avoided by crating!

Never, ever, under any circumstances, should a dog be permitted to ride uncrated in the back end of an open pick-up truck. I have noted, with disgust and horror, that some people do transport their dogs in this manner, and I think it cruel and shocking. How easily such a dog can be thrown out of the car by sudden jolts or an impact. And I am sure that many dogs have jumped out at the sight of something exciting along the way, quite possibly into the path of an oncoming car. Some unthinking individuals tie the dog, probably not realizing that if he were to jump under those circumstances, his neck could be broken, he could be dragged alongside the vehicle or get under its wheels, or he could be hit by another vehicle. If you are for any reason taking your dog *anywhere* in an open back truck, *please* have sufficient regard for that dog to provide a crate to protect him. Also please remember that with or without a crate, a dog riding exposed to the sun in hot weather can really suffer and have his life endangered by the heat.

If you are staying in a hotel or motel with your dog, please exercise him somewhere other than in the parking lot, along the walkways, or in the

Am., Can. Ch. Peachy's Technical Knockout, owned by Ginny Boyle, Charms Goldens.

Mary Lou Burke's first Golden, Samantha Burke, front, at ten years of age, and Hogan Burke, three years of age.

flower beds of the property. People walking to and from their rooms or cars really are not thrilled at "stepping in something" left by your dog and should not be subjected to the annoyance. Should an accident occur, pick it up with tissues or a paper towel and deposit it in a proper receptacle; don't just let it remain there. Usually there are grassy areas on the sides or behind motels where dogs can be exercised with no bother to anyone. Use those places rather than the busy, more conspicuous, carefully tended areas. If you are becoming a dog show enthusiast, you will eventually need an exercise pen to take with you to the show. They are ideal to use when staying at motels, too, as they permit you to limit the dog's roaming space and to pick up after him easily. Should you have two or more dogs, such a convenience is truly a "must!"

Never leave your dog unattended in a room at a motel unless you are absolutely, positively, sure that he will stay quiet and not destroy anything. You do not want a long list of complaints from irate fellow-guests, caused by the annoying barking or whining of a lonesome dog in strange surroundings or an overzealous watch dog barking furiously each time a footstep passes the door. And you certainly do not want to return to torn curtains or bedspreads, soiled rugs, or other embarrassing (and sometimes expensive) evidence of the fact that your dog is not really house-reliable.

Am., Can. Ch. Morningsage Last Tango in 1979, four years old. By Ch. Honor's Let 'Em Have It, C.D., W.C., ex Morningsage Malagold Honey. Bred, owned, and titled by Joanne A. Lastoka.

If yours is a dog accustomed to travelling with you and you are positive that his behavior will be acceptable when left alone, that is fine. But if the slightest uncertainty exists, the wise course is to leave him in the car while you go to dinner or elsewhere and then bring him into the room when you are ready to retire for the night.

When you travel with a dog, it is sometimes simpler to take along his food and water from home rather than to buy food and to look for water while you travel. In this way he will have the rations to which he is accustomed and which you know agree with him, and there will be no problems due to different drinking water. Feeding on the road is quite easy now, at least for short trips, with all the splendid dry prepared foods and high quality canned meats available, not to mention the "just remove it from the packet" convenience foods. And many types of lightweight, refillable water containers can be bought at many types of stores.

If you are going to another country, you will need a health certificate from your veterinarian for each dog you are taking with you, certifying that each has had rabies shots within the required length of time preceding your visit.

Remember that during the summer, the sun's rays can make an inferno of a closed-up car in a matter of minutes, so always leave windows open enough that there is sufficient ventilation for the dog. Again, if your dog is in a crate, this can be done easily and with safety. Remember, too, that leaving the car in a shady spot does not mean that it will remain shaded. The position of the sun changes quickly, and the car you left nicely shaded half an hour earlier may be in the full glare of the sun upon your return. Be alert and be cautious.

When you travel with your dog, be sure to take a lead and use it, unless he is completely and thoroughly obedience trained. Even if the dog is trained, however, using a lead is a wise precaution against his getting lost in strange territory. I am sure that all of us have seen in the "Lost and Found" columns the sad little messages about dogs who have gotten away or been lost during a trip, so why take chances?

Westley Valhalla Noah, C.D. Owned by Kathy Liebler, Valhalla Farms.

Beskabekuk of Maine, W.C., C.D., leaning on the fence. Jennifer Kesner, owner.

CHAPTER SIXTEEN

Veterinarian's Corner

by Joseph P. Sayres, D.V.M.

Susan Breakell, Sutter Creek Kennels, with Ch. Sutter Creek's Libra Bearhug, C.D., and Am., Can. Ch. Sutter Creek Goldrush Flyboy—two obviously healthy and happy Goldens.

Until recent years, there has been a lot of misunderstanding and even animosity between veterinarians and breeders. Some distrust arose on the breeder's part because most veterinarians were not familiar with, or even interested in learning about, purebred dogs. Some of the problems encountered were peculiar to certain breeds and some would crop up at inconvenient times. Veterinarians were then beset by breeders who thought that they knew more about the medical problems of their dogs than the vets did. The veterinarians very often were called only for emergencies or when it was too late to save a sick dog that had been treated too long by people in the kennel. Another problem was that many breeders had never included veterinary fees in their budgets and were slow to pay their bills, if indeed they paid them at all.

Fortunately, these problems, to a large extent, have been solved. Education and better communication between breeders and veterinarians have eliminated most areas of friction.

Today, veterinary education and training have advanced to a point paralleling that of human standards. This resulted from advances in the field of Veterinary Science in the last two decades. Sophisticated diagnostic procedures, new and advanced surgical techniques, and modern well-equipped hospitals all make for improved medical care for our dogs.

Educated breeders now realize that, while they may know more about the general husbandry of their dogs and the unique traits of the Golden Retriever, they should not attempt to diagnose and treat their ailments.

In choosing your veterinarian, be selective. He or she should be friendly, should be interested in your dogs, and, in the case of breeders, should be interested in your breeding programs. Veterinarians should be willing to talk freely with you. Such things as fees, availability for emergencies, and what services are and are not available should be discussed and understood before a lasting relationship with your veterinarian can be established.

You can expect your veterinarian's office, clinic, or hospital to be clean, free of undesirable odors, well equipped, and staffed by sincere, friendly personnel who willingly serve you at all times. All employees should be clean, neat in appearance, and conversant with whatever services you require. You may also expect your dog to be treated carefully and kindly at all times by the doctor and his staff.

Your veterinarian should participate in continuing education programs in order to keep up with changes and improvements in his field. He should also be aware of his limitations. If he doesn't feel confident in doing certain procedures, he should say so and refer you to qualified individuals to take care of the problem. Seeking second opinions and consultation with specialists on difficult cases is more the rule than the exception nowadays. That is as it should be.

You will know that if your veterinarian is a member of the American Animal Hospital Association, he and his facility have had to measure up to high standards of quality and are subjected to inspections every two years.

Many excellent veterinarians and veterinary hospitals by choice do not belong to the American Animal Hospital Association. You can satisfy your curiosity about these places by taking guided tours of the facilities and learning by word of mouth about the quality of medicine practiced at these hospitals.

So far, we have discussed only what you should expect from your veterinarian. Now, let's discuss what the veterinarian expects from his clients.

Most of all, he expects his clients to be open and frank in their relations with him. He doesn't like to be double-checked and second-guessed behind his back. He also wants you to handle your pet so that he, in turn, can examine him. He also expects you to leash your dog, to control him, and to keep him from bothering other pets in the room. He expects to be paid a fair fee and to be paid promptly for services rendered. Fees in a given area tend to be consistent, and variations are due only to complications or unforeseen problems. Medicine is not an exact science; therefore, things unpredictable can happen.

If you are dissatisfied with the services or fees, then ask to discuss these things in a friendly manner with the doctor. If his explanations are not satisfactory or he refuses to talk to you about the problem, then you are justified in seeking another doctor.

The veterinarian expects to provide his services for your animals during regular hours whenever possible. But he also realizes that in a kennel or breeding operation, emergencies can occur at any time, and his services will be needed at off hours. You should find out how these emergencies will be handled and be satisfied with the procedures.

No veterinarian can be on duty twenty-four hours of every day. Today, cooperative veterinarians group together to take turns covering each other's emergency calls. Some cities have emergency clinics that operate solely to take care of those catastrophes that seem usually to happen in the middle of the night or on weekends.

Ch. Laurell's Honey 'n' Spice, well-cared-for by the Klings at Laurell's Goldens.

My conclusion, after thirty years of practice, is that most disagreements and hard feelings between clients and veterinarians are a result of a breakdown in communication. Find a veterinarian that you can talk to and can be comfortable with, and you'll make a valuable friend.

In using veterinary services to their best advantage, I believe that you will find that prevention of diseases and problems is more important than trying to cure these things after they occur. In other words, an ounce of prevention is worth a pound of cure.

Congenital Defects

Golden Retrievers have their share of congenital defects. From the publication *Congenital Defects in Dogs* published by Ralston Purina Company, as well as other reliable sources, the following conditions are listed as congenital defects in Golden Retrievers:

a. Cataracts, Bilateral—Opaque lenses.

b. Central Progressive Retinal Atrophy—Mottling and increased reflectivity in retina resulting in loss of central vision affecting dogs three to five years old. Difficulty in seeing still objects. Affected individuals can see best in dim light.

c. Von Willebrand's Disease—Prolonged bleeding episode..

d. Cryptorchidism—Non-descent of testicles.

e. Hip Dysplasia—See section on this subject near the end of this chapter.

f. Hyperammonemia—Excess ammonia in blood due to urea cycle enzyme deficiency.

g. Entropion—Inverted eyelids.

Vaccines

By proper and vigilant vaccination programs, the following contagious diseases can be eliminated: distemper, hepatitis, parainfluenza, leptospirosis, rabies, and parvovirus enteritis.

The vaccination schedule described below should be set up and strictly followed to prevent infectious diseases.

Distemper: Vaccinate when six to eight weeks old, with the second inoculation to be given at twelve to sixteen weeks of age. Revaccinate annually.

Hepatitis (Adenovirus): Follow the same schedule as for distemper.

Parainfluenza (Kennel cough): Follow the same schedule as for distemper.

Leptospirosis: Give first vaccine at nine weeks of age. Revaccinate with second DHLP (distemper, hepatitis, leptospirosis, parainfluenza) at twelve to sixteen weeks of age. Revaccinate annually.

Rabies: Give first inoculation at three to four months of age; then revaccinate when one year old, and at least every three years thereafter. If dog is over four months old at the time of the first vaccination, then revaccinate in one year and then once every three years thereafter.

Parvovirus: Give first vaccine at seven to eight weeks of age, second vaccine four weeks later, and third vaccine four weeks later. Duration of immunity from three injections established at one year at the time of this writing. See explanation below. Revaccinate annually.

Vaccines used are all modified live virus vaccines except for leptospirosis, which is a killed bacterium. New and improved vaccines to immunize against parvovirus have appeared recently. The long-awaited modified live virus vaccine of canine origin was made available recently. It is safe and will produce immunity lasting one year.

Other communicable diseases for which no vaccine has been perfected as yet are: canine coronavirus, canine rotavirus, and canine brucellosis.

Infectious and Contagious Diseases

Distemper

Distemper is caused by a highly contagious, airborne virus. The symptoms are varied and may involve all of the dog's systems. A pneumonic form is common, with heavy eye and nose discharges, coughing, and lung congestion. The digestive system may be involved as evidenced by vomiting, diarrhea, and weight loss. The skin may show a pustular type rash on the abdomen. Nervous system involvement is common, with convulsions, chorea, and paralysis as persistent symptoms. This virus may have an affinity for nerve tissue and cause encephalitis and degeneration of the spinal cord. These changes, for the most part, are irreversible and death or severe crippling ensues.

We have no specific remedy or cure for distemper; and recoveries, when they occur, can only be attributed to the natural resistance of the patient, good nursing care, and control of secondary infections with antibiotics.

That's the bad news about distemper. The good news is that we rarely see a case of distemper in most areas today because of the efficiency of the vaccination program. This is proof that prevention by vaccination has been effective in almost eradicating this dreaded disease.

Hepatitis

Hepatitis is another contagious viral disease affecting the liver. This is not an airborne virus and can only be spread by contact. Although rarely seen today because of good prevention by vaccination programs, this virus is capable of producing a very acute, fulminating, severe infection and can cause death in a very short time. Symptoms of high temperature, lethargy, anorexia, and vomiting are the same as for other diseases. Careful evaluation by a veterinarian is necessary to confirm the diagnosis of this disease.

The old canine infectious hepatitis vaccine has been replaced by a canine adenovirus type 2 strain vaccine which is safer and superior. The new vaccine seems to be free of post-vaccination complications such as blue eyes, shedding of the virus in the urine, and some kidney problems.

Parainfluenza

This is commonly called kennel cough. It is caused by a throat-inhabiting virus that causes an inflammation of the trachea (windpipe) and larynx (voice box). Coughing is the main symptom and fortunately it rarely causes any other systemic problems. The virus is airborne and highly contagious, and it is the scourge of boarding kennels. A vaccine is available that will protect against this contagious respiratory disease and should be given as part of your vaccination program, along with the distemper, hepatitis, leptospirosis, and parvovirus shots. Pregnant bitches should not be vaccinated against parainfluenza because of the possibility of infecting the unborn puppies. As there may be more than one infectious agent involved in contagious upper respiratory diseases of dogs, vaccination against parainfluenza is not a complete guarantee to protect against all of them.

Leptospirosis

This is a disease that seriously affects the kidneys of dogs, most domestic animals, and man. For this reason, it can become a public health hazard. In urban and slum areas, the disease is carried by rats and mice in their urine. It is caused by a spirochete organism which is very resistant to treatment. Symptoms include fever, depression, dehydration, excess thirst, persistent vomiting, occasional diarrhea, and jaundice in the latter stages. Again, it is not always easy to diagnose so your veterinarian will have to do some laboratory work to confirm it.

We see very few cases of leptospirosis in dogs and then only in the unvaccinated ones. The vaccine is generally given concurrently with the distemper and hepatitis vaccinations. Preventive inoculations have resulted in the almost complete eradication of this dreaded disease.

Rabies

This is a well-known virus-caused disease that is almost always fatal and is transmissible to man and other warm-blooded animals. The virus causes very severe brain damage. Sources of the infection include foxes, skunks, and raccoons, as well as domesticated dogs and cats. Transmission is by introduction of the virus by saliva into bite wounds. Incubation in certain animals may be from three to eight weeks. In a dog, clinical signs will appear within five days. Symptoms fall into two categories, depending on what stage the disease is in when seen. We have the dumb form and the furious form. There is a change of personality in the furious form; individuals become hypersensitive and overreact to noise and stimuli. They will bite any object that moves. In dumb rabies, the typical picture of the loosely hanging jaw and tongue presents itself. Diagnosis is confirmed only by a laboratory finding the virus and characteristic lesions in the brain. All tissues and fluids from rabid animals should be considered infectious and you should be careful not to come in contact with them. Prevention by vaccination is a must because there is no treatment for rabid dogs.

Canine Parvovirus (CPV)

This is the newest and most highly publicized member of the intestinal virus family. Cat distemper virus is a member of the same family but differs from canine parvovirus biologically, and it has been impossible to produce this disease in dogs using cat virus as the inducing agent; and conversely canine parvovirus will not produce the disease in a cat. However, vaccines for both species will produce immunity in the dog. The origin of CPV is still unknown.

Canine parvovirus is very contagious and acts rapidly. The main source of infection is contaminated bowel movements. Direct contact between dogs is not necessary, and carriers such as people, fleas, and medical instruments may carry and transmit the virus.

The incubation period is five to fourteen days. The symptoms are fever, severe vomiting and diarrhea, often with blood, depression, and dehydration. Feces may appear yellowish gray streaked with blood. Young animals are more severely affected, and a shock-like death may occur in two days. In animals less than six weeks old, the virus will cause an inflammation of the heart muscle, causing heart failure and death. These pups may not have diarrhea. A reduction in the number of white blood cells is a common finding early in the disease.

The virus is passed in the feces for one to two weeks and may possibly be shed in the saliva and urine also. This virus has also been found in the coats of dogs. The mortality rate is unknown.

Dogs that recover from the disease develop an immunity to it. Again, the duration of this immunity is unknown.

Control measures include disinfection of the kennels, animals, and equipment with a 1 to 30 dilution of Clorox and isolation of sick individuals.

Treatment is very similar to that for coronavirus, namely: intravenous fluid therapy, administration of broad spectrum antibiotics, intestinal protectants, and good nursing care.

Transmission to humans has not been proven.

Clinical studies have proven that vaccination with three injections of the new modified live virus vaccine of canine origin, with four weeks between injections, will be over ninety percent effective. Recent work at the James A. Baker Institute for Animal Health at Cornell University has shown that maternally derived antibodies can interfere with the immunizing properties of our vaccines for as long as fifteen to sixteen weeks. This means that some of our puppies, especially those from dams with good immunity, will not become susceptible to successful vaccination until they are sixteen weeks old. It is also known that the maternal protection afforded these puppies, while enough to prevent successful vaccination, may not be enough to protect them from an exposure to the virus. The best advice is to give our puppies three inoculations of a canine origin modified live virus vaccine four weeks apart, starting when they are eight weeks old. Then, hope for the best and revaccinate annually.

Canine Coronavirus (CCV)

This is a highly contagious virus that spreads rapidly to susceptible dogs. The source of infection is through infectious bowel movements. The incubation period is one to four days, and the virus will be found in feces for as long as two weeks. It is hard to tell the difference sometimes between cases of diarrhea caused by coronavirus and parvovirus. Coronavirus generally is less severe or causes a more chronic or sporadic type of diarrhea. The fecal material may be orange in color and have a very bad odor; occasionally, it will also contain blood. Vomiting sometimes precedes the diarrhea, but loss of appetite and listlessness are consistent signs of the disease. Fever may or may not be present. Recovery is the rule after eight to ten days, but treatment with fluids, antibiotics, intestinal protectants, and good nursing care are necessary in the more severe watery diarrhea cases. Dogs that survive these infections become immune but for an unknown length of time.

To control an outbreak of this virus in a kennel, very stringent hygienic measures must be taken. Proper and quick disposal of feces, isolation of affected animals, and disinfection with a 1 to 30 dilution of Clorox are all effective means of controlling an outbreak in the kennel.

There is no vaccine yet available for prevention of canine coronavirus. Human infections by this virus have not been reported.

Canine Rotavirus (CRV)

This virus has been demonstrated in dogs with a mild diarrhea but again with more severe cases in very young puppies. Very little is known about this virus.

A milder type of diarrhea is present for eight to ten days. The puppies do not run a temperature and continue to eat. Dogs usually recover

Pepperhill's First Class, co-owned by Charles and Patricia Bradley and Pepperhill Farms, handled by Jeff Pepper at the Potomac Valley Golden Retriever Club in 1982.

naturally from this infection. There is no vaccine available for this virus.

Canine Brucellosis

This is a disease of dogs that causes both abortions and sterility. It is caused by a small bacterium closely related to the agent that causes undulant fever in man and abortion in cows. It occurs worldwide.

Symptoms of brucellosis sometimes are difficult to determine, and some individuals with the disease may appear healthy. Vague symptoms such as lethargy, swollen glands, poor hair coat, and stiffness in the back legs may be present. This organism does not cause death and may stay in the dog's system for months and even years. The latter animals, of course, have breeding problems and infect other dogs.

Poor results in your breeding program may be the only indication that brucellosis is in your kennel. Apparently, normal bitches abort without warning. This usually occurs forty-five to fifty-five days after mating. Successive litters will also be aborted. In males, signs of the disease are inflammation of the skin of the scrotum, shrunken testicles, and swollen tender testicles. Fertility declines and chronically infected males become sterile.

The disease is transmitted to both sexes at the time of mating.

Other sources of infection are aborted puppies and birth membrane and discharge from the womb at the time of abortions.

Humans can be infected, but such infections are rare and mild. Unlike in the dog, the disease in humans responds readily to antibiotics.

Diagnosis is done by blood testing, which should be done carefully. None of the present tests are infallible and false positives may occur. The only certain way that canine brucellosis can be diagnosed is by isolating the *B. canis* organism from blood or aborted material and for this, special techniques are required.

Treatment of infected individuals has proven ineffective in most cases. Sterility in males is permanent. Spaying or castrating infected pets should be considered as this will halt the spread of the disease and is an alternative to euthanasia.

At present, there is no vaccine against this important disease.

Our best hope in dealing with canine brucellosis is prevention. The following suggestions are made in order to prevent the occurrence of this malady in your dogs.

a. Test breeding stock annually and by all means breed only uninfected animals.

b. Test bitches several weeks before their heat periods.

c. Do not bring any new dogs into your kennel unless they have had two negative tests taken a month apart.

d. If a bitch aborts, isolate her, wear gloves when handling soiled bedding, and disinfect the premises with Roccal.

e. If a male loses interest in breeding or fails to produce after several matings, have him checked.

f. Consult your veterinarian for further information about this disease; alert other breeders and support the research that is going on at the James A. Baker Institute for Animal Health at Cornell University.

External Parasites

The control and eradication of external parasites depends on the repeated use of good quality insecticide sprays or powders during the warm months. Make a routine practice of using these products at seven-day intervals throughout the season. It is also imperative that sleeping quarters and wherever the animal habitates be treated also.

Fleas

These are brown, wingless insects with laterally compressed bodies and strong legs, and they are bloodsuckers. Their life cycle comprises eighteen to twenty-one days from egg to adult flea. They can live without food for one year in high humidity but die in a few days in low humidity. They multiply rapidly and are more prevalent in the warm months. They can cause a severe skin inflammation in those individuals that are allergic or sensitive to the flea bite or saliva of the flea. They can act as a vector for many diseases and do carry tapeworms. Control measures must include persistent, continual use of flea collars or flea medallions, or sprays or powders. The dog's bedding and premises must also be treated because the eggs are there. Foggers, vacuuming, or professional exterminators may have to be used. All dogs and cats in the same household must be treated at the same time.

Ticks

There are hard and soft species of ticks. Both species are bloodsuckers and at times cause severe skin inflammations on their host. They act as a vector for Rocky Mountain Spotted Fever, as well as other diseases. Hibernation through an entire winter is not uncommon. The female tick lays as many as one thousand to five thousand eggs in crevices and cracks in walls. These eggs will hatch in about three weeks and then a month later become adult ticks. Ticks generally locate around the host's neck and ears and between the toes. They can cause anemia and serious blood loss if allowed to grow and multiply. It is not a good idea to pick ticks off the dogs because of the danger of a reaction in the skin. Just apply the tick spray directly on the ticks which then die and fall off eventually. Heavily affected dogs should be dipped every two weeks in an anti-parasitic bath. The premises, kennels, and yards should be treated every two weeks during the summer months, being sure to apply the insecticide to walls and in all cracks and crevices. Frequent or daily grooming is effective in finding and removing ticks.

Lice

There are two kinds of lice, namely the sucking louse and the biting louse. They spend their entire life on their host but can be spread by direct contact or through contaminated combs and brushes. Their life cycle is twenty-one days, and their eggs, known as nits, attach to the hairs of the dog. The neck and shoulder region, as well as the ear flaps, are the most common areas to be inhabited by these pesky parasites. They cause itchiness, some blood loss, and inflammation of the skin. Eradication will result from dipping or dusting with methyl carbonate or Thuron once a week for three to four weeks. It is a good idea to fine-comb the dogs after each dip to remove the dead lice and nits. Ask your veterinarian to provide the insecticides and advice or control measures for all of these external parasites.

Mites

Less commonly occurring parasitic diseases such as demodectic and sarcoptic mange, caused by mites, should be diagnosed and treated only by your veterinarian. You are wise to consult your doctor whenever any unusual condition occurs and persists in your dog's coat and skin. These conditions are difficult to diagnose and treat at best, so that the earlier a diagnosis is obtained, the better the chances are for successful treatment. Other skin conditions such as ringworm, flea bite allergy, bacterial infections, eczemas, and hormonal problems, among others, all have to be considered.

Internal Parasites

The eradication and control of internal parasites in dogs will occupy a good deal of your time and energy.

Puppies should be tested for worms at four weeks of age and then six weeks later. It is also wise to test them again six weeks following their last worm treatment to be sure the treatments have been successful. Annual fecal tests are advisable throughout your dog's life. All worming procedures should be done carefully and only with the advice and supervision of your veterinarian. The medicants used to kill the parasites are, to a certain extent, toxic, so they should be used with care.

Ascarids

These include roundworms, puppy worms, stomach worms, and milk worms. Puppies become infested shortly after birth and occasionally even before birth. Ascarids can be difficult to eradicate. When passed in the stool or thrown up, they look somewhat like cooked spaghetti when fresh or like rubber bands when they are dried up. Two treatments at least two weeks apart will eliminate ascarids from most puppies. An occasional individual may need more wormings according to the status in its system of the life cycle of the worm at the time of worming. Good sanitary conditions must prevail and immediate disposal of feces is necessary to keep down the worm population.

Hookworms

Hookworms are bloodsuckers and also cause bleeding from the site of their attachment to the lining of the intestine when they move from one site to another. They can cause a blood-loss type of anemia and serious consequences, particularly in young puppies. Their life cycle is direct and their eggs may be ingested or pass through the skin of its host. Treatment of yards and runs where the dogs defecate with 5% sodium borate solution is said to kill the eggs in the soil. Two or three worm treatments three to four weeks apart may be necessary to get rid of hookworms. New injectable products administered by your veterinarian have proven more effective than remedies used in the past. Repeated fecal examinations may be necessary to detect the eggs in the feces. These eggs pass out of the body only sporadically or in showers, so that it is easy to miss finding them unless repeated stool testing is done. As is true with any parasite, good sanitary conditions in the kennel and outside runs will help eradicate this worm.

Ch. Willow Lane's Sunswept Luke, handsome winning Golden Retriever, owned by Mr. and Mrs. Charles Bradley, Wilton, Connecticut. Handled by Bob Stebbins.

Whipworms

These are a prevalent parasite in some kennels and in some individual dogs. They cause an intermittent mucousy type diarrhea. As they live only in the dog's appendix, it is extremely difficult to reach them with any worm medicine given by mouth. Injections seem to be the most effective treatment, and these have to be repeated several times over a long period of time to be effective. Here again, repeated fresh stool samples must be examined by your veterinarian to be sure that this pest has been eradicated. Appendectomies are indicated in only the most severe chronic cases. The fact that cleanliness is next to Godliness cannot be emphasized too often; it is most important in getting rid of this parasite.

Tapeworms

They are another common internal parasite of dogs. They differ in the mode of their transmission as they have an indirect life cycle. This means that part of their cycle must be spent in an intermediate host. Fleas, fish, rabbits, and field mice all may act as an intermediate host for the tapeworm. Fleas are the most common source of tapeworms in dogs, although dogs that live near water and may eat raw fish and hunting dogs that eat the entrails of rabbits may get them from those sources. Another distinguishing feature of the tapeworm is the suction apparatus which is the part of the head which enables the tapeworm to attach itself to the lining of the intestine. If, after worming, just the head remains, it has the capability of regenerating into another worm. This is one reason why tapeworms are so difficult to get rid of. It will require several treatments to get the entire parasite out of a dog's system. These worms are easily recognized by the appearance of their segments which break off and appear on top of a dog's feces or stuck to the hair around the rectal area. These segments may appear alive and mobile at times, but most often they are dead and dried up when found. They look like flat pieces of rice and may be white or brown when detected. Elimination of the intermediate host is an integral part of any plan to rid our dogs of this worm. Repeated wormings may be necessary to kill all the adult tapeworms in the intestine.

Heartworms

Heartworm disease is caused by an actual worm that goes through its life cycle in the blood stream of its victims. It ultimately makes its home in the right chambers of the heart and in the large vessels that transport the blood to the lungs. They vary in size from 2.3 inches to 16 inches. Adult worms can survive up to five years in the heart.

By its nature, this is a very serious disease and can cause irreversible damage to the lungs and heart of its host. Heart defect and lung pathology soon result in serious problems for the dog.

The disease is transmitted and carried by female mosquitoes that have infected themselves after biting an infected dog; they then pass it on to the next dog with which they come in contact.

The disease has been reported wherever mosquitoes are found, and cases have been reported in most of the United States. Rare cases have been reported in man and cats. It is most prevalent in warmer climates where the mosquito population is the greatest, but hotbeds of infection exist in the more temperate parts of the United States and Canada also.

Ch. Sir Richard of Fleetwood, C.D., a fine Golden owned by the Jeffrey Peppers, Pepperhill Farms. An Alton Anderson photo.

Concerted effort and vigorous measures must be taken to control and prevent this serious threat to our dog population. The most effective means of eradication I believe will come through annual blood testing for early detection, by the use of preventive medicine during mosquito exposure times, and also by ridding our dogs' environment of mosquitoes.

Annual blood testing is necessary to detect cases that haven't started to show symptoms yet and thus can be treated effectively. It also enables your veterinarian to prescribe safely the preventive medicine to those individuals that test negative. There is a ten to fifteen percent margin of error in the test, which may lead to some false negative tests. Individuals that test negative but are showing classical symptoms of the disease such as loss of stamina, coughing, loss of weight, and heart disease should be further evaluated with chest X-rays, blood tests, and electrocardiograms.

Serious consequences may result when the preventive medication is given to a dog that already has heartworm in his system. That is why it is so important to have your dog tested annually before starting the preventive medicine.

In order to be most effective, the preventive drug diethylcarbamazine should be given in daily doses of 2.5 mg. to 3 mg. per pound of body weight or 5 mg. per kilogram of body weight of your dog. This routine should be started fifteen days prior to exposure to mosquitoes and be continued until sixty days after exposure. Common and trade names for this drug are Caricide, Styrid-Caricide, and D.E.C. It comes in liquid and tablet forms.

This drug has come under criticism by some breeders and individuals who claim that it affects fertility and causes some serious reactions. Controlled studies have shown no evidence that the drug produces sterility or abnormal sperm count or quality. Long-term studies on reproduction, when the drug was given at the rate of 4.9 mg. per pound of body weight (two times the preventive dose level) for two years, showed no signs of toxic effects on body weight maintenance, growth rate of pups, feed consumption, conception rate, numbers of healthy pups whelped, ratio of male to female pups, blood counts, and liver function tests. It is reported to be a well-tolerated medication, and many thousands of dogs have benefitted from its use. From personal experience, I find only an occasional dog who will vomit the medicine or get an upset stomach from it. The new enteric coated pills have eliminated this small problem.

However, if you still don't want to give the preventive, especially to your breeding stock, an alternative procedure would be to test your dogs every six months for early detection of the disease, so that it can be treated as soon as possible.

Heartworm infestation can be treated successfully. There is a one to five percent mortality rate from the treatment. It can be expected that treatment may be completed without side effects if the disease hasn't already caused irreversible problems in the heart, lungs, liver, kidneys, or other organs. Careful testing, monitoring, and supervision is essential to success in treatment. Treatment is far from hopeless these days and if the disease is detected early enough, a successful outcome is more the rule than the exception.

In conclusion, remember that one case of heartworm disease in your area is one too many, especially if that one case is your dog. By following the steps mentioned here, we can go a long way in ridding ourselves of this serious threat to our dogs.

Home Remedies and First Aid

You have repeatedly read here of my instructions to call your veterinarian when your animals are sick. This is the best advice I can give you. There are a few home remedies, however, that may get you over some rough spots while trying to get professional help.

I think it is a good idea to keep on hand some medical supplies in a first aid kit. The kit should contain the following items: a roll of cotton, gauze bandages, hydrogen peroxide, tincture of metaphen, cotton applicator swabs, BFI powder, rectal thermometer, adhesive tape, boric acid crystals, tweezers, and a jar of petroleum jelly.

A word here on how to take a dog's temperature may be in order. Always lubricate the thermometer with petroleum jelly and carefully insert it well into the rectum. Hold it in place for two to three minutes and then read it. The thermometer should be held firmly so that it doesn't get sucked up into the rectum.

To administer liquid medicines to dogs, simply pull the lips away from the side of the mouth, making a pocket for depositing the liquid. Slightly tilt the dog's head upward and he will be able to swallow the liquid properly. Giving liquids by opening the mouth and pouring them directly on the tongue is an invitation to disaster because inhalation pneumonia can result. Putting it in the side of the mouth gives the dog time to hold it in his mouth and then swallow it properly.

Tablets are best administered by forcing the dog's mouth open, and pushing the pill down over the middle of the tongue into the back of his mouth. If put in the right place, a reflex tongue reaction will force the pill down the throat and thus be swallowed. There is no objection to giving the pills in favorite foods as long as you carefully determine that the medicine is surely swallowed with the food.

Vomiting

To stop vomiting, mix one tablespoon of table salt to one pint of water and dissolve the salt thoroughly; then give one tablespoonful of the mixture to the patient. After waiting one hour, repeat the procedure and skip the next meal. The dog may vomit a little after the first dose, but the second dose works to settle the stomach. This mixture not only provides chlorides but also acts as a mild astringent and many times in mild digestive upsets will work to stop the vomiting.

Diarrhea

In the case of adult Goldens, give three or four tablespoons of Kaopectate or Milk of Bismuth every four hours. Use one-fourth of this dosage for puppies. Skip the next meal, and if diarrhea persists, then start a bland diet of boiled ground lean beef and boiled rice in the proportions of half and half. Three or four doses of this medicine should suffice. If the diarrhea persists and, particularly, if accompanied by depression, lethargy, and loss of appetite, your veterinarian should be consulted immediately. With all these new viral-caused diarrheas floating around, time is of the essence in securing treatment.

Mild Stimulant

Dilute brandy half and half with water, add a little sugar, and give a tablespoonful of the mixture every four to five hours. For puppies over three months old, reduce the dosage to a teaspoonful of the mixture every four to five hours.

Mild Sedative

Dilute brandy half and half with water, add a little sugar, and give a tablespoon of the mixture every twenty to thirty minutes until the desired effect is attained. For puppies over three months old, reduce the dosage to a teaspoonful of the mixture every twenty to thirty minutes.

Using brandy for both sedation and stimulation is possible by varying the time interval between doses. Given every four to five hours, it's a stimulant; but given every twenty to thirty minutes it acts as a sedative.

Minor Cuts and Wounds

Cleanse them first with soap and water, preferably Tincture of Green Soap. Apply a mild antiseptic such as Bactine or Tincture of Metaphen two or three times daily until healed. If the cut is deep, and fairly long and bleeding, then a bandage should be applied until professional help can be obtained.

Whenever attempting to bandage wounds, first apply a layer or two of gauze over the cleaned and treated wound. Then apply a layer of cotton and then another layer or two of gauze. The bandage must be snug enough to stay on but not so tight as to impair the circulation to the body part. Adhesive tape should be applied over the second layer of gauze to keep the bandage as clean and dry as possible until you can get your dog to the doctor.

Tourniquets should be applied only in cases of profusely bleeding wounds. They are applied tightly between the wound and the heart, in addition to the pressure bandage that should be applied directly to the wound. The tourniquets must be released and reapplied at fifteen-minute intervals.

"Don't lick those sutures!" Beskobekuk of Maine, W.C., C.D., is wearing an "Elizabethan collar" used to protect wounds while they heal. Jennifer Kesner, owner.

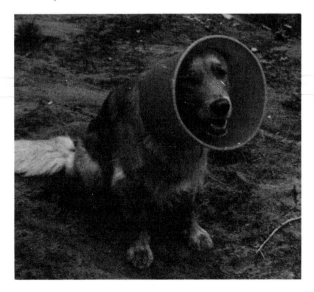

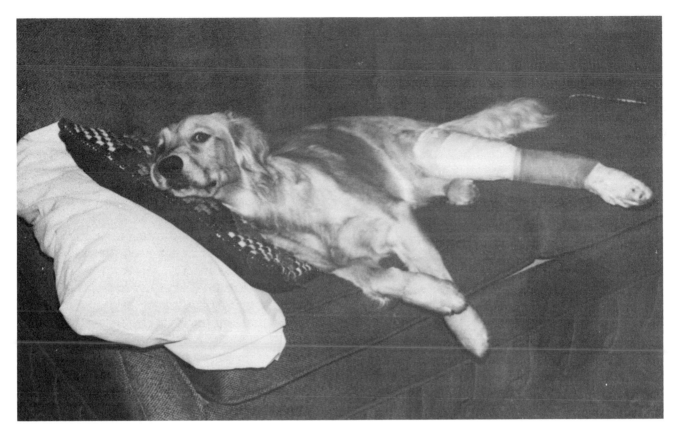

Recovering from a leg injury, one of Connie Gerstner's Goldens shows how the breed appreciates the comforts of home.

Burns

Application of ice or very cold water and compresses is the way to treat a skin burn. Apply cold packs as soon as possible and take the dog immediately to your vet.

Frostbite

Frostbite is a rarely occurring problem. The secret in treating this condition is to restore normal body temperature gradually to the affected parts. In other words, use cold water, then tepid water, to thaw out the area slowly and restore circulation. In cases of severe freezing or shock due to bitter cold temperature, take the animal to the veterinarian as soon as possible.

Abscesses and Infected Cysts

Obvious abscesses and infected cysts that occur between the toes may be encouraged to drain by using hot boric acid packs and saturated dressings every few hours until professional aid can be secured. The boric acid solution is made by dissolving one tablespoon of crystals to one pint of hot water. Apply frequently to the swollen area. Further treatment by a veterinarian may involve lancing and thoroughly draining and cleaning out the abscess cavity. As most abscesses are badly infected, systemic antibiotics are generally indicated.

Heatstroke or Heat Exhaustion

A word about the serious effects of heat on a dog is timely. It never ceases to amaze me how many people at dog shows have to be warned and advised not to leave their dogs in cars or vans on a warm day.

A dog's heat-regulating mechanism is not nearly as efficient as ours. Consequently, dogs feel the heat more that we do. Keep them as cool and as well ventilated as possible in hot weather. Another inducement for shock is taking your dog out of a cool air-conditioned vehicle and exposing him immediately to the hot outdoors. Make that change as gradual as you can because a rapid change can cause a shock-like reaction.

In cases of suspected heatstroke, which manifests itself with very high body temperatures (as high as 106° to 108°F. sometimes), severe panting, weakness, shaking, and collapse, act quickly to get him into a cold bath or shower or put ice-cold compresses on his head. Then, again without delay, rush him to the nearest veterinarian for further treatment. Prevention is the key here and with a little common sense, heatstroke and exhaustion can be avoided.

Poisons

Many dogs are poisoned annually by unscrupulous people who hate dogs. Many others are victims of poisoning due simply to the careless use of rat and ant poisons, insecticides, herbicides, anti-freeze solutions, drugs, and so forth. Dogs also frequently eat poisonous plants, either in the house or outdoors, which can lead to serious consequences. Common sources of these toxic products are named below.

Plants that can be a source of poison for dogs include the following (this list contains only the most common ones): daffodils, oleanders, poinsettas, mistletoe, philodendron, delphiniums, monkshood, foxglove, iris, lilies of the valley, rhubarb, spinach, tomato vines, sunburned potatoes, rhododendron, cherry, peach, oak, elderberry, black locust, jack-in-the-pulpit, Dutchman's-breeches, water hemlock, mushrooms, buttercups, poison hemlock, nightshade, jimson weed, marijuana, locoweed, and lupine.

Poisonous animals include such snakes as vipers, rattlesnakes, copperheads, water moccasins, and the coral snake. Lizards like the Gila monster and Mexican beaded lizard are bad. Some toads, spiders, insects, and fish also are potential sources of trouble.

Chemicals comprise perhaps the largest and most common source of poisoning in our environment. These are hazards that our dogs may be exposed to every day. Careful handling and awareness of these products are essential.

Toxic materials are found in arts and crafts supplies, photographic supplies, and automotive and machinery products and include such things as antifreeze and de-icers, rust inhibitors, brake fluids, engine and carburetor cleaners, lubricants, gasoline, kerosene, radiator cleaners, and windshield washers. Cleaners, bleaches and polishes, disinfectants, and sanitizers all contain products that potentially are dangerous.

Even health and beauty aids may contain toxic materials if ingested in large enough quantities: some bath oils, perfumes, corn removers, deodorants, anti-perspirants, athlete's foot remedies, eye makeup, hair dyes and preparations, diet pills, headache remedies, laxatives, liniments, fingernail polish removers, sleeping pills, suntan lotions, amphetamines, shaving lotions, colognes, shampoos, and certain ointments.

Paints and related products also can be dangerous. Caulking compounds, driers, thinners, paints, paint brush cleaners, paint and var-

This picture originally illustrated a magazine article, entitled "Dangers of Antifreeze and Your Dog," by Jennifer A. Kesner.

nish removers, preservatives, and floor and wood cleaners all fit into the category.

Pest poisons for the control of birds, fungi, rats, mice, ants, and snails all can be toxic and sometimes fatal to dogs.

Miscellaneous items like fire extinguishers and non-skid products for slippery floors can be unsafe. Almost all solvents like carbon tetrachloride, benzene, toluene, acetone, mineral spirits, kerosene, and turpentine are bad.

The previous paragraphs serve only to illustrate how many products in our everyday environment exist which can be hazardous or fatal to our dogs.

In cases of suspected poisoning, be aware of what to do until professional help can be obtained:

a. Keep the animal protected, quiet, and warm.

b. If a contact is on the skin, eye, or body surface, cleanse and flush the area with copious amounts of water. Do this also if the dog gets something in his eye. Protect him from further exposure.

c. Inducing vomiting may be dangerous and should be done only on the advice of a veterinarian. Giving peroxide may induce vomiting in some cases. It is better to allow the animal to drink as much water as he wants. This will dilute the poison. Giving milk or raw egg whites is helpful many times to delay absorption of the toxic products.

Do not attempt to give anything by mouth if the patient is convulsing, depressed, or unconscious.

Do not waste time getting veterinary service. Take any vomited material and suspected causative agents, and their containers with you to the vet. When the suspected product is known, valuable time can be saved in administering specific treatment.

A word to the wise should be sufficient. Keep away from your dog all products that can harm him in any way.

Bloat

One of the most serious and difficult problems and real emergency situations that can occur is that of bloat. Other names for this condition are torsion and acute indigestion. This condition generally occurs in larger breeds after the consumption of a large meal (usually dry feed) and then the drinking of a lot of water immediately after eating. If this is followed by a vigorous exercise period, the stage is set for bloat. The stomach, being pendulous and overloaded at this point, can become twisted or rotated. This, of course, cuts off the circulation to the stomach and spleen and may also interfere with the large blood vessels coming to and from the liver. A shock-like syndrome follows and death may ensue shortly if heroic measures are not undertaken to save the stricken animal. If ever there was an emergency, this is truly one. Dry heaves, painful loud crying, and abdominal enlargement, take place in a very short time. Relief of the torsion requires immediate surgery to right the stomach to its normal position and to keep it there. Circulation may then return to normal.

In cases of acute indigestion without torsion, the distress and bloat may be relieved by passing a stomach tube to allow the gas to escape. At the risk of being redundant, it must be said that this condition is very acute and requires immediate and heroic action to save the victim.

Preventive measures for bloat include dividing the normal diet of these dogs into three or four meals a day. Water should not be given for one hour before and one hour after each meal, and no exercise is advisable for an hour or two after eating.

With breeders and veterinarians becoming more aware of the bloat syndrome, I feel that more of these cases will be saved than were in the past.

Whelping

We cannot leave the subject of emergencies without considering the subject of whelping. Most bitches whelp without any problems. It is wise, however, to watch them closely during this time. I feel that no bitch should go more than two hours in actual labor without producing a puppy. This includes the time before the first one as well as between puppies. If more than two hours elapse, then the dam should be examined by a veterinarian. It will then be determined if she is indeed in trouble or is just a slow whelper. This rule of thumb gives us time to find out if there is a problem, what it may be, and have time to save both dam and puppies in most cases.

It is good practice to have your bitches examined for pregnancy three and a half to four weeks after mating, as well as at term around the fifty-eighth to fifty-ninth day. These procedures will enable the veterinarian to discover any troubles that may occur during pregnancy, as well as alerting him as to when the whelping is going to take place. Knowing this, he can plan to provide service, if needed during off hours.

Bitches that are difficult to breed, miss pregnancies, or have irregular reproductive cycles should have physical exams including

Laurell's Gadabout Grandee, by Ch. Honor's Grandeur, C.D.X., from Ch. Duckdown's Veronica Laker, C.D. Laurell Goldens.

laboratory tests to determine the cause of the trouble. These tests may be expensive, but a lot of breeding and sterility problems due to sub-par physical condition, hormonal imbalances, or hypo-thyroidism can be corrected. If a valuable bitch is restored to her normal reproductive capacity, the reward more than offsets the medical costs.

Another important thing to remember about whelping and raising puppies is to keep them warm enough. This means a room temperature of 75° to 80°F. for the first ten days to two weeks until the puppies are able to generate their own body heat. Be sure the dam keeps them close; leave a light burning at night for the first week so she won't lose track of any of them or accidentally lie on one of them. Chilling remains the biggest cause of death of newborn puppies. Other causes are malnutrition, toxic milk, hemorrhage, and viral and bacterial infections. Blood type incompatibilities have been understood lately as causes of trouble.

Consultation with your veterinarian concerning these and any other breeding problems you've had in the past may result in the solution of these problems. This may result in larger litters with a higher survival rate.

Care of the Older Dog

Providing medical services from cradle to grave is the slogan of many veterinarians, and rightly so. The average life expectancy for our dogs these days is about thirteen years. Sad to say, this is a short time compared to our life span. Larger breeds historically do not live as long as the medium-sized or smaller breeds. However, I think that with proper care your Goldens should be expected to reach this expectancy.

Probably the most common ailments in older dogs are arthritis, kidney disease, heart problems, and cataracts; hip dysplasia may also become evident as the dog ages.

Arthritis

When your pet has trouble getting up in the morning, jumping up, or going upstairs, you can bet that some form of a joint problem is starting. Giving two enteric coated aspirin tablets three times a day for five days very often will help these individuals. This dosage is for adult dogs. It is relatively free of side effects and as long as nothing else is wrong, your dog will get a bit of relief.

Kidney Disease

Signs of kidney weakness are excessive drinking, inability to hold urine through the night, loss of weight, lack of appetite, and more than occasional bouts of vomiting and diarrhea. If any of these signs present themselves, it would be worthwhile to have a checkup. Very often corrective measures in diet and administering some medicine will prolong your dog's life.

Heart Problems

Some form and degree of heart problems exist in a lot of older animals. Symptoms of chronic congestive heart failure consist of a chronic cough, especially after exercise, lack of stamina, lethargy, abdominal enlargement, and labored breathing at times. If diagnosed and treated early in the disease, many heart patients live to a ripe old age.

Cataracts

Cataracts form in the lenses of most, if not all, old dogs. They are a part of the normal aging process. Total blindness from cataracts generally does not result for a long time. Distant and peripheral vision remain satisfactory for the expected life span of the dog. Rarely is total blindness produced by these aging cataracts before the dog's life expectancy is reached. There is no effective treatment for cataracts other than their surgical removal which is not recommended in the older patient that has any vision at all left.

Hip Dysplasia

It is becoming more evident that most of the arthritis in older dogs in large breeds is the result

This handsome senior citizen is the famous Ch. Sir Richard of Fleetwood at thirteen-and-a-half years of age, still a well-loved family member of Pepperhill Farms owned by Barbara and Jeff Pepper.

458

of problems in bone growth and development when the individual was very young. Problems such as panosteitis, hip dysplasia, elbow dysplasia, and osteochondrosis dessicans all are often precursors of arthritis. In Goldens, according to information from the Orthopedic Foundation for Animals, circa 1974, hip dysplasia is found in 25.7% of the cases presented to them.

At any rate, hip dysplasia seems to be a developmental condition and not a congenital anomaly. It is thought to be an inherited defect, with many genes being responsible for its development. Environmental factors also enter into the severity of the pathology in the hip joints. Nutrition during the growth period has been an important factor. Overfeeding and oversupplementation of diets have caused an abnormal growth rate with overweight puppies. These individuals, if they were susceptible to hip dysplasia in the first place, show more severe lesions of hip dysplasia. Restricted feeding of growing dogs is necessary for normal bone growth and development.

Signs of hip dysplasia vary from one dog to another, but some of the more common ones are difficulty in getting up after lying for awhile, rabbit-like gait with both rear legs moving forward at the same time when running, lethargy, and walking with a swaying gait in the rear legs. In many cases, a period of pain and discomfort at nine months to one year of age will resolve itself; and even though the dysplasia is still there, most of the symptoms may disappear.

It is recommended that dysplastic individuals not be bred, that they not be allowed to become overweight, and that they have moderate exercise.

The selection of dysplastic-free individuals for breeding stock eventually will result in the production of sounder hip joints in affected breeds. This factor, of course, is only one consideration in the breeding and production of an overall better Golden Retriever.

Canine Nutrition

After mentioning the problem of overfeeding and oversupplementation of puppies' diets with vitamins and minerals in the discussion of hip dysplasia, a few words about canine nutrition are in order.

It is generally agreed that great strides have been made in canine nutrition in the past few years and that most of our well-known commercial dog foods provide all the essential ingredients of a well-balanced diet for our dogs. Probably the greatest problem is providing good quality protein in proper proportions. It behooves us to read dog food labels and to know what we are feeding and how much is necessary to provide the requirements for a lean healthy individual. The tendencies in our society today are to overfeed and under exercise both our dogs and ourselves.

We must know the energy content or caloric value of the foods we are feeding. Then we must determine the energy requirements of our dogs. These will vary with time and circumstances. Your adult Golden requires about twenty-five calories per pound of body weight daily for maintenance.

Generally speaking for the average adult Golden house dog, a diet consisting of 16% high quality protein, 10% fat, and 44% carbohydrates is a good mix. For the working dogs, dogs being shown, or pregnant bitches, increase the protein and fat percentages by about 25% and decrease the carbohydrate proportion by 25%. To meet the needs of the increased stress of growth in young puppies and nursing bitches, the protein and fat components should be increased yet another 10 to 15% and the percentage of carbohydrates should be decreased by the same amount. Any stress situation means a rise in caloric requirement. For example, in the case of pregnancy, it is advisable to increase the amount of food intake by 20% after four weeks of gestation and by 75% after six weeks of gestation, and so forth.

We are assuming that the vitamins and minerals in the foods used are complete and balanced.

You may have to combine, mix, and juggle various types and brands of food to attain the desired diet, but don't despair; it can be done. Prescription and special diet foods are available through your veterinarian. These probably cost more initially but may pay off in the long run.

As to exactly how much to feed each individual dog, no one can give you a magic formula that works in all cases. My best advice is to use common sense and a scale. The guidelines on dog food containers have a tendency to be overinflated. It is better to err on the low side than to overfeed. Remember, keep your dog slim and fit with a proper diet and plenty of exercise. That's not a bad idea for your own well-being also.

BECKWITHS GOLDEN BLAZE,C.D.
(Our first golden)

Beckwith's Golden Blaze, C.D., the first Golden owned by Mr. and Mrs. R.E. Beckwith and the sire of the great Ch. Beckwith's Copper Coin, demonstrates his versatility, paws on the typewriter.

Glossary

To the uninitiated, it must seem that fanciers of purebred dogs speak a special language all their own, which in a way we do. The following is a list of terms, abbreviations, and titles which you will run across through our pages which may be unfamiliar to you. We hope that this list will lead to fuller understanding and that it will additionally assist you as you meet and converse with others of similar interests in the world of purebred dogs.

A.K.C. The commonly used abbreviation of American Kennel Club.

Albino. A deficiency of pigmentation causing the nose leather, eyerims, and lips to be pink.

Almond eye. The shape of the tissue surrounding the eye, which creates the almond-shaped appearance required by some breed standards.

American Kennel Club. The official registry for purebred dogs in the United States. Publishes and maintains the Stud Book, handles all litter and individual registrations, transfers of ownership, and so on. Keeps all United States dog show, field trial, and obedience trial records; issues championships and other titles in these areas as they are earned; approves and licenses dog show, obedience trial, and field trial judges; licenses or issues approval to all championship shows, obedience trials, and recognized match shows. Creates and enforces the rules, regulations, and policies by which the breeding, raising, exhibiting, handling, and judging of purebred dogs in the United States are governed. Clubs, not individuals, are members of the American Kennel Club, each of which is represented by a delegate selected from the club's own membership for the purpose of attending the quarterly American Kennel Club meetings as the representative of the member club, to vote on matters discussed at each meeting and to bring back a report to the individual club of any decisions or developments which took place there.

Angulation. The angles formed by the meeting of the bones, generally referring to the shoulder and upper arm in the forequarters and the stifle and hock in the hindquarters.

Apple head. An exaggerated roundness of the top-skull.

Apron. Frill, or longer hair, below the neck.

Bad bite. Can refer to a wryness or malformation of the jaw, or to incorrect dentition.

Bad mouth. One in which the teeth do not meet correctly according to the specifications of the breed standard.

Balance. Symmetry and proportion. A well-balanced dog is one in which all of the parts appear in correct ratio to one another: height to length, head to body, skull to foreface, and neck to head and body.

Beefy. Overmusculation or overdevelopment of the shoulders or hindquarters or both.

Benched Show. Dog show at which the dogs are kept on benches while not being shown in competition.

Best in Show. The dog or bitch chosen as the most representative of any dog in any breed from among the group winners at an all-breed dog show. (The dog or bitch that has won Best of Breed next competes in the group of which its breed is a part. Then the first-prize winner of each group meets in an additional competition from which one is selected the Best in Show.)

Best of Breed. The dog that is adjudged best of any competing in its breed at a dog show.

Best of Opposite Sex. The dog or bitch that is selected as the best of the opposite sex to the Best of Breed when the latter award has been made.

Best of Winners. The dog or bitch selected as the better of the two between Winners Dog and Winners Bitch.

Bitch. A female dog.

Bite. The manner in which the upper and lower jaws meet.

Bloom. The sheen of a coat in healthy, lustrous condition.

Blue-ribbon winner. A dog that has won first prize in the class for which it is entered at a dog show.

Bone. Refers to the girth of a dog's leg bones. A dog called "good in bone" has legs that are correct in girth for its breed and for its own general conformation. Well-rounded bone is round in appearance, flat bone rather flattish. Light bone is very fine and small in diameter, almost spindle-like in appearance; legs are extremely slender. Heavy bone refers to legs that are thick and sturdy.

Brace. Two dogs, or a dog and a bitch, closely similar in size, markings, color, and general appearance, moving together in unison.

Breed. Purebred dogs descended from mutual ancestors refined and developed by man.

Breeder. A person who breeds dogs.

Breeding particulars. Name of the sire and dam, date of breeding, date of birth, number of puppies in the litter, their sex, and name of the breeder and of the owner of the sire.

Brisket. The forepart of the body between the forelegs and beneath the chest.

Brood bitch. A female dog used primarily for breeding.

CACIB. A Challenge Certificate offered by the Federation Cynologique Internationale towards a dog's championship.

Canine. Dogs, jackals, wolves, and foxes as a group.

Canine teeth. The four sharp pointed teeth at the front of the jaws, two upper and two lower, flanking the incisors; often referred to as fangs.

Carpals. Pastern joint bones.

Castrate. To neuter a dog by removal of the testicles.

Cat foot. The short-toed, round tight foot similar to that of a cat.

C.D. An abbreviation of Companion Dog.

C.D.X. An abbreviation of Companion Dog Excellent.

Ch. Commonly used abbreviation of champion.

Challenge certificate. A card awarded at dog shows in Great Britain by which championship there is gained. Comparable to our Winners Dog and Winners Bitch awards. To become a British champion a dog must win three of these Challenge Certificates at designated championship dog shows.

Champion. A dog or bitch that has won a total of fifteen points, including two majors, the total number under not less than three judges, two of which must have awarded the majors at A.K.C. point shows.

Character. Appearance, behavior, and temperament considered correct in an individual breed of dog.

Cheeky. Cheeks which bulge out or are rounded in appearance.

Chest. The part of the body enclosed by the ribs.

Chiseled. Clean-cut below the eyes.

Choke collar. A chain or leather collar that gives maximum control over the dog. Tightened or relaxed by the pressure on the lead caused by either pulling of the dog or tautness with which it is held by the handler.

Chops. Pendulous, loose skin creating jowls.

Cloddy. Thickset or overly heavy or low in build.

Close-coupled. Compact in appearance. Short in the loin.

Coarse. Lacking in refinement or elegance.

Coat. The hair which covers the dog.

Companion Dog. The first obedience degree obtainable.

Companion Dog Excellent. The second obedience degree obtainable.

Condition. General health. A dog said to be in good condition is one carrying exactly the right amount of weight, whose coat looks alive and glossy, and that exhibits a general appearance and demeanor of well-being.

Conformation. The framework of the dog, its form and structure.

Coupling. The section of the body known as the loin. A short-coupled dog is one in which the loin is short.

Cow-hocked. Hocks turned inward at the joint, causing the hock joints to approach one another with the result that the feet toe outward instead of straight ahead.

Crabbing. A dog moving with its body at an angle rather than coming straight at you; otherwise referred to as side-wheeling or side-winding.

Crest. The arched portion of the back of the neck.

Crossing action. A fault in the forequarters caused by loose or poorly knit shoulders.

Croup. The portion of the back directly above the hind legs.

Cryptorchid. An adult dog with testicles not normally descended. A dog with this condition cannot be shown and is subject to disqualification by the judge.

Cynology. A study of canines.

Dam. Female parent of a dog or bitch.

Dentition. Arrangement of the teeth.

Derby. Field trial competition for young novices, generally up to two years of age.

Dewclaws. Extra claws on the inside of the legs. Should generally be removed several days following the puppy's birth. Required in some breeds, unimportant in others, and sometimes a disqualification—all according to the individual breed standard.

Dewlap. Excess loose and pendulous skin at the throat.

Diagonals. The right front and left rear leg make up the right diagonal; the left front and right rear leg the left diagonal. The diagonals correctly move in unison as the dog trots.

Dish-faced. The tip of the nose is placed higher than the stop.

Disqualification. A fault or condition which renders a dog ineligible to compete in organized shows, designated by the breed standard or by the American Kennel Club. Judges must withhold all awards at dog shows from dogs having disqualifying faults, noting in the Judges Book the reason for having done so. The owner may appeal this decision, but a disqualified dog cannot again be shown until it has officially been examined and reinstated by the American Kennel Club.

Distemper teeth. Discolored, badly stained, or pitted teeth. A condition so-called due to its early association with dogs having suffered from this disease.

Divergent hocks. Hock joints turn outward, creating the condition directly opposite to cow-hocks. Frequently referred to as bandy legs or barrel hocks.

Dock. Shorten the tail by cutting it.

Dog. A male of the species. Also used to describe collectively male and female canines.

Dog show. A competition in which dogs have been entered for the purpose of evaluation and to receive the opinion of a judge.

Dog show, all-breeds. A dog show in which classification may be provided, and usually is, for every breed of dog recognized by the American Kennel Club.

Dog show, specialty. A dog show featuring only one breed. Specialty shows are generally considered to be the showcases of a breed, and to win at one is a particularly valued honor and achievement, owing to the high type of competition usually encountered at these events.

Domed. A top-skull that is rounded rather than flat.

Double coat. A coat consisting of a hard, weather-resistant, protective outer covering over soft, short, close underlayer which provides warmth.

Down-faced. A downward inclination of the muzzle toward the tip of the nose.

Down in pastern. A softness or weakness of the pastern causing a pronounced deviation from the vertical.

Drag. A trail having been prepared by dragging a bag, generally bearing the strong scent of an animal, along the ground.

Drawing. The selection by lot to decide in which pairs dogs will be run in a specific field trial.

Drive. The powerful action of the hindquarters which should equal the degree of reach of the forequarters.

Drop ear. Ears carried drooping or folded forward.

Dry head. One exhibiting no excess wrinkle.

Dry neck. A clean, firm neckline free of throatiness or excess skin.

Dual champion. A dog having gained both bench show and field trial championships.

Dudley nose. Flesh-colored nose.

Elbow. The joint of the forearm and upper arm.

Elbow, out at. Elbow pointing away from the body rather than being held close.

Even bite. Exact meeting of the front teeth, tip to tip with no overlap of the uppers or lowers. Generally considered to be less serviceable than the scissors bite, although equally permissible or preferred in some breeds.

Ewe neck. An unattractive, concave curvature of the top area of the neckline.

Expression. The typical expression of the breed as one studies the head. Determined largely by the shape of the eye and its placement.

Eyeteeth. The upper canine teeth.

Faking. The altering of the natural appearance of a dog. A highly frowned upon and unethical practice which must lead, upon recognition by the judge, to instant dismissal from the show ring with a notation in the Judges Book stating the reason.

Fancier. A person actively involved in the sport of purebred dogs.

Fancy. The enthusiasts of a sport of hobby. Dog breeders, exhibitors, judges, and others actively involved with purebred dogs as a group comprise the dog fancy.

Fangs. The canine teeth.

F.C.I. Abbreviation of the Federation Cynologique Internationale.

Feathering. The longer fringes of hair that appear on the ears, tail, chest, and legs.

Federation Cynologique Internationale. A canine authority representing numerous countries, principally European, all of which consent to and agree on certain practices and breed identification.

Feet east and west. An expression used to describe toes on the forefeet turning outward rather than directly forward.

Fetch. Retrieving of game by a dog, or the command for the dog to do so.

Fiddle front. Caused by elbows protruding from the desired closeness to the body, with the result that the pasterns approach one another too closely and the feet toe outward. Thus, resembling the shape of a violin.

Field champion. A dog that has gained the title field champion has defeated a specified number of dogs in specified competition at a series of American Kennel Club licensed or member field trials.

Field trial. A competition for specified Hound or Sporting breeds where dogs are judged according to their ability and style on following a game trail or on finding and retrieving game.

Finishing a dog. Refers to completing a dog's championship, obedience title, or field trial title.

Flank. The side of the body through the loin area.

Flat bone. Bones of the leg which are not round.

Flat-sided. Ribs that are flat down the side rather than slightly rounded.

Fld. Ch. Abbreviation of field champion, used as a prefix before the dog's name.

Flews. A pendulous condition of the inner corners of the mouth.

Flush. To drive birds from cover. To spring at them. To force them to take flight.

Flyer. An especially exciting or promising young dog.

Flying ears. Ears correctly carried dropped or folded that stand up or tend to "fly" upon occasion.

Flying trot. The speed at which you should *never* move your dog in the show ring. All four feet actually briefly leave the ground during each half stride, making correct evaluation of the dog's normal gait virtually impossible.

Forearm. The front leg from elbow to pastern.

Foreface. The muzzle of the dog.

Front. The forepart of the body viewed head-on. Includes the head, forelegs, shoulders, chest, and feet.

Futurity. A competition at shows or field trials for dogs who are less than twelve months of age for which puppies are nominated, at or prior to birth. Highly competitive among breeders, usually with a fairly good purse for the winners.

Gait. The manner in which a dog walks or trots.

Gallop. The fastest gait. Never to be used in the show ring.

Game. The animals or wild birds which are hunted.

Gay tail. Tail carried high.

Get. Puppies.

Goose rump. Too sloping (steep) in croup.

Groom. To bathe, brush, comb, and trim your dog.

Groups. Refers to the variety groups in which all breeds of dogs are divided.

Gun dog. One that has been specifically trained to work with man in the field for retrieving game that has been shot and for locating live game.

Guns. The persons who do the shooting during field trials.

Gun-shy. Describes a dog that cringes or shows other signs of fear at the sound or sight of a gun.

Hackney action. High lifting of the forefeet in the manner of a hackney pony.

Ham. Muscular development of the upper hind leg. Also used to describe a dog that loves applause while being shown, really going all out when it occurs.

Handler. A person who shows dogs in competition, either as an amateur (without pay) or as a professional (receiving a fee in payment for the service).

Hard-mouthed. A dog that grasps the game too firmly in retrieving, causing bites and tooth marks.

Hare foot. An elongated paw, like the foot of a hare.

Haw. A third eyelid or excess membrane at the corner of the eye.

Heat. The period during which a bitch can be bred. Also referred to as being in season.

Heel. A command ordering the dog to follow close to the handler.

Hie on. A command used in hunting or field trials, urging the dog to go further.

Hindquarters. Rear assemblage of the dog.

Hock. The joint between the second thigh and the metatarsus.

Hocks well let down. Expression denoting that the hock joint should be placed quite low to the ground.

Honorable scars. Those incurred as a result of working injuries.

In season. *See* **Heat.**

Incisors. The front teeth between the canines.

Int. Ch. An abbreviation of international champion.

International champion. A dog awarded four CACIB cards at F.C.I. dog shows.

Jowls. Flesh of lips and jaws.

Judge. Person making the decisions at a dog show, obedience trial, or field trial. Judges residing in the United States must be approved and licensed by the A.K.C. in order to officiate at events where points toward championship titles are awarded; residents of another country whose governing body is recognized by the A.K.C. may be granted special permits to officiate in the United States.

Kennel. The building in which dogs are housed. Also used when referring to a person's collective dogs.

Knee joint. Stifle joint.

Knitting and purling. Crossing and throwing of forefeet as dog moves.

Knuckling over. A double-jointed wrist, or pastern, sometimes accompanied by enlarged bone development in the area, causing the joints to double over under the dog's weight.

Layback. 1) Describes correctly angulated shoulders. 2) Describes a short-faced dog whose pushed-in nose placement is accompanied by undershot jaw.

Leather. The ear flap. Also the skin of the actual nose.

Level bite. Another way of describing an even bite, as teeth of both jaws meet exactly.

Level gait. A dog moving smoothly, topline carried level as he does so, is said to be moving in this manner.

Lippy. Lips that are pendulous or do not fit tightly.

Loaded shoulders. Those overburdened with excessive muscular development.

Loin. Area of the sides between the lower ribs and hindquarters.

Lumber. Superfluous flesh.

Lumbering. A clumsy, awkward gait.

Major. A win of either Winners Dog or Winners Bitch carrying with it three, four, or five points toward championship.

Mane. The long hair growing on the top and upper sides of the neck.

Match show. An informal dog show where no championship points are awarded and entries can usually be made upon arrival, although some require pre-entry. Excellent practice area for future show dogs and for novice exhibitors as the entire atmosphere is relaxed and congenial.

Mate. To breed a dog and a bitch to one another. Littermates are dogs which are born in the same litter.

Milk teeth. The first baby teeth.

Miscellaneous class. A class provided at A.K.C. point shows in which specified breeds may compete in the absence of their own breed classification. Dogs of breeds in the process of becoming recognized by A.K.C. may compete in this class prior to the eventual provision of their own individual breed classification.

Molars. Four premolars are located at either side of the upper and lower jaws. Two molars exist on either side of the upper jaw, three on either side below. Lower molars have two roots; upper molars have three roots.

Monorchid. A dog with only one properly descended testicle. This condition disqualifies from competition at A.K.C. dog shows.

Muzzle. 1) The part of the head in front of the eyes. 2) To fasten something over the mouth, usually to prevent biting.

Non-slip retriever. A dog not expected to flush or to find game; one that merely walks at heel, marks the fall, then retrieves upon command.

Nose. Describes the dog's organ of smell, but also refers to his talent at scenting. A dog with a "good nose" is one adept at picking up and following a scent trail.

Obedience trial. A licensed obedience trial is one held under A.K.C. rules at which it is possible to gain a "leg" towards a dog's obedience title or titles.

Obedience trial champion. Denotes that a dog has attained obedience trial championship under A.K.C. regulations by having gained a specified number of points and first place awards.

Oblique shoulders. Shoulders angulated so as to be well laid back.

Occiput. Upper back point of skull.

Occipital protuberance. A prominent occiput noted in some of the Sporting breeds.

O.F.A. Commonly used abbreviation for Orthopedic Foundation for Animals.

Orthopedic Foundation for Animals. This organization is ready to read the hip radiographs of dogs and certify the existence of or freedom from hip dysplasia. Board-certified radiologists read vast numbers of these files each year.

O.T. Ch. An abbreviation of obedience trial champion.

Out at elbow. Elbows are held away from the body rather than in close.

Out at shoulder. Shoulder blades set in such a manner that joints are too wide and jut out from body.

Oval chest. Deep with only moderate width.

Overshot. Upper incisors overlap the lower incisors.

Pacing. A gait in which both right legs and both left legs move concurrently, causing a rolling action.

Paddling. Faulty gait in which the front legs swing forward in a stiff upward motion.

Pad. Thick protective covering of the bottom of the foot. Serves as a shock absorber.

Paper foot. Thin pads accompanying a flat foot.

Pastern. The area of the foreleg between the wrist and the foot.

Pedigree. Written record of dog's lineage.

Pigeon chest. A protruding, short breastbone.

Pile. Soft hair making a dense undercoat.

Plume. A long fringe of hair on the tail.

Poach. To trespass on private property when hunting.

Point. The position assumed by a hunting dog indicating the discovery and location of game.

Pointed. A dog that has won points toward its championship is referred to as "pointed."

Police dog. Any dog that has been trained to do police work.

Put down. To groom and otherwise prepare a dog for the show ring.

Quality. Excellence of type and conformation.

Racy. Lightly built, appearing overly long in leg and lacking substance.

Rangy. Excessive length of body combined with shallowness through the ribs and chest.

Reach. The distance to which the forelegs reach out in gaiting, which should correspond with the strength and drive of the hindquarters.

Register. To record your dog with the American Kennel Club.

Registration Certificate. The paper you receive denoting that your dog's registration has been recorded with the A.K.C., giving the breed, assigned names, names of sire and dam, date of birth, breeder and owner, along with the assigned Stud Book number of the dog.

Reserve Winners Bitch or **Reserve Winners Dog.** After the judging of Winners Bitch and Winners Dog, the remaining first prize dogs (bitches or dogs) remain in the ring where they are joined by the bitch or dog that placed second in the class to the one awarded Winners Bitch or Winners Dog, provided she or he was defeated only by that one bitch or dog. From these a Reserve Winner is selected. Should the Winners Bitch or Winners Dog subsequently be disallowed due to any error or technicality, the Reserve Winner is then moved up automatically to Winners in the A.K.C. records, and the points awarded to the Winners Bitch or Winners Dog then transfer to the one which placed Reserve. This is a safeguard award, for although it seldom happens, should the winner of the championship points be found to have been ineligible to receive them, the Reserve dog keeps the Winners' points.

Roach back. A convex curvature of the topline of the dog.

Rocking horse. An expression used to describe a dog that has been overly extended in forequarters and hindquarters by the handler, *i.e.*, forefeet placed too far forward, hind feet pulled overly far behind, making the dog resemble a child's rocking horse. To be avoided in presenting your dog for judging.

Rolling gait. An aimless, ambling type of action correct in some breeds but to be faulted in others.

Saddle back. Of excessive length with a dip behind the withers.

Scissors bite. The outer tips of the lower incisors touch the inner tips of the upper incisors. Generally considered to be the most serviceable type of jaw formation.

Second thigh. The area of the hindquarters between the hock and the stifle.

Septum. The vertical line between the nostrils.

Set up. To pose your dog in position for examination by the judge. Same as "stack."

Shelly. A body lacking in substance.

Shoulder height. The height of the dog from the ground to the highest point of the withers.

Sire. The male parent.

Skully. An expression used to describe a coarse or overly massive skull.

Slab sides. Flat sides with little spring of rib.

Soundness. Mental and physical stability. Sometimes used as well to denote the manner in which the dog gaits.

Spay. To neuter a bitch by surgery. Once this operation has been performed, the bitch is no longer eligible for entry in regular classes or in Veterans Class at A.K.C. shows.

Special. A dog or bitch entered only for Best of Breed competition at a dog show.

Specialty club. An organization devoted to sponsoring an individual breed of dog.

Specialty dog show. *See* **Dog show, specialty.**

Spring. To flush game.

Stack. *See* **Set up.**

Stake. A class in field trial competition.

Stance. The natural position a dog assumes in standing.

Standard. The official description of the ideal specimen of a breed. The Standard of Perfection is drawn up by the parent specialty club, usually by a special committee to whom the task is assigned, approved by the membership and by the American Kennel Club, and then serves as a guide to breeders and to judges in decisions regarding the merit, or lack of it, in evaluating individual dogs.

Stifle. The joint of the hind leg corresponding to a person's knee.

Stilted. The somewhat choppy gait of a dog lacking correct angulation.

Stop. The step-up from nose to skull; the indentation at the juncture of the skull and foreface.

Straight behind. Lacking angulation in the hindquarters.

Stud. A male dog that is used for breeding.

Stud book. The official record kept on the breeding particulars of recognized breeds of dogs.

Substance. Degree of bone size.

Swayback. Weakness, or downward curvature, in the topline between the withers and the hipbones.

Sweepstakes. Competition at shows for young dogs, usually up to twelve or eighteen months of age; unlike Futurity, no advance nomination is required.

Tailset. Manner in which the tail is placed on the rump.

T.D. An abbreviation of Tracking Dog.

T.D.X. An abbreviation of Tracking Dog Excellent.

Team. Generally consists of four dogs.

Thigh. Hindquarters from the stifle to the hip.

Throatiness. Excessive loose skin at the throat.

Topline. The dog's back from withers to tailset.

Tracking Dog. A title awarded dogs who have fulfilled the A.K.C. requirements at licensed or member club tracking tests.

Tracking Dog Excellent. An advanced tracking degree.

Trail. Hunt by following a trail scent.

Trot. The gait at which the dog moves in a rhythmic two-beat action, right front and left hind foot and left front and right hind foot each striking the ground together.

Tuck-up. A natural shallowness of the body at the loin creating a small-waisted appearance.

Type. The combination of features which make a breed unique, distinguishing it from all others.

U.D. An abbreviation of Utility Dog.

U.D.T. An abbreviation of Utility Dog Tracker

Unbenched show. Dog show at which dogs must arrive in time for judging and may leave anytime thereafter.

U.D.T.X. An abbreviation of Utility Dog and Tracker Excellent.

Undershot. The front teeth of the lower jaw reach beyond the front teeth of the upper jaw.

Upper arm. The foreleg between the forearm and the shoulder blade.

Utility Dog. Another level of obedience degree.

Utility Dog and Tracker. A double title indicating a dog that has gained both utility and tracking degrees. Also known as Utility Dog Tracking.

Utility Dog and Tracker Excellent. A double title indicating a dog that has gained both utility and advanced tracking degrees.

Walk. The gait in which three feet support the body, each lifting in regular sequence one at a time off the ground.

Walleye. A blue eye, fish eye, or pearl eye caused by a whitish appearance of the iris.

W.C. An abbreviation for Working Certificate.

Weedy. Lacking in sufficient bone and substance.

Well let down. Short hocks, hock joint placed low to the ground.

Wet neck. Dewlap, or superfluous skin.

Wheel back. Roached back with topline considerably arched over the loin.

Winners Bitch or Winners Dog. The awards which are accompanied by championship points, based on the number of dogs defeated, at A.K.C. member or licensed dog shows.

Withers. The highest point of the shoulders, right behind the neck.

Working Certificate. An award earned by dogs who have proven their hunting ability and are not gun-shy.

Wry mouth. Lower jaw is twisted and does not correctly align with the upper jaw.

Index

This index is composed of three separate parts: a general index, an index of kennels, and an index of names of people.

General

Kennels

(page reference in **bold** face indicates location of kennel story)

People

A

Adams, Jan, 89
Anderson, Elizabeth (Betty) M., 148, 309, 318
Anderson, Judye, 364
Andrews, R. Steve and Betty R., 128, 280
Arbuthnot, Karen, 259
Armstong, Mr., 24
Arnold, Hobart S., 260
Arszman, Hank, 165, 269
Arszman, Henry and Michelle, 61, 103, 272
Ashby, N. Bruce, 28, 268
Austin, Mrs. James M., 32
Ayers, Roy, 129

B

Baihly, Art and Caroline, 126-27, 278
Baird, D. Jean, 172, 262, 279, 380
Baker, Maurice, 135
Bakewell, III, Paul, 370
Barbour, Mrs. H.D., 28, 39, 268
Barlow, Bobby B., 117, 119, 300
Baruch, Alan and Marilyn, 371
Beale, Raymond, 301
Bechfelt, Stephanie J., 312
Beckwith, Ludell L. (Mrs. R.E.), 100, 295, 345
Beckwith, Ludell L. and R.E., 76-79, 140, 192, 220, 223, 262, 268, 269, 290, 419, 460
Beckwith, Lynn Marie, 76, 264, 268
Beckwith, R.E., 190, 295
Belsaas, Dean, 122
Belsaas, Nancy Kelly, 44, 120-22, 341, 345, 392
Beran, Vicki, 133
Berger, Cherie, 142-44, 263
Bergloff, Gerald and Fleur, 40, 41
Betteridge, Mr. R.G., 192
Beuer, Judy, 109
Bickford, Kay, 54, 285, 293, 294
Billings, Michele, 86, 179
Bischoff, R.M., 28, 269
Bischoff, Mr. & Mrs. Reinhard M., 31
Bissette, Anne, 55, 167

Bissette, John and Anne, 73-75, 233
Blair, Cheryl, 171, 378
Blanchette, Tommy, 435
Bluford, Dave and Suzi, 48, 59, 97-100, 221, 223, 228, 340, 356, 396, 418
Boalt, Ben L., 25, 267
Boalt, Mr. & Mrs. Ben L., 27
Boalt, Ralph G., 24, 27
Borrow, Elizabeth, 74, 75
Boyce, Georgia, 330
Boyle, Virginia (Ginny) A., 58, 227, 230, 297, 327, 349, 364, 383, 412, 420, 438, 439, 442
Bracy, Ed, 301
Bradley and Schofield, 200
Bradley, Charles and Patricia, 246, 312, 333, 449, 451
Brady, John W., 33
Braybook, Mr., 15
Breakell, Susan, 10, 90, 105, 167-72, 203, 204, 262, 266, 267, 275, 279, 299, 317, 328, 333, 341, 361, 378, 380, 381, 400, 409, 445
Breakell, Susan and Larry, 167-72, 237
Brocket, Lord, 16
Brooks, Leslie C., 268
Brown, Mrs. F.C., 25
Brown, Jeannie, 157
Brown, William D., 11
Brown-Leger, Ed and Susan, 267
Bruce, Robert, 268
Bryant, Ed and Edith, 89
Bryon, Mr. L., 20
Buechting, LaVerne and Earl, 259
Bunce, Mrs. Janet L., 46, 147, 185-86, 229, 254, 256, 261, 293, 333, 377, 413, 414
Burhans, Alice A., 393
Burke, Mary Lou, 411, 439, 442
Burkholder, Delores, 126

C

Cahoor, Arthur D. and Shirley, 399
Carnegie, Mrs., 15, 16
Carson, James, 124
Case, Lloyd M., 26, 27, 28, 29, 30, 34, 35, 36, 37, 38, 39, 86, 115, 116, 117, 119, 296, 388

Case, Mr. & Mrs. Lloyd M., 29-30, 37
Cathey, Kitty, 156-57, 338
Charlesworth, Mrs. M.W., 11, 14-15, 16, 17-19, 20, 27
Chase, Polly, 36
Chichester, Lord, 13
Christian, Mr. & Mrs. Henry B., 24
Churchill, Mrs. Janet, 300, 329, 382
Ciganek, Judith, 65
Clark, Anne Rogers, 54
Clark, C.H., 25
Clark, Houston, 140
Clark, Mrs. R.G., 20
Clark, Jr., Mrs. Robert V., 90, 93, 104, 108, 126, 205, 269, 283
Clemans, Michael A., 24
Cohns, the, 165
Colgate, Miss Adele, 44
Collier, Chester A., 291
Cooper, Dick, 103, 164, 165, 272
Corey, Mrs. Patricia, 31-32
Correll, H. Terry, 23, 33, 147, 149, 301
Correll, Harold, 29
Cortesia, Gail, 122
Cortright, Lyn and Dave, 259
Cottingham, Mrs. J.D., 19
Cowie, James A., 31
Cox, Herman, 126
Cox, Mrs. Jay S. (Nancy), 123, 277, 430
Crane, Charles (Chuck), 36, 42, 116
Cronheim, Charles A., 395
Crowley, Jean Baird, 259
Cummings, Linda, 92
Cummings, Mrs. Mary W., 47, 63, 91-94, 145, 235, 336, 386, 387, 389, 425
Custer, Elmer, 257
Czameski, Pauline, 266

D

D'Alessandro, T., 165, 262
Dallaire, Nancy, 219, 242, 260, 302
Dallaire, Nancy and Robert, 89, 178-79
Danenhauer, Bob and Jerri, 136
Dartt, George and Betsy, 131-33

473